Experiencing God
in the
Gospel of John

Experiencing God in the Gospel of John

ANTHONY J. KELLY, C.SS.R.

AND

FRANCIS J. MOLONEY, S.D.B.

Paulist Press
New York/Mahwah, N.J.

Cover design by Valerie Petro
Book design by Lynn Else

Library of Congress Cataloging-in-Publication Data

Kelly, Anthony J.
    Experiencing God in the Gospel of John / Anthony J. Kelly and Francis J. Moloney.
        p.   cm.
    Includes bibliographical references.
    ISBN 0-8091-4140-X
    1. Bible. N.T. John—Theology. I. Moloney, Francis J. II. Title.
BS2615.52 .K45 2003
226.5'07—dc 21

                                                         2002156403

Published by Paulist Press
997 Macarthur Boulevard
Mahwah, New Jersey 07430

www.paulistpress.com

Printed and bound in the United States of America

Contents

Contents

Contents

Contents

Contents

Contents

Preface

In the late 1980s, as the Jesus Seminar became front-page news, the authors of this book, one a biblical scholar and the other a systematic theologian, wondered about the theological significance of what has become known as "the third quest." We chatted about the possibility of a collaborative work that might study the question. However, other tasks, both scholarly and administrative, rendered this collaboration impossible. We still dreamt of a shared study, and the appearance of Frank Moloney's three-volume narrative commentary on the Gospel of John has provided this opportunity. The Fourth Gospel has long been the source of much Christian theology, and this large-scale commentary from one of the authors provided the basis of a theological work that exploited the Johannine narrative. The work that follows is a long way from a biblical-theological reflection upon the contemporary quest for the Jesus of history. Yet it is an attempt by two Christian scholars to produce theological study that is strongly determined by contemporary biblical scholarship.

The title, *The Experience of God in the Johannine Writings*, indicates the direction of our study. We undertook it in the hope of not only underscoring the fundamental Godward dimension intrinsic to the Johannine texts, but of reinvigorating theology with that deeply spiritual or experiential sense inherent in this remarkable part of the New Testament. This dimension, far from being an optional extra, or worse, a soft option in the intellectually demanding work of theology in its efforts to objectify and clarify the meaning of God, is the vital datum from which theology emerges and to which it returns in its special ministry to the church under the guidance of the Spirit of Truth.

The authors are friends and colleagues of long standing. Only a conversation extending over many years could steel us for the risk implied in this collaborative undertaking, for risk it was. The biblical and theological disciplines have their own distinctive languages and criteria, and it required a patient effort on the part of both of us as we sought to respect and enlarge the perspectives of one another. But what kept us working together was the sense of the gift—the *donum,* the *datum*—greater than any discipline, and certainly greater than the both of us as it overflowed any pattern or method of exploration. In this sense, too, God is outside any genus of classification (St. Thomas Aquinas, *Summa Theol.* 1, 5, 5).

Francis Moloney, S.D.B., professor of New Testament at the Catholic University of America, Washington, D.C., is the author of many studies on John, climaxing in his three-volume study: *Belief in the Word: Reading John 1–4; Signs and Shadows: Reading John 5–12,* and *Glory not Dishonor: Reading John 13–21,* the basic reference point for the Johannine narrative throughout this study. Tony Kelly, C.SS.R., is professor of theology at Australian Catholic University (a position previously occupied by Frank, immediately prior to his appointment in Washington, D.C.) and likewise the author of numerous theological publications on subjects that include the Trinity, eschatology, spirituality, and theological method.

As explained above, the opportunity for collaboration occurred when each of us was looking beyond the restricted confines of our respective disciplines for something more. We realize that such moments seldom occur in academic life when there are so many demands to keep reasonably up-to-date in our differing specializations. But we were not prepared to let go of the dream

Preface

that we should work collaboratively to produce a systematic reflection based upon contemporary biblical scholarship. It is good to risk something in a larger scope—not to undermine the sophisticated division of labor necessary today, but to profit from it—and in the process to remind ourselves that it is the one faith seeking understanding, however awkwardly differing scholarly methods might be. There comes a time when you simply do it; in the hope that what has been done might prove profitable—not only for the two collaborators concerned, but also for a potentially broad range of readers.

For this purpose, we decided not to overload the text with a huge apparatus of footnotes and references. A wide-ranging presentation of the never-ending scholarly reflection upon the Johannine Gospel can be found in the three volumes referred to above, and the theological references given are meant to be pointers toward further possibilities of theological elaboration and dialogue. While references to biblical scholarship are minimal, there are a number of references, for example, to Bernard Lonergan's *Method in Theology,* and to such commanding theological figures as Hans Urs von Balthasar. The reader will also find pointers to dozens of other writers, past and present. But such references do not complicate the text unduly, and they are usually kept to footnotes. There is plenty of room for further studies, either from the biblical or theological perspective; we had no intention of exhausting the possibilities in this particular effort. Nonetheless, we have written this collaborative work as a genuinely academic contribution on a crucially important theme, trusting, nevertheless, that a general reader might dip into it with profit and even inspiration.

Anthony J. Kelly, C.SS.R.
Francis J. Moloney, S.D.B.

1

The Experience of "God"

The theological concerns of our exploration into the experience of God arise from the Johannine writings themselves. The Gospel declares that Jesus, his disciples, and the generation of believers who succeed them, all share the one mission: to make God known (John 17:3, 10, 18, 21, 23) in a world that has not known God (John 17:25). Despite the present momentous changes in human culture, there is no reason to think that the mission has changed or, for that matter, that the world's ignorance of God has been finally overcome. The only way of countering the lure of the idols against which the First Letter of John warns (1 John 5:21) is the continuous effort to reappropriate at a new depth "the gift of God" (John 4:10).

The writings of John are an uninterrupted encouragement for believers to turn to God, not as to a remote cosmic force, nor as to an inaccessibly transcendent deity, but as to the Father revealed through him who is "the way, the truth and the life" (14:6). It is not a matter of entering some invisible realm that somehow volatilizes the realities of this world, but of finding this world loved, inhabited, and saved by an original and universal love. More than once in recent times, theology has been powerfully reproached for losing confidence in the uniqueness of the Christian revelation of God by taking refuge in the "God" of dominant ideologies.[1] The experience of God is not had in merely thinking about God, however sophisticated such thinking has been, and indeed needs to be. The experience proper to faith resides rather in something far more immediate and personal. It requires not merely thought, but the complete self-surrender of the believer to the God who remains, as far as ideas and words are concerned, beyond the range of human comprehension and speech. Nicholas Lash, drawing wry inspiration from *Alice in Wonderland,* has observed, "As the God of modern deism fades from view like Lewis Carroll's Cheshire Cat, his only trace a smile of vague and indeterminate benignity, some people construe ineffability to mean that we may say, concerning God, whatever takes our fancy."[2] When either preachers or politicians irenically assure their hearers that "after all, we are all God's children," other and destructive possibilities of paternity nevertheless remain (cf. John 8:42; 1 John 3:8–15). All the more reason, then, to return to the data and explore what the experience of God might mean, at least in terms of the Johannine testimony.

1. Accenting Experience

In opting to explore the *experience* of God, we have no intention of disregarding church doctrines. Nor do we wish to ignore the vast systematic effort of theologies that have sought to bring the data of scripture and the doctrines of Christian tradition into a coherent, intelligible presentation at different stages in the history of the church. The accumulated experience of its apostles, evangelists, martyrs, confessors, and doctors is the immeasurably larger field of experience that this particular exploration presupposes. Notably influenced by the Johannine writings, the early councils of Nicaea (325), Constantinople (381), and Chalcedon (451) are classic instances of faith struggling to free itself from the domain of myth and anthropomorphism, and to transcend the limits that any one philosophy

2

might impose.[3] Christian faith had to disassociate itself from the old gods of polytheism, and even the new gods of the philosophers, if it were to respect the uniqueness of its experience of the one true God revealed in Jesus Christ. The purpose of both doctrine and theology is to enable the original Gospel to be told and retold in the varied cultural situations through which the history of the church has moved.

Still, it is possible to have the meaning—understood as a series of doctrinal formulations—and yet to miss the experience. Unless the distinctive experience of God that the Gospels invite us to is appropriated, doctrinal definitions appear abstract and arbitrary. Such appears to be the case especially in the present cultural context. What was once universally unquestioned, namely, the existence of God and the spiritual dimension of human being, is now widely problematical. When "the truths of faith" drift free from traditional moorings, a sea of relativity seems to be the only option, while the question of meaning is endlessly deferred.[4]

Moreover, if the Christianity of the new millennium is to be increasingly in spiritual dialogue with the great religions of the East,[5] it will be necessary to reclaim the Christian experience of God as it is documented in the New Testament. Without a reclamation of the Godward movement of conversion inscribed in Christian experience, the doctrines of faith cannot but appear increasingly superficial, abstract, and exotic, while theology will look like a more or less sophisticated distraction from the gift which the Gospel witnesses to. It must be remembered that the evangelists were not intent on providing material for conciliar definitions, nor were Jesus and his disciples theologians giving seminars. In their respective ways, they were witnessing to the all-transforming gift of God. The more believers are refreshed in their experience of God, the more doctrines of faith will be seen as signposts pointing into the inexpressible mysteries they are

meant to serve; and the more theology will be continually rein-
vigorated to explore the deepest meaning of what has been
revealed within the history of human experience.

2. Different Approaches to Experience

Admittedly, *experience* is an especially slippery term, above
all when the question bears on the experience of God. The variety of possible meanings is immediately evident in the Johannine
writings. On the one hand the Gospel of John is written from the
decisive experience of a community of original witnesses who
can claim, "...we have gazed upon his glory, glory as of the only
Son from the Father" (John 1:14b; cf. 1 John 1:1–3). On the
other hand, there is another kind of experience into which
believers are summoned: "Blessed are those who have not seen
and yet believe" (20:29b). This latter implies more an ongoing
journey or "experiment" in the truth of what has been given:
"...these things are written that you might go on believing that
Jesus is the Christ, the Son of God, and that believing you might
have life in his name" (20:31).

Aquinas: Experiencing the Divine Persons in Grace

Not surprisingly, the notion of experience figures in different, but complementary, fashions in theology, past and present.
St. Thomas Aquinas, and the medieval doctors generally, spoke
of a certain kind of experimental knowledge of the divine persons. In the gift of grace, the Father is "given,"[6] and the Son and
Spirit are "sent." The graced soul is thus said to be conformed
to the divine persons through the missions. Through the gifts of
charity and infused wisdom the soul is likened to the Spirit and
the Son respectively. The Son, however, is not any kind of word,
but a "Word breathing love." Following Augustine, Thomas

interprets the consciousness of grace as *"a kind of experimental knowledge."*[7] At the heart of the intense speculative intellectuality of medieval theology, this kind of experience assures theology of its status, not only as a *science,* but as a *wisdom.* The Christian contemplative "suffers things divine" *(patiens divina).*[8] Though the emphasis on experience passes often unnoticed in summaries of Thomist theology, it is far from irrelevant to our investigation as our occasional references to Aquinas's commentaries on the Gospel of John will suggest.

Lonergan: Grace as Radical "Being in Love"

Building positively on such a tradition, astute theological methodologists such as Bernard Lonergan have attempted to transpose the medieval theoretical achievement into a contemporary context. His approach is critically underpinned by the experience of human consciousness itself. For example, Lonergan interprets religious experience from which all theological objectifications flow as a radical, gifted experience of "being in love." That, for Lonergan, is the phenomenological equivalent of "the state of grace."[9] Such a dynamic state of loving occurs as a gift, so affecting the human capacity for self-transcendence that it becomes an unrestricted self-surrender to the giver of the gift. This unconditional experience of loving and being loved pervades all levels of consciousness. As it animates and subsumes all other forms of loving, it gives intelligence a clouded awareness of a mystery that provokes its own kind of questions and leads to its own kind of answers.[10] The gift of love occurs as something of a holy disruption in the routine flow of life. Conversion results with religious, moral, and intellectual consequences.[11] Lonergan writes:

That fulfillment is not the product of our knowledge and choice. On the contrary, it dismantles and abolishes the horizon in which our knowing and choosing went on and it sets up a new horizon in which the love of God will transvalue our values and the eyes of that love will transform our knowing....Though not a product of our knowing and choosing, it is a conscious dynamic state of love, joy and peace that manifests itself in acts of kindness, goodness, fidelity, gentleness and self-control.[12]

Lonergan's methodological treatment of religious experience will prove rewardingly applicable to the Johannine writings. For instance, John writes to bring his readers to the point where they sense the dismantling of their former limited horizons, only to be drawn into an unrestricted horizon illumined by the Father's love.

Further recent examples of a theological turn to experience are found in the works of Karl Rahner and Hans Urs von Balthasar, to mention but two.[13]

Karl Rahner: "The Heart of Christianity"

Rahner, in the mystagogic and pastoral emphasis of his vast output, repeatedly points to a prethematic experience of God, occurring in the often unnamed intimations of "the Mystery." This kind of overture to the transcendent is instanced in our living encounter with such issues as truth, responsibility, forgiveness, death, and love of another. In a key article,[14] Rahner writes, "Today it is becoming clearer, and that too within Christianity at the doctrinal and institutional level, that *this experience of God...really constitutes the very heart and center of Christianity itself and also the ever living source of that*

6

conscious manifestation which we call 'revelation'"[15] [emphasis added]. After locating the experience of the God of all at "the very heart and center of Christianity," he goes on to say, "It is, therefore, a task precisely for Christianity itself to point ever anew to this basic experience of God, to induce man to discover it within himself, to accept it and also to avow his allegiance to it in its verbal and historical objectification."[16]

This present investigation into the experience of God will concentrate on its "verbal and historical manifestation" in the Johannine writings. Where Aquinas spoke of the experience of God in grace, and Lonergan located it in the otherworldly but transforming gift of love, Rahner opens up the whole domain of Christian mysticism rooted in a variety of experiences of the transcendent. Each of these approaches will have its place in our study.

Von Balthasar: Experience as Journey

This brief note on faith's experiential sense of God would be incomplete without referring to von Balthasar, who showed a special interest in the Johannine writings. He elaborated the meaning of experience through the "journey" metaphor. Divine glory can be experienced only by surrendering oneself to the movement of the journey inherent in faith itself.[17] The self-surrender inherent is such an experience is characterized by a certain self-dispossession and expropriation, in the movement from self to God:

> In faith and through it, rather, I am made open and dispossessed of self....*The important thing is the movement away from myself, the preference of what is other and greater* [emphasis added], and precisely the person who has been expropriated for God does

not want to become fully secure with regard to this Other and Greater."[18]

For von Balthasar, faith is not concerned with a self-image. It is looking into, but away from, any form of self-possession. He appositely remarks, "...looking in the mirror of the self would incur the loss of love. For 'truth,' as John understands it, is to be found in the unconditional abandonment of what is one's own for the sake of the Beloved."[19] Observing that the multifaceted character of Christian experience can never be reduced to this or that aspect, he goes on to make an important point about the Johannine pattern of experience:

> Christian experience, rather, implies *a progressive entrance of the believing person into the total reality* of faith and the progressive "realization" of this reality. Pascal, Kierkegaard and Newman understood Christian experience in no other way. The best justification for this are *the criteria of experience that in John continually circle around each other,* always pointing one to the other. And the impossibility of ordering John's different aspects at the theoretico-theological level into a manageable system...*points us in the direction of another level of synthesis, that of Christian experience as the fruit of a faith lived in obedience to God.*[20] [All emphasis added.]

The challenge, then, is to locate the experience of God as John presents it within what von Balthasar called in the above quotation "that other level of synthesis," which is accessible only within the journey of faith. Where Aquinas connected the experience of God with the gift of sanctifying grace; where Lonergan located it in unconditional love permeating every level

8

of human consciousness; and where Rahner focused the whole
of Christian faith in the mystical experience of God; von
Balthasar points to the pilgrim nature of that experience. We
could add that it demands of believers, in all their modes of seeing, hearing, and touching "what was from the beginning" (cf.
1 John 1:1–4), something like the tact which Coleridge understood to be the special gift of the poet:

> He may not have it in logical coherence, in his Brain
> & Tongue; but he must have it by *Tact:* for all sounds
> and forms of Nature he must have the *ear* of a wild
> Arab listening in the silent Desert—the *eye* of a North
> American Indian tracing the footsteps of an Enemy
> upon the Leaves that strew the Forest; the *Touch* of a
> Blind Man feeling the face of a darling Child.[21]

Such a quality of exploration is not unrelated to the way
opened up by the writings of John himself. Here Von Balthasar
helpfully notes two further dimensions of the experience we are
attempting to discern. The first is the dramatic structure of our
experience of God; the second is that of the radiance of divine
glory. A word, then, on each of these.

3. Dimensions of Experience: Drama and Glory

The Drama

To appreciate more fully the manner in which John introduces his readers into the experience of God we must appreciate
its dramatic quality. This would mean attending to the Gospel
especially as a *play,* as a divinely authored drama. God is revealed
to the world by drawing believers into a dramatic experience,
designed to transform the meaning of life itself. The dramatic

form of Christian experience has been impressively elaborated by von Balthasar, as his *Theological Aesthetics* leads into the *Theo-drama*.[22] In the drama of divine communication, the playwright is the Father (the author of "the work"), while the divine author's purpose is communicated under the direction of the Spirit. Thus, Jesus, as the Son and Word, enacts in his role or mission what both the author and director intend.[23] There is an interplay of three freedoms, each showing its own initiative. The director serves the play as it was conceived by the author; and the actor serves them both with his own gifts—if the audience is to experience what the author and director intended. In an extended meditation on John, von Balthasar exploits the dramatic metaphor, while underscoring the unique and original event of God's self-revelation in Christ:

> The Spirit who leads Jesus is the Spirit of the Father, the Spirit who as a divine person is free to "breathe where he will" (John 3:8) and who, precisely in that freedom, is given to the Son "without measure" (3:34). It is hardly likely that the Son will obstruct the Spirit of the Father with any prior decisions of *his* own, or determine in what direction his inspirations will blow, or sketch for himself the plan which the Spirit is to unfold for him. It would be better to compare him to an actor playing a part for the first time, receiving it by inspiration, as it were, scene-by-scene, word-by-word. *The play does not exist in advance, but is conceived, produced and acted all in one. The incarnation is not the nth performance of a tragedy already lying in the archives of eternity. It is an event of total originality, as unique and untarnished as the eternally here-and-now birth of the Son from the Father.*[24] [Emphasis added.]

This "event of total originality" is at the heart of the Johannine experience of God. All metaphors limp, as does that of likening God's saving act to a human drama. In the usual case, a human limitation has to be recognized in that the role to be acted and the person of the actor can never fully coincide. There is always an element of artistic fiction and suspension of belief. After all, actors have their own lives to lead—the off-stage private life when the role is dropped and the greasepaint wiped away. But von Balthasar, quoting Theodor Haecker, brings us back to the uniqueness of Jesus' acting out the role the Father has given him in such a way that his person and role are one and the same in the great drama of world's salvation:

> In this play there can be a tragic or comic dichotomy between the actor and the role; and this produces the tragedies and comedies of world history—and farces too, of which today we are both spectators and actors, as we have always been. Only in the drama of the God-Man do we find identity between the sublime actor and the role he has to play.[25]

If the experience of God is formed within a dramatic movement of divine communication, an alert appreciation of that kind of experience is required in anyone aiming to discern its movement and direction.

The Radiance of Glory

A further dimension of the Johannine experience of God is the paradoxical nature of the term *glory*, in reference to the unique divine glory that is revealed in the drama of the Johannine narrative. Here we make only the briefest remark since the theme of glory will return so many times as our investigation unfolds.

In a general sense, glory is a primal symbol of the experience of the most prized meaning and value of one's life in the world. It is associated with the public radiance and social acknowledgment of one's role and achievement. It is reputation writ large, confirming and celebrating someone's identity as the author of what is commonly taken to be a remarkable achievement. One way or another, culture assigns to glory a certain death-defying quality. It resides in the splendor of a life destined to live on in human memory, and continuing to affect human history—despite the erosion of time, and the power of death to annul and diminish all else. Though glory is opposed to death in this sense, it can make strange alliances with mortality, as when, say, a death is declared glorious in the service of a great cause; or when the glory of a person, a group, or a people comes to demand the death of others in order to maintain or intensify its glorious status.[26] To this degree, "glory," as the radiant symbol of personal worth and identity, is apt to provoke questions on what constitutes personal identity, lasting life, true judgment, and the "god"—if any—who glorifies, or is glorified by, us human beings.

The Gospel is quite direct in distinguishing two radically opposed forms of glory. John makes rich use of the unique biblical word *doxa*. God's visible saving actions (the parting of the Reed Sea, the fire in the night, the manna in the morning) are called, in Hebrew, the *kabod YHWH*. When the Hebrew Bible was translated into Greek, the word *kabod* was consistently translated by the Greek word *doxa*. Only in the Bible does it mean both the social acknowledgment of one's reputation and role, and the unique saving revelation of God.[27] For John, nowhere is this contrast more eloquent than in John 12:43. Puzzling over the failure of "the Jews" to accept Jesus, the narrator comments, "They loved the *doxa* of human beings, rather than the *doxa* of God." Jesus asks his adversaries, "How can you believe, who receive glory from one another, and do not see

12

the glory that comes from the one who sent me?" (5:44). There is the glory proper to this world and its ruler.[28] It contrasts to the properly divine glory that will climactically shine forth in the self-giving of Jesus on the cross.[29]

An unsettling point, yet ever more relevant to believers in later ages of faith, is that the experience of God happens in the midst of intense, defiant, counter-cultural confrontations. Losing face in the prevailing culture seems to be a condition for experiencing the reality of "the only true God" (17:3). The dynamics of human glory and reputation (5:41–44; 7:18), the cultivation of the ruler of this world,[30] the power of human respect (8:15; 12:43), the culture of violence and hatred,[31] the idolatrous subservience to imperial authority (19:15), all are heart-numbing realities that make faith in the Son and obedience to the Father impossible (5:37b). The Paraclete comes to contend against these self-justifying mundane forces (16:8–11).[32] The promised "opened heaven" (1:51) of communion and dwelling in God, of mutual love, and the gifts of truth, joy, peace, and life to the full (14:15–27) are in stark contrast to the way of the world (1 John 2:15–18). Nonetheless, as will be seen as our investigation unfolds, the pressure of false gods of the dominant culture is intense. Believers come to know the one true God "in spirit and in truth" (John 4:23–24) only when they are prepared to make a stand of practical adoration in the face of the powers ranged against them. God is known in the ongoing struggle of the believers to keep themselves from idols (1 John 5:21).

While the great arc of Johannine theology stretches all the way from what was "in the beginning" (1:1) to Jesus' return to the glory that was his "before the foundation of the world"(17:5, 24; 20:17), it dips into the depths of where believers find themselves: "in the world" (17:14–16). However exalted the reach and sweep of John's vision, it is always grounded in the actuality of our worldly existence. While it ends in glory (17:24), it never ceases to engage the darkness, ambiguity, conflict, and scandal of our present being-in-the-world. Whatever the splendor of divine revelation, it has allowed for rejection, betrayal, scandal, hatred, and violent killing. Yet the deadly effects of rejection and unbelief play their part in the drama of the divine design. The glory of the Father is revealed in the Son. He is lifted up on the cross (8:27–29) to draw all to himself (12:32)—not only despite, but from within, the influence of what is anti-Christ and anti-God at work in the human heart and society.

The community's faith in the true God will continue to demand great courage in the face of a huge antagonistic resistance. The impetus to appropriate the original experience of God is generated in the Gospel by difficulties that arise from outside the community. In the Letters, the conflict and division occurring within the community with the passage of time demanded a radical recentering of that community's faith.[33] In both cases, a community's problems are resolved only by turning to God.

4. The Singularity of the Johannine Experience

A Distinctive Concreteness

For all its transcendent focus, there is a notable concreteness in the Johannine pattern of experience. Venerable traditions of philosophical and religious thought feel an immediate kinship with such key notions as God, Word, Spirit, the world, life, light, truth, spirit, flesh, unity, glory, and so forth. Yet the Johannine author shows a critical awareness of the danger of such themes being easily co-opted to other purposes. The unsurpassable singularity of "the fullness of the gift that is truth" (1:14b) can be lost in metaphysical and religious generality—if either the incarnation (1 John 4:1–2) or its effective meaning (cf. 1 John 2:6–11; 3:11–22) slip out of focus.

John invites his readers to enter into a horizon transformed in the light of Word made flesh among us (1:14a). Seeing no longer means ordinary vision. The hearing of faith exceeds our usual acoustic range. True life is more than our death-bound biological existence. Even such prized values as love, unity, peace, glory, and joy are newly defined; and the truth that contests human judgment comes from beyond any judicial system we know. The meaning of "the world" is so notoriously ambiguous that one must wait on the succession of contexts rather than restrict it to any one description. All these meaning and values are different because the God whom the Word reveals is so startlingly different. Without attending to that difference, any interpreter risks misrepresenting the whole aim and purpose of his Gospel. The meaning of God is not simply read off from a text, but a reality to be discovered, by entering into the realm of life and love which emanates from the Father.[34] Likewise, any form of metaphysical ascent to what is above and beyond the reality of Jesus, however religious in intent, is a distortion.

At the point where the writings of John seem to tempt the reader into some idealized "beyond," they turn us back to a real world, to the Word incarnate in that world, and to the cruciform truth of God there revealed. There is no escape from the flesh into a world of pure spirit, for the reality of "the flesh" is penetrated by the Word and Spirit (1 John 4:2). And if the Gospel acknowledges the shock of death in the biological sphere, as in the case of Lazarus (11:4), it is for the sake of revealing another life, beyond the threat of death (11:25–26). Even though the Gospel begins (1:1) and ends (17:5, 24) its narrative in a time-transcending realm, it is only to send us back to the world in the sounding of that hour that has changed the whole drifting meaning of time itself (17:1b).

An Unsayable Excess

As with all the classics of art and religion, the writings of John attest to an excess of experience that can never be fully appreciated or objectified.[35] When believers read the classic writings of John, they are drawn into an experience that is really one of endless deferral. Any interpretation is judged in the light of the fullness of the gift of truth (1:14b). The horizon of faith opens into an experience that is always "greater."[36] The "gift of God" (4:10) leaves no worldly horizon or identity untroubled.[37]

By reading of how God so loved the world (3:16), and of how the world was made through the Word himself (1:10b), faith learns its own reserve, in deferring to what is beyond any horizon of interpretation. Would-be interpreters must exercise their own tact in entering into a realm outside all mundane categories. While Jesus has been sent to be the savior of the world (4:42), his kingdom is not of this world (18:36). Within the immeasurable extent of that excess, the Word comes from the realm of God to enliven and enlighten the world of the flesh, to be received by disciples, friends (15:14–15) and brethren (20:17a). Yet even within that gifted familiarity, he points to the One who is utterly other, God himself: "...my Father and your Father, my God and your God" (20:17b).

"The Jews"...?

In John's narrative, the distinctive designation, "the Jews," refers to those who headed the forces opposing Jesus.[38] John's way of naming the opposition was of course not without its irony, for those so named are by no means a monolithic block, since, after all, "...salvation is from the Jews" (John 4:22). Besides, Mary, John the Baptist, and the Beloved Disciple are Jews, as are an overwhelming number of the early disciples and witnesses. Further, there are instances of more neutral usages (cf. John 8:31; 11:19, 31, 36, 45; 18:20, 33, 39). But in the experience of contradiction and estrangement, the full nature of which will probably always elude full explanation, *hoi Ioudaioi* became a catch-phrase in the adversarial rhetoric of the particular Johannine community in which the Gospel originated. It suggests something of the nature of a family row.[39] It goes without saying that this peculiar usage in no way excuses the virulent anti-semitism of later ages. By the time of 1 John, "the Jews," as the agents of opposition, no longer figure, yielding to another source of contradiction—"...the many antichrists who have come...[who] went out from us" (1 John 2:18–19).

What seems to be central to the experience of intense polarization that these writings convey is a feeling of piercing disappointment. Those whom believers most expected to accept Jesus and his disciples, in some remarkably scandalous instances, did not: "...and his own people received him not" (John 1:11). Those who most belonged to "us" by reason of common religious and historical origins, either ended by excluding "us" from their gatherings (9:34; 16:2), or by leaving "our" community (1 John 2:19). It is a matter of living with the scandal of a revelation that in some obvious sense has failed (John 16:1). The community of faith is promised no free ride on the back of a general consensus. Believers have to make an option more radical than they had previously realized—at that point when it becomes clear that there are those in their midst who are unwilling to see the glory of God *in this way,* and to be converted to the novelty and universality of the Father's love, manifest in the banal particularities of mundane existence. When expected sources of support prove threateningly contrary, the community is exposed to opposition from the closest of quarters. Though a community of mutual love is both the ideal and the imperative flowing from belief in God (John 13:34; 14:12; 17:26; 1 John 3:11, 16–18; 4:7, 11, 20), God

17

alone, revealed in the paradoxical glory of the cross, is the motive of faith. It is God's love that saves the world, and brings about the unity of faith (John 17:20–23), not calculations based on human expectations or resources.

A troubling possibility emerges. At any stage in the history of faith, the effective meaning of "the Jews" of the Gospel of John might well be translated in more familiar terms. It is not unknown, either in the past or in the present, that deeply committed disciples of Jesus, alive to the universal, unreserved self-giving of God's love for the world, suffer a scandal to their faith, not only from secular forces outside the Christian fold, but from some within it. These could understandably be named, depending on the situation, not only "the antichrist," but "the Catholics," "the Orthodox," "the Protestants," "the fundamentalists," "the Left/Right," even "the hierarchy," or "the clergy"—or, be it humbly confessed, "the theologians"! Since the problem of "the Jews" will occur so often in our treatment of the narrative sections of the Gospel, it is just as well to clear the air on this point, so that the real issue is not obscured: namely, the challenge to surrender to the only true God in a world dominated by false absolutes, and a willingness to be converted to unreserved universality of the Father's love.

5. Focus on God

Theocentric Christology

Lest this exploration seem pretentious, given that "no one has ever seen God" (1:18), or otiose—since all the books of the world cannot contain the Word of God (21:25)—it is worth pausing over the special problem we meet in an investigation such as this. Johannine studies have been thematized around many distinct issues—Christology, pneumatology, ecclesiology, ethics, and so forth. But the problem always seems to remain: the more the investigation of the Gospel is thematized, the more its central concern—presumed to be obvious to all—fades into the background. The Gospel is about God.[40] But such a transcendent and pervasive theme resists any easy delimitation. John's theology can never be unrelated to his Christology, nor, given the pervasive witness of the Spirit, disconnected from his pneumatology, and the "discernment of spirits" (1 John 4:1) in the conduct of the community. Most puzzling, "the world," an ever present theme, never escapes a vexing polyvalence of meaning. It is once the object of God's saving love (3:16), and yet the reality most resistant to the Word, and most oppressive of the typically beleaguered Christian community (9:22; 12:42; 16:2; 17:14–16; 1 John 2:15–17).

It is worth, then, trying another tack, in an effort to focus on what John himself is evidently concentrating on, and, even more deeply, on the express aim of Jesus himself. For instance, Jesus has not come to show himself to the world, but to make God known to the world (17:3, 10, 18, 21, 23). The flow of the personal consciousness of Jesus is irreducibly "Father-ward." The experience of God is the God of Jesus' experience, "...my Father and your Father, my God and your God" (20:17). The vitality of his mission draws its energy from an Other: "My food is to do the will of him who sent me and to complete his work" (4:34). In this regard, the "high Christology" of John is essentially relational.[41] As the only Son, Jesus lives from and for the Father. Jesus is not a cult figure, let alone a religious idol, nor a mere object of devotion in his own right (20:17). His "going away" is declared to be an advantage (16:7) and an occasion for rejoicing (14:28). The Word turned toward God in the beginning (1:1), who came from God and returns to God (13:3), has come to awaken the world to a new consciousness of the Father, through a worship in Spirit and in truth (4:23–24).

Every phase of the testimony of Jesus points to an utterly relational existence totally defined in terms of his being-from-and-
for the Father. He is "the Way," not the end (14:6). An authentic
Christology, then, is faced with the necessity of establishing, not
the *relativity* of the place of Jesus (as though there were some
other Word or some other "only Son"), but the *relationality* of
his identity and mission. In all that Jesus does, and in all that
happens to him leading him to the hour, God is present. The
grammatical sign of the authorial presence of the Father in the
drama of the world's salvation is the frequent use of "the divine
passive," as in the case of the "opened heaven" (1:51). Apart
from being one of the favorite symbols from the prophetic and
apocalyptic traditions, it is also present in early Christian tradition.[42] The "opened heaven" of John's Gospel indicates that the
unseen God is no longer hidden beyond the mysterious dome of
the sky, but will be "seen" in Jesus, the Son of Man.[43] Even at
the culminating point in the Gospel, when Thomas confesses the
Risen Jesus to be "my Lord and my God" (20:28), the nature of
his lordship and divinity still derives from his origin in the
Father (13:3–4; 14:28).

Jesus—Not Idol but Icon

In this regard, Jesus is not a blank screen onto which religious concerns are projected in the light of human needs and messianic hopes. Nor is he a mirror reflecting back our own faces. In
him believers behold not themselves, but the Father, the Other in
whose gaze they live (14:9–10). In this way, the Word incarnate
is not an *idol* set up even in innocent opposition to the infinity of
God, but the *icon* of the Father, backlit, as it were, by the light
that shines through him from a transcendent source into the
darkness of the world.[44] Human consciousness, now more than
ever, feels alone in the vast time space of the fifteen billions years

of cosmic emergence. Earthed on this tiny planet circling the sun—one of the hundred billion stars of our galaxy (in a universe of probably a hundred billion galaxies)—the human spirit may exhibit a peculiar creativity in fabricating an idol to assuage its dread, to project onto it some consoling meaning in order to fill the emptiness and to shrink the infinite to the measurable. But that is not the role of Jesus Christ in the Gospel of John. The infinite origin of the universe has uttered itself in the Word, and this Word has entered the world of human limitation. Far from being a human projection, the Word is God's own self-utterance into the darkened theater of the world.

The most accurate word, then, to describe our explorations is *theological,* in its original and strongest meaning. *Theos* and *Logos* are mutually conditioning terms. In the Gospel narrative, the Father, as the only true God, is invisible and inaudible save in light of the Word incarnate in the Son. And the Word-Son is unintelligible except as coming from, being for, and returning to the Father. For God is revealed in the flesh, in the full-bodied reality of the life and death of Jesus. In this sense, there is nothing *meta,* or "beyond," about the Gospel narrative. It is not God who is "beyond" the realities witnessed to, but the world of non-believers who are on the outside—blind, deaf, and defensive in regard to the glory of love that is being revealed (5:37–38). The journey of faith leads to an inside knowledge of God, into a communion with the Father and the Son in their unity (17:20–26). Within this communion, believers "see" the Father by seeing the Son (14:9), and come to know God through an active participation in the love that God is (1 John 4:8).

The Invisibility of God

Nonetheless, the invisibility of God remains, along with the impossibility of reducing the divine to an object or a particular factor within the world. Though the Johannine writings speak in strikingly intimate terms of our coming to know God (John 17:3; 1 John 4:7), being born of God (1:13; 1 John 3:9), and dwelling in God (1 John 4:16), there is a certain reserve when it comes to speaking about "seeing God." In fact, the Gospel states the opposite (e.g., 1:18; 1 John 4:12).[45] Aquinas continues this tradition by speaking of being joined to God as to one radically unknown who always transcends the limits of human knowledge. God is known only through the contemplation of the "effects" of his action. In other words, God is known in what he does, not directly, and never comprehensively.[46] Still, loving familiarity with God is possible, since love for God can go further than knowledge,[47] to "join" us to what always exceeds our knowing. As an explicitation of the Johannine experience of God ("everyone who loves is born of God and knows God" [1 John 4:7b]), this medieval position is far from irrelevant, as will be seen.[48]

6. The Gospel and the "Theology" of the Letters

We note here that the Letters of John have one particular relationship to the Gospel that is worth stressing at this early stage. If the experience of God brought home to believers in the Gospel narrative were to be sustained and appropriated by the later communities to whom the letters are addressed, a bold theological effort was needed. In the Letters, the intricate complexity of the Gospel narrative telling of the signs and words and deeds of Jesus yields to a series of intensely theological statements, though there is no question of attenuating the incarnational realism of the Gospel (cf. 1 John 2:2, 22; 3:16, 23; 4:2, 10; 5:6). The communities addressed in the Letters are more remote from the memory of historical presence of Jesus, and are feeling deprived of living eyewitnesses to all that had happened.

In this context, the experience of God comes to be central in a new way. Various affirmations of, or about, Jesus as the light (1:4–5; 8:12), the truth (14:6), the source of life (4:14; 6:57), and the embodiment of love (13:15) are now transposed into statements about God himself as light (1 John 1:5), as the source of life (1 John 5:11b), as the truth (1 John 5:20), and as love (1 John 4:8, 16b). Thus, the theological mystagogy of the Letters focuses many of the themes pervading the Gospel, to highlight the special character of the Christian experience of God. These later writings act as a kind of therapy for a community grown distracted, divided, or despondent in its faith: "Little children, keep yourselves from idols" (1 John 5:21).[49]

The relationship between the Gospel and the First Letter suggests one aspect of the method we will employ in the pages to follow. The decision to concentrate on the experience of God in the Johannine writings precludes the option of treating only a few choice "theological" passages. Naturally, this will pose its own problems, since it will not be possible to give an exhaustive commentary on the Gospel, even from this point of view. Still, the commentary work has been done,[50] and it enables us to move on to the topic of our special interest. After all, it is our basic contention that the fundamental concern of the Gospel and of Jesus himself is to lead into a living experience of God: "...this is eternal life, that they may know you the one true God" (John 17:3). But in the concreteness and, indeed, in the ongoing drama of Christian life in the world, the experience narrated in the Gospel must be brought into new focus. For the community of 1 John, that theological effort resulted from the counter experience of division, sinfulness, and failure, with the consequently intensified allure of a world that appeared too big, too self-assured—and too violent—for the God of faith to be true. Idols threatened. In the world immeasurably more vast than that accessible to the Johannine communities, our experience is different; and our idols, especially given the cultural atheism of modernity, are perhaps more imposing and enticing. And yet, even here, at this later time, we can return to what John invites us to, if only to ask: What if *this* were true; and that *here,* in fact, true life were to be found?

Notes

1. For example, Michael J. Buckley, *At the Origins of Modern Atheism* (New Haven: Yale University Press, 1987); Joseph S. O'Leary, *Questioning Back: The Overcoming of Metaphysics in the Christian Tradition* (New York: Seabury, 1985); John Milbank, *Theology and Social Theory: Beyond Secular Reason* (Oxford: Blackwell, 1993); William C. Placher, *The Domestication of Transcendence: How Modern Thinking about God Went Wrong* (Louisville: Westminster, 1996).
2. Nicholas Lash, *The Beginning and the End of Religion* (Cambridge: Cambridge University Press, 1996) 58.
3. Particularly relevant to specific aspects of doctrinal development are the following: John Courtney Murray, *The Problem of God* (New Haven: Yale University Press, 1964); Joseph Ratzinger, *Introduction to Christianity,* J. R. Foster, trans. (London: Search Press, 1969), 67–127; Jaroslav Pelikan, *The Emergence of the Catholic Tradition (100–600)* (Chicago: University of Chicago Press, 1971) 27–41; 172–266; Basil Studer, *Trinity and Incarnation: The Faith of the Early Church,* Matthias Westerhoff, trans., Andrew Louth, ed. (Collegeville, Minn.: Liturgical Press, 1993).
4. With regard to the range of problems—and challenges—associated with post-modernity, and the "deconstructive" methods associated with it, see Graham Ward, ed., *The Post-Modern God: A Theological Reader* (Oxford: Blackwell, 1997). The Editor's "Introduction" is particularly stimulating (xv–xlvii).
5. The need to be attuned to the experiential dimensions of Christian truth is challengingly brought out by Joseph O'Leary, *La vérité chrétienne à l'âge du pluralisme religieux* (Paris: Cerf, 1994).
6. *Summa Theologiae* 1, 43, 4 ad 1.

7. *Summa Theol.* 1, 43, 5 ad 2. See John Dedek, *"Quasi-Experimentalis Cognitio:* An Historical Approach to the Meaning of St Thomas," *Theological Studies* 22, 1961, 363–370.
8. *Summa Theol.,* 1, 1, 6 ad 3. The experiential component of Thomas's theological method is more obvious in his biblical commentaries, as we will see in reference to his commentary on John, *In Evangelium B. Joannis Expositio.* Our references will be to the Marietti edition of 1925. Translations from the Latin text are our own.
9. Bernard J. F. Lonergan, S.J., *Method in Theology* (London: Darton, Longman and Todd, 1972) 107, 120–123.
10. Ibid., 105–106. Cf. also, 340–343.
11. Ibid., 267–270.
12. Ibid., 106. While Lonergan here confines his biblical references to the Pauline letters, he evidences, especially in his later writings, a growing appreciation of John. See Frederick E. Crowe, S.J., ed., *A Third Collection: Papers by Bernard J.F. Lonergan, S.J.* (New York: Paulist Press, 1985), 53, 79, 84, 85, 88, 92, 93, 94, 97, 189, 191, 192, 194, 197, 220, 230, 231, though his earliest references are far from insignificant: for example, in an article written in 1943, "Finality, Love and Marriage," *Collection: Papers by Bernard Lonergan, S.J.* (London: Darton, Longman and Todd, 1967), 31.
13. Significant, too, for our study is Edward Schillebeeck's *Christ: The Christian Experience in the Modern World,* John Bowden, trans. (London: SCM Press, 1980). This monumental study of contemporary Christian experience devotes some 120 pages to the Johannine experience of God as love. As far as the notion of experience goes, he notes that the basic meaning of the Dutch word *ervaren* means "travelling through the country and thus—through exploration—being taken up into the process of learning...learning through direct contact with people and things" (31).
14. Karl Rahner, "The Experience of God Today," *Theological Investigations XI,* David Bourke, trans. (London: Darton, Longman and Todd, 1974), 149–165.
15. Ibid., 164.
16. Ibid., 165.
17. Hans Urs von Balthasar, *The Glory of the Lord: A Theological Aesthetics: I: Seeing the Form,* Erasmo Leiva-Merikakis, trans. (New York: Crossroad Publications, 1982), 228.
18. Ibid., 22.

19. Ibid., 237.
20. Ibid., 238–239.
21. Letter to William Sotheby, in volume II, p. 810, of *Collected Letters of Samuel Taylor Coleridge,* I–VI, E. L. Griggs, ed., New York: Oxford University Press, 1956–71.
22. Hans Urs von Balthasar, *Theo-Drama: Theological Dramatic Theory,* I–III, Graham Harrison, trans. (San Francisco: Ignatius Press, 1988–1992). A valuable overview is found in Edward T. Oakes, *Pattern of Redemption: The Theology of Hans Urs von Balthasar* (New York: Continuum, 1994), 211–250.
23. Oakes, *The Pattern of Redemption,* 218–221.
24. Von Bathasar, *A Theology of History* (London: Sheed and Ward, 1964), 33.
25. Von Balthasar, *Theo-Drama I,* 646.
26. In this regard, see the unsettlingly insightful Ernest Becker, *The Denial of Death* (New York: The Free Press, 1973).
27. See G. von Rad and G. Kittel, *"dokeo ktl." Theological Dictionary of the New Testament (TDNT)* 2 (Grand Rapids, Mich.: Eerdmans, 1964) 232–255.
28. John 5:41–44; 9:24; 12:43; 16:2; 1 John 2:15–17.
29. John 1:14b; 2:11; 7:39; 8:50, 54; 11:4, 40; 12:16, 28; 13:31; 14:13; 15:8; 16:14; 17:1, 5, 22, 24.
30. John 13:27; 14:30; 16:11; 17:12; 1 John 5:19.
31. John 8:40, 44; 10:31; 11:50; 12:10; 16:2–3; 1 John 3:11–15.
32. See James Alison, *Raising Abel. The Recovery of the Eschatological Imagination* (New York: Crossroad, 1996), especially 57–75, 138–145; and Gil Bailie, *Violence Unveiled: Humanity at the Crossroads* (New York: Crossroad, 1997), 217–234.
33. Raymond E. Brown, *The Community of the Beloved Disciple: The Lives, Loves and Hates of an Early Christian Community* (New York: Paulist Press, 1979).
34. With regard to the inclusive "our," and the self-giving character of "the Father" in the Johannine writings, see Dorothy A. Lee, "Beyond Suspicion? The Fatherhood of God in the Fourth Gospel," *Pacifica* 8/2, June 1995, 140–153, as it faces a range of feminist concerns.
35. On the meaning of a "classic," see David Tracy, *The Analogical Imagination: Christian Theology and the Culture of Pluralism* (New York: Crossroad, 1981) 99–202; B. Lonergan, *Method...,* 161–162. Here Lonergan cites Friedrich Schlegel's statement, "A

classic is a writing that is never fully understood. But those who are educated and educate themselves must always want to learn more from it" (161).

36. Note the prevalence of the Johannine comparative, "greater" (John 1:50; 4:11; 5:20, 36; 14:12, 28; 1 John 3:20; 4:4; 5:9). Cf., von Balthasar, *Theo-Drama* II, 128–130. See also the perceptive remarks of B. R. Gaventa, "The Archive of Excess: John 21 and the Problem of Narrative Closure," in R. A. Culpepper and C. C. Black, *Exploring the Gospel of John: In Honor of D. Moody Smith* (Louisville: Westminster John Knox Press, 1996) 240–252, especially pp. 240–249.

37. How the gift of God breaks in, and out of, all horizons determined by worldly exchanges has been well presented by Robyn Horner, *Rethinking God as Gift: Marion, Derrida and the Limits of Phenomenology* (Fordham: Fordham University Press, 2001). Of special interest here are her references to Marion's notion of "the saturated phenomenon" (cf., Jean-Luc Marion, "Le phénomène saturé," *Phénomènologie et théologie* [Paris: Criterion, 1992], 79–128). Fixed notions of objectivity and clearly determined horizons, along with any securely established subjectivity are overwhelmed, as it were, by the gift of God in Christ. The believer can only receive in an act of self-surrender, thereby being constituted as a subject (89–90, 116–118, 121).

38. See John Ashton, "The Identity and Function of the *Ioudaioi* in the Fourth Gospel," *Novum Testamentum (NT)* 27 (1985) 40–75.

39. John Ashton, *Understanding the Fourth Gospel* (Oxford: Clarendon, 1991), 151.

40. For an approach to the theology of the Fourth Gospel, which takes this as a starting point, see F. J. Moloney, "Johannine Theology," in R. E. Brown, J. A. Fitzmyer, and R. E. Murphy, eds., *The New Jerome Biblical Commentary* (Englewood Cliffs: Prentice Hall, 1989) 1417–26.

41. For a useful biblical-theological treatment of these issues, see Jean Galot, *Abba, Father: We Long to See Your Face. Theological Insights into the First Person of the Trinity*, trans. M. Angeline Bouchard (New York: Alba House, 1992). For a more challenging systematic exposition, see Robert W. Jenson, *Systematic Theology I: The Triune God* (New York: Oxford University Press, 1997) 93, 109–110, 165 *passim.*

42. See Gen 7:1, Isa 24:18; 64:1; Ezek 1:1; Mark 1:10; Matt 3:16; Luke 3:21; Rev 4:1.

43. W. Cadman, *The Open Heaven. The Revelation of God in the Johannine Sayings of Jesus,* G. B. Caird, ed. (Oxford: Blackwell, 1969); F. J. Moloney, *The Johannine Son of Man* (Second Edition; Biblioteca di Scienze Religiose 14; Rome LAS, 1978) 24–31.

44. Jean-Luc Marion, *God Without Being: Hors-Texte,* Thomas A. Carlson, trans. (Chicago: University of Chicago Press, 1991), 7–22.

45. Though 3 John 1:11b does associate doing good with "seeing God," it is most likely that the author is speaking in reference to God's revelation in Christ.

46. Summa Theol., 1, 12, 13 ad 1; *Summa contra Gentiles,* 3, 48. For his extended comment on John 1:18, see *In Evangelium B. Johannis...,* c.1, lect. 9.

47. *Summa Theol.,* 1–2, 27, 2 ad 2.

48. Especially when linked to the Thomist analyses of grace as an "interior instinct" (*In Evangelium B. Johannis,* c. 6, lect. 5, n. 3), as a conformity to the divine persons (*Summa Theol.,* 1, 43, 3–6), of charity as a participation in God's own love (2–2, 24, 2), and of the rules for the discernment of the state of grace (1–2, 112, 5).

49. D. Rensberger, *1 John, 2 John, 3 John* (Abingdon New Testament Commentaries; Nashville: Abingdon Press, 1997), 39–40; A. Kelly, "'God is Love': A Theological Moral Reading of 1 John," *Studia Moralia* XXVII/ 1, June 1999, 35–72.

50. In terms of translation, exegesis, and commentary, we are, understandably, following the three-volume work of Francis J. Moloney, S.D.B., *Belief in the Word: Reading John 1–4* (Minneapolis: Fortress Press, 1993); *Signs and Shadows: Reading John 5–12* (Minneapolis: Fortress Press, 1996); *Glory not Dishonor: Reading John 13–21* (Minneapolis: Fortress Press, 1998); and the recent commentary, F. J. Moloney, *The Gospel of John* (Sacra Pagina 4; Collegeville: The Liturgical Press, 1998).

2

The God of "The Prologue":
A *Theological* Reading
(1:1–18)

This "prologue" of the Gospel is designed to serve the Word it declares. It is a form of words that looks beyond itself to God's own self-expression and utterance. It declares a divine communication surpassing all inspired human words. Through God's Word the universe of "all things" (1:3a) is created, illumined, and enlivened. Yet it is this Word, successively designated as "this one" (1:2), the only Son (1:14c), and Jesus Christ (1:17b), who enters the flesh of our worldly existence to embody and tell the story of God.

From one angle the prologue of John's Gospel is not really a "prologue" at all. It suggests nothing "fore-Word." It is a direct celebration of "the Word," given from a realm beyond the "beginning-middle-end" of the various scripts that make up world history and human lives. This original and all-originating Word comes to make known the otherwise ineffable God. In this perspective, the Gospel narrative that follows is "epilogue," "after-Word." It fleshes out the presence of the Word among us—as his unbroken communion with the Father draws into itself all who come to believe (17:20–24; 20:17b). At every stage of the Gospel narrative, the Word incarnate is the teller and the telling-point of the story of the unseen God (1:18c).

As the Gospel story progresses, it repeatedly leads to a crisis. Is the original vision of the prologue being realized? Can the readers of the Gospel still believe in that vision as the story unfolds in all its drama? Can they continue to understand that story in the light of the original vision? Indeed, the final verses of the Gospel (20:30–31) could be paraphrased in the form of a question, "Now that you have been through the story of the life and light coming into the world, does the prologue make sense?" From our perspective, we ask, What kind of experience of God does the prologue suggest?

1. What Kind of Beginning?

1. In the beginning was the Word, and the Word was turned toward God; and what God was the Word also was. 2. He was in the beginning with God.[1]

In Contrast to Genesis

The "beginning" implied in these opening verses is in remarkable contrast to "the beginning" of Genesis (Gen 1:1), despite the obvious literary parallels. In the first verse of Genesis, we read, "In the beginning God created the heavens and the earth...." God is introduced as the creator of everything in the beginning of creation. It is a beginning *in* time, and even *of* time—as the week of creation unfolds in its ordered sequence of the Priestly account (Gen 1—2:3). But in the first verses of the Gospel, the beginning is otherwise.

God is not, first of all, the creator. He is not set in opposition to what is other, namely, "a formless void" and a "darkness covering the face of the deep" (Gen 1:2) into which the divine light-giving word is uttered. The other-than-God in the Genesis account is the *creandum,* the yet-to-be-created. If this other

30

exists formlessly together with God, as it were, it is not ostensibly turned toward God—except, perhaps, that in its very formlessness and in the depths of its darkness, it is crying out for order and light. The beginning of Genesis evokes a sense of the chaos awaiting a transformation into the cosmos. To these depths, despite their darkness, the source of light turns. Even so, as that which is to be formed and illumined, the chaos is in no sense divine.

To take note of the above, is to become aware of the totally other beginning that the prologue describes. First of all, God is not directly referred to. All received notions of God are held in reserve, since the Word is the immediate point of reference. It is not as though the world is to be created, as in Genesis, but that God is to be disclosed in reference to this Word. The *Logos* is outside time and creation; it already *was*. Not only is it there, outside of time and the whole order of creation, as something originally spoken, something communicable, the source of revelation about God, but it stands in its utter originality as "turned toward God" (1:1b). So complete is this original turning, so communicative and receptive is this relationship, that "what God was, the Word was" (1:1c). God will be revealed in a new originality through this Word that will be spoken into creation and into human history.

The extreme concision of the statement, "what God was, the Word was," even while defying a wholly satisfactory translation, is a reminder not to absolutize any culturally received notions of God. Typically, these evoke images of divine reality as alone in infinite perfection, as uncommunicative and unattainably aloof in regard to creation—as Greek philosophy and Gnostic spirituality might imply. What God is, is yet to be revealed. The Word, however, uniquely turned toward God as receptive and expressive of what God is, implies that the God of this beginning is turned, as speaker and communicator, not only to the Word, but to all who will receive what has been so uttered from the beginning.

And yet, as pointing forward to what has its beginning in him, the Word points back to what precedes the beginning. "This one" is turned toward the unsayable God in a relationship implying both communion with and distinction from the origin beyond all origin: "He was in the beginning with God" (1:2). The relationship implied is subtly nuanced affirmation of identity which, while guaranteeing the status of the Word as divine expressiveness, evidently leaves room for receptivity on the part of the Word and of relationship to the one who is uttered in him: "what God was the Word also was" (1:1c). Hence, the *enarchic* (in-the-beginning) Word is the self-expression of God.

Any prior privileged comprehension of God—positively, in terms of being, life, light, truth, love, and glory; or negatively, as opposed to the domain of "flesh"—is, following the logic of the prologue, doubly ruled out. First, the Word is himself indefinable save in relationship to the inexpressible source out of which he is uttered. And, second, this God-referred Word enarchically precedes and comprehends all human words and created realities. All human meanings are to be transformed in the light of another Meaning; and all human values will be revalued by what is to be revealed. It is little wonder, then, that the revelation about to be made in association with the measureless gift (3:34) is of the divinely autonomous Spirit (3:8).

Since "what God was, the Word also was" (1:1c), this Word is divine communication. There is no need to look beyond this Word for what God is and intends. Though the prologue will affirm that "the Word became flesh and dwelt among us" (1:14a), the identification of this Word with God is the original point of the Gospel. Hence, there arises the question fundamental to our investigation: What kind of Word *of God* is this Word? He is "of God" in the sense of being "from God," and "turned toward God" (1:1) in the beginning. He will tell "about God" in making the Father known (cf. 1:18). And being "what God was" (1:1c), he is the unique self-utterance of the divine. Thus the reader of the Gospel is brought to the brink of the most radical question: Who is the God of this Gospel? The most direct and simple answer must frame itself in reference to "the Word." God is primarily the one who speaks, and is spoken, but not only as "Word-ing" creation into light and life in a way similar to Genesis. For the divine mystery words itself, in a dimension antecedent to all creation in time. The divine self-utterance in the Word is not restricted to any temporal beginning. It evokes another realm of originality—that of the eternal divine vitality and communication, manifest in him who was "turned toward God," and was "in the beginning with God." In his *enarchic* character, the Word is turned in communion to God with whom, in a sense yet to be expressed, he is identified (1:1c). Yet who the God is to whom he is turned is still to be disclosed.

A later theology will refer to this as that eternal procession of the Word in God, grounding the temporal mission of the Word in history, as, for instance, Aquinas.[2] In "the beginning" of the prologue, God is not first named but yields place to this unique original *Logos*. Here we have a hint of the Gospel's original *"Logic"*—as it will be expressed in reference to the reciprocal glorification of the Father and the Son, and to the Son's return to the glory that was his "before the foundation of the world" (17:24).

The Johannine emphasis suggests that all cultural-religious notions of God are suspect, unless they are brought into reference to the Word that is to be revealed. Faith cannot start with a notion of "God," as if waiting to see how its previous conception is filled out, as it were, in relation to the Word. The reverse is demanded. To know the true God, faith must begin with the Word which was in the beginning, only to let that Word reveal what God is truly like. What is anticipated here is brought to lapidary expression in the words of Jesus, "Believe in God, believe also in me" (14:1–2).[3]

2. The Word and Creation

3. All things were made through him, and without him, nothing was made. What took place 4. in him was life, and the life was the light of humankind. 5. The light shines in darkness, and the darkness has not overcome it.

Though the prologue now unfolds into the sphere of creation, the primordial Word remains the focus. In the beginning, God is not presented immediately as the creator, but God-in-communion with the Word, communicating on the uncreated level of divine life and being. For the Word "...was in the beginning with God" (1:2). Out of this communion and communication, there results the existence of the universe: "All things were made through him, and without him nothing was made" (1:3).

Since "the Word was turned toward God" (1:1b), the original communication and self-utterance that the Word is transcends all modes of human conversation. In the vocabulary of faith, the meaning of "God" begins from and returns to this Word who is "with God" in the beginning. Nonetheless, the Word is not an abstract principle, but "he," *this one* (1:3–4, 10–11). An actual addressable subject is implied, one whose original identity will unfold only in the conversational world of human subjects. The people he meets, confronts, and calls will know him as "you." Here, too, later theology and doctrinal definitions will turn to the question of how there can be one subject belonging both to the divine realm of being, and to the realm of finitude and humanity. Previous notions structured on a great dividing line between God and finite existence will be relocated in a new horizon opening around "one and the same Our Lord Jesus Christ" who is "one in being with the Father as to the divinity and one in being with us as to the humanity."[4] Thus the falsely limiting options of Docetism, Arianism, Nestorianism, and Monophysitism are transcended. The eventual doctrinal solution is implicitly present in this personal pronoun, *houtos,* "he," "this one" (1:2), even if it would be anachronistic to expect that either the technical questions or the doctrinal resolutions that will emerge over the next four centuries are explicitly addressed. Yet it is on the basis of this vital biblical evidence, the later church, true to the direction of the Paraclete, will take its stance.[5] John's statement of the identity of the Word is concrete and compact. When *this one* who is the Word acts, speaks, prays, and suffers in the person of Jesus, "what God was" (1:1c) from the beginning is invoked, engaged, and revealed.

"All things were made through him" (1:3a): despite the differences existing among all created things, and despite their difference, even alienation, from God, the *Logos* is the genetic and unifying principle of the universe. The diversity of creation is a "uni-verse" because of its origin and coherence in the Word. All of creation is a field of divine communication, being "Word-ed" into being. This is the fundamental "logic" of the Gospel: nothing has meaning outside the divine *Logos.* Nothing and no one stands in its own right outside the primordial Word.[6]

A Dia-Logical World

The *Logos,* by reasons of his origin, incarnation, and mission creates an ever-shifting *dia-logical* space in which Jesus will enter into conversation with all the range of *dramatis personae* who will populate the dramatic unfolding of the Gospel narrative. Addressed by this Word, they will evince either acceptance, incomprehension, hesitation, doubt, questioning, or rejection, or any combination of such attitudes. The Word, dwelling among us (1:14b), thus opens a unique field of communication. The "Godward" *(pros ton theon)* status of Word in the first verse of the prologue presumes a certain dialogical dimension within the divine mystery itself. Certainly, as we shall see in John 17, when the God-Word relationship is unfolded in the prayer of the Son to the Father, this will be more evident. Coming out of this original communion, the Word enters the world to make it an expanding field of dialogue.[7] The living "flesh" of the world is made up of communication with others. Into such a conversation the Word is uttered, and into the dialogue originally existing between the Father and the Son the various actors of the Gospel drama are drawn. As this process reaches out to include believers of every age, God's unrestricted love for the world provokes the full play of human conversation as it turns on the meaning of life, God, human identity, and the destiny of the world itself.[8]

The Gospel, as a document of many conversations, enters the conversation that makes up the church in this present stage of its history. With its emphasis on unity and witness, it is a necessary inspiration to continuing ecumenical conversation taking place in all its modes. As the Word is the life and light of all peoples (1:3–5, 9), it radiates in interreligious dialogue, to open the possibilities of communication to a new register of meaning.[9] In faith's dialogue with contemporary science, it is not insignificant that "all things were made through him, and without him nothing was made" (1:3). The genesis of the cosmos and the ultimate unity of the universe, have their source in him.[10] In these and other instances, the Word has entered into the world of our communication and into the flesh of our conversation.

36

The God of "The Prologue"

An Ana-Logical Universe

In general terms, analogical language is designed to support intelligence as it attempts to formulate the unknown in terms of the already known.[11] In traditional philosophical instances, the human mind, participating in the wholeness of creation, moves from what is immediately experienced and expressible to a clouded knowledge of the creative mystery from which all things have come. In the prologue of the Gospel, such a pattern is reversed. The Word is presented as the first meaning in relation to which all our efforts to know must defer. All other *logoi*—words, sciences, philosophies, and theologies—are radically referred to this *Logos*.[12] As a result, there can be no self-sufficient theology pretending to capture the divine meaning within a limited human realm of meaning.

And yet we are confronted with a paradox at this point. How is the Word to be known, since he is turned to God in the beginning, and we human beings are not? The answer must wait on what theology refers to as to the incarnation of the Word (1:14). In this case of divine communication, the Word is at once like and unlike what falls within the range of our experience. While human and religious preconceptions will be repeatedly challenged in the light a new realm of experience—a "kingship which is not from this world" (18:36)—there remains a likeness through which the Word becomes accessible to the consciousness of faith. For the Word becomes flesh; he enters the world of words and deeds that make up the flesh of our existence. The Word becomes flesh; and the flesh becomes a story. As the Gospel will show, that story is made up of the conversations of Jesus with all the variety of those who receive or reject him. It unfolds in terms of their questions and all their experience of need, affliction, death, isolation, and defeat. Consequently, all the human conversations about who God is and what God wills are set in the context of the Word spoken and speaking "among us" (1:14). The extremes of enclosing God and creation within the sameness of human experience, on the one hand, and the sense of an unbridgeable gulf permitting no communication between God and the world, on the other, are met with what is implicit in the Johannine vision. The ultimate meaning of God and the radical meaning of the universe are intelligible only in reference to the incarnate *Logos*. The knowledge of faith is, therefore, in the deepest sense, "ana-*logical*."

When the Word is located "in the beginning" and immediately related to the reality of God (1:1), and when it has been identified as "this one" (1:2–3), a new kind of religious language demands to be forged. If *he* is the Word of God, and of the creation, life, and light which happen as a result, a new way of speaking about God is set in motion. The classic themes of Word, being, life, and light common to all ancient philosophies and religions are subsumed into a new mode of meaning. God is not known by a further refinement or extension of notions inherent in any human tradition. Rather, they are given a new twist, as it were, by being "earthed" in the story of the man, Jesus Christ. Divine revelation is received by encountering the Word made flesh and hearing the story he tells and embodies. God is thus "ana-*logically*" knowable as the one to be revealed in the expression and resonance of this Word.

The Integrity of Creation

This does not mean that creation is downplayed when its meaning and existence are centered in the divine Word. What it does mean, however, is that the true character of creation is known only in reference to the Word in whom the universe came to be. It is brought to fulfillment only when that Word is fully incarnated in the flesh of creation, when Jesus cries out on the cross, "It is finished" (19:30a).[13] Only when heaven is opened (1:51) does creation fulfill its destiny. Furthermore, the Word, as the light of all (1:4, 9), constitutes human identity in a holistic relationship both to God from whom he comes, and to the "all things" he creates and illumines. Since the Word is turned toward God, all that has been worded into being and life and light in him are drawn into his God-ward "turning." The Word is inscribed into the existence of all that is, just as all creation communicates in him in whom it originates, coheres, and converses.

This experience will lead to a vision of heaven made open, and "the angels of God ascending and descending on the Son of Man" (1:51). Once the Word has become flesh, the horizons of past history are reoriented in the light of this unique event of God's self-revelation. There is nothing on the outside of this event. Everything and everyone is enfolded in the creative Word. There is no originally exterior darkness, no zone of existence outside the domain of the Word. It will appear also, because of "the life that took place in him" (1:3–4), that there is even no clear disjunction between life or death (cf. 6:47, 50, 54, 57–58; 11:26). Even the ostensibly clear metaphors of up or down, "from above" and "from below" must now be refocused in the event of the Word become flesh, dwelling "among us" (1:14). The primeval struggle between darkness and light is given a new sense through the primordial light already in possession (1:5). Most important, there is no separation between what God is and what he has revealed, for that, too, has been transcended in the statement, "and what God was the Word also was" (1:1c). Likewise any traditional distinction of flesh from spirit is called into question. The flesh is not only included in the genetic totality of "all things" coming to be in the Word. For flesh is what that same Word has become. Likewise, "faith and reason" are no longer mutually exclusive. Through the Word and its light, such a dichotomy yields to another economy of knowing: "The true light that enlightens everyone was coming into the world" (1:9), to be "the fullness of the gift that is truth" (1:14a). Most challenging, the conflict of divine and human freedoms, no matter how dramatic and seemingly terminal that conflict appears as the Gospel unfolds, occurs in the spaciousness of a universe cohering in the Word who is the light and life of all. The creative Word enters into a world of created freedoms (1:11–13), as addressed to freedom and for the sake of freedom. The disciples of Jesus will not only "know the truth" (8:32a), but "the truth will make you free" (8:32b). In the "Word-ed" universe, freedom is a reality that will come to its own fulfillment: to those who believe in him, he gives "the power to become children of God" (1:12).

Genesis recounts how human beings had, in their pride, once aimed "to build ourselves a city, and a tower with its top in the heavens; otherwise we shall be scattered abroad upon the face of the whole earth" (Gen 11:4). God goes down to intervene (11:6–8), with the result that the abandoned city "was called Babel, because there the LORD confused the language of all the earth" (11:9). The "Babelization" of language at the origins of human history are now confronted with another kind of speaking, that of the Word in the beginning before all human beginnings.[14] The words of the Word will promise both unity and true glory to those who receive him (John 12:32; 17:20–25). It is a God-given language since the Word, as the only Son of the Father, will speak only what he has heard from the Father (7:16; 12:49). In contrast to the attempt to mount to heaven by building a tower, John's Gospel will present a lifting up of quite another kind (8:28).

Life and Light: A Decisive Happening

Something utterly decisive has occurred. It is suggested in the subtle change of tense in the use of the verb "to become."[15] Hence, the declaration: "What took place in him was life"

40

(1:3b–4). In contrast to any understanding of the Word as an englobing cosmic presence, the focus shifts to an event within creation and its history. Where before all things came to be in the Word, now the Word comes to be within that universe.[16] A specific happening of the Word as the source and form of true life has occurred. This life is evidenced in the new consciousness made possible by what has happened: "and the life was the light of humankind" (1:4). The vitality of the Word will throw light on who God is, on what the world of creation is, and on the promise inherent in human destiny. The Word enters the flow of time as the embodiment of life; and expands the meaning of creation in the radiance of light.[17] Existence now has a new vital energy at work within it, and is illumined by a new meaning and direction. All this has been made possible within creation in the happening of primordial life among us of the Word-become-flesh.

What, then, does the gift of "life" which happens in the Word add to that fact that all things were made in him? Another level of relationship to God is implied. Through what has taken place, creation is made open to the original liveliness and vitality of God and the Word (1:1c). It can share in the Word's "being-turned" toward God in the beginning (1:1b), in receptivity, and communion. The enlivening presence of the Word is utterly alien to death-bound *bios* of isolated and self-assertive existence of a world closed in on itself.[18] In the coming of the Word, human existence is brought into the radiant field of its divine origin and God-ordained destiny.

Still, the Gospel of the Word is neither theological information nor a contemplative escape from the drama of being in the world: "The light shines in the darkness, and the darkness has not overcome it" (1:5). The prologue recognizes the threat of an enveloping darkness, and the impending realities of suffering and rejection. But the light continues to shine. In the interplay of the symbols of light and darkness, the evangelist depicts the luminous presence of the Word as the abiding source of Christian faith and hope. Nonetheless, there is a non-divine darkness which is somehow a counter-principle to the original being, life, and light inherent in the divinely originated Word, and in the origin of all things in him. The ruler of this world (16:11) is an agent of darkness and deception, organizing the world to reject its true life (cf. 1 John 2:15; 3:8); and the domain of the flesh is a chiaroscuro of countervailing influences. There is a struggle of light against a darkness blind to all that is truly of God.

Though an inevitable conflict awaits the appearance of the Word, a serene confidence is expressed: "...and the darkness has not overcome it" (1:5b). The conviction that light will continue to shine in an inextinguishable radiance suggests that the Gospel is written out of an experience both luminous and liberating. Even at this early stage, the subversive light of the Cross is intimated. The darkest moment of the world's rejection of the Word will be the hour when the glory of God's love will be shine forth.

3. The Witness of John the Baptist

In this first interruption of the flow of the prologue, an instructive contrast to the role of the Word is given. Reference is made to another actor in the Gospel drama, who also enjoyed a unique divine mission:

> 6. **There was a man sent from God, whose name was John. 7. He came for testimony, to bear witness to the light, that all might believe through him. 8. He was not the light, but came to bear witness to the light.**

The previous exalted account of the origin of the Word is now compared with an eminent religious figure—perhaps emblematic of all great "God-people" who are named in human history. That this John was especially known and revered is clearly recognized by the writer and first readers of the Gospel. While in this case there is no implication of divine origins, this John is declared to be "sent by God" (1:6). He has been given a unique mission and vocation within the religious history of Israel and the world. But this is intelligible only in relation to the original Word. John came to bear testimony, however, not to God directly, nor even to the Word in general, but to the luminous event through which the Word of God has entered the world "to bear witness to the light"—that "all might believe through" the one who is uniquely the Word and light. Just as the Word is turned toward God, John, in his mission from God, is turned toward the Word who is the light. If through the Word all things were made, John's role consists in calling "all" to believe in the one through whom they were created. Though not the light himself, John, in his God-given mission taking place in the temporal unfolding of events, "came to bear witness to the light" (1:8). He is a historical witness to the historic fact that the Word has entered our history, to dwell among us. John is indeed a luminous presence, but only by reflecting the original light— who is not yet identified with a human name.

4. The Word Within a World of Conflict

9. The true light that enlightens everyone was coming into the world. 10. He was in the world, and the world was made through him, yet the world knew him not. 11. He came to his own home, and his own people received him not. 12. But to those who received him, who believed in his name, he gave power to become children of God; 13. who were born,

**not of blood nor of the will of the flesh nor of the will
of man, but of God.**

The presence of the Word in the world, soon to be
expressed in the climactic terms of incarnation, is at this stage
described as a universal illumination (1:9). The paradox implicit
in the divine origin of the Word entering the world is now
brought out. He enters the world as a particular figure, even
though "the world was made through him" (1:10b). The Word
of divine origin and the principle of universal creation is not presented as some abstract universal truth. *He* is "in the world," the
embodiment of its meaning and destiny. A further irony exacer-
bates the paradox, for "yet the world knew him not" (1:10c). In
not recognizing him, the world not only does not recognize his
divine origin, but also misses the point of its own original meaning. In failing to appreciate the "Word-ed" reality of its existence, it cannot receive the life being offered.

The Word Immanent within Human History

It should be noted that the Word "was in the world"
(1:10a) in a way that God is never said to be "in the world."
Though philosophical and theological thought envisages the
immanence of the Creator to creation, God is never an object
within the sphere of creation, or a reality contained within the
universe. Yet, if the Word is what God is, a new dimension of
divine immanence is being suggested. He is *in* the world as the
one through whom the world exists (1:3, 10b). Spatial and
instrumental metaphors break down in the face of a divine order
of communication and immanence in regard to creation. The
world did not know him through whom it was created (1:10c),
as the many confrontations narrated in the Gospel will bring
out. The representatives of the "the world" were looking for

God in the wrong place—in a transcendent above, rather than in the heaven opened in its midst (1:51).

He came "to his own home," into a creation in whose meaning and existence the Word was already inscribed. The *ta idia,* the true dwelling place envisaged by the Gnostics situated beyond the realm of vulgar experience, is here given a new meaning. Spiritual initiates are not transported into a transcendent realm; for it is the transcendent and creative Word that comes into the world. The true home is not attained by escaping the flesh of this world in a kind of stratospheric spiritual self-realization. When the Word enters the world to meet his own people he finds them enthralled in their own other-worldly projections. Reaching for a God and a salvation of their own making, they reject him through whom they were made, their life and light.

With the Word coming to his own home and meeting rejection from his own people, a further revision of the Genesis story occurs. Adam and Eve, by their disobedience, had shut out the Word of God's command from the garden (Gen 2:16–17; 3:1–7). As a result, they are themselves expelled from paradise by God's decree (Gen 3:22–24). But, in the context of the prologue, it is the Word who is expelled from what was his, for "his own people received him not" (1:11).

The Empowering Word and the Children of God

Yet such rejection is not universal. The light is not overcome by the darkness. There are "those who received him, who believed in his name" (1:12). Amongst these are those by whom and for whom the Gospel is written. By believing in his name, even though the name of the Word is still to be given, they have received him as the source of new life. Already, the Word, by virtue of his original intimacy with God and of the communication of life that has happened in him, has exercised a generative power of divine dimensions. Those receptive to it have been empowered to participate in the divine life as God's children (1:12c). The prologue thus attests that the Word embodies not merely a promise of future salvation, but is already effective and generative with regard to whose have become God's children.

The gift of divine filiation is declared to be utterly outside the domain of earthly biology, sexual procreation, and human control. It comes from beyond the mundane powers of *bios, eros,* and *techne.* The genesis of this new relationship to God is brought about by the Word, for "in him was life" (1:4). But at the same time it is brought about by God: "...but of *God*" (1:13b). The manner in which those who receive the Word and believe in his name are quickened into new life cannot be reduced to some form of intraworldly genesis. This gift comes only from the giver whose power to give is outside the limits of all human giving and receiving.[19] The extent of the giving and the capacity to receive hinge on the astonishing intimacy of the Word become flesh, with the "us" of creation.

The Incarnation of the Word

14. And the Word became flesh and dwelt amongst us, the fullness of the gift that is truth. We have gazed upon his glory, glory as of the only Son from the Father.

This declaration brings into sharpest focus the previous themes of the prologue. Though all things had been made through him (1:3), the creative Word has entered the world of creation, to coexist, in the sphere of finitude and distance from God, with us human beings. While "what took place in him was life, and the life was the light of humankind" (1:3–4), the life that

46

happened in him is now presented as enfleshed in our worldly existence. As "the true light that enlightens everyone was coming into the world" (1:9), the Word is now declared as coming to be in the world of flesh. He is the light, not merely from outside, but from inside, the earthly domain of our human existence.

The shock of the statement, "and the Word became flesh," will be felt through the whole Gospel story. Both the Wisdom literature of Israel and ancient philosophical traditions would have had little trouble assimilating the idea of a *Logos* as a creative principle, the source of life and light and union with the divine. But the specific and scandalous contention of Christian faith is that the divine Logos has become *flesh*. The result is a new and startling genesis—of the Word coming to be within the physical, alienated, finitude of human being. While this "flesh" has in no sense brought forth the Word (cf. 1:13), the Word is nonetheless brought forth in the flesh.

The symbol of "flesh" is thus revalued. Even though it retains its negative connotations, more typical of Pauline thought as a domain of human experience closed to the "spiritual" realm of God,[20] a new positive meaning, hospitable to the Spirit, blooms in this incarnational becoming (1 John 4:2). What was imagined and experienced to be most separated and alienated from God, is now appropriated by the Word as a domain of saving communication. As a consequence of his incarnation, his flesh will give life (6:51b, 53–58).

The hitherto closed world of the "flesh" is broken open in two directions, from above and from within. From above, because the Word who "was what God was" has become flesh. The incarnate Word provokes humanity to a new self-appropriation of itself within the universe that coheres in him. From within, because this Word disrupts any sense of self-containment and fulfillment deriving from human capacities (1:13), and even gifts given in the past (1:16). What we are as human beings is defined by the as yet indefinable God. As children *of God,* believers find themselves in turning toward God in the God-ward-ness of the Word himself (1:1). To this extent, the experience evoked in the prologue jars any tendency to locate God or even ourselves within the bounded worlds of routine human experience.

5. The All-Fulfilling Gift

The uniqueness of the genesis of the Word in the world is further brought out in that he "dwelt amongst us" (1:14b). It evokes Old Testament associations with the divine wisdom dwelling in the midst of the people of Israel (cf. Sir 24:8–10), and with the divine glory resting on the tabernacle (cf. Exod 25:8; 40:35). Yet the dwelling of the Word among us is a new kind of gift, "the fullness of a gift which is truth" (1:14c).

The Gift of the Truth

What has appeared in the incarnation of the Word is both the fulfillment and the plenitude of the divine gift. It is described as "truth," a key word in the Gospel narrative to follow. It will exhibit various meanings as it reveals God, engenders new life, brings light, effects judgment, offers freedom, calls to faith, nourishes the hungry, heals, commands mutual love, forgives sin, and promises the Spirit—to mention the more obvious instances. The truth is a reality, indeed, *the* reality, for the Word through whom all things were made has now become flesh. The prologue witnesses neither to a new divine attitude to the world, nor to a new philosophical comprehension of God by the world. It is about a climactic communication of divine Word—to the world, but by dwelling "among us." The Word, having entered history, occasions a judgment on everyone in so far as they receive or reject him. In his light, a believer becomes someone other compared to previous horizons of understanding. Through the gift of the truth, everyone is now addressed by the Word.[21] And God is no longer the all-transcending supreme truth of the philosophers, but the "you," addressed by Jesus, and addressing believers, through him (17:1–26; 20:17). While the immediate focus is on the gift embodied in the incarnate Word, the giver of such a gift is implied—the God to whom the Word is turned. Recipients of the gift are brought into a new relationship with the giver. They are made "children of God" (1:12), by no earthly agency (1:13), solely in terms of the divine act of giving.

The Only Son

The gift of the truth brings its own experience of divine glory: "We have gazed upon his glory, glory as of the only Son from the Father" (1:14c, d). Throughout the Bible, the divine glory was presented as the visible manifestation of the presence of God.[22] Through the advent of the Word in the flesh, a community of faith has come into being, gifted with an all-fulfilling manifestation of the divine presence. Those who have been made "through him" (1:3, 10b), who have been quickened by the life that has happened "in him" (1:4a), who have been illumined with the light of that life (1:4b), who have received power to become the children of God from him (1:12), now contemplate the glory that he receives as the only Son of the Father (1:14c).

In contrast to worldly reputation and earthly glory, themes often visited in the Johannine writings (12:43; 1 John 2:15; 5:21), believers recognize another kind of glory. The distinctiveness of this radiance is brought home by means of a fresh metaphor that will pervade the whole Gospel narrative. The Word is "the only Son from the Father" (1:14d). Thus, the (already) symbolic designation of Jesus as Word now extends into an expressly interpersonal, familial analogy. The Word "turned toward God" (1:1b) is now affirmed as the only Son issuing from the Father. The interrelationship of this Father and this Son will allow for the expression of the drama of both God's own self-giving love for the world (3:16) and the role of the Son as an actor within it.

In this regard, it is noteworthy that the "we" of the witnessing community referred to here has beheld, not the glory of God directly, nor the glory of the Word turned toward God, nor of the Son *with* the Father (e.g., John 17:5), but the glory of the only Son as he comes *from* the Father. Believing readers of the Gospel are here being exposed to the divine activity of revelation, and drawn into it. In this sense, the divine glory is beheld, not first of all as the radiance of intradivine communion, but in terms of the Father's communication to the world through his only Son. The "we" of this prologue declares that God's revelation is in progress.

6. John and the "Time" of the Word

The mysterious genesis of the divine eternal Word in time is underscored once more by the witness of John [the Baptist]:

15. John bore witness to him, and cried, "This was he of whom I said, 'He who comes after me ranks before me, for he was before me.'"

The cry of the Baptist witnesses to the mysterious origin of the one he witnesses to. Even though the Word has come into the world after John, his coming transcends any temporal sequence, or any dependence on the mission of his predecessor. For the Word from the beginning is located before all history and human witness. Thus, the witness of this man, John, a historically identifiable person, brings out the uniqueness of the Word's coming in the flesh. On the one hand, John testifies to him as here, in the fabric and flow of human history. On the other hand, the Word and Son is confessed to be from beyond the span of space and time. Thus John, himself sent by God (1:6), defers to the primordial Word he witnesses to. While the Baptist uses the categories of "after" and "before" to describe his testimony in relation to the Word, there is no such implication of any before and after in the relationship of that Word to God (cf. 1:1–3).

7. The Gift in Place of All Gifts

16. And from his fullness we have all received, a gift in place of a gift. 17. For the Law was given through Moses; the gift that is the truth came through Jesus Christ. 18. No one has ever seen God; the only Son, who is turned toward the Father, he has made him known.

In the compenetration of eternity and time implied in the witness of John [the Baptist], the "we" of believers who have "received him, who believed in his name" (1:12a, b), who have been transformed into "the children of God" (1:12c), have thereby received the gift of a unique fulfillment and plenitude: "And from his fullness have we all received" (1:16). It is a plenitude in that the invincible light (1:5), the true light (1:9), has shone. But the fulfillment is in fact described as a replacement of former gifts, "a gift in place of a gift" (1:16). The former gift is directly linked to Moses and, thereby, to Israel. Implicitly, too, it evokes, on a more cosmic register, the gift of creation including humankind as a whole within the domain of the Word-created universe. In this time of fullness, the restriction inherent in former gifts is surpassed. The new gift is available to "all." It replaces the former limited dispensation. In this "fullness," as in the categories of being, life, light, and Logos, the prologue undermines the lofty pretensions of a gnostic vocabulary. "His fullness" is not a *pleroma*—a self-realization reserved for initiates into the heavenly sphere. It is a gift made in the actuality of our human history, indeed, in the very flesh of our existence. In the incarnation of the Word, in the advent of the only Son from the Father, gnostic flights are brought back to earth. The fullness of the truth is among us.

With two names, the prologue situates the saving gifts of God within human history, Moses, and Jesus Christ (1:17). Though the Mosaic gift is not demeaned, it is presented as succeeding to the unsurpassable gift embodied in Jesus Christ. How the one gift is to yield to the other will be described in the Gospel in many ways. It is worth noting, nonetheless, that the complete character of the final gift is emphasized. The law was given; hence a gift; but what succeeds it is "the gift which is the truth." This does not mean that the Mosaic gift was not genuinely God-given, but that a plenitude of divine revelation has occurred through the Word and only Son, now finally identified as "Jesus Christ." In this man, Jesus Christ, Word with God and Son from the Father, God's giving has reached a climactic generosity. Limitless dimensions of God's creation were previously presented in reference to the Word, the life, and light that have entered the world in the "glory as of the only Son from the Father" (1:14d). These are now earthed in a man with a name. On him, in conversation and conflict with many others to be named in the Gospel, the drama of salvation will turn. God's self-revelation has become a matter of history.

8. Making Known the Invisible Giver

The prologue ends by directing its readers from the gift to the giver. If God has uttered his Word in the flesh, if the Father has sent his only Son, if God is so unreserved in giving, how are we to imagine the God who is the source of such grace? The answer is to be found in the gift: "No one has ever seen God; the only Son, who is turned toward the Father, he has made him known" (1:18). The invisible mystery of God the giver is made known in the flesh of history. By initially focusing on the Word, the prologue suggests that God is to be heard, rather than seen. Even as it rejoices in "gazing" on the glory of the only Son, the visibility in question is of the Son *from* the Father (1:14cd). God is invisible and the Father inexpressible—except by becoming visible and expressible through his Word and Son. Because Jesus Christ alone is turned toward God as the Word (1:1b), and turned toward the Father as the only Son (1:18b), he embodies the gift of the truth and tells the story of God.

The remarkably direct denial of any human capacity to see God, with which the prologue concludes, is not only an affront to the Jewish piety of the day; it also undercuts prevalent gnostic pretensions of knowing the absolute One and the True. Yet the negativity of this denial serves the positive plenitude of God's self-revelation in Jesus Christ. The negation works in the believer to inspire a sense of receptivity and surrender before the mystery of the Father and his will. Faith brings no controlling knowledge of God. What it does bring is a relationship to Jesus Christ—soon to be revealed as the way, the truth, and the life (cf. 14:6). To know him is to know the Father (14:7, 9–11). In his heart-to-heart, Fatherward relationship (1:18b), the only Son is unreservedly receptive to the divine will, and to all that God is. The eternal character of Jesus' identity as Word is thereby acted out in a relationship extended through his whole historical existence. Through this dialogical relationship the Father will be revealed; and his love for the world (3:16) will be enacted and expressed in the events that make up the Gospel story.

The Gospel prologue has not aimed primarily to teach a new idea of God, but to introduce a story leading to an all-surpassing new experience of God—who is yet to be disclosed in the glory of Jesus. Thereby, it stands as declaration demanding to be countersigned by innumerable generations of others in their experience of the life, the light, and the love that has come to them.

This is to say that, though the Word does not reduce human speech to silence, it does affect human powers of expression with a kind of unrelenting negation in the light of the excess that marks the glory to be revealed. It is unlike what "we know" (cf. 1:41, 45; 3:2, 9–10; 5:37b, etc.), always outside the horizon of human anticipation and experience. Until its hearers come to the hearing and seeing of faith, all lesser levels of hearing and seeing are radically called into question. On the other hand, neither previous revelation nor the original coherence of all things in the Word are negated. The great positives remain. Jesus will still be numbered among "the Jews [from whom] comes salvation" (4:22). The Word he embodies and communicates is still the fulfillment of the Scriptures (1:23; 6:45; 17:12; 19:24, 36). The world continues to be the object of God's love (3:16). Even with his historical departure, Jesus is still present, to the advantage of his disciples, in the gift of the Spirit (16:7), and in the blood and water of the sacraments (19:34–35). Above all, the original glory which was proper to the Son "before the foundation of the world" (17:24) breaks on that world in the final hour of fulfillment. And the genesis of all creation in the Word comes to its fulfillment in his exultant cry, "It is finished" (19:30).

Christian reflection, in attempting to mediate the original meaning of the Word to later historical contexts, must be continuously creative. It must necessarily strive to keep alive a sense of the vitality and originality of the One who is revealed in

Christ. For the Word comes as a judgment on all history and on every age, in its faith and unbelief alike. The essential theological task is one of bringing back the reflection of faith to its essential mystery—*reductio in mysterium*[23]—to the Godward Word, the only Son from the Father, coming into the world to make God known.

9. Four Dimensions of Meaning

The Word becomes flesh, and thus enters into the world of human meaning. Lonergan identifies four dimensions of the meaningful world: the cognitive, the constitutive, the communicative, and the effective.[24] Each of these is applicable to the task of bringing out the meaning of the Word among us.

First, *cognitive* meaning. This dimension of meaning implies a definable content grasped in an objective judgment. It is inherent in faith's answer to the questions: Who is the one true God? How is this God revealed? How is the divine will to be discerned? Meaning functions under the weight of an evidence that inclines faith to judge yes or no; here, not there; in this, not that; thus, and not otherwise. It culminates in an assent to the truth to which, in an objective sense, we are beholden, the light in which we are judged, the unrestricted character of the love that has revealed itself. In this cognitive dimension, the Word enters our experience as an objective *datum*, provoking questions, and demanding an assent to the reality of the God he reveals.

Second, meaning functions in a *constitutive* manner. The meaning of the Word affects the experience of human identity. In this dimension, the Word of God "informs us," not just as telling us about God, but as forming our identity in the light of the divine meaning. This meaning "constitutes" us believers, in an awareness of ourselves as "the children of God," and recipients of the gift of the truth. The believer "indwells" the divine meaning to find a new self in the light of what God is. In that light we have a new identity as the whole horizon of our living is radically affected. Alive to this dimension of meaning, we can read the Gospel with the question, "What new identity do we have as believers in the light of the God who is self-revealed in Jesus Christ?"

Third, the meaning of the Word is *communicative*. A community of common experience, conviction, and identity is the result of a shared possession of the deeply meaningful. We are "meant" into a coexistence founded in our common experience of God. This dimension of meaning is evidently of prime importance in all of the New Testament, and notably in this Gospel, and the other writings connected with it. The very choice of the name "the Word" in the first verse of the prologue underlines the communicative dimension, pervading the Gospel right to its end (20:31). At a moment of climactic intensity, Jesus asks the Father that the disciples and their successors be one as he and the Father are one (17:20–24). In and through the Word, the meaning of God is communicative. Hence, questions inevitably arise out of the Johannine experience of God: how does the God revealed in Jesus Christ affect the way we relate to one another? How is the experience of God an experience of communication and community?

And last, the meaning of the Word is *effective*. Jesus Christ, and the God revealed through him, enable Christians to transform the world in new and hopeful ways. The experience of God brings with it an orientation, a conversion, a commandment, and a way of life affecting every aspect of existence. So central to the Johannine experience of God is this effective dimension that John can write, in as many words, that the three other dimensions of divine meaning collapse if the effective meaning is not at work. To pretend to love God while hating a member of the community is to be in darkness (1 John 2:9, 11). We cannot love the invisible God without loving the all-too-visible human other (1 John 4:20). Hence, the exhortation, "Let us love one another, because love is from God. Everyone who loves is born of God and knows God" (1 John 4:7). Given the eminence of effective meaning inherent in the experience God in John's writings, an important hermeneutical question is this: How does the experience of God inspire and even depend on a world-shaping praxis?

All this is to suggest that the Word "words" the divine meaning in accord with these four dimensions. They are interwoven and interpenetrate in a holographic manner within the density of the Word's incarnate reality. While they can never constrict the utter originality of the Word to the limited dimensions of human meaning, the articulation of these four dimensions is a valuable tool in interpreting the experience of God as attested to in the writings we are considering.

While the shifting texture of the consciousness of Johannine faith cannot be straitjacketed by these dimensions of meaning, still, the four dimensions—God-given objectivity, identity, community, and praxis—are always present. Cognizance of them can only make our interpretation of the Johannine witness more nuanced and comprehensive. It is rare that scholars treat more than one or the other of these dimensions. They thereby unwittingly shrink the multi-dimensional field of meaning inherent in the Johannine writings, and so impoverish their sense of faith's experience of God.

After this extended reflection on the prologue, and the experience of God it frames, we now pass to "epilogue," to the ways in which the Son has made the Father known.

Notes

1. The translations of the original Greek are taken from the commentary of F. J. Moloney, *The Gospel of John* (Sacra Pagina 4; Collegeville: The Liturgical Press, 1998).
2. *Summa Theol.*, 1, 27, 1; 34, 1–3; 43, 1–8; *In Evangelium B. Joannis*, c.1, lect. 1.
3. Von Balthasar, in *The Glory of the Lord 1*, observes, "Only God can express God authentically. Thus, the 'ontological difference' in the first verse of John's prologue...immediately indicates the total reality at stake here: it is, so to speak, the act of putting on those eyeglasses that allow us to observe the phenomenon in a stereoscopic and plastic fashion" (615).
4. J. Neuner and J. Dupuis, eds., "The Symbol of Chalcedon," *The Christian Faith in the Doctrinal Documents of the Catholic Church* (London: Collins Liturgical, 1982) #614, p. 154.
5. Or, as the Fathers of Chalcedon expressed it, "He is one and the same only-begotten, God the Word, the Lord Jesus Christ, as formerly the prophets and later Jesus Christ have taught us about him and has been handed down to us by the Symbol of the Fathers," *The Christian Faith...*, #611, p. 153.
6. *Summa Theol.*, 1, 34, 3: "Because God understands both himself and all things in one act, the single divine Word is expressive, not only of the Father, but also of all creatures."
7. In reference to an influential Jewish philosophy of dialogue, see L. Augustine Brady, "Martin Buber and the Gospel of John," *Thought* 201, September 1978, 283–292.
8. For the hermeneutical (and human) importance of the play of conversation, see David Tracy, *The Analogical Imagination*, 101, 446–455; *Pluralism and Ambiguity. Hermeneutics, Religion, Hope* (San Francisco: Harper and Row, 1987), 16–27.
9. J. O'Leary, *La vérité chrétienne*, 21–47, 163–194.
10. See Anthony J. Kelly, *An Expanding Theology: Faith in a Word of Connections* (Newtown, NSW: E. J. Dwyer, 1993. Ridgefield, Conn.: Morehouse Publishing, 1993). In reference to the Prologue, 69–90.
11. For an excellent critical survey of the significance of analogy in contemporary theology, see Philip A. Rolnick, *Analogical Possibilities: How Words Refer to God* (Atlanta: Scholars Press, 1993).

12. The relationship of the *Logos* to the *logoi* of creation is one aspect of the great cosmic vision of Maximus Confessor. See Lars Thunberg, *Man and the Cosmos: The Vision of Maximus the Confessor* (Crestwood, N.Y.: St Vladimirs Seminary Press, 1985), and Andrew Louth, *Maximus the Confessor* (London: Routledge, 1996) for texts and critical comment.

13. J. Alison, *Raising Abel*, 72–74, and Gil Bailie, *Violence Unveiled: Humanity at the Crossroads* (New York: Crossroad, 1997), 219–228: both make telling points regarding the Johannine sense of creation.

14. This is not to suggest that the shifting contexts of theological language ever achieve a total expression of the Word. That would only replace the Babelized situation with the pretensions of logomania. In fact, the transcendence of the Word over all human words and contexts keeps the language of faith ever open to new possibilities of interpretation. See Joseph O'Leary, *La vérité chrétienne*, 81–90.

15. The versatile Greek verb, *ginomai,* has many possible meanings. In 1:3ab it refers to the *panta*, the "all things" of creation, in the aorist form of *egeneto*. But in its tense in 3c, *gegonen:* the reference is no longer to the act of creation, but to an act which happened in the past and continues its influence into the present, namely, the "happening" of life and light in the incarnation.

16. For this interpretation of 1:3b–4, see F. J. Moloney, *Belief in the Word: Reading John 1–4* (Minneapolis: Fortress Press, 1993), 30–34. For a magisterial overview of the Word's coming to be within the becoming and evolving universe, see Karl Rahner, "Christology within an Evolutionary View of the Word," *Theological Investigations* V, Karl-H. Kruger, trans. (Baltimore: Helicon, 1966), 157–192. Rahner's article can be read as a particularly effective transposition in an evolutionary worldview of Aquinas's words: "The mission of divine person can be taken as implying, from one point of view, a procession of origin from the sender; and from another perspective, a new way of being in what is other. Thus the Son is said to be sent by the Father into the world, in that he begins to be in the world in the visibility of the flesh he has taken to himself" (*Summa Theol.*, 1, 43, 1).

17. For an extended biblical and patristic meditation on the symbol of light, see Jaroslav Pelikan, *The Light of the World: A Basic Image in Early Christian Thought* (New York: Harper and Brothers, 1962).

18. This point could be further developed in reference, from a neo-Freudian perspective, to E. Becker, *The Denial of Death,* 47–66; and, in dependence on the anthropology of René Girard, J. Alison, *Raising Abel,* 29, 41–42, 58.

19. See R. Horner, *Rethinking God as Gift: Marion, Derrida, and the Limits of Phenomenology* (Fordham: Fordham University Press, 2001), 241–344.

20. Joseph A. Fitzmyer, "Paul's Anthropology," *The New Jerome Biblical Commentary,* Raymond E. Brown, Joseph A. Fitzmyer, and Roland E. Murphy, eds. (London: Geoffrey Chapman, 1989), 1402–1412.

21. A theme extensively explored by Karl Rahner, *Hearers of the Word,* J. B. Metz, ed., Ronald Walls, trans. (London: Sheed and Ward, 1969).

22. Exod 33:22; 1 Kgs 8:11; Isa 10:1; Hab 2:14.

23. Karl Rahner, "The Concept of Mystery in Catholic Theology," *Theological Investigations,* IV, Kevin Smyth, trans. (Baltimore: Helicon Press, 1966), 36–73.

24. B. Lonergan, *Method in Theology,* 76–81.

3

God in Love with the World
(1:19—3:36)

In this chapter, we move from the "analogical" discourse of
the prologue to the key elements in the dramatic narrative of
how "God so loved the world" (3:16).[1] Four incidents leading
up to the dialogue between Jesus and Nicodemus—which will be
our main consideration—deal respectively with John the Baptist,
the early disciples, the Mother of Jesus at Cana, and the cleansing of the Temple. A brief reflection on each of these episodes
will serve to sketch the context in which the exchange between
Jesus and Nicodemus takes place.

1. Setting the Stage: John the Baptist

25. They asked him, "Why are you baptizing if you
are neither the Messiah, nor Elijah, nor the prophet?"
26. John answered them, "I baptize with water.
Among you stands one whom you do not know, 27.
the one who is coming after me; I am not worthy to
untie the thong of his sandal." (1:25–27)

In the remainder of the Gospel's first chapter, all the
actors in the unfolding drama are present: John the Baptist
(1:19–33), the God who has sent the Baptist and spoken to
him (1:33), the Holy Spirit (1:32–33), Moses and the prophets
(1:45), the disciples (1:35–51), "the Jews" (1:19)—and, of

61

course, the evangelist himself. In a quite literal sense, John the Baptist sets the stage on which the drama will be enacted, and the experience of God will occur.

John's Witness to Israel

A dramatic dialogue, which takes place between the Baptist and the representatives of Israel (priests, Levites, Jews, Jerusalem authorities), articulates what the prologue has already stated about John as a man *sent* by God to bear witness to the light (1:6–9). John has been *sent* by God (1:6); and priests and Levites have been *sent* by the Jerusalem authorities to ask, "Who are you?" (1:19). Two kinds of missions are on a collision course. The question put to John calls into question the identities of four main actors in the story: John himself, the Jews who question him, Jesus to whom the he defers, and, most radically, the Father from whom Jesus has come. As the light begins to shine in the darkness, the struggle between light and darkness is intensified (1:5).

The narrative moves in a kind of *theologia negativa.* John vigorously rejects any effort to project onto him either a messianic or prophetic role. Such categories would restrict the originality of what he is witnessing to (1:20–21). Insistent questioning on the part of his interlocutors (1:19, 21, 22) indicates a theological anxiety to gain control over what is happening. The delegation must have an answer to take back to the distantly positioned authorities (1:22). But no answer can be given, except in terms that go beyond all previous experience. The witness of John cannot be fitted neatly into the expectations of Jewish history; for he stands in the light of another beginning. John's "I am not"(1:20) clears the way for the one who will come as "I am he" (4:25). The Baptist is not a prophet as other great precursors were. He has even located himself outside the confines of the Holy City. Yet he declares, in the words of one of the great prophets, that he has been sent to be "the voice of one crying in the wilderness to make straight the way of the Lord" (1:23). Still, the emissaries of the Pharisees seek an explanation of his baptismal activity (1:25). John breaks the mold of their expectations. He has confessed himself to be neither the Messiah, nor one of the Messiah's recognized precursors—neither Elijah nor the prophet (1:25b). He stands beyond the horizon of what the priests, Levites, "the Jews," the Pharisees, and the religious establishment of Jerusalem itself (1:25) can find acceptable. The way of the Lord does not follow familiar landmarks in the history of Israel. The Lord will move in their midst as one who is as yet unknown to them (1:26). No one comes to the Father but by him (14:6).

In response to the questions put to him, John states that, though he baptizes with water, there is an unknown one among them (1:26) who will succeed him, and baptize with the Spirit (cf. 1:33). To him John, as one unworthy to untie the thong of his sandal (v. 27), is prepared to yield totally. John's persistent admission of "not knowing" indicates the path that faith must follow, as he clears the ground for the way of the Lord in a new and final revelation to Israel.

The Lamb of God

29. The next day he saw Jesus coming toward him and declared, "Here is the Lamb of God who takes away the sin of the world! 30. This is he of whom I said, 'After me comes a man who ranks ahead of me because he was before me.' 31. I myself did not know him; but I came baptizing with water for this reason, that he might be revealed to Israel." (1:29–31)

John's witness to Jesus as the Lamb of God disrupts the perspective of the past from two directions. First, Jesus is the lamb *of God.* The divinely-given lamb is unknown to those who are unable to look beyond the traditional ritual sacrifice of the Temple. This God-given victim will expiate for human evil and be the agent of reconciliation with God. Second, this lamb of God "takes away the sin *of the world.*" To accept him is to be taken into a new realm of universal reconciliation. In that world of divine forgiveness, all are sinners, whether pagans or Jews. It admits no possibility of self-justification (cf. 1 John 1:7–8). To all is offered the unrestricted redemption made possible by the Lamb that God provides. All other sacrificial lambs have prefigured the ultimate sacrifice that God alone can make out of love for the world (3:16).

John solemnly defers to the Lamb of God as ranking before him (1:30a). He belongs to to the divine realm of "the beginning" (1:1), since "he was before me" (1:30b). Unknown to the Jews and their representatives (1:26), Jesus has also been unknown to John himself (1:31, 33a). A *docta ignorantia* has guided him to baptize in order that this hitherto unknown one might be revealed to Israel (1:31b).

The Descent of the Spirit

In a reference to an otherwise unreported baptism of Jesus, the Baptist speaks of a vision:

> 32. I saw the Spirit descending from heaven like a dove, and it remained on him. 33. I myself did not know him, but the one who sent me to baptize with water said to me, "He on whom you see the Spirit descend and remain is the one who baptizes with the Holy Spirit." 34. And I myself have seen and testified that this is the Son of God. (1:32–34)

For John, not knowing the identity of the one who was to come, the Spirit descending and remaining on Jesus is the divine mark of identification. From now on, the continuing witness of the Spirit is a dimension of the truth that will be revealed. Whereas John's mission from God had collided previously with the mission of those sent to him from Jerusalem (1:19, 24), it now converges with this other divine mission, that of the Lamb of God who ranks before him. John's baptizing with water looks to the new time of a baptism with the Spirit—to be performed by him who is now seen and confessed to be "the Son of God" (1:34). The Lamb of God is the Son of God. The Lamb that God gives to take away the sin of the world is empowered to undo the world's evil because God is giving what is so intimately his own, namely, his Son. He enters the world of darkness and sin possessed by the Holy Spirit of a new baptism.

The Baptist's double declaration of Jesus as the Lamb of God (vv. 29, 35) frames his vision of the descent of the Spirit on Jesus, and his hearing of the divine testimony. The hitherto unknown one will baptize with the specifically divine "element," in contrast to the Baptist's mission to baptize with water. This raises the question of the relationship between the "Lamb" and the "Spirit." As the Gospel proceeds, the glory of God will be made clear only when this Lamb gives himself for his own in a new Passover (13:1). Glorified by being lifted up on the cross, he becomes the source of the Spirit for the church (19:30). So it is that the Spirit is given only when the sacrifice of the Lamb is complete. The coming of the Spirit will witness to the divine origin of Jesus' self-giving love (John 16:7–15), and inspire a life conformed to the love and service that characterized the existence of Jesus (1 John 3:24; 4:2, 13). In him, crucified and risen, the Spirit will be found.[2]

Only God's special revelation to John can prepare him to witness to the unknown one. The initiative rests always with God. In sending John, the divine Sender is revealed as the God of the Baptist, of the Lamb, of the Son, and of the descending Spirit. God is the giver of gifts surpassing the previous religious imagination of Israel.

2. The Path of the Disciples

35. The next day John again was standing with two of his disciples, 36. and as he watched Jesus walk by he exclaimed, "Look, here is the Lamb of God!" 37. The two disciples heard him say this, and they followed Jesus. 38. When Jesus turned and saw them following, he said to them, "What are you looking for?" They said to him, "Rabbi" (which translated means Teacher), "where are you staying?" 39. He said to them, "Come and see." They came and saw where he was staying, and they remained with him that day. (1:35–39)

The First Words of the Word

Jesus, the Lamb, and Son of God, moves forward in his God-given mission. His passing by draws the disciples into their journey of faith. But, in the initiative proper to the Word, Jesus turns back to them, and asks, "What are you looking for?" (1:37). The first words of the Word are a question, designed to keep the movement toward him open to what is to be revealed. The disciples' response indicates the limited perspectives in which they are moving: "Rabbi,...where are you staying?" (1:38). The second utterance of the Word invites the future disciples to go beyond their preconceptions, and to make contact with the living truth of what is taking place: "Come and see" (1:39). They go with him, and stay with him for the rest of the day.

Their report of what happened indicates that their journey is in these first steps far from complete. One of them, Andrew,

claims that "we have found the Messiah" (1:41). The disciples
have not, in fact, gone beyond their own part in what took
place. They have not understood the significance of Jesus' initiative in turning to them, addressing them, and calling them
beyond the ambit of their own intentions and expectations. It is
not that they have found the Messiah, but they have been sought
and found by the Father (cf. 4:23). The divine initiative is indicated in the next words of the Word. When Andrew brings his
brother, Simon, to him, Jesus declares that Simon will be called
"Cephas," Peter—the Rock (1:42). To encounter the Word of
God, to follow the Lamb of God, to listen to the Son of God, to
be baptized in the Spirit of God, will bring about a new identity
in those who receive him.

Promise of Heaven Opened

In the pursuit of his mission, Jesus decided to go Galilee.
There he "finds" Philip, and summons him: "Follow me" (1:43).
Other lesser "findings" follow, serving to point up the contrast
between the initiative of Jesus and the claims and inventions of
the disciples: "...Philip *found* Nathanael, and said to him, 'We
have *found* him about whom Moses in the law and also the
prophets wrote, Jesus son of Joseph from Nazareth'" (1:45).
Philip's reference to Jesus, not as the Lamb and Son "of God,"
but as the progeny of Joseph with origins in Nazareth, indicates
that he is introducing one whom he does not really know yet. He
has not yet come to identify Jesus as originally turned toward
God, and with God in the beginning (1:1).

> 46. Nathanael said to him, "Can anything good come
> out of Nazareth?" Philip said to him, "Come and see."
> 47. When Jesus saw Nathanael coming toward him, he
> said of him, "Here is truly an Israelite in whom there

is no deceit!" 48. Nathanael asked him, "Where did
you get to know me?" Jesus answered, "I saw you
under the fig tree before Philip called you." 49.
Nathanael replied, "Rabbi, you are the Son of God!
You are the King of Israel!" 50. Jesus answered, "Do
you believe because I told you that I saw you under the
fig tree? You will see greater things than these." 51.
And he said to him, "Amen, amen, I say to you, you
will see heaven opened and the angels of God ascending and descending on the Son of Man." (1:46–51)

Nathanael, in the directness for which he will be commended, seems to sense the self-assertiveness of the disciples and
the narrowness of their expectations. He poses his ironic question, "Can anything good come out of Nazareth?" (1:46). Still, a
significant contact has been made. Philip's invitation, "Come and
see" (1:46), is a precise echo of the previous invitation of Jesus to
the two disciples (1:39). The Word can speak despite, and even
through, the limitations of human communication. When Jesus
now sees the new disciple approaching, he utters words of praise
about him. Nathanael is coming in a way that contrasts with the
blinkered approach of the other disciples. Yet he too exhibits limitations. He asks Jesus, in a language restricted to human possibilities and particular places, "Where did you get to know me?"
(1:48). Given the logic of the prologue, such a question is already
answered. All things exist through the Word who is the light of
all (1:3, 5, 9). Consequently, Jesus had seen Nathanael under the
fig tree even before Philip called him to this meeting (1:48).

Astonished by the intimacy of Jesus' knowledge of him, this
newest disciple makes an ecstatic but still limited confession. He
speaks in terms that combine the restrictions of the old with the
promise of the new: "Rabbi!...Son of God!...King of Israel!"
(1:49). As the drama of God's self-revelation unfolds, Jesus will

give new meaning to each of these titles: this Rabbi will show himself as a servant washing his disciples' feet (13:1–16). This Son of God will be revealed as God's loving gift to the world for its life and salvation (3:16). This King of Israel will declare that his "kingdom is not from this world" (18:36). The experience of God will overflow all historical containers.

The excess of this experience of God is now adumbrated in the first use of the comparative—"greater," in the Johannine writings.[3] If Nathanael is astonished by Jesus seeing him under the fig tree, this guileless Israelite is promised a greater vision: "You will see greater things than these" (1:50). Jesus then solemnly promises that the disciples "will see heaven opened and the angels of God ascending and descending on the Son of Man" (1:51). Jesus will be the new Jacob's ladder (Gen 28:12–17), connecting what is above with what is below (cf. 3:13). The Son of Man will become the new place of meeting, the new "gate of heaven." He will be the realization of a new communication between God and the world. What is most intimate to God will be accessible in the flesh of this world; and what in this world has been most distant from God will now find a way to the Father, and a dwelling in his house (14:1–4). In all this, the Father is at work opening heaven, the realm of God, to all who follow the way of Jesus. Heaven, therefore, is not opened by any human effort or wisdom, wrestling with God to gain access to the realm of light. It is the result of the Word's dwelling "among us" (1:14).

3. Cana: The Faith of the Mother of Jesus

3. When the wine failed, the Mother of Jesus said to him, "They have no wine." 4. And Jesus said to her, "O woman, what have you to do with me? My hour

has not yet come." 5. His mother said to the servants, "Do whatever he tells you." (2:3–5)

The "third day"—on which the wedding at Cana is celebrated—evokes that other "third day" on which the glory of God was revealed in Israel's past (cf. Exodus 19). At the Cana celebration, the authentic recognition of that glory occurs in the response of the Mother of Jesus to the Word who is her Son. In her the bounds of natural and religious experience are confronted with the reality of the opened heaven already mentioned. Her acceptance of the Word is unreserved. When Jesus reproaches her for attempting to hasten or determine the hour of salvation, she comes to a point of total, even if necessarily uncomprehending, surrender to the Word—who is her Son: "Do whatever he tells you" (2:5). In effect, she expresses, in a self-surrender that goes beyond all human conditions, the essential pattern for obeying the Word, heard now in the voice of Jesus.

While the first words of the Word were a question, the first act of the Word is a transformation. Jesus meets a human need in a way exceeding the capacities of any human agency. The result is that the Jewish water of purification is transformed into a new and perfect wine which all can enjoy—even if its source is incomprehensible (2:6–10). In the fact that the servants knew who had drawn the water that was changed into wine (2:9), the reader of the Gospel is teased into appreciating the link between the occurrence of the new and those who had not forgotten the role of past revelation to prepare for the fulfillment which is to happen. Mary, the servants, and the disciples, therefore, saw his glory revealed—"and believed in him" (2:11). A new family of Jesus is being brought into existence in the light of the hour that is about to strike. In the power of the Word, the purifying water of the Old Testament (2:6) will be changed into the wine of the New Covenant.

4. The Cleansing of the Temple

As the feast of the Passover draws near (2:13), Jesus goes up to Jerusalem. The great feast will, in the end (13:1; 19:36), be transformed by "the fullness of a gift that is truth" (1:14a). The path of Israel, so long centered on the Temple in Jerusalem, must now become a continuing journey of conversion. For the sake of the opened heaven (1:51), Israel must turn from the familiarly known, from the settled arrangement of its ritual celebrations—with their attendant "business as usual," in the most literal meaning of the phrase (cf. 2:14, 16)—to the freeing and fulfilling acceptance of "the truth," however disruptive it will prove to be. In contrast with the Synoptic accounts, John's Gospel places Jesus' intervention in the Temple at the beginning of his ministry.

16. "...you shall not make my Father's house a house of trade." 17. His disciples remembered that it was written, "Zeal for your house shall consume me." 18. The Jews then said to him, "What sign have you to show us for doing this?" 19. Jesus answered them, "Destroy this Temple, and in three days I will raise it up." 20. The Jews then said to him, "It has taken forty-six years to build this Temple, and you will raise it up in three days?" 21. But he spoke of the Temple of his body. 22. When, therefore, he was raised from the dead, his disciples remembered that he had said this; and they believed the Scripture and the word that Jesus had spoken.

Jesus acts to clear his Father's house of its immersion in an old economy grown forgetful of its true purpose, in order to make accessible "the many dwelling places in my Father's house" (14:2). While protest turns on Jesus and his disruptive activity, he himself is focused on the God from whom he comes. The disciples will remember his dramatic intervention as an instance of the zeal for God's house that will consume him, and bring about his death (2:17). The dwelling of the true God among us demands that our human world be more than a marketplace with God safely contained in a material building. God is outside the calculated exchanges of any human economy. The rule of the Father's household will be shown to be otherwise. The Word originally contains all that is; and, by his coming in the flesh, he opens the world, and any place or site within it, to that beginning in which he is "with God."

As for Jesus, "his own people" still do not receive him in "his own home" (1:11). To keep what has drawn so disconcertingly near at bay, "the Jews" demand an authenticating sign (2:18). The old economy of signs sees only threat in "the fullness of a gift which is truth" (1:14b). The fullness of the gift cannot be contained in a building of stone erected over the years by human design, even if for the most sacred purpose *(hieron)* (2:20). It can be contained only in an edifice *(naos)* of God's design (2:19), to be constructed in the "three days" of God's good time. The material Temple will be subject to the laws of death and eventual destruction. But what God is building is something quite different. How this will come about will be made clear to the disciples through their later and fuller grasp of the Scriptures (2:17). Then they will understand that Jesus was speaking of "the Temple of his body" (2:21). In the light of the resurrection, as they read the Scriptures and ponder the words of the Word recalled therein, they will appreciate that God's new house was in the making (2:22).[4]

In the meantime, the old ways will die hard. "The Jews," now having emerged as a force antagonistic to Jesus, had received his baffling statement about raising the temple anew with sarcasm and contempt (2:20). This man, whatever his pretensions and signs, cannot rebuild the temple of their glory. But after the resurrection, the followers of Jesus will been given entry into his Father's house (14:2), despite the wholesale destruction of the Temple that had occurred by the time the Gospel came to be written.

"The Jews," looking for a sign on their own terms (2:18), are contrasted with the true Israelites who come to believe in his name because of the signs he actually performs during the Passover: "...in the festival crowd many believed in his name because they saw the signs that he was doing" (2:23). Yet the economy of signs is incomplete. The Word who is the light of all (1:4), in whom all are made (1:3), is not enclosed or limited by a world of signs or dependent on such. In his original identity, he has an immediate knowledge of "all people" (2:24), and is never reduced to their fragmentary and provisional perceptions (2:25). Just as neither his identity nor mission depend on any human confirmation, his witness transcends the economy of signs, to attract those who have begun the journey of faith to its fulfillment. He draws attention away from the signs he does to the truth that he is. The original question, the first words of the Word, still resonate: "What are you looking for?" (1:38).

5. Nicodemus: Coming in from the Dark

The above versions of the crisis inherent in the journey of faith provide the context in which Jesus' dialogue with Nicodemus can be more fully appreciated. This exchange, in turn, will be followed by the final appearance of John the Baptist (3:22–30).

Nicodemus is described as "a Pharisee" and "a leader of the Jews" (3:1). The Gospel is thereby alerting its readers to expect both some kind of reprise of the conflictual situation that

73

has gone before (2:20), and to anticipate what is to come in the many confrontations in store. But in this case, there is a difference: "the Jews" do not send messengers, as happened with John (1:19, 24). Nicodemus comes himself—even if it is "by night" (3:2). His nocturnal arrival on the scene symbolizes the limitations inherent in his approach to Jesus: "Rabbi, we know that you are a teacher who has come from God" (3:2b). Though his assured "we know" has confrontational overtones, there is also evidence of an initial good will—which in other future disciples marks the beginning of the journey of faith. Nonetheless, the fact that Nicodemus is well disposed to Jesus conceals an effort to fit him into a ready-made religious worldview. For him the mission of Jesus can be assimilated to the way things are known to be. His signs—"no one can do these signs that you do, unless God is with him" (3:2)—are being interpreted in simple continuity with the long line of signs of divine presence already marking Israel's history. His concern for the past is blocking his receptivity to the new.

New Birth

3. Jesus answered him, "Amen, amen, I say to you, no one can see the kingdom of God without being born again, from above." 4. Nicodemus said to him, "How can a person be born after having grown old? Can one enter a second time into the mother's womb and be born?" 5. Jesus answered, "Amen, amen, I say to you, no one can enter the kingdom of God without being born of water and the Spirit. 6. That which is born of the flesh is flesh, and that which is born of the Spirit is spirit. 7. Do not marvel that I said to you, 'You must be born anew.' 8. The wind blows where it wills, and you hear the sound of it, but you do not know whence

**it comes or whither it goes; so it is with everyone who
is born of the Spirit." (3:3–8)**

For Nicodemus, both the possibility of being "born again,
from above" (3:3) and the actual presence of Israel's God incarnate in the *Logos,* are now slipping beyond the accepted bounds
of possibility. For Jesus stands within a horizon determined by
God's action "from above," exploding the calculations and criteria formed "from below." A new realm of life, light, and divine
initiative occasions a "vertical" change of horizon.[5] It cannot be
reduced to a developmental outcome within the known history
of Israel.

The metaphor of a new birth suggests the generative activity of God as the source of new life. Jesus is not here presup-
posing either a general notion of God, or even Israel's particular
millennial experience of God in its history. Apart from this new
birth he speaks of, no can "see" the Kingdom of God (3:3) as it
is taking place. Despite his respectful appreciation of Jesus,
Nicodemus shows, as yet, no recognition that God himself is
involved in this new birth. Trapped within the limitations of his
vision, Nicodemus exploits the ambiguity of the phrase "from
above." He takes it to mean to be born again in a way continuous with the life he had lived up to his meeting with Jesus. He
has grown old, and no other birth is possible. Why should he be
so infantilized as to leave behind the accumulated, age-old wisdom of the tradition in which he is an acknowledged leader and
teacher? To be reduced to the state of a newborn child would
leave him and his people with nothing.

But Jesus is insistent. The condition required for entering
this new divine realm is to be born of water and the Spirit (3:5).
Implied here is a rupture in the history of religious experience.
The action of God "from above" will change things *from within*
the flesh of this world, to bring a new kind of both "seeing" and

"entering into" the realm of God. Reference to "water" bespeaks an identifiable baptismal practice on the part of a new community of believers mediating the divine initiative. Seeing and entering God's kingdom is related to the flesh-and-blood reality of a visible community of Jesus' disciples—those in whom this new birth has occurred. Notwithstanding the place of water in this initiation, Jesus concedes that no upward reach from below, from the sphere of "flesh," can ever bring about the divine initiative "from above," of "Spirit" (3:6). New life comes only as a God-given gift.

And yet it would appear that the activity of the Spirit gives new scope to what is "from below." In continuity with John the Baptist, Jesus and his disciples will *baptize* (3:22). An identifiable human action, baptism by water, is subsumed into the sphere of the Spirit. The flesh need not be an enclosed reality; for it owes its existence to the Word (1:3), and is possessed by the Word in the incarnation (1:14). On the other hand, the Spirit is the transcendent agent of the new, working in the world but beyond any of its capacities and categories (3:7). God works in the world but not as agent contained by it. Hence, this new birth is a real happening, within the life of an identifiable community which baptizes. It is by water *and* the Spirit.

At this point, Jesus counsels Nicodemus not to be astonished at this divine action "from above," irrupting into the ordinary course of human life. Unreserved acceptance of the ways of God is a necessary condition for this new birth, even if much is left unexplained and outside human control. Jesus exploits the metaphor of the wind (3:8). A sudden gust or the shifting breeze exceed any normal prediction or control. In the realm of new life, it symbolizes the free air of another world. But Nicodemus is thrown back on his own sense of what is possible: "How can these things be?" (3:9). By setting limits on how revelation can happen, he is blocked in his capacity to be divinely surprised. It proves too much for this "teacher of Israel" (3:10). Although divinely-wrought transformations of unheard-of proportions figure in Israel's own tradition,[6] this religious teacher does not allow for them. By pretending to master the meaning of the tradition, he is found to be missing the experience it witnesses to. The lesson is driven home: something beyond all previous horizons is now occurring. A teacher of Israel does not understand "these things" (3:10). The wisdom of Israel is now meeting "the fullness of a gift that is truth" (1:14).

Witnesses to "Heavenly Things"

11. Amen, amen, I say to you, we speak of what we have known and bear witness to what we have seen; yet you do not receive our testimony. 12. If I have told you about earthly things and you do not believe, how can you believe if I tell you heavenly things? (3:11–12)

The ambiguities experienced by Nicodemus in Jesus' promise of a new birth and a new vision of the kingdom of God now lead to the key question: Where is the true God to be found? At this juncture (3:11–12), both speaker and listener are abruptly multiplied: the "I" of Jesus becomes the "we" of the believing community; the singular "you" of the baffled Jewish leader now comes to include the group he represents. This group—"the Jews"—are now caught up in a radical alternative. They must either deny the word that Jesus speaks and rid themselves of his provocation; or accept him, and be reborn to another life. The collective "we know" (3:2b) that Nicodemus had voiced is now confronted with another "we know," voiced by those who received Jesus' testimony as Word and light (3:11). The communion of the church (we) speaks to the community of Israel (you). The questions asked by Nicodemus (3:4, 9) in the face of the implausibility of Jesus' claim, are now pushed back to a more radical point of interrogation. The Word has become a question for Israel and its leaders.

Admittedly, the "earthly things" in question are not in fact purely "earthly" at all. They are the sacred promises familiar to the tradition of Israel. But they were being enclosed within the shell of a tradition that does not allow for the fulfillment that can come only as God's surpassing gift. This gift cannot be obtained through an ascent to heaven powered, as it were, by the accumulated resources of previous tradition. None of the great prophetic figures of the past reached up to what is now being given (3:13). The ancient wisdom of Israel has reached its limits; heaven was still not opened (1:51). No one has ever seen God (1:18). But God is now being made known by him who comes down from the realm of the Father, to become flesh (1:14), as the Son of God (1:18) and the heaven-revealing "Son of Man" (1:51; 3:13).

Yet, while such revelation is made from the realm of a hitherto inaccessible heaven, it will be accomplished within the brute, resistant reality of the world. The Word, coming from the Father, is indeed made flesh. As a consequence, the incarnation of the Word will be connected with a "lifting up" within the world of human violence and struggle and death, in order to make the heaven of eternal life with the Father a reality. The healing sign of Moses, the serpent lifted up in the desert, is replaced by another lifting up: that of the Son of Man himself: "And just as Moses lifted up the serpent in the wilderness, so must the Son of Man be lifted up, that whoever believes in him may have eternal life" (3:14–15). Revelation, healing, faith, and eternal life are hereby mentioned, though the full meaning of each of these themes is yet to appear. An ominous *double entendre* plays in the significance of the predicted "lifting up," with its intimations of both glorification and crucifixion. How the glory of God will shine forth in the cross is still to be revealed.

6. The Extent of God's Love for the World

16. For God so loved the world that he gave his only Son, so that everyone who believes in him may not perish but may have eternal life. (3:16)

Every word in this verse is loaded with significance, in its reference to the author of the cosmic drama, the main actor within it, and the world as the object of God's love. It is a summary of the story so far, and a recapitulation of what was stated in the prologue itself. But now a word is used which the prologue, with its emphasis on truth and revelation, did not itself employ, namely, *love*. This suggests that God's culminating communication with the world through the Word is to be judged, in its motive and its measure, by one criterion: the extent of God's love. This theme will be developed most notably in 1 John 4. But here we have its powerful first notes. Moreover, the extent of the Father's giving anticipates the unreserved self-giving of Jesus unto death.

Given the protean use of the term, *the world,* in the Johannine lexicon, here it has a singularly positive and inclusive connotation. What God loves is the world (3:16a). The *kosmos,* as the object of divine love, joins with the primary meaning of creation as it is presented in the Prologue (1:3, 10). The universe of "all things [that] came into being through him" (1:3)—the Word, as the source of being, life, and light (1:3–4)—finds its further explanation in the, as yet, unexpressed reality of God *so* loving the world. Moreover, the limitless connotation of *the world* reaches beyond its present embodiment in the representatives of

Israel to include the Samaritans and the Gentiles, soon to figure in the Gospel narrative (4:1–54).

In the light of such love, directed to the world that has its being in the Word, earthly things can shine with heavenly significance. The meanings of "existence," "life," "flesh," and "glory" are transformed. The creaturely character of the world itself—instanced in parents and children, or in the lamb of the flock or the dove flying above, in the play of light and darkness, in the flowing water or the shifting wind, in the wine of the wedding feast and the bread of daily sustenance—can now mean something else. Even the Temple of Jerusalem, the place of God's dwelling, will be relocated into another world of meaning. All this is made to point into the origin of "all things" in the Word of God, and, in a sense, even beyond that, to the Father's love.

God's Unreserved Giving

The key affirmation of God's love for the world is linked with a remarkable statement of excess: "God so loved the world *that he gave his only Son*" (v. 16b). God's love is that of the Father giving his only Son. What is most intimate and vital to God's character as Father—his Son—is given for the life of all. By this measure, divine love for the world is a self-giving of a most unconditional kind. There is no reserve on the Father's part in making such a gift. Nor is there any restriction in the number eligible to receive it—"the world," and "everyone who believes in him." Nor is there any limitation in the goal of the giving: "eternal life." Nor is such limited by the self-destructive capacities of human freedom: it reaches out to evildoers that they "may not perish...." The Father is made known to the world as the God of unstinted giving.[7]

Love, in this sense, does not mean simply that the world is bathed in a general divine benevolence. The Son, as the one who is most intimate to the divine being and life, incarnates the Father's saving love "among us" (1:14), right at the point where darkness most threatens (1:5). In what the only Son is, does, and suffers is found the realization of *this* Father's, *this* God's, all-embracing love (cf. 1 John 4:8–10).

Some points deserve emphasis. God gives *his* only Son. The Gospel of John can be interpreted as contrasting God's gift of *his* Son with two notable instances in the Old Testament describing the sacrifice of sons. The first instance—the most commonly agreed on—deals with God's testing of Abraham (Gen 22:1–19). God commands: "Take your son, your only son, Isaac, whom you love, and offer him there..." (22:2). As the sacrifice is being prepared, Isaac addresses Abraham, "Father!"; and the latter replies, "Here I am, my son" (22:7). To the boy's question as to where the lamb of sacrifice is to be found, his father replies, "God himself will provide the lamb for a burnt offering, my son" (22:8). The rest of the story unfolds: the angel of God intervenes just as Abraham is about to kill his son in sacrifice, and declares, "...for now I know that you fear God, since you have not withheld your son, your only son, from me" (22:12). Then the great patriarch looks up and, seeing the ensnared ram, "offered it as a burnt offering instead of his son" (v. 13). Thereupon he names the place, "The Lord will provide" (22:14). The following verses (22:14–19) confirm the blessings promised to Abraham, "our father in faith," because of his unreserved surrender to the divine will.

John, in this reference to a classic story of Israel's past, shows himself to be a supreme theological ironist. In the wider theater of "the world"—extending beyond the history of Israel and its sacred sacrificial rituals—the Lord now provides another kind of victim destined for another kind of atonement, and for another purpose. To prove *his* love, the Father gives *his* only Son. It is no longer a case of God testing the patriarch's faith, but

God allowing his love to be tested by the world. By reflecting on the classic stories of Israel's past in the light of "the Lamb *of God*" (1:29, 36), the Gospel presents the ever-transcendent mystery of the divine as newly defined and finally revealed in terms of God's self-giving and unreserved love.

In a second example of contrast (2 Sam 21:1–14),[8] David inquires of the Lord as to the cause of the three-year famine affecting the land. He is informed that "there is blood guilt on Saul and on his house, because he put the Gibeonites to death" (21:1), a people whom Israel had sworn to spare (21:2). So David asks the survivors what would be needed to make expiation so that they might "bless the heritage of the Lord" (21:3). It emerges that the only acceptable reparation would demand that Saul's seven sons be handed over to be executed by impalement "before the Lord at Gibeon on the mountain of the Lord" (21:6). David, with some qualifications, agrees to hand over seven members of Saul's family (21:6–9). After this grisly exchange, "God heeded supplications for the land" (21:14).

The sense of God implied in God in Love with the World the rough justice and fierce religion of the warrior society of tribal Israel emerges in the starkest contrast with what is now revealed: God so loved the world, not only Israel, to take away the blood-guilt of nations. The Father brings this about, not by the sacrifice of someone else's sons, but by giving his own Son— to be lifted up on the cross (3:14): in that hour of glory, "They shall look on him whom they have pierced" (19:37).

The Father gives *his* only Son. In the death of this Son, the glory of God's self-giving love shines forth. Though from the world's perspective, this death is an event of extreme darkness in a world of violence and ignorance of God, to the vision of faith it will be understood as the extreme of self-giving love, a manifestation of the light "that darkness has not overcome..." (1:5).

The experience of God's love for the world radically subverts the violent theology of certain historical phases of the Old Testament—that still influenced the world within and behind the text of the Gospel, and still tragically continues to influence the world of today. Any "peace process" is confronted with a fundamental problem: How can the violence cease without inflicting more violence on the parties concerned? In a world of lethal absolutes, what is the source of self-giving love capable of disarming the heart's violent idolatries and of allowing the impossibly new to happen? Whatever the sins committed by Christians, the Gospel recalls us to what is most fundamentally "scandalous" to the self-serving proclivities of every society: "God so loved the world...."

Beyond Theological Positions

The theological density of John's Gospel modifies the context of the traditional theological question regarding "the motive of the Incarnation": *Cur Deus Homo?* St Anselm's question has been addressed in different ways by "the Thomists"—with an emphasis on the redemptive love of God, and the "the Scotists"—with their emphasis on the intrinsic finality of the creation looking to this divine fulfillment.[9] If the former tended to absolutize the penal predicament of humanity unable to make an infinite recompense for the infinite evil of which it was guilty, the latter absolutized the notion of a good creation as inherently hospitable to the Word. Both views can appeal to the Gospel of John for support. "Thomists" can point to the redemptive extreme of God's self-giving love rescuing humankind from its predicament, as in texts cited above (3:16; 1 John 4:8–10). "Scotists" can base their view on the first verses of the Prologue (1:1–5). Despite the value of both these perspectives, Johannine theology is, in some radical sense, far more *theo-logical* and more *theo-dramatic*.[10] It summons faith out of the human logic of motives into the original *theo-logy* of the Word who, in his utter originality, is the only "definition" of what God is and what creation is. Secondly, it is more *theo-dramatic*. The *Theos* is revealed in a divinely-authored drama of love. The Father loves the Son and gives all things into his hands; and loves the world, to give his only Son into the tangled motives of human existence in order that creation awaken to what God intends it to be: the opened heaven of everlasting communion with God, realized in the "It is finished" (19:30) of Jesus on the cross.[11] From this perspective, it is not a matter of theology clarifying divine motives, but of God clarifying human motives by shining "the light" into the world's darkness. Though the "Scotist" view approximates to the Gospel's *theo-logic,* though the "Thomist" view is closer to the John's *theo-drama,* the lived concreteness of the Johannine experience of God transcends them both. The locus of all theological speculation must be the gift that God has given, never to be mastered by a logic extrinsic to it, only to be appreciated as "the saturated phenomenon" eluding and reorienting all horizons of other gifts and other worlds.[12]

7. Love and Judgment

17. **For God sent the Son into the world, not to condemn the world, but that the world might be saved through him. 18. Those who believe in him are not condemned; those who do not believe are condemned already, because they have not believed in the name of the only Son of God. 19. And this is the judgment, that the light has come into the world, and people loved darkness rather than the light, because their**

deeds were evil. 20. For all who do evil hate the light, and do not come to the light, so that their deeds may not be exposed. 21. But those who do what is true come to the light, that it may be clearly seen that their deeds have been done in God. (3:17–21)

Whatever the violence and idolatry found in human history, God does not act to condemn the world. In the light of God's unreserved gift, the world is not condemned in its ambiguities and dead ends. It is offered salvation—"that the world might be saved through him" (3:17).

And yet there remains the threat of judgment and condemnation, even if it is not God who either judges or condemns. The Father and the Son reject no one. God's loving gift of his Son places him beyond the domain of any "god" who judges and condemns. How, then, does judgment and condemnation occur, if such acts are not the business of God? In John's answer to this question, the bias of differing habitual patterns of action is candidly acknowledged. Those who have habitually acted in accord with the light will, phototropically, recognize its fulfillment in Jesus. On the other hand, a photophobic aversion to the light will lead to condemnation—for those who, by rejecting the Word, flee from the radiance of the love that has been disclosed, and refuse to be part of it.

The Ultimate Criterion

What kind of God is thus revealed? As 1 John will affirm, God so loves the world because "God is love" (1 John 4:8–10). Knowing the true God is to find all existence illumined: "God is light and in him there is no darkness at all" (1 John 1:5). The heavens have been opened (1:51). Anyone opting to remain outside this new world of love and light is self-condemned. For a decision has been made—to live in the world of self-justification and worldly glory (12:43), at the expense of the glory of the love that has been revealed. The consequence of such a decision is to find that heaven, the realm of love and life that God has opened, in fact remains closed and threatening. When darkness is a familiar habitat, the world of light means the glaring exposure of worldly identities structured on what is contrary to God's self-giving love. The God of Jesus cannot but be a threat to those who have a stake in remaining in the dark. God's self-giving love for the world, therefore, does not ratify mundane self-promotion and violence. That ever-darkening world serves another "god." Within that world of darkness, "the ruler of this world" (14:30) holds sway.

In contrast, doing the truth—with the continuing conversion that this entails—homes to a realm of light in which the way God acts, and the way those act who accept Jesus, are in ultimate agreement: for "their deeds have been done in God" (3:21).

Unreserved acceptance of Jesus locates believers in the realm of light and love: "Those who believe in him are not condemned…" (3:18). Though the conversion of faith will have its moral, intellectual, and religious aspects,[13] its crucial criterion is the Father's self-revelation in Jesus. He is not, in the first place, a teacher of a new morality or the exponent of a new theology; nor is he the promoter of a new religion, philosophy, or spirituality. He is the incarnate presence of God's love for the world. There is no room for some other criterion, whether this be a gnostic criterion of knowledge, or an ethical criterion of moral attainment, or a religious criterion of devotion to a historical tradition—unless it be that such criteria are transformed in the light of the Word. These extrinsic criteria displace the reality of judgment from the truth of the Father's love for the world onto some form of human estimate or human glory. Such standards of judgment would enclose "the gift of God" (4:10) within a horizon inhospitable to the limitless love that has been revealed. The outreach of God's all-inclusive cosmic love would be diminished. A gnostic criterion excludes the ignorant or uninitiated. A purely moral criterion could be brandished against the immorality of those judged to be sinful by the righteous. And even a purely religious criterion could be maintained only by excluding all others who had not been the recipients of divine election. In contrast, coming to the light means accepting the full dimensions of God's gift to the world. God has acted not to condemn the world, but, by giving his Son, to save it (3:17). To judge by other criteria would be in fact relegating the world to condemnation, and excluding oneself from the domain of God's love.

8. Jesus and John

As Jesus and the disciples move into "the Judean countryside" (3:22), and John is now located in a Samaritan setting, a wider circle of involvement is suggested (3:22–23). Also implied, in the reference to John's impending imprisonment (3:24), is the increasing risk; dissension and violence now poison the atmosphere (cf. 4:1–4, 9, 43–44). A tension has occurred between the groups gathered around Jesus and John, instanced in the "discussion about purification" taking place between the followers of John and "a Jew" (3:25). It is possible that this figure had witnessed Jesus' baptismal activity in the Judean countryside, and had been affected by the negative or even envious attitude of "the Jews" previously mentioned. But John's response to his disciples' report points to the necessity of realizing the revelatory moment of what is happening, and of transcending the criteria of worldly calculation. A distance, beyond the geographical sense, has opened between John, reverentially addressed as

"Rabbi," and "the one who was with you across the Jordan, to whom you testified" (3:26a). Now this Jesus is baptizing and "all are going to him" (3:26b). Such a description of events may well express the all-too-human phenomenon of rivalry between the two groups, and the anxiety of John's disciples over their master's waning influence. At a deeper level, there in an implication that God's love for the world (3:16–17) is having a measurable effect, and eroding the ascetical criteria of the Baptist's followers regarding what having a good standing before God might mean.

Whatever the historical situation, John's response gives expression to the economy of a divine gift. What God is bringing about can be appreciated only by those who lay themselves open to the incalculable abundance and surprise of the opened heaven (1:51)—as opposed to the closed heaven of any restricted economy of salvation. The Baptist places the emphasis, not on the merits of human actors, but on the initiative of the divine giving: "No one can receive anything except what has been given from heaven" (3:27). In this economy of sheer giving, John reminds his disciples that they have never witnessed him claiming to be the Christ, even though he has been sent by God ahead of him to whom he must witness (3:28). In this regard, John understands himself to be, not the bridegroom, but the "best man." His role is to witness the marriage between the Son and the Sion of God's people. In performing this role, the joy of John is fulfilled (3:30). He has stood by and heard the Word of God; and now he rejoices in the bridegroom's voice, that of the Word-made-flesh speaking "in the first person." At this turning point, the Baptist must give way to the grace of the final truth: "He must increase, but I must decrease" (3:30).

The conversion demanded of the whole of Israel is brought to expression in these words. What has occurred in the case of the Mother of Jesus at Cana, what has been demanded of

Nicodemus and in the call of the disciples, is here continued in the self-transcendence of John in the presence of the original Word. Former identities, former assurances of the divine promises, must now yield to something new. All previous existence must be re-meant in the light of the Word. The authentic faith of John is manifested in a joyous consent to the glory of the surpassingly new. Though he too has been sent, he does not cling to his own project. His role has not led to failure, but to fulfillment realized in his unconditional self-surrender to the economy of God's all-fulfilling gift. Implied in John's attitude is an unrestricted adoration of the Giver, in receptivity to the gift—given in the way God chooses to give, surprising all human expectation and control.

9. The Gift Beyond Measure

The commentary that now follows in the Gospel text underscores the transcendence of the gift in relation to all previous categories, even as it brings them to an unexpected completion:

> 31. The one who comes from above is above all; the one who is of the earth belongs to the earth and speaks about earthly things. The one who comes from heaven is above all. 32. He bears witness to what he has seen and heard, yet no one receives his testimony. 33. Whoever has received his testimony sets seal to this, that God is true. 34. He whom God has sent speaks the words of God, for it is not by measure that he gives the Spirit. 35. The Father loves the Son and has given all things into his hand. 36. The one who believes in the Son has eternal life; the one who does not obey the Son shall not see life, but the wrath of God rests upon such a one. (3:31–36)

The Son, coming "from above" to give eternal life, lives in communion with the divine source of such a gift and such a giving. Those locked into the economy of earthly things cannot appreciate this, for "He bears witness to what he has seen and heard, yet no one receives his testimony" (3:32). The Word comes and speaks out of an original seeing and hearing. The truth he embodies looks back to its "heavenly" source. His authority does not consist in being one more earthly authority or worldly power asserting itself against others as though jealous of its own privilege. For he comes as one who has received, obedient to a truth that is not of this world, even if it means suffering rejection within this world. On the other hand, "Whoever has received his testimony sets seal to this, that God is true" (3:33). The truth incarnate in him, which flows from what he has seen and heard, is authenticated by the counter-signatures written in the lives of the original witnesses and those who will come after them. That God so loved the world, that God gave his only Son, that the Word turned toward God in the beginning has been made flesh—is each an aspect of the revealed truth of God. As the Son makes known the Father, he brings about a new identity in believers as they are born from above, and draw near the light.

Thus, "He whom God has sent speaks the words of God, for it is not by measure that he [God] gives the Spirit" (3:34). The unique revelation of the truth of God depends on an original sending proper to the Word and Son: only such a Word can "word," in the fullest sense, the truth of God. His mission and person are one and the same.[14] Because he has seen and heard, because he is with God in the beginning and sees and hears on that other level, he can mediate "among us" what is truly from above, and thus incarnate God's love for the world.

The divine communication here implied is bound up with the immeasurable gift of the Spirit. This is the "breath" by which the Word is spoken and speaks, which has descended and remained on Jesus (1:32). By this Spirit, those who accept Jesus are reborn (2:5) and led into the fullness of truth (16:13). The Spirit is also the gift of the Risen Jesus (20:22). In this "divine atmosphere" of superabundance, a primordial communication is at work: "The Father loves the Son and has given all things into his hand" (3:35).[15] For the first time in the Gospel, mention is made of the Father's love for the Son and of giving "all things" into the Son's possession. The Father's giving is unstinted (3:35, 13:3; 17:7). It includes his name (17:11), glory (17:22, 24), authority over all flesh (17:2), having life "in himself" (5:26), works or the work (5:36; 17:4), words (17:8), authority and judgment (5:2, 27), everything that he asks for (11:22), and believers in the present and of the future (6:37, 39; 10:29; 17:2, 6, 9, 12, 24; 18:9).

The metaphor of the Word with God in the beginning (1:2) is now refocused in the Father's loving relationship to the Son, and in his personal giving of "all things" to him.[16] Behind the immeasurable reality of God's love for the world, instanced in the gift of his only Son, is an even more intimate and original communication: the Father's love for the Son and the gift of all things into his possession. The Father's love for the Son in handing over all things to him is acted out, as it were, in the drama of God's love for the world. In the truth that "God so loved the world that he gave his only Son" (3:16b) is contained a more original love and a more radical giving. The Father loves the Son; and, in the giving of all things to the Son, gives him his saving mission to the world. Love for the world flows from the love the Father has for the Son. His giving of the Son for the world flows from his giving *to* the Son in the immeasurable dimensions of the Spirit (cf. 1 John 4:7–8).

Who Condemns?

The gift of eternal life that God intends for those who accept the Son is already actual. But to refuse to believe in him as the form and source of life forecloses on the possibility of "seeing" life in its most radical and enduring promise. In starkest contrast, to close one's ears to the Word that the Son embodies and speaks is to live under God's wrath (3:36). An exegetical reading of this phrase, alert to different strata in this section of the commentary, acknowledges the possibility that "God's wrath" may belong to an earlier stage in the Johannine tradition not yet fully focused on the primacy of God's love, as is the case in John 3:16. Still, in the text as it stands, the divine wrath, despite its connotation of an active divine judgment, has in fact been already "demythologized," and so shorn of anthropomorphic penal overtones. When God's love for the world has been so unconditionally affirmed (3:16), and when any implication that God is intent on judgment has been so firmly denied (3:17), the anger of God must be understood as a description of the human situation resulting from a personal option for darkness over light. Cut off from the Son as the light, those who reject Jesus are actively creating a world of violence and death that is certainly not willed by God. They are living in a world of darkness, envy, and self-justification in which God can only be experienced as a threat to all that they have chosen to be. To the degree that they have locked themselves into a state of ultimate refusal, they experience the world, not as loved by God, but as enclosing them in a prison of their own making.

10. The Meaning of the Experience

The Gospel's narrative and its theological commentary are designed to lead the reader more deeply into the experience of

God. Following the terminology already employed, we draw attention to the four dimensions of meaning that permeate the experience of God in question. In brief, the Gospel account functions *effectively* in that it demands an unreserved hearkening to the Word—"do whatever he tells you" (2:5)—and calls actual and potential to come to the light (3:21).

Second, the Gospel documents new intensities of *constitutive* meaning radiating from the light. Born from above in the power of the Spirit, judged in the presence of the light, believers are constituted in a new identity: Simon is renamed (1:42). To follow Jesus is to be dispossessed of former views, criteria, securities, and expectations. Contact with the Word means a radical self-transformation. In that new self-making, believers receive a gift that both dispossesses and leads to a new self-possession in a world loved by God.

Third, the experience of God as John depicts it means a new belonging. It *communicates,* and forms solidarities and communities that did not exist before. The family of God grows (2:11–12). To believe in Jesus means being initiated into a community of his followers (3:5). It is to live in a world unreservedly loved by God (3:16).

Last, such experience is directed and nourished by an objectivity focused on who God is, what God does, and what God wills. In this *cognitive* dimension, the Lamb *of God,* the Son *of God,* the Spirit *of God,* come from God to lead to the vision of opened heaven (1:51) and to entry into the Kingdom of God (3:3, 5). The God of this heaven and kingdom is the Giver, acting out of unreserved love, by giving all things to the Son (3:35), and by giving the Son as the source of eternal life (3:16). The *data* of Christian experience provoke a concern for self-transcending objectivity. They demand that the believer pass from the range of incalculable gifts—*dona*—to acknowledge the

Giver—the *donor*—who gives in the Spirit of measureless generosity (3:34).

In moving now to the next chapter of John's Gospel, we will examine further aspects of the originality and extent of "the gift of God" (4:10).

Notes

1. In a more general theological context, Ghislain Lafont, *God, Time and Being,* Leonard Maluf, trans. (Petersham, Mass.: Saint Bede's Publications, 1992) imaginatively connects analogical knowledge with the principle of narrativity.
2. See Gary D. Badcock, *Light of Truth and Fire of Love: A Theology of the Holy Spirit* (Grand Rapids, Mich.: William Eerdmans, 1997), 27–35, especially p. 33, n. 23. Overall, this book is an excellent study in contemporary pneumatology.
3. Cf. chapter 1, note 33.
4. Mary L. Coloe, *God Dwells with Us: Temple Symbolism in the Fourth Gospel* (Collegeville Minn.: Liturgical Press, 2001) applies the Temple symbolism not only to Jesus, but to the Christian community in its experience of God dwelling in its midst. In reference to John 2:13–25, see pp. 65–84.
5. Lonergan's reference to Joseph de Finance's distinction between two contrasting modes of exercising freedom, namely, the "horizontal" and the "vertical," have a special significance at this point: "A horizontal exercise is a decision or choice that occurs within an established horizon. A vertical exercise is the set of judgments and decisions by which we move from one horizon to another...it is also possible that the movement into a new horizon involves an about face; it comes out of the old by repudiating characteristic features; it begins a new sequence that can keep revealing ever greater depth and breadth and wealth. Such an about face and new beginning is what is meant by conversion." (B. Lonergan, *Method in Theology,* 237–238.)
6. See, for example, Exod 15:8; Isa 40:7, 44:3, 59:21; Ezek 11:19–20, 36:26–27; Joel 28:29; Job 34:14; Pss 18:15, 51:10; Wis 9:16–18.

7. St. Thomas Aquinas, in *Summa Theol.* 1, 20, 2, gives crystalline expression to the unconditioned character of the love of God in the statement: *amor Dei est infundens et creans bonitatem in rebus* ("The love of God is infusing and creating the good in things").

8. Particularly suggestive here is James Alison, *Raising Abel,* 44–49. The author acknowledges his debt to Robert Hammerton-Kelly, *Sacred Violence: Paul's Hermeneutic of the Cross* (Minneapolis: Augsburg Fortress, 1992), 78–79.

9. As an indication of the complexity of the question, and for an abundance of relevant texts and comment, Humbert Bouësse, O.P., *Le Sauveur du monde: La place du Christ dans le plan de Dieu* (Chambéry-Leysse: College Théologique Dominicain, 1951).

10. Both terms are borrowed from the theology of Hans Urs von Balthasar.

11. For insightful criticism of the model, "creation, fall, redemption, heaven," see James Alison, *Raising Abel,* 49–56.

12. Jean-Luc Marion, "Le phénomène saturé," 89–90, 103–105, 113–127.

13. In Lonergan's terms, the conversion of faith "sublates" the aspects of conversion proper to the intellectual, moral, religious, and psychological dimensions. Following Karl Rahner on this point, he describes what happens thus: "what sublates goes beyond what is sublated, introduces something new and distinct, puts everything on a new basis, yet so far from interfering with the sublated or destroying it, on the contrary needs it, includes it, preserves all its proper features and properties, and carries them forward to a fuller realization within a richer context" (B. Lonergan, *Method in Theology,* 241).

14. This is a central feature of von Balthasar's *Theo-Drama.* See especially "Christ's Mission and Person" in *Theo-Drama III: Dramatis Personae: Persons in Christ,* Graham Harrison, trans. (San Francisco: Ignatius Press, 1992), 149–229.

15. The manner in which the Spirit not only proceeds from the Father and the Son but is the Spirit of their mutual love and self-giving is creatively presented by François-Xavier Durrwell, *The Spirit of the Father and the Son: Theological and Ecumenical Perspectives,* Robert Nowell, trans. (Middlegreen, Slough: St Paul Publications, 1990). For a fuller treatment by the same author, see *Holy Spirit of God: An Essay in Biblical Theology,* Benedict Davies, trans. (London: Geoffrey Chapman, 1986).

16. In the traditional Thomist trinitarian scheme, the Second Person of the Trinity is understood as Son precisely because he is the perfect living self-expression of God as Word, a "certain intellectual emanation" (*Summa Theol.*, 1, 34, 2). Though the Prologue legitimates this way of understanding to some extent, the Gospel here invites theology to further its exploration of the divine life as one of interpersonal relationships between the Father and the Son.

4

The God of the Wider World (4:1–54)

The hearing (or non-hearing) of the Word has been described to this point in an explicitly Jewish context. The prophet is indeed being found to be without honor in his own country (4:44); and the Jewish leaders are increasingly disturbed by an outbreak of baptismal activity independent of their authorization, as they anxiously ponder on what or who was behind it.

1. The Gift of God

10. Jesus answered her, "If you knew the gift of God, and who it is that is saying to you, 'Give me a drink,' you would have asked him, and he would have given you living water." 11. The woman said to him, "Sir, you have no bucket and the well is deep. Where do you get that living water? 12. Are you greater than our father Jacob, who gave us the well, and with his children and flocks drank from it?" 13. Jesus said to her, "Everyone who drinks from this water will be thirsty again, 14. but whoever drinks from the water that I will give them will never be thirsty. The water that I will give will become in them a spring of water welling up to eternal life." 15. The woman said to him, "Sir, give me this water, so that I may never be thirsty or have to keep coming here to draw water." (4:10–15)

But now the circle widens. The Father's love for the world moves Jesus on: "He had to go through Samaria" (4:4). At this stage of his journey, Jesus is found at Jacob's well, outside the city of Sychar. He is described as exhausted by his travels. His mission is proving costly to him. His tiredness and thirst foreshadow his passion (cf. 19:28), and "the lifting up" by which he would draw all to himself (12:32). Left behind by his disciples who had gone off to buy food, he is alone, until a Samaritan woman comes to draw water from the well. He initiates a conversation with an abrupt demand: "Give me a drink" (4:7). A disconcerting other is entering her life. She registers the anomaly, for cultural and religious boundaries are being broached: "How is it that you, a Jew, ask a drink of me, a woman of Samaria?" (4:9). Though, by the end of this episode, this stranger would be acknowledged by her people as "the Savior of the world" (4:42), he is at first dismissively reduced by the woman to his obvious ethnic and religious status. For his part, Jesus does not accept the segregated world that allowed no communication between a Jew and a Samaritan—let alone between a man and a woman in these circumstances. Despite the prohibition of contact between these two antagonistic groups (4:9), Jesus is obedient to another will. He will not be part of such a polarized world. Accordingly, he responds to the woman in terms of the Father's all-inclusive, self-giving love (3:16).

The woman is being invited into another realm of divine grace and life. The well was historically connected with former blessings ("...our father Jacob who gave us this well" (4:12; cf. Gen 33:19; 48:22; Josh 24:32). Now it emerges as a symbol of the life-giving depths of another kind—the gift of "living water" as "a spring...welling up to eternal life" (4:14). It is the divine gift which alone can slake all human thirst in ways that surpass all past forms of divine giving. The Word who speaks is now breaking open the world molded by the privileges and antagonisms of the past. Sensing a novel interruption of the way things were, the woman responds in a tone of measured respect: "Sir, you have no bucket and the well is deep. Where do you get that living water?" (4:11).

Still, she is confused, unable to respond on the level at which Jesus promises the gift he speaks of. Taking refuge in defense, she insists that what is in store for her is governed by what is already in possession. All else is impossible; there is no room for the "greater": "Are you greater than our father Jacob?"(4:12). She reduces the proffered "gift of God," the promised "living water," to her own mundane needs, demanding in her turn: "Sir, give me this water…" (4:15). Despite the barrier of initial impossibility holding her back, the impossible possibilities of the gift of God are about to open up.

In the exchange that Jesus initiated, God's giving is the source and explanation of his behavior. This gift is ever more inclusive: "Go, call your husband, and come back" (4:16). God is being revealed—in a love that dissolves all boundaries. At the other extreme is the woman herself. She finds herself anew, as one known and addressed by the Word (4:16–18). Her somewhat evasive self-description, "I have no husband" (4:17a), is confronted with his declaration, "…you have had five husbands, and the one you have now is not your husband" (4:18). As a result she is shocked into new realization. She is being intimately addressed by one who truly knows her (cf. 1:48—with regard to Nathanael). At the same time, Jesus appreciates her capacity to receive the truth: "You are right in saying…" (4:17b); and "what you have said is true" (4:18b). The revelation of God is the truth that comes to the true. Jesus knows what is within God and "what is within everyone" (2:25). The woman, now disorientated in the expanding horizon of "the fullness of the gift which is truth" (1:14b), comes up against a truth about which there is no ambiguity. He knows her, and sees more in her than she has previously dared admit. His presence is unsettling, as if to stimulate her real questions and her real search—in a way reminiscent of the first words of the Word to the disciples in the question, "What are you looking for?" (1:38).

Accepting that she has been truly known by this stranger, the woman comes to new appreciation of Jesus. He is no longer "you, a Jew" (4:9) or even "Sir" (4:11, 15, 19a). She is brought to a religious level of engagement with him: "Sir, I see you are a prophet" (4:19). He is identified as one who speaks sympathetically in the name of God, even if, presumably, the God he speaks for is associated with the Temple of Jerusalem. And so she invites him to clarify the radical point of antagonism between Jew and Samaritan: "Our fathers worshipped on this mountain but you say that the place where people must worship is in Jerusalem" (4:20). Under the shadow of the holy Mount of Gerizim, she is limited to the categories of her ancestral religion. Samaritan tradition associated this mountain with Abraham's sacrifice of Isaac and Jacob's dream, and so revered it as a special dwelling place of God. Jesus addresses her out of a light "from above," unshadowed by the purely human perspective with its succession of sacred times and its geography of sacred places. Jacob's dream of the ladder between heaven and earth, and his waking declaration that "this is no other than the house of God and this is the gate of heaven" (Gen 28:12, 16–17) is about to be reshaped in the light of the vision of "opened heaven" (1:51), centered on Jesus himself.

2. The Father Seeks True Worshipers

21. Jesus said to her, "Woman, believe me, the hour is coming when you will worship the Father neither on this mountain nor in Jerusalem. 22. You worship what

you do not know; we worship what we know, for salvation is from the Jews. 23. But the hour is coming, and now is, when the true worshipers will worship the Father in spirit and in truth, for such the Father seeks to worship him. 24. God is spirit, and those who worship him must worship in spirit and in truth." 25. The woman said to him, "I know that the Messiah is coming, he who is called Christ. When he comes, he will show us all things." 26. Jesus said to her, "'I am' is the one speaking to you." (4:21–26)

The Worship of the Father

The hour has arrived when God would be definitively revealed as the God of everyone, irrespective of the limitations of the cherished traditions of the past. In this sense, Jesus is not concerned to act in the traditional prophetic role of confessing the one true God against what is false and idolatrous. For all previous modes of worship, both the genuine and the defective, are relativized. He is at once more than a prophet and greater than the patriarch Jacob. He presents God as no longer contained within the limitations of the past ("our fathers"), but as "*the* Father" whose worship is not restricted to particular places, however holy, nor confined to those who have been part of the privileged economy of divine revelation in the past: "...neither on this mountain nor in Jerusalem" (4:21).

While transcending previous traditions in this new hour of grace, Jesus nonetheless locates himself within the history of God's giving. As a Jew (cf. 4:9), he acknowledges the "anonymous Judaism" of the Samaritans: "You worship what you do not know" (4:22a). Such worship has been without the benefit of the universal dimension of God's design. In contrast, "we worship what we know, for salvation is from the Jews" (4:22b).

In the history of Israel, the saving will of God has been manifest in the many gifts preparing for this hour when an ultimate universal salvation would appear: "Turn to me and be saved, all the ends of the earth! For I am God, and there is no other" (Isa 45:22). Jesus' use of the inclusive "we" in regard to the faith of Israel intensifies the sense of all that was positive in its long history of familiarity with the one, true God. That history has included the Word "coming to his own" (1:11). Despite rejection and incomprehension that mark his relations with "the Jews," the darkness has not overcome the light (1:5), with the result that "We worship what we know...."

A new time of grace has arrived when true worshippers will come into their own. They will adore God, not as one contained in the hallowed sanctuaries of either Gerizim or Jerusalem, but as the Father to whom they will turn in unreserved intimacy and assurance. They will worship the Father "in spirit and truth" (4:23a). This promise of universal access to God is already being realized: "and now is here" (4:23b). A new consciousness of God had already been intimated in the Gospel: "The true light, which enlightens everyone" (1:9) has been coming into the world. The Word has become flesh and lived among us, bearing the full and final gift of the truth (1:14). In this plenitude, God is made known by his only Son who enjoys an original and intimate relationship with the Father (1:17–18). Whoever accepts the testimony of Jesus becomes convinced that "God is true" (3:33), with the implication that the human search for the true God, and the truth of God's revelation, meet in the radiance of the light: "...that it may be clearly seen that these deeds have been done in God" (3:21). As the one who speaks and embodies the true word of God, Jesus is the personal evidence that God is giving "the Spirit without measure" (3:34), the mysterious agency that transforms human existence in a "new birth" (3:5).

In Spirit and Truth

As the Gospel unfolds, the meaning of both "truth" and "spirit" will be progressively filled out. For example, Jesus will promise to send "the Spirit of truth" from the Father, to testify on his behalf (15:26). In the Johannine range of reference, the significance of these two key words unfolds like fractal patterns, endlessly replicating themselves in wider dimensions. In the immediate context of Jesus' encounter with the Samaritan woman, worshipping the Father "in spirit and truth" is first of all contrasted with her narrow and distant sense of God. She is being drawn out of herself into a new realm of relationship to God. For the worship of the Father "in spirit" implies going beyond all previous localizations and objectifications of the divine. The true God can never be an instrument of self-glorification, nor an individual or national possession. The Father is not kept anywhere nor owned by anyone. He is worshipped in his self-giving love for the world (3:16)—in the truth incarnate in his Word, and in the Spirit of his measureless generosity (3:34). Faith must now live in the expanse of the opened heaven, and not within the world enclosed in its history of antagonisms and rivalries.

In apposition to worship in "Spirit" is worship in "truth." The gifts, restrictions, and ambiguities of former situations are now brought to their moment of truth. Through Jesus, God is proving true to himself in an all-surpassing communication. His Son will declare himself to be the way, *the truth* and the life (14:6). Holding to his word will mean "to know the truth, and the truth will make you free" (8:32). Previous economies structured on rigid exclusion mean nothing in the presence of the Word. He has come into the human situation, and speaks; for he is the hinge on which a new final phase of the revelation of God will turn. As the communication of the truth, his words to this woman reach out to all actual and potential believers.

Jesus' own relationship to the Father is preeminently one of "spirit and truth." In the Spirit which has descended and remained on him (1:33), he makes God known, and embodies the gift of God in those measureless dimensions which now extend into the "enemy territory" outside the bounds of Israel itself. He makes God known "in truth" in the intimacy of his knowledge as "the only Son of the Father, who is close to the Father's heart" (1:18). His truth pierces to the heart of those he encounters—Nathanael, the disciples, his mother, Nicodemus; and, in this instance, the Samaritan woman. Far from teaching a new theology, he truly embodies the gift of God. The "spirit and truth" of genuine worship is conformed to the "spirit and truth" manifest in the person and mission of Jesus himself.

Still, while Jesus is the revelatory focus of what is happening, his words and actions always look to the Father, the origin of all his communication. What he offers is the gift *of God*. As if to emphasize the divine origin of his mission, he explains, "...for the Father seeks such as these to worship him" (4:23). This statement suggests the very purpose of John's Gospel, which is to witness to the Father actively seeking out those who will relate to him as he relates to the world. The Father's seeking enables his genuine worshippers to respond in accord with his unreserved love—the measureless generosity of the Spirit in which he has given his Son. God is revealed as the love that knows no bounds and acknowledges no boundaries. Hence, "God is spirit, and those who worship him must worship in spirit and in truth" (4:24). The indefinable reality of God must be met with the unconditional self-giving of true adoration. The Father himself has defied the measure of all earthly criteria, breaking open the little worlds of "religion" to another sense of proportion. His seeking out true worshippers is an aspect of his unreserved love for the world, as it invites believers to participate in such love and to witness to it (cf. 1 John 4:11–12). This "gift of God," given in the spirit of all-embracing love, given in the truth of all that it claims to be, inspires a response proportionate to it.

3. "I Am He"

Hesitating at the frontier of some wondrous new land of promise, the woman grasps for some manageable category in which to continue the conversation and to comprehend "who it is that is speaking" to her (4:10). Her appreciation of his identity has progressed from "you, a Jew," from the respectful "Sir," from the designation of him as "prophet," to what, given his amazing knowledge of who she is, is for her an ultimate possibility: "I know that the Messiah is coming, he who is called Christ. When he comes, he will show us all things" (4:25).

In a way paralleling the restrictive "we know" of Nicodemus (3:2), her "I know..." represents a last-ditch effort to contain him within the categories of a received messianic tradition. Since Jesus has revealed so much about her, is he the messianic figure who will reveal all kinds of marvelous things? Is she to be the privileged recipient of an even more dazzling display of secret knowledge? Setting aside Jesus' reference to the Father and the qualities of true worship, she tries to bring Jesus back to her world. His response is the radical explanation of their conversation. God is at work. In a way that surpasses all categories of expectation, he identified himself, " 'I am he' is the one speaking to you" (4:26). He does not claim, given the ambiguity and limitation inherent in her frame of reference, to be "Christ." Rather, he speaks of himself in terms of the most sacred name of God himself: "I am he" (cf. 8:24, 28, 58; 13:19; 18:5). By giving his name (Exod 3:14), God had made himself invocable in the history of Israel as its savior, to lead the Chosen People to the

105

future fulfillment of their calling. The God, invoked and confessed through this name, transcends all history in his creative and saving power (Isa 43:10; 45:18), compared to which all other "gods" are nonentities. What is now implied is that this God is finally made known in Jesus, and made intimately invocable in him. He is the new "burning bush" in which the living God is encountered. Jesus thus presents himself to the woman, not merely through the fascinating disclosure of secrets bearing on her past, but as opening up for her God-given possibilities in what is now taking place.

4. Completing God's Work

The Disciples Return

A dramatic interruption in the moment of revelation occurs, suggested by a beautifully timed irony in the Gospel account when the disciples return, and are deeply shocked at the scene: has he even been eating with a Samaritan woman? Their suspicion of impropriety surfaces in their unexpressed question, "'Why are you speaking to her?'" (4:27b). The frozen categories of their habitual religious, cultural, ethnic, and sexual segregations melt in the warmth of this new world of the Word's communication. The "gift of God" is more disconcertingly inclusive than even the disciples could allow. God's revelation comes on its own terms, and respects no human conventions. The disciples must learn that, though they will witness to God's Word, they do not own it.

In the meantime, the woman, despite her growing appreciation of this man who went out of his way to speak to her, still evidences a lack of understanding as she leaves the scene. In her report to her fellow citizens, she is no missionary or evangelist. Yet she does carry an invitation to them: "Come and see a man who has told me everything I have done" (4:29a). In her puzzlement, she shares her question, "Can this be the Christ?" (4:29). And this is sufficient to get them started on the way.

After the woman has gone, there is an intermezzo. The disciples have come back after buying food; the Samaritans are yet to arrive. The disciples, laboring with the same limitations shown by the woman, address Jesus as "Rabbi," and press him to eat (4:31). His response reaches beyond the dramatis personae of the immediate narrative to speak of larger mysteries, and of an origin and a future which the present circle of disciples cannot at the moment comprehend: "I have food to eat which you do not know" (4:32). He rejects his disciples' insistence to eat something. He is given over to another will, and sustained by other food—about which they are deemed to be ignorant. When what is happening is beyond them, they are forced back to their scandalized assessment of the situation: "Has anyone brought him food?" (4:33). What has been going on between him and the woman who has just left? These question suggest that the woman has made more progress in understanding Jesus than they have.

But Jesus redeems the situation by offering his own explanation of what has been really taking place: "My food is to do the will of him who sent me, and to complete his work" (4:34). His explanation is given only in terms of his relationship to the Father. What sustains him ("my food") is outside the world of human respect and expectation; beyond all the limited cultural and religious categories in which people have lived; even beyond the physical reality of food and drink. The Father's love for the world (3:16) is the energizing factor in his mission. It is this that sustains him in weariness and thirst, explains his journey to Samaria, and his reaching out to the Samaritans. Coming from the Father (1:14, 18, 34; 2:16; 3:16–17, 35–36), the origins and terms of his mission are beyond human calculation and control. He comes from the one who cannot be understood—"God no one has ever seen" (1:18)—as sent to where, in the judgment of his disciples, he should not be. Because "God is spirit," Jesus, as God's Son and Word, acts in ways that leave the human scope of understanding and expectation bewildered. Because the Father seeks worshipers in spirit and in truth (4:21–24), his action in people's lives will mean an experience of God's freedom and surprising truth that are apt to leave human expectation and human judgment at a loss for words. Only the Word is the language of God. All other meanings and interpretations fall short. Only in the Word as revealer of God, and only in the Son as the agent of the Father's will, can the behavior of Jesus be understood. God's will takes him beyond all boundaries—beyond the limits of the Jewish world, into the alien region of Samaria.

Sustained by his mission, Jesus is intent on bringing to perfection the work of the Father, "and to complete his work" (4:34b). The work of God moves the Son toward a God-willed future fulfillment. The Son's particular "works," as in the present instance of his dealings with the Samaritans, anticipate his completion of the Father's work. His mission turns on that hour when he will be lifted up (3:14), and turn to the Father with the words, "I have glorified you on earth by finishing the work that you gave me to do" (17:4). In the meantime, the works and signs he performs flow from his obedience to the Father in order to bring God's saving work to completion.

Laborers in the Harvest

With the impending arrival of the Samaritans, that divine work is progressing. The long season of waiting for harvest time has been divinely abbreviated. By contradicting the conventional expectations of his followers, Jesus introduces them into a new time-scale—measured now by God's saving power at work: "Do you not say, 'Four months more, then comes the harvest?' I tell you, lift up your eyes, and see how the fields are already ripe for harvest" (4:35). The time of salvation is not linked to earthly seasons, nor predictable according to the world's patterns of growth. When the Father seeks worshipers "in spirit and truth," the time of waiting for an indefinite future is over. The disciples are bidden to lift up their eyes to see the arrival of the Samaritans who "were coming to" Jesus (4:30). The "gift of God" is being given; and now that the time of God is ripe, "He who reaps receives wages, and gathers fruit of eternal life, so that the sower and reaper may rejoice together" (4:36).

The Word has seeded the world already, for the Samaritans are approaching, despite all that has hitherto prejudiced their access to him (4:8, 9, 27). Moreover, Jesus is including his disciples in his work in a manner hitherto beyond their capacities or expectations. But joy awaits them; for they will gather the fruit of eternal life because Jesus has labored to sow the grain. The metaphor of the harvest looks back to the symbol of "living water welling up to eternal life" (4:14). The spring of water flows; the grain has grown; the harvest is now ready; and God's work is coming to completion. The sower, the reaper, and the gatherer all share in the one joy of accomplishment. This is to anticipate the terms of Jesus' last discourse when he declares the purpose of witness, "...that my joy may be in you, and your joy may be complete" (15:11). The wisdom of the old proverb, "One sows, and another reaps" (4:37), is now understood to articulate a special truth: what the Word has sown, and what the disciples will reap, are both aspects of the one "work of God" being brought to fulfilment in ways that transcend the present understanding of Jesus' followers. But the urgency of God's work presses, as has been instanced in the divine necessity under which Jesus himself has made contact with the Samaritans (4:4).

Since the Father works and seeks, so also does Jesus, in making contact with the Samaritans and in summoning his disciples to share in his mission. The scope of his mission includes the whole world (cf. 3:16–17). The Samaritans will soon confess him to be, in fact, "the savior of the world" (4:42). He sends his disciples as he too was sent: "I sent you to reap that for which you did not labor" (4:38a). The disciples have not yet experienced the fatigue, hunger, and thirst of their master (4:6)—all indications of the passion he is to undergo—nor have they been part of his initiative with regard to the Samaritan woman. But now, sent by him, they will reap the harvest. As his being sent meant complete surrender to the Father's will, so their commission will entail obedience to the will of Jesus who has come "from above." Behind both the mission of Jesus and the envisioned mission of the disciples is the Father's initiative.

In the work of God, "others have labored, and you have entered into their labor" (4:38b). The "others" referred to by Jesus, as he addresses the "you" of all who would come to believe in him, has many possible references. In their respective manners, God, the prophets of Israel, those who have been baptizing with Jesus beforehand, and even this present circle of disciples, in their wary dealings with the Samaritans, have been "working." But preeminent among those who have labored for this future harvest are the two have been "sent" by God, John the Baptist (1:6), and Jesus himself (3:17; 4:34). John has made way for Jesus; and Jesus is making way for the completion of the Father's work. For all concerned, the work has proved costly. In the labor of love for the world, the Father has given his only Son (3:16); John has accepted to "decrease" that the role of Jesus might increase (3:30); Jesus has known the exhaustion and thirst which foreshadow his final "lifting up" on the cross. The disciples do not simply enter into the joy of the harvest, but into the labor of gathering it in. In each instance, an unreserved self-giving is demanded. For the disciples, it will mean leaving behind all past securities if they are to collaborate in the work of God, for they now are the only baptizers: the baptismal activity of both John and Jesus has come to an end (3:24; 4:2).

The Arrival of the Samaritans

But the work of God goes on. The Samaritans arrive on the scene, inspired by their fellow citizen's astonished testimony: "Many Samaritans from the city believed in him because of the word of the woman's testimony, 'He told me everything I have done.'" (4:39). They have come with their own questions and expectations, influenced by the woman's question, "Can this be the Messiah?" (4:29). They are drawn by one of the signs Jesus performed, namely, his amazing knowledge of one of their number. In this they instance a form of religious belief based on the testimony of another, but it is not yet faith in the Word himself. There is a further step to take in their journey. Though still in the economy of signs, they invite him to stay with them, in a gesture of welcome and hospitality. The Word has been in this world too (1:10), which, up to this point, has not known him. Here, too, he has come to what was his own. While he has encountered rejection from his own people, these foreigners are accepting him (1:11). To these he will give the power to become the children of the Father (1:12), to worship "in spirit and in truth," in a way not determined by race, tradition, or human antagonisms, but by God (1:13): "So when the Samaritans came to him, they asked him to stay with them; and he stayed there for two days" (4:40).

Not only does Jesus not acknowledge the ancient antagonisms between Jew and Samaritan, but the Samaritans themselves appear to have forgotten such divisions. They are prepared to enter into the universality of God's design. The Father's search for true worshipers is being realized in their hospitality offered to the Word, with the result that "...many more believed because of his word" (4:41).

The "many more" implies that no automatic outcome is envisaged. The Word is addressed to human freedom. Worship "in spirit and truth" is an act of the free. While the economy of signs can have its dangers—such as a fascination with the marvelous, or claims by a few to privileged knowledge or special favor—the criterion of true faith is obedience to the Word that Jesus is and speaks. Hence, the newly believing Samaritans now dissociate themselves from their previous form of belief, to base their faith squarely on its only foundation: "They said to the woman, 'It is no longer because of your words that we believe, for we have heard for ourselves, and know that this is indeed the Savior of the world'" (4:42).

They now confess themselves to know, in contrast to previously recorded self-assertive claims to know (cf. 1:41, 45; 3:2), that Jesus is in fact the savior of the world. This truth has been revealed to them. In their hearing of the Word, their consciousness of God's saving action has expanded to include the whole world (3:17). God is identified no longer in terms of the tradition of their "fathers" (4:12, 20), but as "the Father" seeking true worshipers. They are no longer simply fascinated by a charismatic figure divining a woman's secrets, for they have found themselves in the presence of "I-am-he" communicating with them. They have risen above the rivalries between the sacred places of Gerizim and Jerusalem into the wide world of God's action. Beyond the boundaries of Israel, a new community of believers has come into being, witnessing to the God of the whole world (3:16). The one sent by God has been found to speak the words of God (3:34a). The Father is giving the Spirit "without measure" (3:34b). By welcoming the Word, the Samaritans have begun to live in the world in a new way, displaced with regard to old religious markers, yet at home now within the limitless horizon of God's gift.

The Samaritan episode is complemented by the story of Jesus' healing of the royal official's son (4:46–54), and his coming to faith "along with his whole household" (4:53). Here, too, God is reaching beyond the boundaries of Israel, even as Jesus is conscious that "a prophet has no honor in his own country" (4:44). With his son's cure, the official's subsequent witness is once more based, not on signs, but on the fact he " believed in the word that Jesus spoke to him and started on his way" (4:50).

The way of the Son, sent by the Father, has provoked a number of journeys so far, within Israel and beyond its boundaries, as the work of God is being brought to completion.

5. An Expanding Experience of God

As the Gospel leads its readers further into the depth and breadth of the Christian experience of God, it moves along lines shaped by the disconcerting otherness that Jesus brings into the situation. It looks back and upward—to his origin with the Father; and out—to the scope of what the Father is bringing about. Jesus' communication to the woman works in dimensions deeper than her cherished well, and broader than the horizon bounded by the local and historical markers of the past. He has drawn near, bearing "the gift of God," sent by the Father to seek out true worshipers. Jacob's dream of the opened heaven has become a reality. The dialogue with the woman began around a well in the shadow of Mount Gerizim. The Temple of Jerusalem, though geographically distant, is an oppressively present reality in the Samaritan imagination as the polar opposite to what they are. Now this geography of mutual antagonism, rivalry, and exclusion is redrawn to another scale. Another has entered the scene, opening it to dimensions of "spirit and truth," not centered on a well, but in the flow of the living water of life without end. Jesus' unconventional outreach to one of their own has led the Samaritans to acknowledge him as the Savior of the world. Their world has been remade. The God of their "fathers" is now revealed as "the Father," loving the whole world and seeking them out as true worshipers.

The symbols figuring in this episode—the spring of living water, the food sustaining Jesus, the harvest that lies ready—work not so much as describing the reality of God's presence and action, but as inviting into an experience affecting the imagination of faith with a sense of the bounty of the gift of God. Each of these symbols stimulates a sense of the "greater" (4:12) as the work of God moves to its completion. The inexhaustible life-giving spring contrasts the precarious limits of life centered around a well. The food sustaining Jesus, soon to be linked to Jesus' own gift to his disciples, contrasts with food that the hungry disciples had gone off to buy. The fields now ripe for the harvest contrast to the slow, uncertain time of working the fields and waiting on the seasons. Abundance, nourishment, and ripeness mark faith's experience of the Father here being revealed.

5

The God of the Sabbath (5:1–47)

The relationship of Jesus to God and of God to Jesus emerges as the fundamental question—in the Holy City (5:1), in the Temple itself (5:14), and on this holy day (5:9).

1. The Son Heals on the Sabbath

5. One man was lying there who had been ill for thirty-eight years. 6. When Jesus saw him lying there and knew that he had been there for a long time, he said to him, "Do you want to be healed?" 7. The sick man answered him, "Sir, I have no one to put me into the pool when the water is troubled, and while I am making my way, someone else steps down ahead of me." 8. Jesus said to him, "Rise, take your mat and walk." Now that day was a Sabbath. (5:5–8)

Jesus has come up to Jerusalem (5:1), and appears at this place of healing frequented by numerous invalids—the Sheep Pool, Bethesda, opposite the Antonia fortress in the northern part of the city. He takes the initiative in regard to one of the more hopeless cases who had been suffering for some thirty-eight years. He "knew he had been there a long time" (5:6), thereby showing the prescience of him "who knew what was in everyone" (2:25). This case recalls similar instances of such knowledge—of Nathanael (1:47–48), and of the Samaritan woman (4:18). Once more, too, in a way characteristic of the Word whose first recorded words in the Gospel were a question (cf. 1:38b), Jesus asks the sick man a question, "Do you want to be healed?" (5:6b). The sufferer acknowledges that he is without human help to do what he sees as necessary. Left to himself, locked in defeat and incapacity, he can see no further. He is as yet unaware of any divine possibilities in the situation.

Nonetheless, Jesus' initiative discloses a new economy of healing and salvation for the crippled man. It begins with hearing the word of the Word. Jesus commands him to stand, to take up his mat and walk; and the man is healed and obeys. On this Sabbath, the Word is at work in the world. On this day dedicated to the Creator, he brings about a healing that transcends all human capacity.

> 10. So the Jews said to the man who had been cured, "It is the Sabbath; it is not lawful for you to carry your mat." 11. But he answered them, "The one who healed me said to me, 'Take your mat and walk.'" 12. They asked him, "Who is the one who said to you, 'Take your mat and walk'?" 13. Now the one who had been healed did not know who it was, for Jesus had withdrawn, as there was a crowd in the place. (5:10–13)

The laws governing Sabbath observance now give rise to a conflict regarding the God of the Sabbath. Jesus' healing of the sick man on the holy day is interpreted as an act of provocation. He is breaking open a primary symbol of Jewish tradition to a startlingly new significance. At the outset of this episode, the Word incarnate is immersed, in the logic of the prologue, in reality of the "flesh." He makes contact with the world of the suffering—the blind, the lame, and the paralyzed (5:4), who have come for a cure in a traditional place of healing. On this level he is simply "the one who healed me" (5:11), then to be swallowed up in the crowd (v. 13).

The significance of Jesus' action is not lost. The representatives of Jewish orthodoxy could not but interpret what he did as running counter to the clear meaning of the Sabbath. The healing Jesus performed, and the man carrying the mat at his command, both were flaunting the Sabbath observance. How can any human agent possibly pretend to be honoring God or doing God's will by acting in this way? For the words of the law were clear:

> 8. Remember the Sabbath day and keep it holy. 9. Six days you shall labor and do all your work. 10. But the seventh day is a Sabbath to the LORD your God....11. For in six days, the LORD made heaven and earth, the sea, and all that is in them, but rested the seventh day; therefore, the Lord blessed the seventh day and consecrated it. (Exod 20:8–11)

Neither the healer nor the healed were observing what was essential to Jewish identity and practice. The God of Israel was clearly being dishonored, if the words of Jeremiah were to be respected:

> 19. Thus said the LORD God to me: Go and stand at the People's gate....20. And say to them: Hear the word of the LORD....21. Thus says the LORD: For the sake of your lives, take care that you do not bear a burden on the Sabbath or bring it in by the gates of Jerusalem. 22. Do not carry a burden out of your houses on the Sabbath, or do any work, but keep the Sabbath day holy, as I commanded your ancestors....(Jer 17:19–22; cf. Deut 5:15)

The ensuing discussion between the guardians of the Law and the man who had been healed kept two planes of reference resolutely apart. God was on one level, deserving Sabbath veneration. But, on another level, there was the man who had been healed and the one who made him whole on the Sabbath. Moreover, Jesus now loses himself in the crowd, unidentifiable in the mass of faceless humanity surrounding him. While the believer is being invited to see the Word in action, those immediately affected by his provocative action cannot. They have not yet learned to identify God's Son acting in the world of human suffering. Jesus is merely a mysterious provocateur who disappeared in the crowd.

14. After this, Jesus found him in the Temple and said to him, "See, you have been healed! Do not sin anymore, so that nothing worse happens to you." 15. The man went away and told the Jews that it was Jesus who had healed him. (5:14–15)

But Jesus later seeks out the man who had been cured, and finds him in the Temple. The scene has shifted, both for the former invalid and for Jesus himself. Their place of meeting is no longer a traditional place of healing, but the sacred place of God's presence. In this place of God, Jesus carries his work of healing further. His words transcend the current interpretation of the Sabbath law while, at the same time, they challenge the one who had been ill to see himself as more than someone defined simply by his previous suffering and subsequent cure. Something more than physical healing is at stake: "Do not sin anymore, so that nothing worse happens to you" (5:14). Implicitly, Jesus is contesting the traditional theology of linking physical suffering to divine displeasure. His action suggests another kind of judgment, which becomes apparent in the discussion to follow.

2. On Trial for the Father

16. And this is why the Jews persecuted Jesus, because he did this on the Sabbath. 17. But Jesus answered them, "My Father is still working, and I am working." 18. This is why the Jews sought all the more to kill him, because he is not only breaking the Sabbath but was also calling God his own Father, thereby making himself equal to God. (5:16–18)

The issue is crystallized: for "the Jews," it is no longer a matter of a supposedly cured man carrying his mat on the Sabbath, but the transgression of this other man who had commanded him so to behave. The guardians of the law now actively move against Jesus. They begin to harass Jesus with every means, legal or otherwise. The meaning of the Sabbath and its God were at stake. If God had hallowed the Sabbath day, if God had rested on that day, who was this man to work by doing and commanding the contrary? The Law was clear:

2. And on the seventh day, God finished the work that he had done, and rested on the seventh day from all the work that he had done. 3. So God blessed the seventh day and hallowed it, because on it God rested from all the work he had done in creation. (Gen 2:2–3)

Jesus' answer to the charge contests the received Sabbath theology: "My Father is still working, and I also am working" (5:17). Here, the prosecution must have recognized, he was exploiting the divine exception to the rule. For it was acknowledged in theological tradition that, despite the words of Genesis 2:2–3, God, and only God, could transcend his own law. Jewish reflection on the Sabbath rest led to a decision that, while all must rest on the Sabbath, God alone performed two essential tasks. As children were born and people died on the Sabbath, God continued to give life and to judge. Without the action of God, even on a Sabbath, the whole of creation would simply cease to be.[1] Such properly divine activities knew no law. If, then, Jesus was putting his action on the same level as God's Sabbath activity, then here was a clear case of blasphemous transgression.[2]

In the case against him, besides the obvious infractions of performing a work of healing on the Sabbath, and commanding another to break the law, a deeper level of malice was apparent. This Jesus was invoking God as his own Father. He thereby claimed an exclusive and original relationship with the God of the Sabbath—which is exactly what the Gospel had presented from the beginning (cf 1:1, 14, 18). Further, he is alleged to be "making himself equal to God" (5:18). But this phrase was fraught with ambiguity. To "the Jews" it expressed a blasphemous pretension on the part of a man usurping the divine authority. To the emerging circle of disciples, it was the logical outcome of Jesus' existence as the Word and Son of God.[3]

The problem, however, progressively implied in the unfolding of the Gospel story, given its unhesitating affirmation of the One God (17:3), is the meaning of "equal." Only his opponents claimed that Jesus was making himself equal *(isos)* to God. He never claimed such equality, but spoke of his relationship with God as the Son to the Father. There is never question of his standing apart from God in an independent and competitive sense. However, an alternative interpretation was inaccessible to his accusers—namely, that he was acting in relationship to his Father in a reciprocity of love and life, in which everything he is and does is received from the Father who has sent him into the world. If that were recognized, far from breaking the Sabbath, he is breaking it open to its true meaning. He is actively keeping holy the seventh day by making his "holy Father" (17:11b) known in a new and final way, as a consequence of the unity that exists between the Father and the Son: "My Father is still working, and I also am working" (v. 17). Thus, the holiness of the Sabbath is, in fact, not being denied. But an inevitable question has been posed. Does the received tradition so limit and exhaust the meaning of the Sabbath day that Jesus' action must be judged blasphemous? Or, in the light of what he has done and of the God he makes known, is its meaning enlarged and redefined?

The latter possibility had to be profoundly threatening to upholders of traditional Sabbath law; hence their decision to remove him (v. 18a): "One who blasphemes the name of the Lord shall be put to death" (Lev 24:16). Jesus is judged as an imposter, deserving the full weight of the law: "Whoever acts high-handedly...affronts the Lord, and shall be cut off from among the people" (Num 15:30–31). The exchanges that follow continue in the form of a trial scene. The escalating antagonism of "the Jews" toward Jesus solidifies around the issue of God and of who is entitled to speak in his name (cf. 1:19; 2:13–22). Yet Jesus, though speaking in the name of his Father, will not only defend his action, but bring his judges to the point where they themselves are judged.

3. Witness to the Father's Love

19. Jesus said to them, "Amen, amen, I say to you, the Son can do nothing on his own authority, but only what he sees the Father doing; for whatever he does, that the

121

Son does likewise. 20. For the Father loves the Son, and shows him all that he is doing; and greater works than these shall he show him, that you may marvel. (5:19–20)

In answer to the charges against him—working on the Sabbath, calling God his Father, making himself God's equal—Jesus does not involve himself in casuistry. What is remarkable is the nature of his defense. He speaks of his Father who is acting on this Sabbath, so that the initiative of God is the major factor. Moreover, Jesus does not directly answer the charge of making himself God's equal. If anything, he shifts the accent back onto the Father; for it is the Father himself who has made Jesus his equal in giving him such works to perform.

Yet the notion of equality with God is not left hanging in the air. The receptivity and dependence of the Son in regard to the Father is solemnly emphasized in the opening words of Jesus' "defense": "Amen, amen, I say to you, the Son can do nothing on his own authority" (5:19). The most emphatic words of the Word point away from himself to the Father, leaving him with "nothing"—with no capacity to act unless it is given. What he does arises out of his vision of what the Father is doing. The Son's action deliberately reproduces the activity of the Father "...for whatever he [i.e., *that one* as in the Greek, *ekeinos*] does, that the Son does likewise" (5:19b). These opening words of Jesus' defense absolutely preclude any suspicion that he is somehow invading the divine transcendence, or displacing the all-initiating authority of "that one" onto himself. Any semblance of rivalry is thereby banished. The Son is not asserting himself against his Father, but asserting the true character of God as "his Father," as the God and Lord of the Sabbath. What Jesus does as the Son must be in perfect accord with the initiative of the ever-acting Father.

Not only does the Son defer to the Father in loving obedience and imitation. A further, more mysterious element enters in
the presentation of the God of the Sabbath. Correlative to the
Son's seeing what the Father is doing, is the Father's love in
showing the Son what he is doing. Jesus' obedience is conditioned by the demonstrative love of the Father: "the Father loves
the Son and shows him all that he himself is doing" (5:20a). This
extends a previous statement in the Gospel declaring that "the
Father loves the Son, and has placed all things in his hands"
(3:35). Thus, the Son's humility in "do[ing] nothing on his own"
(5:19a) is matched by the Father's dispossession by putting
everything in his hands. God acts out of unreserved love. The
love of God that gave his only Son for the life of the world (3:16)
is also the love that the Father shows by placing all thing in the
hands of the Son.

The economy of the Sabbath is predicated on a transcendent divine giving—of the Father to the Son, of the Son to the
Father, of the Father to the world—and, as will appear especially
in John 6, of the Son "for the life of the world" (6:51). The
superabundance of the gift, not the narrow limit of the law, is
the divine measure. In what Jesus says and does as the Son, a
measureless gift is being made (3:34).

The exchange between the Father and the Son is notably
characterized by their oneness in "the work" of mutual glorification. While the mission of the Son is to glorify the Father, the
Father is intent on glorifying the Son in his mission to the world.
The very notion of the one God is being transformed in the light
of a primordial communion into which believers are to be drawn.
For Jesus there is no question of dishonoring the Sabbath God,
but of honoring the real God, and of doing what God is doing in
the world. In the works the Father does and shows the Son,
"greater" dimensions will appear (5:20b). Beyond the marvel of
healing the sick man, the open circle of divine communication is

expanding, working to draw even the most resistant into it: "and greater works than these will he show him that you may marvel" (5:20b).

Marvelous and Greater Works

21. For as the Father raises the dead and gives them life, so also the Son gives life to whom he will. (5:21)

The true God of the Sabbath is to be revealed, not only as the God of healing, but the source of eternal life (5:21). The exclusive life-giving power of the God of Israel cannot be alienated.[4] That is not denied here; but what is affirmed is a new dynamic in the way God gives life: the Father has shown and given to the Son a uniquely divine power, even to the point of allowing for the Son's own freedom to make such a gift: "so also the Son gives life to whom he will" (5:21). The sovereign power of the Sabbath God has been passed on to the Son and put at his disposal. The initiative of Jesus in curing the sick man on the Sabbath is now seen as an adumbration of his God-given, life-giving power. The free activity of the Son in seeking out this particular sufferer suggests that Jesus has been given the power to give life and to raise the dead. It is not a question of some form of slavish imitation of the Father or of a kind of automatic overflow from a divine source, by-passing the free activity of the Son. Though he can do nothing except it be given and shown by God, he is *someone*—acting and speaking in the world with his own freedom. He is not God's puppet, nor a mask behind which the real God is hiding. He is the Son, acting in his own person, as it were, to overcome death and give life. In him both person and mission coincide: he is what he does; he acts out his original identity. Even though he is utterly dependent on the being, action, and will of the Father, Jesus acts as a free agent, consciously confronting other freedoms in the world in which he communicates.[5] Loved by the Father, shown what the Father is doing, given over to his Father's will, Jesus works freely to make his Father known. Paradoxically, his unreserved total surrender to the one who sends him, and his complete deference to the Father's authority, result in a freedom which is profoundly disturbing to all other authorities.

As a result, the Jewish upholders of the Sabbath law are treated to a shocking irony. In the words of the Law, the God of Israel has spoken: "And see now that I, even I, am he; there is no god beside me. I kill and make alive; I wound and I heal; and no one can deliver from my hand" (Deut 32:39). How could this man act in the role of "god beside God"? How can he pretend to be the source of life alongside the "I am," YHWH, who has spoken so clearly? Why is it that the transcendent power of God to take life away or to give it has become, in Jesus, an act of healing on the Sabbath and a promise of resurrection? What is happening to God's judgment on all who pretend to usurp the divine power? The dreadful, baffling power of God acting from beyond this world in the domain of death and life is now appearing in another guise—in the mission of the Son to heal and to give life.

4. The Father "Resting" from the Work of Judgment

> 22. The Father judges no one, but has given all judgment to the Son, 23. that all may honor the Son, even as they honor the Father. Anyone who does not honor the Son does not honor the Father who sent him. (5:22–23)

Jesus continues as if to emphasize that a kind of divine dispossession has taken place. The Father does not judge at all, but has given all judgment over to his Son. An age-old conception of a "God of judgment" awaiting the sinner in the realm of death is being met with the revelation of the life-giving Father who judges no one. In this regard, God is no longer imagined as asserting his majesty against all others, but as sharing his divine prerogatives with a loved other: he judges no one, but gives all judgment to the Son (5:22).[6] The activity of judging had been hitherto understood as another Sabbath activity reserved to God alone.[7] However, on this Sabbath of divine self-revelation in the Son, Jesus has become the true interpreter of the Sabbath and its God. Because God is still working and because Jesus himself is working, he is to be honored as the Son. In him, the Father is present and acting, "so that all may honor the Son just as they honor the Father" (5:23a). Jesus precludes any suggestion that he can act against or outside the source from which he comes. Everything is referred back to his origin: "Anyone who does not honor the Son does not honor the Father who sent him" (5:23b). Not to recognize the Son is to dishonor the character of God as Father. For the Father is the original Giver. He has given what is only his to give—the power to give life and to judge—to him who alone can receive it, his only Son. Therefore, to move against the Son (5:16) is to remain outside the gracious economy of the true God's Sabbath activity.

5. The Giving of Life

24. Amen, amen, I say to you, anyone who hears my word and believes him who sent me, has eternal life, and does not come into judgment, but has passed from death to life. 25. Amen, amen, I say to you, the hour is coming, and now is, when the dead will hear the voice of the Son of God, and those who hear will live. 26. For as the Father has life in himself, so he has

**granted the Son also to have life in himself, 27. and
has given him authority to execute judgment, because
he is the Son of Man. (5:24–27)**

As if to underscore Jesus' role as the focus and expression
of the Father's activity, the Gospel now depicts him speaking,
with solemn emphasis, in the first person. To hearken to his
word and to accept him as the communication of God—by
believing in "the one who sent me" (5:24)—is to enter into a
communion of deathless life. Believers are removed from the
sphere of judgment altogether. The divine work of giving life and
judging which continues on the Sabbath is now incarnate in the
Son. The life of the world to come, of the eternal Sabbath, has
already begun. Death and judgment have ceased to be the all-
determining realities for human existence. When the decisive
reality now consists in the acceptance of God's action in the Son,
death and judgment are negative realities only for those who
reject God's life-giving communication.[8] The gift of eternal life
with God and the moment of divine judgment are no more
located at some menacing point outside this world. When "the
Word was made flesh and dwelt among us" (1:14), both life and
judgment are revealed within this world: eternal life has already
begun; judgment is already being made. The decisive hour has
already begun (5:25).

Even the future reality of physical death is subsumed into
the divine vitality emanating from the Son. The power of God is
exercised through the Son *of God*. The Father himself is the
main agent of resurrection (5:26a). The stream of eternal life has
begun to flow. The fact of physical death, however, is not
repressed: all will die as far as this world is concerned. Still, the
fact of human mortality is relativized. The voice of the Son
reaches the dead already—wherever they are imagined to be.
Even in the realm of death the voice of life is heard. The silence

of death is penetrated by the life-giving Word. The grace of this Sabbath is a gift which extends to all regions, to all time, and to all the generations: "...the dead will hear the voice of the Son of God, and those who hear will live" (5:25b). The life that comes through the Son affects every experience of death: "...in him was life, and the life was the light of all people....And darkness did not overcome it" (1:4–5).

From the deathless vitality of the Father, Jesus himself receives the power to be a source of life in a death-bound world: "Just as the Father has life in himself, so he has granted the Son to have life in himself" (5:26). For Jesus, as for those who hear him, death is not the final factor. While death is given its due as a human fact, it is shorn of its symbolic power. Human mortality is no longer a menacing realm of darkness enclosing the world in the domain of the "ruler of this world" (16:11), and causing those haunted by its power to seek a spurious life of worldly glory and influence. As the incarnation of God's own vitality, Jesus destabilizes the world determined by the culture of death. He has the authority to execute judgment "because he is the Son of Man" (5:27). The use of this title alludes to chapter 7 of Daniel. The prophet, watching through the visions of the night in the darkness of Israel's previous history, had declared:

> I saw one like the Son of Man coming with the clouds of heaven. And he came to the Ancient One and was presented before him. To him was given dominion and glory and kingship, that all peoples and nations and languages should serve him. His dominion is an everlasting dominion that shall not pass away, and his kingship is one that shall never be destroyed. (Dan 7:13–14)

While the Son as God's "Human One" is "from above" and occupies a realm that embraces all human history and the whole world ("coming on the clouds of heaven"), he has now come; and is here and now at work. He has already contacted the world beyond Judaism in his dealings with the Samaritan woman and pagan official. He is the bearer of God's final gift which will not yield to some other stage. The Son does not come to "the Ancient One" to be presented to him by some other intermediary. For "the Ancient One" is now revealed as the Father who, in a remarkable sense, is presenting his Son to the human world as savior, life-giver, and judge. The reason has already been given: for the Father "loves the Son and shows him all that he himself is doing" (5:20a), and places "all things in his hands" (3:35).

Earlier references to Jesus' role as the Son of Man necessarily affect the present context. Nathanael, like the Jews in the present episode, will see "greater things" (1:50b; 5:20b). The heavens, as the realm of God hitherto closed to the death-bound vision of the world, will be opened; and the Son of man will be the new Jacob's ladder of communication between God and the world (1:51). In Jesus, the God of the Sabbath is present and acting. As the communicator of the things of God, the Son of Man has "come down" from the realm above in which he communes with God, his Father, in a unique and exclusive way (3:13). He has come down to be "lifted up" as sign of healing like the serpent of Moses in the desert (3:14; 5:2–9), and as the source of "the greater things" of eternal life (3:15; 5:26). In this, he is already God's judgment on the world. Those who reject him and choose to remain in an alienated darkness (3:16–21), will find themselves separated from those who freely accept him as the gift of life and light.

28. "Do not marvel at this; for the hour is coming when all who are in the tombs will hear his voice 29. and come forth, those who have done good to the resurrection of life, and those who have done evil to the resurrection of judgment." (5:28–29)

129

When Jesus states that the Father does not judge, it does not mean that God is indifferent to human fate, or simply tolerant of human perversity. What it does mean is that there is no mysterious divine judgment being made from beyond the world in which the Son dwells among us as the Word. The judgment of the truth occurs in the acceptance or rejection of the one who is sent by God, and in whom he is present and acting. Our attitude to the Son transforms existence in the present, and reaches into the depths of the grave itself. To accept the Son is to be confirmed in hope for the future, even if that future necessarily involves the fate inherent in our common mortality. For the life that he already gives is not diminished or interrupted by death—unless judgment has been called down on oneself by opting for a world deaf to the voice of the Son. In the coming of the Son, not in the occurrence of death, God's judgment is made. Thus, to accept the Son as healer, life-giver, judge, and revealer, is truly to honor the true God of the Sabbath, to adore the Father "in spirit and truth" (4:23).

Though the voice of the Son that will sound in the tombs of the dead, Jesus reiterates his complete dependence on the Father: "I can do nothing on my own. As I hear, I judge" (5:30; cf. 5:19). The Son's voice is not one of self-assertion. In the violent situation of competing wills intent on their own respective justifications, Jesus professes unreserved obedience to him who sent him. The one who is sent is always looking back to the one who sends, so that his "judgment is just, because I seek not my own will but the will of him who sent me" (5:30b). Because he is so attuned to the ever-acting God of the Sabbath, he utters true judgment. As sent by the Father, he makes the Father present as the God who newly hallows this holy day.

6. Judgment on the Judges

31. "If I bear witness to myself, my witness cannot be verified; 32. there is another who bears witness to me, and I know that the testimony that he bears to me is true. 33. You sent to John, and he has borne witness to the truth. 34. Not that I accept such human testimony, but I say this that you may be saved. 35. He was a lamp that was kindled and shining, and you were willing for a while to rejoice in his light. 36. But the testimony that I have is greater than that of John; for the works that the Father has granted me to accomplish, these very works that I am doing, bear me witness that the Father has sent me. 37. And the Father who sent me has himself borne witness to me. His voice you have never heard, his form you have never seen, 38. and you do not have his word abiding in you, for you do not believe him whom he has sent. 39. You search the scriptures because you think that in them you have eternal life; and it is they that bear witness to me; 40. yet you refuse to come to me that you may have life." (5:31–40)

With Jesus affirming his complete dependence on God, his erstwhile judges themselves begin to feel the sharp edge of judgment. If the source of Jesus' judgment lies in his being totally beholden to the Father (5:31–32), the perversity of other judgments is diagnosed as a foreclosure on vital evidence (5:33–47). The Father-centered attitude of the Son is contrasted to the egotistical glory-seeking of those who are rejecting him.

Moreover, besides the witness of the Father on Jesus' behalf, there have in fact been other witnesses. First of all, those who were now rejecting Jesus had, pursuing evidence proper to their traditional world, "sent messengers to John who testified to the truth" (5:33). Though witness of John is not on the same level as the Father's witness (5:34a), the Baptist's witness does play its special role in the accomplishment of God's saving intention: "...that you may be saved" (5:34b). After all, John was "a man sent by God" (1:6), and "the Jews," acknowledging this possibility, had sent messengers to him (1:19). But John had "testified to the truth" (5:33b), by witnessing to Jesus as God's Lamb (1:19, 35) and Son (1:34), and the one on whom the Holy Spirit had descended (1:32–33). The light of John, though not the light of the Word, radiated with its own evidence—as Jesus himself acknowledges (5:35). It brings its own sense of joy, in that God is acting for the salvation of Israel, and because the messiah was coming (LXX Ps 131: 16b–17). Receptive to the light, people are made open to the possibilities of salvation in the world of searching and listening. God works in the given situation, even though there is more to be revealed. The Word has his witnesses in the world "from below," as God works to bring about the fullness of what is being revealed "from above" (5:34b; cf. 1:14; 3:16–17). But now what was once an occasion of joy for those who received John's witness to Jesus has turned to a mood of deadly antagonism. What further witness remains?

Jesus proceeds to indicate another kind of witness that is "greater than John's" (5:36a). The Gospel's use of the comparative "greater" was previously associated with "the works that the Father has given me to complete..." (5:20b). These works provide the evidence that the Father has sent him (5:36b). "The work of God" (4:34) is realized in the many "works" that Jesus brings to perfection. Even here, the signs and actions Jesus performs are never simply *his* works, but *the* works. In them, the Father is active as the original author of what is yet to be completed

(5:36b). "These very works" are crucial additional evidence of Jesus' mission. His actions are underwritten by the Father (5:37).

Notwithstanding the value of John's witness and that of "the works" performed by Jesus, it remains that the Father is the irreplaceable and essential witness without whom Jesus cannot be recognized or received. Other kinds of witness could be seen and heard and appreciated on their own level; but, as far as the Father's witness goes, Jesus' antagonists are found to be deaf and blind: "His voice you have never heard, his form you have never seen" (5:37b; cf. Deut 4:12, 15). If God is silent and invisible for them, how can they receive the Son who is the Word and luminous presence of God among them? However much they may believe that they have received the word of God—"the word of God abiding in you" (5:38a)—they are unaware of the source of that word in the deafness and blindness that has overtaken them: "you do not believe in him whom he has sent" (5:38b).

By rejecting Jesus, his antagonists have become alienated even from what they hold to be most precious. Their "searching of the scriptures" in the hope of eternal life (5:39) has enclosed them in the past, rather than opening them to the present in which the reality of eternal life has already begun. In their supposed mastery of the words of scripture, they have missed the Word to which the scriptures witness (5:39b). By holding to the former gift of the law, they are refusing the fullness of the gift of truth. Deaf to the voice of God, blind to the divine form, dead to the true promise of life, these masters in Israel misread what they most pretend to grasp. Unable to accept God's communication to them in this present hour, in a way that transcends all past traditions (4:23), they are meeting, not with salvation, but judgment. So impervious to the way of the true God have they become that they have interpreted the Sabbath in a manner fraught with lethal consequences for him who has been sent to them (5:17–18)—and for themselves as well (5:40). They are using their tradition to block God's reaching out to them in the Son. They are accused of choosing human glory over the glory of God (5:41–44).

> 41. "I do not accept glory from human beings. 42. But I know that you have not the love of God within you. 43. I have come in my Father's name, and you do not receive me; if another comes in his own name, him you will receive. 44. How can you believe, who receive glory from one another and do not seek the glory that comes from the one who alone is God? 45. Do not think I shall accuse you to the Father; it is Moses who accuses you, on whom you set your hope. 46. If you believed Moses, you would believe me, for he wrote of me. 47. But if you do not believe his writings, how will you believe my words?" (5:41–47)

Jesus contrasts his attitude to that of his accusers. By declaring that he does not accept human glory, he places himself outside the network of human reputation and self-justification that is making his hearers impervious to divine glory being revealed.[9] His identity is not defined by the death-bound culture of human respect, for the fundamental dynamism of his existence is to be from and for the Father. Unbeholden to human criteria, the sole measure of his action and judgment is the will of God. As a result, on the mundane level, his life is inglorious; he is left with a bad reputation in a world structured on self-justification. In that world, the law of God is invoked by those who obey it for the sake of bolstering their sense of self-worth—to the exclusion of the real God who is being revealed.

Jesus recognizes that his persecutors lack the love of God (5:42). Their existence is centered, not in God, but in themselves, and in the reputation that a loveless world can offer. Closed in on themselves, they turn from the ever "greater" action of God (5:20b, 36), thus rendering themselves incapable of receiving him who comes in the Father's name (5:43). He is alien to them because they are alien to God. He has come to his own, but his own do not accept him (1:11). Shut out of the social and religious realm of their valuation, the Son is deemed to be a dangerous nobody representing one to whom they are blind, deaf, and dead (5:37b–40). Anyone complacently inhabiting the world of the religiously inert is welcomed as one of its own (5:43b). Because Jesus is profoundly disturbing to such a world, he comes across as a stranger and a threat. How can they have faith in him when the whole horizon of their lives is closed against the One who is at the heart of his identity and mission?: "How can you believe..."? (5:44). If worth is calculated only in terms of mundane reputation, the subversive glory of God does not figure. A culture of self-promotion cannot allow itself to be disturbed by God: for its inhabitants "do not seek the glory that comes only from the one who alone is God" (5:44b). Their interpretation of the Sabbath is incapable of recognizing "My Father is still working, and I also am working" (5:17).

Despite the fact that the Father has handed over all judgment to the Son, Jesus is not about to make himself the accuser of his adversaries (5:45a). The keenest edge of the judgment against them arises from the figure they most revere, Moses himself, "on whom you have set your hope" (5:45b). Since the scriptures bear witness to Jesus (5:39b), there is a relationship between the Mosaic witness and the words of Jesus (5:47). The gift of the law both prepares for a new gift and is replaced by it (1:16–17). In rejecting the Son, these Jews are refusing the testimony of Moses and their own law—as well as missing out on the fulfilment it promised. That is the judgment that has come upon them.

This Sabbath day has ended in crisis. The issue throughout is how the Lord of the Sabbath is to be honored and known.

YHWH continues to work when the guardians of the Law insist that he rest. But the Lord of the Sabbath is still working through Jesus, the Son. His adversaries have insisted that the work of God is already complete. Their mastery of the Law has foreclosed on the possibility of God's final revelation. Anything "greater" is unimaginable.

7. The Sabbath Experience and the Meaning of God

Other feasts will be referred to over the next five chapters of the Gospel, and each one will provoke a more profound understanding of the God revealed in the words and works of the Son (5:1—10:42; cf. 5:9; 6:4; 7:2; 10:22). The mood pervading this Sabbath experience is one of intense antagonism. Implicit in the dramatic exchanges taking place between Jesus and "the Jews" is the presence of an early Christian community suffering a painful exclusion from the synagogue, and the consequent cessation of its traditional feasts. The other implied presence is that of the representatives of the Jewish people who had not only lost the temple and seen Jerusalem destroyed (70 A.D.), but were being confronted with what purported to be a new and final phase in the history of God's dealings with Israel; and, indeed, with the world itself, through the coming of Jesus Christ.

Each of these conflicting parties is living with its own grieving recollection of a God-given past. Now, some decades later, each is being faced with its own disturbing questions. Who, and where, is God, in this perilous moment of history? The old order had been so devastatingly demolished. And even if the new order had arrived in Jesus Christ, he has come and gone, now absent from the contentious world he had been sent to save. If Israel had lost the Temple, these early followers of Jesus, now long deprived of his historical presence, had a sense of being uprooted and disoriented, in a waning sense of continuity with their past.

In its way, the Christian community was experiencing a double negativity in this new situation. Not only did early believers—in response to the Father who had sought out true worshipers "in spirit and truth" (4:23)—have to leave behind the clarity and security of their diverse traditions, be they Jewish, Samaritan, or pagan, but they had to enter a history fraught with conflict and threat. They were not spared the vicissitudes and weaknesses inherent in human existence. With their past seemingly obliterating and their future increasingly precarious, where was God in all this? The Temple was destroyed; the synagogue has become inhospitable; and Jesus was no longer with them.

No doubt a sense of fulfilment endured. The faithful continued to confess the fullness of the gift of truth that had come through Jesus Christ. But there was grief as well. The new age had dawned only to make them more isolated in the world they had known. How then was the worship of the Father in spirit and truth to be genuinely enacted? Did the great feasts of their past now mean nothing to them? Or, did they now need to find the true meaning of what such celebrations were anticipating, in a way that would be worthy of the cosmic, all-inclusive love of God (3:16)? Faith had to enter history; and believers had to suffer the realities of time and conflict, in order to be converted to the true proportions of what God had brought about in Jesus Christ.

We conclude on a more explicitly theological note. The experience of God in this episode works toward an enriched *cognitive* sense of the God of Christian faith. In all that happens, the one God of Israel is working. However, the singularity of this one God presumes a unique form of communication and communion between the Father and the Son. The implication that there is a reciprocity of consciousness in regard to the Father who unceasingly works, and the Son who also works, provoked theological outrage (5:17). Undifferentiated monotheism allows for no self-communication either within the divine realm, or beyond it to the world. For mono-dimensional orthodoxy presupposes that God is not only one, but ultimately alone. Such a presupposition in fact cripples the search "for the glory of the one who alone is God" (5:44) revealing himself in the Son. Consequently, "the Jews" see Jesus as not only a breaker of the Sabbath law but, by "calling God his own Father," as blasphemously making himself God's equal (5:18).

This charge stimulates a remarkable expression of the rich and subtle theology underlying every aspect of the Johannine experience of God. The terms of such a theology are always framed by the utterly "Fatherward" relationality of Jesus' existence and action (5:19, 30, 43). And yet the Father's "Sonward" communication is stated in various ways: "The Father loves the Son and shows him all he himself is doing" (5:20). This "showing" includes the "work" of raising the dead and giving life "to whom he will" (5:21, 26). Still, it is not only a matter of the Father's *showing,* but *giving* to the Son—the gifts of "all judgment" (5:22), of having "life in himself" (5:26), of the "authority to execute judgment" (5:27), and of "the works" that are his to accomplish (5:36). Further, the Father both sends and bears witness to the Son (5:37). Though receiving all from the Father as unreservedly surrendered to the Father's will, Jesus is a free agent; and his relationship to the Father is acted out in freedom (5:17). In one respect, the Father "rests" while the Son "works," for "the Father judges no one, but has given all judgment to the Son" (5:22). In this regard, the Father not only gives, but yields, to the Son the properly divine activity of judging. In yielding and giving over judgment to the Son, the divine purpose is "that all may honor the Son, even as they honor the Father" (5:23).

The intentional reciprocity and the mutuality of relationships here described will give rise, in the centuries to come, to a full-blown Athanasian trinitarianism of the post-Nicene doctrine.[10] For the moment, it is sufficient to observe that, in the cognitive meaning informing faith's experience of Jesus' personal authority as inseparable from the Father—who sends, loves, shows, gives, and even yields to the Son—it is transforming former religious and philosophical notions of undifferentiated divine unity. What emerges is a differentiated unity enlivened by mutual relationships and intersubjective communication. Though the axis of the inter-relationship is here presented along the lines of the Father above and the Son below, the Prologue (cf. 1:1–2) has already expressed the supra-temporal dimension of divine communion that will be presented more fully in John 17. By attending to the data of this distinctive experience, later theology and church teaching will be led to affirm the distinctive mystery of divine self-communication therein implied.

Notes

1. Ancient rabbinic traditions and Philo of Alexandria gave eloquent witness to this debate among Jewish thinkers. For further detail, see Jewish, Philonic, and secondary references in F. J. Moloney, *Signs and Shadows: Reading John 5—12* (Minneapolis: Fortress Press, 1998), 8.
2. Cf. Gen 3:5; Isa 14:14; Ezek 28; Dan 11:31–36; 2 Macc 9:12.
3. For a comment on the theological significance of this problem of "equality," see Wolfhart Pannenberg, *Systematic Theology,* Volume 2, Geoffrey W. Bromiley, trans. (Grand Rapids, Mich.: William B. Eerdmans, 1994), 334–343.
4. 1 Sam 2:6; Deut 32:39; Isa 25:8; Wis 16:13; 2 Kgs 5:7.
5. For a profound discussion of Jesus' freedom and inspiration, see Hans Urs von Balthasar, *Theo-Drama III,* "Mission as the Measure of the Knowledge and Freedom of Jesus," 191–202.
6. Here St Thomas Aquinas, in his commentary on these verses, bids us attend to "a marvelous variety of words: where before we are presented with the Father working and the Son resting *(Pater operans et Filius vacans),* now it is the opposite: the Son is working and

the Father rests. The Father will not appear in judgment because God in his own nature cannot appear to all who are to be judged. Since the vision of God is our beatitude, for the wicked to see God would mean that they were already in bliss. Therefore, only the Son will appear for he alone has assumed our nature. He alone is the judge who alone will appear to all" (*In Evangelium B. Joannis,* c. 5, lect. 4). Despite the medieval garb of expression, profound Johannine truths are implied: judgment is related to the Incarnation, and the Father in himself is the source of life and beatitude.

7. Pss 67:5, 94:2, 105:7; Isa 2:4, 26:9, 33:2; Mic 4:3; Ezek 30:3.
8. See James Alison, *Raising Abel,* 138–144, for a perceptive reflection on judgment in John's Gospel.
9. Ibid., 180–181, in which a telling interpretation of John 5:41–44 is offered.
10. For an excellent account of the theological development involved, see T. F. Torrance, *The Trinitarian Faith: The Evangelical Theology of the Ancient Catholic Church,* 47–75.

6

━━━━

The Bread of God in the New Passover (6:1–71)

Our perception of the Johannine experience of God is notably enriched in John 6. The incarnate Word, now presented mainly in the rich symbolism of bread, shocks the religious experience of his hearers even to the roots of their conceptions of "life" and "death." Israel's experience of God had been deeply affected by divine negations originating with the Genesis prohibition, "but of the tree of knowledge of good and evil you shall not eat, for the day you eat of it, you shall die" (Gen 2:17).[1] But now a new time of hitherto unimaginable positivity has arrived: for "the Father gives the true bread from heaven" (6:32), the "bread of God" for the life of the world (6:33).

1. The Prodigality of the Gift

5. Lifting up his eyes, then, and seeing that a multitude was coming to him, Jesus said to Philip, "How are we to buy bread, so that these people may eat?" 6. This he said to test him, for he himself knew what he would do. 7. Philip answered him, "Two hundred denarii would not buy enough bread for each of them to get a little." 8. One of his disciples, Andrew, Simon Peter's brother, said to him, 9. "There is a lad here who has five barley loaves and two fish; but what are they among so many?" 10. Jesus said,

141

"Make the people sit down." Now there was much grass in the place; so the men sat down, in number about five thousand. 11. Jesus then took the loaves, and when he had given thanks he distributed them to those who were seated; so also the fish, as much as they wanted. 12. And when they had eaten their fill, he told his disciples, "Gather up the fragments left over, that nothing may be lost." 13. So they gathered them up and filled twelve baskets with the fragments from the five barley loaves, left by those who had eaten. 14. When the people saw the sign he had done, they said, "This is indeed the prophet who has come into the world!" 15. Perceiving then that they were about to come and take him by force and make him king, Jesus withdrew again to the mountain by himself. (6:5–15)

The chapter begins by unfolding in what seems to be a completely horizontal dimension limited to the world of human need and desire. The previously described activity of the God of the Sabbath is not apparent; "the other side of the Sea" is, at first glance, remote from the realm of the Father. On the other hand, a large crowd is following Jesus because of his healing signs, one of which took place on the Sabbath day: "...because they saw the signs which he did on those who were diseased" (6:2). Here, too, the Father is unceasingly at work, drawing all to the Son (6:37, 44–45) as Jesus will soon declare. By describing him going up the mountain like Moses, and sitting down with his disciples, there is an evocation of new gift that will change forever the meaning of the Passover (cf. 1:16–17).

In the miraculous feeding of the large crowd that now takes place, there is still no direct mention of the Father. Yet, as Jesus looks up and sees the large crowd approaching, he tests Philip with a question that resonates paradoxically with the words of Moses' complaint to YHWH (Num 11:13): "How are we to buy bread, so that these people may eat?" (6:5b). Like the Father, he is continuing to work, and will not drive away anyone the Father has given him (cf. 6:37b). In that green springtime, he tells his disciples to make the people recline on the grass, thereby evoking the "green pastures" to which the Lord shepherds his flock (Ps 23:1–3). The crowd is about to share in an economy infinitely surpassing what can be bought or supplied out of human resources. The world of the flesh—of need and limitation typified in the five loaves and two fish—is to receive another gift, as Jesus turns to God in thanksgiving. In contrast to the former gift (cf. Exod 16), a new, inexhaustible abundance of food has become available to feed the hungry. Nothing of it—a symbol of the true bread which will nourish the church through the ages—must be lost, just as Jesus himself must not lose anything of the Father's gift to him (6:39). But the gift of God (cf. 4:10) is about to exhibit further dimensions of prodigal giving.[2]

The time of fulfilmentfulfillment was to be marked by the gift of new manna from heaven (2 Bar 29:8).[3] A Moses-like prophet had been promised: "The Lord your God will raise up for you a prophet like me from among you...him you shall heed..." (Deut 18:15–18). Hence, the people have reason to judge, "This is indeed the prophet who has come into the world" (6:14). But Jesus resists the premature enthusiasm of the crowd. It leaves out the one who is most significant to his mission—the Father himself. When the Father's will is the food of the Son (4:34), he will not feed off the impulsive movement of the crowd. He therefore withdraws into the heights as if to underline the uniqueness of his mission. His kingdom is not from here (18:36). From this place apart, he is about to descend in the assurance of his true identity.

2. A Divine Intervention

16. When evening came his disciples went down to the sea, 17. got into a boat, and were trying to go across the sea to Capernaum. It was now dark, and Jesus had not yet come to them. 18. The sea rose because a strong wind was blowing. 19. When they had rowed about three or four miles, they saw Jesus walking on the sea and drawing near the boat. They were frightened, 20. but he said to them, "It is I; do not be afraid." 21. Then they were glad to take him into the boat, and immediately the boat was at the land to which they were going. (6:16–21)

The fall of evening brings with it a deeper experience of the darkness of God.[4] Jesus has removed himself from the crowds with their limited understanding, and separated himself from the disciples in a time of darkness and danger. They are experiencing both fear and the reality of his absence, while the people are still anchored to the site where they had seen the sign of the miraculous bread. The disciples, however, in the most graphic sense, are "all at sea," as they encounter heavy weather while crossing the lake against the strong wind. The scene is set for Jesus to rejoin them in the truth of his identity: "I AM. Do not be afraid" (6:20).[5] His coming dispels fear, in a way characteristic of so many divine interventions in the history of Israel.[6] His power over the terrors of the deep evokes the saving might of *YHWH*,[7] as in the declarations of the psalms: "The voice of the Lord is over the waters....The voice of the Lord is powerful; the voice of the Lord is full of majesty" (Ps 29:3), and "Your way was through the sea, your path through the mighty waters, yet your footprints were unseen" (Ps 77:17–19). In the Word through whom all things have come into being (1:3, 10), the world finds its peace, just as wind blowing where it will (3:8) is a figure of the Spirit leading to a revelation of God's working in the world. The God of the new Passover continues to work. And as the boat now reaches the land to which they were going, the saving power of God brings them to a safe place: "He made the storm be still, and the waves of the sea were hushed. Then they were glad because they had quiet, and he brought them to their desired haven" (Ps 107:29–30).

3. Greater Gifts in Store

25. When they found him on the other side of the sea, they said to him, "Rabbi, when did you get here?" 26. Jesus answered them, "Amen, amen, I say to you, you seek me, not because you saw the signs, but because you ate your fill of the loaves. 27. Do not labor for the food that perishes, but for the food that endures to eternal life, that the Son of Man will give you; for on him, God the Father has set his seal." 28. Then they said to him, "What must we do to be devoting ourselves to the works of God?" 29. Jesus answered them, "This is the work of God, that you believe in him whom he has sent." (6:25–29)

The next day (6:22) dawns with the promise of the new bread from heaven, even as it refocuses the cosmic presence of the Word in the scandalous particularity of the flesh-and-blood reality of Jesus' self-giving love. The people have lost contact with both Jesus and the disciples—whom they now follow as they get into boats to go in search of him. While they have not experienced the revelation of Jesus as "I am," as the disciples have done in the intervening time, they are seeking him as the giver of the miraculous supply of bread. In their astonished rec-ollection of what had happened the day before, they have yet to appreciate the bread that was given as a sign of another order of reality. In the logic of the narrative so far, they must live out the question posed to all potential believers, "What are you looking for?" (1:38b). They, like the two disciples before them, are won-dering, "Rabbi, where are you staying?" (1:38c), just as they are about to hear in their own way and in a new setting the invita-tion, "Come and see" (1:39). The revelation of the Father as the giver of this new bread awaits them.

The superficiality of their apparently successful search for Jesus is brought home by the distracted nature of the ques-tion they put to him, "Rabbi, when did you get here?" (6:25). Jesus' emphatic response recalls to them to the demanding reality of the search they have embarked on. Intent on the wondrous physical nourishment, they must come to see it as a sign of something more—not as perishable food for mortal bodies, but as the food of eternal life. Their labor must con-form to the work of the Father and to the works Jesus has been given to do (4:34). This will involve their being nour-ished by another kind of bread. Jesus has food to eat and to give which is unknown, for his food is found in total surren-der to the work of the one who sent him (4:32–34). The food that sustains him and the food he promises will be made of the same ingredients.

As the future giver of this "enduring" bread, he further designates himself as "the Son of Man." In that role, he will be the living communication between what is above and what is below. Heaven will be opened (1:51) through his coming down to make known the things of heaven (3:13), and in the "lifting up" that will be the source of unending life for all who believe in him (3:14).

A new metaphor is introduced, leading from the gift to the giver. Jesus is the source of eternal life because the Father has irrevocably set his seal upon him. This Father has definitively legitimated his mission and underwritten the gift he will give. The Father himself has impressed his own living image on him, *this very one,* who is the Word, the Son, the Lamb (1:29) and the Bread *of God* (cf. 6:33). According to the word of God spoken to the Baptist, Jesus is the one on whom the Spirit has descended and remained (1:33). The Father's seal ratifies the meaning of all the images previously employed, above all the original meaning of the Prologue itself: "What God was, the Word was" (1:1b), as Jesus is turned toward the Father in all that he is and does (1:18). Because he is the living expression of the Father, the Son will make known the unseen God. The Gospel is thus signed with the signature of the Father—just as it will come to be countersigned by the lives of future believers.

Faced with the excess of the promised gift, Jesus' questioners respond out of a sense of obligation determined by the framework of their traditional law: "What must we do, to be devoting ourselves to the works of God?" (6:28). They have not yet glimpsed the novel reality of the gift that is being offered. Their intended commitment to doing "the works of God" is not yet aligned to the work that God is doing in their midst. It is not a question of what *they* must do, but of what the Father is doing. This Passover looks back to a new Sabbath on which "the Father is still working, and I also am working" (5:17). Like the Samaritan woman, the people do not yet know "the gift of God" (4:10), nor the purpose and extent of God's work. Jesus explains, "this is the work of God that you believe in him whom he has sent" (6:29). God works, not to impose a further refinement of the Law, but to give his own Son to the world as the source of life.

4. The Bread of God

Those involved in this encounter with Jesus at least begin to realize that the crucial issue turns on faith in the true God: the miraculous gift of bread is meant as a sign of something more.

> 30. So they asked him, "What sign do you do that we may see it and believe you? What will you do? 31. Our ancestors ate manna in the desert; as it is written: 'He gave them bread from heaven to eat.'" 32. Jesus said to them, "Amen, amen I say to you, it is not Moses who gave you the bread from heaven, but it is my Father who gives you the true bread from heaven. 33. For the Bread of God is he who comes down from heaven and gives life to the world." (6:30–33)

In the Mosaic tradition, the gift of heavenly bread had been a precious sign of the nourishing power of the Law. It looked back to the Passover experience of God leading his people, and, indeed, bringing them to this critical point. The ancestors ate manna in the desert. The God of Moses had acted on their behalf: "He gave them bread from heaven" (6:31b; cf. Exod 16:4,15; Ps 78:24; Neh 9:15). The marvelous gift of manna thus symbolized the unfailing, life-giving bread of the Torah. Is the bread that Jesus promises a continuance of this, or is he promising something more? If he is, how do they know his promise is genuine?

In an emphatic reply to their challenge, Jesus first recalls them to a sense of the ultimate source of what he is promising. God, not Moses, has all along been the principal actor. For even Moses had to pray; and God had acted in answer to his prayer. This God will continue to nourish his people; but now, "it is my Father who gives you the true bread from heaven" (6:32b). Thus, the Father is brought into the story as the main agent both in what had taken place in the past, and in what would be given in the present. It is he who gives the *true* bread, in contrast to all previous forms of nourishment anticipating this time of fulfillment. It is not a question of comparing the bread given by Moses with the miraculous bread given by Jesus; for the true bread from heaven is given by the Father himself. This God-given bread is a gift in the person of Jesus: "...he who comes down from heaven and gives life to the world" (6:33)—a gift not only for Israel, but for the wider world, in the present and for the future.

> **34. They said to him, "Sir, give us this bread always." 35. Jesus said to them, "I am the bread of life; anyone who comes to me shall not hunger and anyone who believes in me shall never thirst. 36. But I said to you that you have seen and yet do not believe. 37. Everyone the Father gives me will come to me; and anyone who comes to me I will not cast out. 38. For I have come down from heaven, not to do my own will, but the will of him who sent me; 39. and this is the will of him who sent me, that I should lose nothing of all that he has given me, but raise it up at the last day. 40. For this is the will of my Father, that all who see the Son and believe in him may have eternal life; and I will raise them up on the last day." (6:34–40).**

The response of the people is still tentative. Their mode of address, though respectful, is not yet that of faith. Their concern is with themselves, not with the larger world of God's love. They are happy to have a continuous supply a bread that will meet their human needs, provided it leave their lives undisturbed. The tone of their request recalls that of the Samaritan woman, "Sir, give me this water, so that I may never be thirsty or have to keep coming here to draw water" (4:15).

Jesus now identifies the "bread of God" with himself: "I am the bread of life" (6:35a).[8] He is, in person, the once and for all, the never-failing and all-fulfilling gift. The closed world of "us" will be broken open to include "anyone who comes" to him, "anyone who believes" (6:35b). No longer is Israel the privileged beneficiary of the bread from heaven. It will be offered to the world of "anyone." Furthermore, the continuing hunger and thirst characteristic of the sages of Israel will now find its satisfaction. In the past, "those who eat me will hunger for more, and those who drink me will thirst for more" (Sir 24:21; cf. Isa 49:10). But, now, in Jesus, that "more" will be made available. He is the bread of life for all. Moses, the manna of Exodus, the Torah, and the Wisdom of Israel's tradition—are all now passing over into their final truth in this Passover time. The final gift, however, resides in an as yet undeclared future. Is it being deferred to "the last day" in terms of common conceptions of religious expectation? If not, how much longer will the present hungering and thirsting have to be borne? While something utterly new is being promised, the question remains: When will that promise be kept?

If the future is elusive, the tug of the past is as clear as it is strong. Jesus finds that his interlocutors are responding only from within the bounds of their human preconceptions and calculations. In clinging to the past and interpreting signs of eternal life merely as worldly marvels, these potential believers are held back from an unconditional acceptance of the gift of God. And yet, there is another influence at work. God is acting. The original gift of the Father, extended to all without exception, is the ultimately critical factor (6:37a). Those coming to Jesus are part of the "all things" given him by the Father (3:35), to be the beneficiaries of God's gift to the world (3:16; 4:10): God gives his only Son to the world, and gives the world—"all things"—to the Son. Because of this original and continuing giving of the Father, believers will come to the Son. Despite his experience of rejection and incomprehension, Jesus is unreservedly at one with the openness of the Father's will. In contrast to that world of many exclusions, in which even he is not accepted by his own (1:11), and his followers suffer excommunication from the synagogue (cf. 9:34; 16:2), he will not shut out anyone (6:37b).

The universal love of the Father remains the rule and motive of his life. A new communion of life with the Father and the Son is in the making (cf. 17:21–24). In his "coming down from heaven" (6:38), in that deepest descent into the world of flesh, suffering, and death, a new order of love, healing, and life is unfolding. At this Passover time, past promises are being kept: "…on the third day, the LORD will come down on Mount Sinai in the sight of the people" (Exod 19:11, 20). Heaven is being opened (1:51). For the Word that has come forth from God "shall not return to me [God] empty, but shall accomplish that which I purpose, and succeed in the thing for which I sent it" (Isa 55:10–11). The Father gives and sends; and the Son, given and sent, acts in accord with the conditions of such a gift and such a mission: to lose nothing of all that the Father has given him (6:39a).

The bread from heaven is life-giving. Its vitality reaches into death, and out to all history, even as the generations come and go. The Father loves the world (3:16), and Jesus keeps all that he has been given to "raise it up on the last day" (6:39b). What takes place in him is life as the light of all humankind (1:3b–4). His quickening influence outlasts death and all imaginable worldly endings. The vital factor in human existence is the Father's life-giving will. Both the historical past of the Mosaic law and the ethnic limitations of Israel are now faced with a promised fulfillment unbounded by death and by the limitations of the past. Jesus promises life to *all*, both *now* and *forever* (6:40).

5. The Father at Work

41. The Jews then murmured at him because he said, "I am the bread that came down from heaven." 42. They said, "Is not this Jesus the son of Joseph, whose father and mother we know? How does he now say, 'I have come down from heaven?'" 43. Jesus answered them, "Do not murmur among yourselves. 44. No one can come to me unless drawn by the Father who sent me; and I will raise that person up on the last day. 45. It is written in the prophets, 'And they shall all be taught by God.' Everyone who has heard and learned from the Father comes to me. 46. Not that anyone has seen the Father except the one who is from God; he has seen the Father. 47. Amen, amen, I say to you, whoever believes has eternal life. 48. I am the bread of life. 49. Your ancestors ate the manna in the wilderness, and they died. 50. This is the bread that comes down from heaven, so that one may eat it and not die. 51. I am the living bread that came down from heaven; whoever eats this bread will live forever; and the bread that I shall give for the life of the world is my flesh." (6:41–51)

With the antagonistic reentry of "the Jews" into the conversation taking place between the Bread of Life and the hitherto larger group, the crucial issue of Jesus' origin reemerges. In the Passover setting of the gift of the new bread from heaven, the murmuring of the present generation of Israelites evokes their ancestors' complaints against Moses. In the past, even in their hour of liberation, they had resisted the promised exodus, dreading the loss of former securities (cf. Exod 15:24; 16:2, 7; 17:3). That resistance continues. How could this man be the bread from heaven and replace the traditional sources of reli-gious sustenance? Their "we know" is all-competent. Just as it enclosed Nicodemus (3:2) in an earthly interpretation of Jesus, so now it disallows the possibility that Jesus is from above: "Is not this Jesus the son of Joseph, whose father and mother we know?" (6:42). In reply, Jesus concedes that his claim is not self-evident; that can be decided only in reference to the One who has sent him. In a piercing allusion to the words of Moses, "Your complaints are not against us, but against the Lord" (Exod 16:8), he declares that the Father who sent him is attract-ing all to him (6:44).[9]

The Father acts by that "drawing" which will be finally realized when Jesus himself is lifted up to draw all to himself (12:32). For those who are so drawn, Jesus will complete the Father's initiative by raising them up on the last day. A new Passover and a new Exodus have begun. Designating him "from below" as the son of Joseph obscures Jesus' true origins "from above." The Father is the source of all the Son is and does and promises. It is the Father who makes it possible for the Son's work to reach its term in the resurrection on the last day. Expanding on the initiative of the Father, Jesus proceeds to make a singular but precious reference to "the prophets" (cf. Isa 54:13), past exemplars of the faith of Israel in its openness to the Word of God: "It is written in the prophets, 'And they shall be taught by God'" (6:45a). God taught Israel through the Law. Now, all who are truly docile to divine instruction—those whom the Father has sought out as true worshippers in spirit and truth (4:23)—will come to him: "Everyone who has heard and learned from the Father comes to me" (6:45b). In the hour of revelation, God, declared to be the Father of Jesus, is no longer limited to the confines of Israel. Though "salvation is from the Jews" (4:22b), it is not limited to them. Israel's faith in the one God of all creation is being disconcertingly realized. Jesus, then, is at once the focus of the Father's action, and the center of the new open circle of life in God.

By conceding that no one has seen the Father, Jesus acknowledges a problem. Despite the nourishing truths of past revelation, God has remained invisible, even to his chosen ones. But now, the exception: a unique, divine "visibility" has occurred, namely, in Jesus himself: "...the one who is from God; he has seen the Father" (6:46b).[10] The problem of being taught by the God whom no one has ever seen has reached an unforeseen solution. The Son, uniquely from the Father, has seen him. He is, therefore, God-made-visible, as the one who is turned toward God in his origins (1:1), and in his life in the flesh (1:18). In contrast to the exalted position of Moses in the giving of the Law (1:17), Jesus brings the gift that is the truth. To be taught by God is to believe in the Son; and to believe in him is already to possess eternal life: "Amen, amen, I say to you, whoever believes in me has eternal life" (6:47).

The question of origins is pursued. His antagonists had played off his "known" genealogy as the son of Joseph against Jesus' claim to be uniquely from God. Having answered on that level, he now introduces another context of contrast—between life and death. The bread he gives, and is, is truly life-giving: "I am the bread of life" (6:48). The manna of former times did not save the ancestors of Jesus' present antagonists from death (6:49). Because the gift of truth had not been given, even the greatest figures of the past were enclosed in an economy of death. Moses, despite his association in Jewish tradition with "the bread the Lord had given them to eat" (Exod 16:15), had himself died outside the Promised Land (Deut 34:5–8). Under the rule of mortality, God was unseen and the divine promises unfulfilled. In the world of "earthly things," there was no experience of what was in store (3:11–15).

But now there is a new economy of life, unrestricted by death. It is introduced by the only one who has seen God. The heavens have been opened; a source of deathless life has becomes accessible in the flesh of worldly existence (6:50). Death, which once exerted its power over human life under a closed heaven, has been deprived of its lethal power. Jesus himself is the source and evidence of true life. He is the truth by which all else is judged, even death itself. For it is not death, but the Word incarnate, the living bread from heaven, that has the last word: "I am the living bread which came down from heaven; whoever eats this bread will live forever" (6:51).

Given the fact that Jesus himself would be put to death, and that future believers would not be spared their mortal fate, the human meanings of both life and death are thrown into question by Jesus' promise of a life that defies death. How will the meaning of death be transformed? How will God's gift subsume the human experience of death into itself, so that even death, in the case of Jesus and in those who believe in him, will become a dimension of the gift of life and the epiphany of the Father's love for the world? Jesus has promised the gift of life in an unconditional manner. The radical factor is the life that flows from the living Father. Death is consigned to the realm of non-reality. The ultimate evidence for what is here promised must however await the glory of the cross.

And yet, the Father's life-giving, all-embracing will has an immediate effect. The gift of life does not wait on some form of postmortem existence. Believers are not to imagine that they must go up to heaven to find true life only after death; for eternal life, in the word and presence of Jesus, is stirring in their midst. Within this world of flesh and death, it is available "in person": "I am the living bread..." (6:51). The natural and cultural symbolism of bread as the nourishment of human life has been transformed: the Word made flesh (1:14) brings life flowing from the Father into the world of flesh.

The Father's originating gift of his only Son carries over into the unconditional giving of the Son himself for the life of the world. He is possessed of a passion both to be and to give the "bread of God" in his own person. In the lethal conflict still building to its climax, he will pursue his Father's design to give life to the world, even though, in a paradox that only the Father can resolve, it will entail the death of his Son. In this, the Father's giving will be matched by his Son's, as the whole worldly reality of his existence, his "flesh," will be offered to accomplish the Father's work. The universality of the divine gift occurs in a field of unreserved self-giving: the invisible Father gives what is most intimately his own, "his only Son" (3:16); and his Son gives what is most intimately his—"my flesh"—all that he is in the world, as the Word made flesh (1:14).

The passionate unreservedness of Jesus' self-giving has already been anticipated in the Gospel. His luminous existence in the flesh has to contend with the power of darkness (1:5). The Baptist has declared him to be "the Lamb of God who takes away the sin of the world" (1:29), even if the malice of the world's sin and the manner in which it will demand the sacrifice of the Lamb of God have yet to be clarified. Jesus is moving toward a final "hour" of revelation (2:5). The Son of Man has yet to be "lifted up" (3:14). The activity of his present antagonists, already recorded in their dramatic confrontation with him in the Temple (2:12–23), and in their plot to kill him (5:18), is set to intensify. Such indications mark the conditions of the complete self-gift that Jesus is to make in the bread of his flesh for the life of the world.

6. Disturbing Possibilities

52. The Jews then disputed among themselves, saying, "How can this man give us his flesh to eat?" 53. So Jesus said to them, "Amen, amen, I say to you, unless you eat the flesh of the Son of Man and drink his blood you have no life in you; 54. for those who eat my flesh and drink my blood have eternal life, and I will raise them up on the last day. 55. For my flesh is food indeed, and my blood is drink indeed. 56. Those who eat my flesh and drink my blood abide in me, and I in them. 57. As the living Father sent me, and I live because of the Father, so the one who eats me will live because of me. 58. This is the bread that came down from heaven, not such as the ancestors ate and died; the one who eats this bread will live forever." 59. This he said in the synagogue, as he taught in Capernaum. (6:52–59)

Now faced with the disconcerting extravagance of this new gift, "the Jews" engage in a dispute among themselves. Their horizon is limited to the flesh of human possibilities. Their mono-dimensional imagination is incapable of entering into the eucharistic imagination inspired by the limitless love of both the Father and the Son. For his adversaries, Jesus is not the bread of God, but one firmly located in their world as *this man:* "How can this man give us his flesh to eat?" (6:52). Jesus' emphatic realism shocks their world into an encounter with the Word, cutting through the barriers imposed by human calculation: "Amen, amen, I say to you, unless you eat the flesh of the Son of Man and drink his blood, you have no life in you" (6:53). It is the flesh and blood of the Son of Man that is in question, not that which gives rise to limited human perceptions and superficial judgments (cf. 7:24; 8:15). Hence, only by truly assimilating what this Son of Man is, in the flesh and blood of his life-giving mission, will the gift of life be given. Admittedly, what that eating and drinking will mean is still to be determined. The communicative reality of his flesh and blood will appear only in his atoning death and in the gifts that flow from it. But the summons to receive the gift of life sounds in the present. Life is not now to be found by clinging to the Law; it will come only from Jesus, as he offers himself to be the source and sustenance of true life.

Moving from a statement of warning to a positive assurance and promise, he declares that those who eat his flesh and drink his blood already have eternal life, and that he will raise them on the last day (6:54). The sheer physicality of this "eating" (no longer *phagein,* but *trōgein,* as in 13:18),[11] underscores the earthly reality of the food that is being offered. The bread of life is not located in some mystical sphere in which what is "from above" is invisible, impalpable, and unattainable. The spiritualization characteristic of the gnostic, and the immateriality of abstract philosophy, are both disconcertingly confronted with the flesh-and-blood reality of the Word dwelling among us in a world of space and time, suffering, and conflict. It is this reality that is to be assimilated by a flesh-and-blood community in the rough-edged reality of the situations in which it continues to celebrate the Eucharist. The world of the flesh that the Word has entered is a world in which he will be killed; his body will be pierced (19:37), and his blood will be poured out (19:34). Thus, the life-giving power of God's love will be disclosed.

The starkly made, universal offer of this food and drink implies a form of life that has already begun, even if it supposes that history will continue toward some definitive moment of completion. The flow of this endless life reaches beyond all temporal endings and deaths—till "the last day." The flesh and blood of Jesus, though marked by his dying in the world of the dead, will transform the meaning of all dying. In this it contrasts with the bread that perishes, the bread that the ancestors of "the Jews" have eaten. Though Jesus will die to bring to completion the work of God, his self-giving in the flesh and his self-outpouring in the blood of the cross in surrender to the Father's will, are the substance and sustenance of true life. His flesh is "food indeed"; his blood is "drink indeed" (6:55).

The eating and drinking of faith leads to an abiding communion with him as the source of life (6:56). The outcome is a mutual indwelling, a distinctive Johannine description of Christian experience. Though the mission of Jesus will take him to death and render him absent from his disciples in terms of worldly appearances, it will also mean for him a new mode of life and presence within the community of those who accept him. The community of faith, for its part, will be united in a new humanity in a way transcending former divisions and separations. As believers dwell in him as the focal point of God's communication, their experience of God, of themselves, and of their world will be transformed.

At the heart of the reciprocity of indwelling between Jesus and his present and future followers is the deathless life of the Father. He is the source of the life now flowing into the world: "As the living Father sent me, and I live because of the Father, so he who eats me will live because of me" (6:57). The primordial vitality of the Father not only is not shadowed by death, but will make the self-giving of the Son in death the form and source of deathless life. In any event, Jesus and his disciples will die. But the Father lives—as the source of Jesus' unqualified promise of eternal life. Here, the Gospel's ostensible denial of the empirical reality of death is inspired by an experience entirely directed to the transcendent vitality of God, and to the manner in which it will be revealed in the Risen One. In view of the living Father, the imminent death of the Son, and the inevitable deaths of those who believe in him, are bound up with the gift of superabundant life (10:10). The limitless vitality of the Father transforms the meaning of death. His life is not held within the limits imposed by the murderous and deceiving ruler of this world (12:31; 14:30; 16:11). When the idol of worldly glory rules the world, it uses the dreadful boundary of death to solidify the domain of the flesh and to make it resistant to the promise of true life. In contrast, from the Father, as the source of endless life, flows the life-giving mission of the Son to the world. The living Father, the living Son, the living community of believers—all are united in one communion of life determined by the deathless vitality of the Father himself. In that realm of life, death loses the deadliness that fear, guilt, and worldly glory project onto it. While death is thus reduced to purely physical reality, it is also a passing from this world to the living Father (13:1).[12] Still, the full meaning of this transformation awaits the arrival of the hour of glory.

The Gospel anticipated what is yet to be revealed in the fact that Jesus himself lives from the divine source, nourished by a food that is unknown to the world (cf. 4:32, 34). Sustained by such food, from "the living Father," he becomes food and life for those who accept him, To eat such bread is to live forever (6:58). Thus, in the synagogue at this Passover time, Jesus witnesses to the arrival of a new and final Passover—a passing-over from the world of death into life in the Father and the Son, from which no one is excluded (6:59).

7. The Crisis of Faith

60. Many of his disciples, when they heard it, said, "This is a hard saying; who can listen to it?" 61. But Jesus, knowing in himself that his disciples murmured,

said to them, "Do you take offence at this? 62. Then
what if you see the Son of Man ascending where he
was before? 63. It is the spirit that gives life, the flesh
is of no avail; the words that I have spoken to you are
spirit and life. 64. But there are some of you who do
not believe." For Jesus knew from the first who those
were that did not believe, and who it was that would
betray him. 65. And he said, "This is why I told you
that no one can come to me unless it is granted by the
Father." 66. Because of this many of the disciples
drew back and no longer went with him. 67. Jesus
said to the twelve, "Do you wish to go away?" 68.
Simon Peter answered him, "Lord, to whom shall we
go? You have the words of eternal life; 69. and we
have believed, and have come to know, that you are
the Holy One of God." 70. Jesus answered them,
"Did I not choose you, the twelve, and one of you is a
devil?" 71. He spoke of Judas the son of Simon
Iscariot, for he, one of the twelve, was to betray him.
(6:60–71)

The Son's promise of eternal life brings with it a moment of
crisis in a world in the thrall of death. The disciples, now drawn
to the brink of unreserved commitment to Jesus, hesitate before
the scandal of such an absolute demand.[13] The promise of life
addressed to human freedom becomes a provocation. There is a
real possibility, despite the unconditional love of the Father for
the world, of acceptance or rejection (cf. 1:11–12; 2:1–4:54;
3:11–21). The opposition, characteristic of the "world," grows
in proportion to the offer of the gift. The initiative of the
Father's love will encounter gratuitous hatred (15:25) and blindness (12:40f). At this juncture, both "the Jews" and the disciples

themselves express their reservations about the reality of what is being offered (6:61).[14]

Though the disciples were privileged witnesses to Jesus' self-revelation during the storm on the sea (6:20), they must continue to hear his command, "Do not be afraid." The fact that they have been saved from physical danger and nourished by physical bread has left some of them restricted to the world of the "fleshly" calculation. If they are to receive the flesh of Jesus and to dwell in him, they must go further. If they are to enter the realm of the Spirit; if they are to receive the gift of God enacted in self-giving of Jesus; they must freely transcend former securities, and surrender to what is given "from above." The prodigality of divine giving appears as an intrusion to a world enclosed in its own possibilities and calculations. The promise of the gift of God is heard as a "hard saying" (6:60).

Because Jesus is the light of all people (1:4), his knowledge reaches into the secret places of hesitation and fear (6:61; cf. also, 16:1). While he claimed to make God known in a way that goes beyond the former gift of the Law, a number of the disciples struggle with this excess. They experience the universality of the new gift as a scandal. Their judgments are limited to the traditions of the past; there is no room for the new. The revelation of God to the world in the Word made flesh, and in the death he will die, are not sufficiently "heavenly." This kind of divine communication is deemed incompatible with traditional ideas of how God is revealed and of how salvation must come about.

Jesus' question meets them at the point of their scandal: "Then what if you were to see the Son of Man ascending to where he was before?" (6:62). The disaffected disciples are looking for an *ascent* to the closed heaven in the manner traditionally characteristic of great revelation figures of the past—Abraham, Moses, Isaiah, and Enoch. In fact, what is taking place is an imaginable *descent* (3:13) from the now-opened heaven (1:51).

162

From the God whom no one has ever seen (1:18; 6:46), an all-surpassing gift has come, and a final revelation been made. Jesus, the living bread from heaven, is the culminating communication between the "opened heaven" and the flesh of the world. In the bread of God, the Word is made flesh; and believers will see "the angels of God ascending and descending on the Son of Man" (1:51). There will indeed be an ascent, but only after a unique descent into the reality of this world is accomplished.

In a sense, the wavering disciples are so caught between heaven and earth as not fully to inhabit either. At one extreme, confined to "the flesh" of their defensive judgments, they are closed to things that are from above. On the other hand, because of a misplaced sense of what is "from above," they are scandalized by the presence of the Word made flesh. In a typically Johannine irony, those most inclined to fall back on the flesh as the norm of judgment are, in fact, most incapable of appreciating the revelation of God in the flesh. Admittedly, the world of the flesh cannot, of itself, generate the deathless life that Jesus offers, for "it is the spirit that gives life, while the flesh is of no avail" (6:63a). Still, the Word has come in the flesh, and communicated, in the midst of what is earthly, the things that are from above (3:12): "The words that I have spoken to you are spirit and life" (6:63b). The life-giving power of the Spirit operates in the world of the flesh, even though there is nothing on the level of the flesh to explain either its origin or its promise. In the free air of God's action, the breath of the Spirit still blows where it wills (3:8).

Thus the believer is led slowly to appreciate the overwhelming novelty of the flesh of Jesus as that of the Word incarnate. The domain of the flesh is subject to death; of itself, it promises no life without end. The Word and bread of God give life deriving not from "blood" nor "the will of the flesh" nor "the will of man," but from God (cf. 1:13). But because the Word, turned in the beginning toward God (1:1), became flesh, "what took place in him was life" (1:3b–4). Thus, Jesus in the flesh, giving himself for the life of the world (6:51), is the language in which the story of the unseen God is told within this world (1:18).

Inherent in the ambiguities of the flesh, there is not only the possibility, but also the fact, of non-belief (6:64). Jesus accepts that, in the world of the flesh in which he speaks and acts, there would be doubt and betrayal. But the all-determining principle is the gift of the Father, which the Son serves in not turning away any who come to him (6:65). The authentic disciple receives the Father's gift, by being drawn to the Son. Seeing his signs and hearing his words are not enough. The Father's "seeking" (4:23) and "drawing" (6:44) leads believers from the signs to the reality of the gift he has made in his only Son; and from the words that are spoken, to the Word who speaks in the flesh.

Though the saving will of God is all-inclusive, all share in the same temptation—the need to make Jesus fit into a familiar world. In this, both those Jesus addresses and those who have become his disciples may well find themselves resisting both Jesus and the Father. The fear of losing former securities and becoming aliens in a world that acknowledges neither Jesus nor his followers (cf. 5:44; 16:1–3; 17:14) is strong. The unhappy outcome is, therefore, predictable: "…many of the disciples drew back and no longer went about with him" (6:66). They fall back into their old worlds undisturbed by the Word, and no longer move with him along the way of a new Passover.

Jesus now poses a question to the inner circle of the twelve: "Do you also wish to go away?" (6:67). Only through a continually renewed decision to follow him can even the chosen disciples continue to experience the gift that is offered. For them, too, it is still possible to turn back to old securities. The Word continues to be a question, as was the case in the first words that Jesus spoke: "What are you looking for?" (1:38). But the Father is at work. His influence is evident in Peter's question, "Lord, to whom shall we go? You have the words of eternal life" (6:68). When the boundaries of human experience begin to touch on the "opened heaven," there is no other resting place in the world as it has been.

Peter acknowledges that the words of Jesus are indeed spirit and life (6:63). He thus echoes the unconditional response of the characters who have appeared on the Cana circuit of Jesus' journey—the Mother of Jesus (2:5), the Baptist (3:29), the Samaritan villagers (4:42), the royal official (4:50). But his confession goes further: "and we have believed, and have come to know, that you are the Holy One of God" (6:69). Thus, for the first time in the Gospel, the purest motive of faith in Jesus is articulated. The divine origin of Jesus is confessed. He is acknowledged to be the Holy One *of God*—consecrated by God in a special intimacy and mission. True faith in Jesus does not consist in situating him in this world, but in recognizing that he comes from beyond this world—from the realm of the unseen, living God himself.

Peter, while speaking for the twelve, gives expression to the demands made on all believers. Even those who have been especially chosen by Jesus himself must live out the reality of a decision. Human freedom is still ambivalent. Indeed, one of the twelve will prove to be "a devil" (6:70), an agent of the ruler of this world (14:30), of the "god" who resists "the living Father." There will be a betrayal: the clouds that have been gathering during the course of this Passover (6:12–13, 15, 27, 51, 53–54) loom toward a future hour when Jesus will meet a violent death and the disciples will be scattered. Yet questions linger. How will the disciples come to recognize that even in that death, indeed most of all in that death, the living Father is revealed? How, in the words of the First Letter of John, will the Father be manifested as "the true God and eternal life" (1 John 5:20b)? And how will the always-vulnerable disciples continue along the way they have begun, and keep themselves from idols? (1 John 5:21).

8. The Ongoing Experience of God

In the unfolding of this chapter of the Gospel, the eucharistic practice of the community of faith is taken for granted, even though its moral implications will be made explicit only in John 13. Still, the Gospel testifies to how "the gift of God" (4:10) enters into the life of the church by means of a sacramental communion with Jesus, the Bread of Life.[15] Metaphors evocative of the experience of God have moved from the healing "signs" performed by Jesus to symbols of vital nourishment. His flesh is given to be eaten and his blood is to be drunk But, as with all the metaphors and symbols drawn either from Jewish tradition or from common human experience (Sabbath, Passover, sacrificial lamb, body and blood, flesh and spirit, food and drink, bread and wine, attraction and witness, and so forth, to include even the manifold resonances of words such as "life" and "death"), a seismic displacement of meaning has occurred: the fullness of a gift that is the truth (1:14) has broken open the range of human experience to the dimensions of the "opened heaven" (1:51). The truth of God's love occurs as an upheaval in the previously imagined world. The varied responses—of incomprehension, acceptance, or scandalized rejection—make the words of the poet Paul Celan especially apposite: "A Rumbling: truth/ itself has appeared/ among humankind/ in the very thick of their/ flurrying metaphors."[16]

166

Notes

1. For a fuller elaboration of these negations, see Ghislain Lafont, *Peut-on connâitre Dieu en Jésus-Christ* (Paris: Les Editions du Cerf, 1969), 236–242.

2. Hans Urs von Balthasar, *The Glory of the Lord VII*, 424: "More is meant in this than in the philosophical adage *bonum diffusivum sui;* here we have the mysterious power to regenerate oneself anew at every instant in the act of giving, or conversely the power to produce incessantly such a fullness in oneself that it can retain its own identity only through giving away the overflow. What has being— and ultimately triune Being itself, as the source of all—is always more than itself...."

3. These writings are considered to be roughly contemporary with John's Gospel; and hence, provide valuable data for understanding the mentality of contemporary Judaism.

4. Christian mystics commonly feel a spontaneous kinship with the Johannine writings. When they employ the metaphor of darkness to describe their experience of God, their language is often couched in terms of Plato's allegory of the cave. The revelation of God in the "I AM" of Exodus, with its own implications of "darkness" (cf. Exod 19:9, 16, 18; 33:19–23), reaches a special intensity in the Gospel of John, so as to emphasize a distinctively biblical and Christian experience. For a stimulating study, see Denys Turner, *The Darkness of God: Negativity in Christian Mysticism* (Cambridge: Cambridge University Press, 1995).

5. Edward Schillebeeckx, *Christ: The Christian Experience...,* 384–397, represents a theologian's struggle to grasp the import of the "I am" sayings. While aware of the complexity of the issues involved, he notes the remarkably "non-gnostic" character of these expressions in John.

6. Gen 15:1; 26:24; 46:3; Isa 41:13–14; 43:1–3.

7. Exod 14–15; Deut 7:2–7; Job 9:8, 38:16; Isa 43:1–5, 51:9–11; Ps 29:3, 65:8, 77:20, 89:10, 93:3–4.

8. The three elements of this statement—"I am," "bread" and "life"— suggest the intensely "saturated phenomenon" through which Jesus mediates the experience of God: the theological self-designation, "I am," is identified with "bread," a primal symbol of human need, which in turn is related to an unobjectifiable totality of experience, "life." Cf. Jean-Luc Marion, "Le phénomène saturé," 89–118.

9. Not only exterior revelation or the object [of faith] has the capacity to draw, but also an interior instinct impels us toward what is to be believed. Thus, the Father draws many to the Son through a divinely wrought instinct moving the human heart to what is to be believed [*per instinctum divinae operationis moventis cor hominis ad credendum*] (*In Evangelium B. Johannis Expositio*, Turin: Marietti, 1925), 6.5.3. Note, too, in the Thomist account of the instinct of faith, the act of faith does not terminate at a proposition, but *ad rem*, in the divine reality itself as in *Summa Theol.* 2-2, 1, 2 ad 2.
10. For a phenomenology of "seeing" in Christian experience, see Hans Urs von Balthasar, *The Glory of the Lord VII*, 286–295.
11. For the significance of the different Greek words for eating, see F. J. Moloney, *Glory not Dishonor: Reading John 13—21* (Minneapolis: Fortress, 1998), 20–22.
12. For a theological reflection on death, see Ghislain Lafont, *Peut-on connaître Dieu...*, 249. Also James Alison, *Raising Abel*, especially pages 29, 41–42, 58–60.
13. Hans Urs von Balthasar, in *The Glory of the Lord VII*, writes: "The kenosis which forms the unique character of Jesus' existence, cannot therefore be traced back to anything that is already known and could explain it; because this is so difficult to discover, he becomes continually a *skandalon*, a 'stumbling-stone'" (221). For further stimulating insights, James Alison, *Raising Abel*, 137, 155–158.
14. See Hans Urs von Balthasar, *The Glory of the Lord VII*, 379–380.
15. On "the eucharistic site" as fundamental to the hermeneutics of Christian experience, see Jean-Luc Marion, *God Without Being*, 149–158. Marion, using a wide range of scriptural references, offers a rich reflection on the eucharistic "site" of theology, even though the ecclesiastical emphasis (153–156) appears extreme, at least in its applicability to the Gospel of John.
16. Paul Celan, *Poems*, M. Hamburger, trans. (Manchester, U.K.: Carcanet, 1980), 202–203. (*EIN DRÖHNEN:* es ist/ die Wahrheit selbst/ unter die Menschen/ getreten,/ mitten ins/Metapherngestöber." Commenting on this passage, John Milbank notes, "At the point where the divine creation establishes the human creation by overtaking and completing it, thereby exposing a realized intention more primitive than human intent and fully its master, there is revelation" (John Milbank, *The Word Made Strange: Theology, Language, Culture*, Oxford: Blackwell, 1997), 131.

7

Between Different
Paternities:
Making the Choice
(7:1—8:59)

The Feast of Tabernacles held a manifold significance. It included elements of an earlier form of harvest festival as temporary outdoor shelters were set up, and the Creator's gifts of water and rain, especially important at autumn time, were celebrated. The flimsy "tabernacles" evoked the memory of the tents of Israel wandering in the desert, but always under the provident care of the God of the covenant. It was the custom for the men to sleep and eat in these dwellings for seven days, as the feast reached its culminating celebration on the eighth day. The festive mood anticipated a messianic fullness of time in which the salvation promised to the patriarchs would be brought to perfection. This most popular of the three pilgrimage feasts was often referred to simply as "the Feast." It was known also as the Feast of YHWH.

Thus, there is a rich symbolic and ritual background for the revelatory discourses of this section of the Gospel. Current research suggests that the conduct of the feast included three main ceremonial actions—the libation of water, the illumination of the temple, and the dawn ritual of turning to the temple. In this festive context, Jesus will be revealed as the source of living water, as the true light of the world, and above all, as the one in whom the true God is present and known.

1. The Father's Will, and Right Judgment

1. After this Jesus went about in Galilee; he would not go about in Judea because the Jews sought to kill him. 2. Now the Jews' feast of Tabernacles was at hand. 3. So his brothers said to him, "Leave here and go to Judea, that your disciples may see the works you are doing. 4. For no one who wants to be widely known acts in secret. If you do these things, show yourself to the world." 5. For even his brothers did not believe in him. 6. Jesus said to them, "My time has not yet come, but your time is always here. 7. The world cannot hate you, because I testify of it that its works are evil. 8. Go to the feast yourselves; I am not going up to this feast, for my time has not yet fully come." 9. So saying he remained in Galilee. (7:1–9)

In the period preceding the feast, Judea had become for Jesus a dangerous place (cf. 5:18). Yet his brothers press him to go into that region, as the feast—with its obligations on all male Jews to attend—draws near. His blood relatives had hitherto been in the background (2:12); now they emerge, impressed by his works, and concerned that he should make up lost ground with those who had left him (6:66). But he distances himself from their understanding of his mission. Self-promotion is not his concern. It would appear that his relatives are a part of a larger group who, having failed to come to faith in him (7:5; cf. 1:11), are unable to grasp that his sole purpose is to make God known;[1] and that his actions are governed by a motive transcending family ambitions and even traditional religious observance. The sole criterion of his mission is the will of the Father.[2] Because his brethren act from other motives, they are complicit in the world's resistance to the truth of what God is revealing. They need not expect violence and rejection. But Jesus does: "My time has not yet fully come" (7:8b). While his relatives are free to go to the feast, Jesus is beholden to another will (4:54; 5:19, 30) and so remains in Galilee.

> 10. **But after his brothers had gone up to the feast, then he also went up, not publicly but in private. 11. The Jews were looking for him at the feast and saying, "Where is he?" 12. And there was much muttering about him among the people. While some said, "He is a good man," others said, "No, he is leading the people astray." 13. Yet for fear of the Jews no one spoke openly of him.** (7:10–13)

Governed only by the Father's will, Jesus reverses his earlier decision. This makes clear that he is now acting, not in accord with worldly calculation or family pressure, but explicitly to carry out the demands of God's will; and in accord with the timing the Father has determined (2:4–7; 4:48–50). Hence, he goes up "privately," that is, not as a member of a family, nor as one of the crowd of pilgrims. In his unique mission, he is not carried along by a general movement, but went up "not publicly but in private" (7:10). There will be another feast when Jesus will publicly go up to Jerusalem, there to be "lifted up" when the hour of glory strikes.

In this instance the will of God moves him into an ominous situation, bristling with conflicts. "The Jews" are looking for him, and there is "much muttering" about him among the people (7:12). The privacy of his mission finds a strange parallel in the fear-enclosed privacy of the discussion surrounding him.

In that secret world, some at least had reached a deadly decision in his regard: "the Jews" whom the people feared.

> 14. About the middle of the feast, Jesus went into the temple and taught. 15. The Jews marvelled at it, saying, "How is it that this man has learning, when he has never studied?" 16. So Jesus answered them, "My teaching is not mine, but his who sent me. 17. Anyone who resolves to do the will of God will know whether the teaching is from God or whether I am speaking on my own authority. 18. Those who speak on their own authority seek their own glory; but the one who seeks the glory of the one who sent him is true, and in him there is no falsehood. 19. Did not Moses give you the law? Yet none of you keeps the law. Why do you seek to kill me?" 20. The people answered, "You have a demon! Who is seeking to kill you?" 21. Jesus answered them, "I did one deed, and you all marvel at it. 22. Moses gave you circumcision (not that it is from Moses, but from the fathers), and you circumcise a man upon the Sabbath. 23. If on the Sabbath a man receives circumcision, so that the law of Moses may not be broken, are you angry with me because on the Sabbath I made a man's whole body well? 24. Stop judging by appearances; adopt right judgment." (7:14–24)

With the celebrations of the festival in full swing, the Gospel reports for the first time that Jesus goes to the temple to teach. "The Jews" express their astonishment at his daring to teach in such an independent fashion. How, and through what recognized authorities, does he link his teaching back to Moses? What is his authority? In response, he reiterates the claims previously expressed: "My teaching is not mine, but his who sent me" (7:16;

cf. 5:19–47). Only by following the will of the one who sent him, and by transcending the bias of inherited certitudes and social reputation, will his hearers appreciate the divinely original character of his teaching. He thus provides the "hermeneutical key" to the meaning of his message: "Anyone who resolves to do the will of God will know whether the teaching is from God, or whether I am speaking on my own authority" (7:17).

Not to be open to the transcendent origin of Jesus' communication is to be locked in the power play and endless disputation about who is authorized to speak of God. Such disputes originate in a defensive concern for one's own authority and reputation within the world. Things are different for anyone whose basic commitment is union with the divine will. The authority that comes from the Son, uniquely seeking the glory of the one who sent him, must ring true for those who are genuinely Godward in their concerns. For his part, Jesus is not trapped in the self-promoting world of worldly glory and prestige: "...in him there is no falsehood" (7:18c). But in the false perspective of worldly glory, even Moses is appealed to so as to legitimate the violent rejection of the Word. Jesus' adversaries are concerned neither with the will nor the glory of God. They fail to appreciate the gift of the Law and the original intention of Moses—to say nothing of the final gift of the truth (1:16–17). Caught up in their own idolatrous projections, they seek to kill Jesus—and to excommunicate his followers (9:22; 12:42; 16:2). They dismiss "the one...who is true" (7:18b) as untrue to their traditions.

The people, unaware of any plan to do away with Jesus, think that his allegation in this regard is a sign of madness (7:20). In reply, he refers back to a previous Sabbath discussion (5:1–18). The question of the legitimacy of his action on the Sabbath thus returns with a special sting, again in reference to the Law. What is its true purpose? Who is the God who has given this gift to Israel? Is God the God of circumcision, or of healing? If circumcision was permitted on the Sabbath in the name of God, why is Jesus' act of healing on the Sabbath not recognized as of God?: "Are you angry with me because on the Sabbath I made a man's whole body well?" (7:3). When legal casuistry is employed to disallow God's healing activity, where does the madness lie?

One of the most dramatic acts in the ritual of the Feast occurred when the assembled crowd turns its back to the rising sun and bows toward the Temple, thereby signifying a renewed dedication to YHWH as the one true God (cf. Ezek 8:16). The rich symbolism of this gesture points to the present crisis inherent in the life of Israel. Will it be found looking in the wrong direction, and fail to recognize the presence of its God in Jesus? A new horizon is necessary within which the invisible God will be seen in a new visibility: "Stop judging by appearances. Adopt a right judgment!" (7:24). A renewed decision in favor of YHWH cannot mean turning away from the Son and rejecting his Sabbath work in healing a sick man. In the present context, a deeper level of sickness is being disclosed, in need of a healing that can come only from him whom God has sent to bring it. Who is mad? Who is sick? When the God of Jesus is acting, such questions are deeply upsetting for those who "judge by appearances," and so disallow divine possibilities.

2. God—or Religion?

25. Certain people from Jerusalem therefore said, "Is not this the man whom they seek to kill? 26. And here he is, speaking openly, and they say nothing to him! Can it be that the authorities really know that this is the Christ? 27. Yet we know where this man comes from." 28. So Jesus proclaimed, as he taught in the

temple, "You know me, and you know where I come from? But I have not come of my own accord; the one who sent me is true, and him you do not know. 29. I know him, for I have come from him, and he sent me." 30. So they sought to arrest him; but no one laid hands on him, because his hour had not yet come. 31. Yet many of the people believed in him; they said, "When the Christ appears, will he do more signs than this man has done?" (7:25–31)

Certain of the citizens of Jerusalem were becoming more aware of the crisis that was brewing. They are aware of the plot to do away with Jesus who is now speaking openly in the temple precincts. Hence their puzzlement over the inaction of the authorities. Had they come to recognize that Jesus was the Christ? (7:26). Eager to counter any such imputation, the religious leaders present their evidence: "We know where this man comes from" (7:27a)—whereas the origins of the Christ are to be unknown (7:27b). The case was closed. There is no room for confusion or conflict.

Once more in the Gospel, the "we know" of prior certitudes about the identity and origin of Jesus are mistaken (cf. 1:41, 45; 3:2; 4:25; 6:42). The Jerusalemites are looking in the wrong direction. They are enclosed in their "theology"—when in "this man" they are being offered the culminating revelation of God! Jesus ironically contests their supposed knowledge of his origins. He does not speak about geographical locations, nor even directly about himself, but about the one who sent him. Jesus knows who this is, but they do not: "...the one who sent me is true, and him you do not know. I know him, for I came from him, and he sent me" (7:28–29). The true God is true to his promises because he is true to himself. The Father reveals his true self through his Son, so to communicate the fullness of truth

(1:14). In contrast, the dawn ritual taking place has become empty posturing. In their impregnable certitudes, these citizens of the Holy City are turned not only from Jesus, but from God. The horizontal perspective of "judging according to appearances" allows no room from the vertical in-breaking of the truth.

When his adversaries attempt to arrest him, Jesus proves, in more ways than one, to be beyond their grasp. His death will occur in that hour determined by the will of God, not by human machinations (7:30). Yet there are some of the people who have arrived at some inkling of his identity, though they are unable to go beyond the signs he has performed. Jesus fits well with their expectations of a Mosaic eschatological prophet, for he has performed signs and wonders associated with the arrival of the messianic age (cf. Isa 11): "When the Christ appears, will he do more signs than this man has done?" (7:31b).

> 32. The Pharisees heard the crowd thus muttering about him, and the chief priests and the Pharisees sent officers to arrest him. 33. Jesus then said, "I shall be with you a little longer, then I go to him who sent me; 34. you will seek me and you will not find me; where I am you cannot come." 35. The Jews said to one another, "Where does this man intend to go that we shall not find him? Does he intend to go to the Dispersion among the Greeks and teach the Greeks? 36. What does he mean by saying, 'You will seek me and you will not find me,' and 'Where I am you cannot come'?" (7:32–36)

While some of the citizens of Jerusalem, worried over the inactivity of the authorities, had attempted to arrest Jesus, the authorities themselves (the Pharisees and chief priests), faced with the muttering of the crowd, now send officers to detain him. Jesus declares that his mission is not subject to their control. First, there is "a little longer" of his time with them that they cannot abbreviate, however much they may wish to do so. Second, there is the realm of his origin and destiny, both of which are impenetrable to them (7:33b–34). They are trying to halt his journey without realizing either its beginning or its end. Nonetheless, the "little time" of salvation remains open to them: "Seek the LORD while he may be found, call upon him while he is near…" (Isa 55:6–7).[3]

If they remove Jesus from their world, they are shutting out a saving possibility. Both the way of Jesus and the realm of the Father will be closed to them (7:34).[4] In attempting to detain him, they are in fact arresting their own movement toward the truth of his testimony.

Who is sick? Who is mad? Who is being arrested? The irony implied in these questions is set to intensify. When Jesus speaks of his return to the Father, they suppose he is talking about moving into the Jewish diaspora in foreign lands (7:35). If they fail to nip his influence in the bud, the whole thing might get out of control. What they do not realize is that he has been sent into the *world* to be "the light of the world" (1:9–13), "the savior of the world" (4:42), and "the bread of God" for the life of the world (6:33)—because God so loved the world (3:16) The decisive factor is not their anxious efforts to restrict his influence, but the unceasing work of the Father in spreading it: "Everyone who has heard and learned from the Father comes to me" (6:45). The Greeks will indeed profit, as will all the scattered children of God (11:52). Despite what Jesus' adversaries are planning to do, even because of it, he will be the agent of a cosmic salvation. In their efforts to restrict his mission, his antagonists are themselves immobilized: they cannot move either upward to the Father, or outward to the whole world of the Father's love.

3. The Living Water of the Spirit

37. On the last day of the feast, the great day, Jesus stood up and proclaimed, "Let anyone who is thirsty come to me, 38. and let the one who believes in me drink. As the scripture has said, 'Out of his heart shall flow rivers of living water.'" 39. Now this he said about the Spirit, which those who believed in him were to receive; for as yet the Spirit had not yet been given, because Jesus was not yet glorified. (7:37–39)

At this point, the Gospel brings us back to the context of the feast. It is the last day of the festival. While the ritual activities of the seven previous days have ceased, this eighth day was similar in atmosphere to the Sabbath with its emphasis on praise and joy. In anticipation of what is to happen, the Gospel terms it "the great day," for Jesus is to be revealed as the source of living water of the Spirit (7:37–38) and the light of the world (8:12).

The words of Jesus resonate with what has already been symbolized in the libation ceremony on each morning of the preceding seven days. Water had been drawn from the Pool of Siloam, mixed with wine, and poured on the altar. It is brought in procession through the Water Gate, identified in rabbinic writing with the south gate of Ezek 47:1–5. The prophets had promised the waters of life flowing forth from the threshold of the temple. Joel, foretelling the outpouring of the Spirit on all flesh (Joel 2:28), went on to speak of a messianic fulfilment "...when all the stream beds of Judah would flow with water; a fountain shall come forth from the house of the Lord..." (Joel 3:18). Zechariah, in the context of the Feast of Tabernacles, evokes the universal significance of what was being celebrated: "If any of the families of the earth do not go up to Jerusalem to worship the King, the LORD of hosts, there will be no rain upon them"

(Zech 14:17). Such associations are woven into the context of Jesus' proclamation: "Let anyone who is thirsty come to me, and let the one who believes in me drink. As scripture has said, 'Out of his heart shall flow rivers of living water'" (7:37b–38).

Where once Jerusalem was hailed as the center of the world, and the Temple regarded as the sacred center of the Holy City from which life-giving waters would flow to the east and to the west, there is a now a new source of life-giving water open to all: "Let anyone..." (7:37b). The Gospel immediately explains this universal gift of water flowing from Jesus as referring to the Spirit: "Now this he said about the Spirit, which those who believed in him were to receive" (7:39). Here John connects the gift of water to the traditional expectation of the outpouring of the Spirit to take place at the end of time.[5]

Specifically, it looks to the hour when Jesus will be glorified: "For as yet the Spirit had not been given, because Jesus was not yet glorified" (7:39b).[6] His heart will be opened in the hour of glory (19:34), when all former gifts will be fulfilled and surpassed. When he is lifted up on the cross (8:28), the glory of God will be revealed as the self-giving love that transforms the doomed world of human glory, and annuls the power of evil. The manner in which the "measureless" gift of the Spirit (3:34) will be given to all believers awaits the full hour of revelation.[7]

4. God's Subversive Paternity

40. When they heard these words some of the people said, "This is really the prophet." 41. Others said, "This is the Christ." But some said, "Is the Christ to come from Galilee? 42. Has not the scripture said that the Christ is descended from David, and comes from Bethlehem, the village where David was?" 43. So

179

there was a division among them over him. 44. Some of them wanted to arrest him, but no one laid hands on him. 45. The officers then went back to the chief priests and Pharisees, who said to them, "Why did you not bring him?" 46. The officers answered them, "Never has anyone spoken like this!" 47. The Pharisees answered them, "Are you led astray, you also? 48. Have any of the authorities or of the Pharisees believed in him? 49. But this crowd, who do not know the law, are accursed." 50. Nicodemus, who had gone to him before, and who was one of them, said to them, 51. "Does our law judge people without first giving them a hearing to know what they do?" 52. They replied, "Are you from Galilee too? Search and you will see that no prophet is to arise from Galilee." (7:40–52)

The disputes that now follow muddy the water. The clash of views regarding Jesus' prophetic or messianic role (7:40–42) suggests something of various ways "the thirsty" are coming to him. Their questions are reminiscent of the reaction of the Samaritan woman (4:13–26). But they also suggest the obstacles lying in the way, due to differing messianic expectations that were in the air during the celebration of the feast. These different "christologies" can be either the inspiration for further journey toward Jesus, or the excuse for going no further. The hidden Messiah of "the Jerusalemites" (7:26–27), the miracle-working Messiah of "many of the people" (7:31), the Messiah who provides living water of "some of the people" (7:37–41a), and the Davidic Messiah of another group (7:41b–42) evidence both the promise and confusion of the situation. Yet Jesus challenges all such messianic hopes in the light of what God is actually bringing about. He has proclaimed the invitation to come to him in order to receive God's all-fulfilling gift (7:37). The messianic categories of the past, variously dealing with the supposed origins of the Messiah, now appear as distractions from that truth that is most essential to the mission of Jesus: he is from God. Because his origins are in God, his life is ruled by a power to which his adversaries are also subject. Their hands cannot lay hold of the one who, coming from above, is essentially beyond them (7:44).

The Temple officials, sent by the chief priests and the Pharisees—who have already made up their minds about what they are going to do about Jesus—fail to bring him back. The officers had found themselves in the presence of someone who escapes both their spiritual and physical grasp: "Never has anyone spoken like this!" (7:46). Encountering the Word, they have begun to appreciate that he is outside all categories. Ironically again, because they have felt the attraction of the Father (6:44), they are accused of being led astray (7:47). They are placed thereby in conflict with the supposedly genuine authorities who, keeping their feet firmly on the ground of the world of "from below," have found no credibility in this man who claims to be "from above" (7:48). The authorities deem that only the accursed crowd, ignorant of the Law and deprived of the glory of true knowledge, has proved suggestible.

One of the Pharisees, the Nicodemus who had previously approached Jesus, is a living disproof of the supposed solidarity of the authorities and Pharisees against Jesus (7:48). He attempts to get a hearing for Jesus in accord with "our law" (7:51), lest the judges be judged by the very law they uphold. In his efforts to gain a hearing for the accused on the basis of his words and deeds, Nicodemus is, in effect, proposing a new interpretation of the Law. It is not merely "our law." It is the gift of God designed to lead to the fullness of the gift of truth (1:16–17). This Pharisee has allowed himself to be affected by the "hermeneutical principle" already stated by Jesus himself: "Anyone who resolves to do the will of God will know whether the teaching is from God…" (7:17). Only by seeking God's will and God's glory can the conditions for right judgment be met—so that Jesus can be judged, not as a violator of the law, but as its fulfillment. For his pains Nicodemus becomes a casualty to the violence in the air. He suffers abuse from his fellows, as did the officers and the crowd. The Temple authorities suggest that Nicodemus himself must have his origins in disreputable Galilee. Not only have they missed the critical point concerning the divine origin of Jesus; they are ignorantly assuming, despite the known origins of Jonah, Hosea, and Nahum, that no prophet comes from Galilee. They are showing an ignorance of their own tradition, even while rejecting Jesus in its name. Despite the brilliant illumination marking the celebration of the feast, a darkness is settling over all who are opposed to the Light.

5. The Light of the Darkening World

12. Again Jesus spoke to them, saying, "I am the light of the world; whoever follows me will not walk in darkness but will have the light of life." 13. The Pharisees then said to him, "You are bearing witness to yourself; your testimony is not true." 14. Jesus answered, "Even if I do bear witness to myself, my testimony is true, for I know whence I have come and whither I am going. 15. You judge according to the flesh. I judge no one, 16. yet even if I do judge, my judgment is reliable, for it is not I alone that judge, but I and the one who sent me. 17. In your law it is written that the testimony of two persons is true. 18. I bear witness to myself, and the Father who sent me bears witness to me." 19. They said to him therefore, "Where is your Father?" Jesus

answered, "You know neither me nor my Father; if you knew me, you would know my Father also." 20. These words he spoke in the treasury, as he taught in the Temple; but no one arrested him because his hour had not yet come. (8:12–20)

In this mood of tension and bewilderment, the Word is once more heard in a world where his own, in the person of Jewish leaders, have failed to receive him. Jesus' proclamation of himself as the light of the world takes place in the illuminated setting of the feast, with the celebration focused on the four menorahs set up at the center of the court of the women. With the exuberance of the thronging pilgrims dancing through the night, the lights of the Temple and its surroundings anticipated the coming of that endless day when the light of God would banish all darkness. The prophecy of Zechariah inspired a mood of joy and hope, as the gifts of light and living water were celebrated:

> On that day there shall not be either cold or frost. And there shall be continuous day (it is known to the LORD), not day and not night, for at evening time there shall be light. On that day living waters shall flow out from Jerusalem....(Zech 14:6–8)

The multifaceted symbolism of light was fraught with significance in the experience of Israel, as it evoked the burning bush from which YHWH spoke (Exod 3:2–6), and the pillar of fire leading the people through the desert (Exod 13:21). But now here was the culminating splendor that had been anticipated in the great hopes of the past:

> How precious is your steadfast love, O God!
> All people take refuge in the shadow of your wings.

They feast on the abundance of your house,
and you give them drink from the river of your
  delights,
for with you is the fountain of life;
in your light we see light. (Ps 36:7–9)

Against this background, Jesus proclaims himself as the
light of the world (8:12). In this light, the world would see
"Light" (1 John 1:5).[8] Jesus shines with the radiance of God's
self-revelation, despite the darkness and confusion his presence
has occasioned. Beneath all the disputes, the question ached:
How is the invisible God related to this Jesus, so disconcertingly
visible within the precincts of the Temple itself? His proclamation actualizes, in fact, the great announcement of the Prologue:
"What has come into being with him was life, and the life was
the light of all people. The light shines in the darkness, and the
darkness did not overcome it" (1:4–5). As "the bread of God"
replaces the manna of old, so too does the light of Christ fulfill
the guiding light of the Law (Wis 18:4; Prov 6:23; Ps 119:105;
Sir 24:27). The radiant symbolism of Israel's past now pales in
the presence of the light of the world.

In the subsequent exchange between Jesus and the Pharisees,
the crucial issue is whether or not in his light they will see light
(cf. Ps 36:9). A legal objection is raised against his apparently isolated testimony (8:13). Ironically, the references in the Law supporting the demand for two or more witnesses actually concern
the death penalty (Num 35:30 and Deut 17:6). The Pharisees had
reason to be sure of their casuistry, since they had already decided
on his death. But, communicating in another dimension, Jesus
had been talking in terms of the gifts of living water and light.
Where the Law has been light for Israel, Jesus is now light for *the
world*. What was limited and provisional must now be judged by
what is universal and definitive. In him the gift of truth has

appeared to judge both the Law and those who follow it: "Even if I do bear witness to myself, my testimony is true, for I know whence I have come, and whither I am going" (8:14a).

As the light of the world, Jesus is first of all luminous to himself—in regard to his origin and destiny in God. This sets him in opposition to his adversaries who do not recognize what is essential to his mission (8:14b). By implication, they have cut themselves adrift from their own God-given origins and destiny, so uncomprehending have they become to the true bearing of the feast they celebrate. They are enclosed in that world of intra-mundane judgment that Jesus does not share: "You judge according to the flesh. I judge no one" (8:15). While they locked into the narrow world of their own criteria—according to which they have decided to get rid of him—his existence is centered on the one who sent him. He is the light of the world because his whole being is transparently turned to the Father in total dependence on God's will.

The light of God shines through him. There is a conse-quence: "Yet even if I do judge, my judgment is reliable, for it is not I alone that judge, but I and he who sent me" (8:16). If his mission does in fact result in judgment on those who close them-selves to his witness (8:17), such a judgment is not the intended outcome of his saving mission to the world. Those for whom there is no criterion of judgment, other than their own self-sufficiency, experience his transparency to God's will as a judgment on themselves (cf. 3:19–21). Their "judgment-constructed" world—"your law" (8:17)—becomes increasingly anomalous as it closes itself to "the light of the world." For, to satisfy their own criterion, two witnesses are, in fact, available; namely, Jesus bearing witness to himself (cf. Isa 43:10), and the Father who sent him and supports his witness (8:18). Has the demand of the God-given law for two supporting witnesses been so reduced to the level of "your law" that the witness of the

Father himself, of the God who gave the Law, has been excluded?

Consequently, the Pharisees' question, "Where is your Father?" (8:19a), indicates a fixation in the order of appearances (7:24) and the flesh (8:15). The Father cannot be located "neither on this mountain nor in Jerusalem" (4:21). The real question turns on who the Father is, and how he is revealed. By presuming to locate the Father in their world as an already known and identifiable witness, they are missing out on the real truth of the one who "so loved the world that he gave his only Son…" (3:16), who seeks for worshippers in spirit and in truth (4:23–24). As a result, a willful ignorance is exposed: "You know neither me nor my Father. If you knew me you would know my Father also" (8:19b). They are placing themselves outside of the "logic" of God's self-revelation, in resistance to both the Father and the Son. By clinging to the former gift, and refusing to let it achieve its purpose in them, they are blocking their reception of the greater gift. Not resolved to doing the will of God (7:17), they cannot know that Jesus' teaching is from God.

The irresistible direction of God's will in the mission of Jesus is highlighted in the fact that his teaching takes place in the illuminated treasury of the Temple, at the very center of the Jewish jurisdiction, and therefore most vulnerable to the power of Temple authorities. But no one arrests him. The will of God is carrying him forward to the hour of the Father's own timing. For the moment, "his hour had not yet come" (8:20).

6. Which Paternity?

21. Again he said to them, "I go away, and you will seek me and die in your sin; where I am going you

cannot come." 22. Then said the Jews, "Will he kill himself, since he says, 'Where I am going you cannot come'?" 23. He said to them, "You are from below; I am from above. You are of this world; I am not of this world. 24. I told you that you would die in your sins unless you believe that I am he." 25. They said to him, "Who are you?" Jesus said to them, "What is the point of talking to you? 26. I have much to say about you and much to judge; but the one who sent me is true, and I declare to the world what I have heard from him." 27. They did not understand that he spoke to them of the Father. 28. So Jesus said, "When you have lifted up the Son of Man, then you will know that I am he, and that I do nothing on my own authority but speak thus as the Father taught me. 29. And the one who sent me is with me; he has not left me alone, for I always do what is pleasing to him." 30. As he spoke thus, many believed in him. (8:21–30)

The conflict-laden narrative of the exchanges that occurred between Jesus, the Pharisees, and the Jews now leads into the dark theme of death—theirs and his. He opens the exchange by pointing to the mortal peril of his adversaries' position: "I go away, and you will seek me and die in your sin; where I am going you cannot come" (8:21). By trying to arrest him they are rendering themselves incapable of following in his path. By plotting his death they are in fact choosing death for themselves. By turning against the Son they have no access to the Father. In an especially ironic turn, they wonder whether he is about to commit suicide, thus interpreting the realm of death as the place that Jesus declares will be barred to them (8:22). In fact, it is they who are in the grip of death—while his death will prove to be the source of life for all who accept him.

The realms of death and true life are polar opposites. Until the heavens are opened (1:51), there is an unbridgeable gap between the Jesus who is from above, and the "you" who are "from below." Still, the way to life still lies open. A refusal to follow it amounts to a spiritual death wish: "…You will die in your sins unless you believe that I am he" (8:24b). To acknowledge that Jesus bears the divine name is to accept that in him the one and only God of Israel is being disclosed. In Jesus, God is made invocable in his divine originality and life-giving power,[9] in a way that fulfills all the promises of the past, even while offering salvation to the whole world.

By using the divine name of himself, Jesus implies that his identity can only be known within the horizon of God's presence and saving action in Israel's history. Faith looks back to what was promised, and upward to what is not of this world. But "the Jews" insist on detaching him both from their past and from the divine realm above, to locate him solely in closed perspectives of the world below: "Who are you?" (8:25a). He reacts against the monotonous presuppositions that make further discussion useless; the barrier of their unbelief remains impregnable: "What is the point of talking to you?" (8:25b). What is required is not endless disputation, but faith in him who lives on the other side of their lies, ambiguities, ignorance, and evasions, in the realization that the whole world is being loved by God into a new realm of life. If they remain within the narrowing confines of their "hermeneutic of suspicion," his witness to the world will fall on deaf ears: "But the one who sent me is true, and I declare to the world what I have heard from him" (8:26). God is true; the Father is authentically revealed in the one he has sent. And Jesus, in declaring this truth to the world, stands before them as one who is truly obedient to the Father's will.

A dawn ritual of turning from the rising sun and bowing toward the temple had been repeated for seven days. It signified

an act of adoration of the one true God, in a renewed dedication
to YHWH above all other gods. This sacred gesture must now
reach toward its ultimate meaning. Israel is being summoned to
turn to its God, now revealed in Jesus. He is sent by God, to be
the source of living water (7:37–38), and the light of the world
(8:12). But if in this time of fulfillment God's self-giving, cosmic
love is rejected, incomprehension results: "They did not understand that he spoke to them of the Father" (8:27).

Their failure to understand sharply expresses the collision
of two opposing worlds of meaning. If the world of his antagonists is to survive, he must go. If he is to be heard and accepted,
then the glory and security of their world is at an end. What is
from above is in terminal conflict with what is from below. Life,
light, and obedience to the divine contrasts with the sinful
refusal that leads to death. The persistent effort to reduce Jesus
to a subversive element within their world blocks the Pharisees'
acceptance of him as the one sent by God to bring life to that
world. Judging by appearances opposes judging in the light of
the truth. The persistent failure to hear him is in contrast to his
hearing from the Father what he declares to the world. Fixation
on the past is not allowing history to reach its fulfillment.

In a final—and, in the event, only partially successful—
attempt to convince his audience of the point they are missing,
Jesus takes a further step into the light and darkness of the hour
which, in different ways, awaits both him and them: "When you
have lifted up the Son of Man, then you will know that I am he"
(8:28a). Even in the violent rejection of the Son, God's love will be
revealed. There will be an all-deciding divine disclosure in the
depth of the world's darkness. In the perspective of "from below,"
this "lifting up" will mean success for those who had plotted his
death, whose religious world he troubled, and whose worldly
glory he undermined, not as a judge, but as the bringer of life and
light. In that other perspective, "from above," in which the Father

has acted out of love for the world, his "lifting up" in death will be the revelation of the excess of divine love "to the end" (13:1b). The glory of God will be revealed as love, manifest within, despite, and even because of, the lethal violence that is closing around him. Jesus will be known as "I am he"—in that the love of God will be revealed as most radiantly divine, as it keeps on being love even at the point of the world's deepest darkness.

Though Jesus will be "lifted up" in this way, he will not be invested with an independent numinous quality. For the divine aspect of his identity will be revealed only in his unreserved receptivity to the Father's will and in a luminous transparency to his communication: "...And that I do nothing on my own authority but speak thus as the Father has taught me" (8:28b). The Father has been the source of all that Jesus has said and done. Though he is "sent" by the Father "from above" into the world "from below," the Father and the Son are in unbroken communion.[10] Sending has not meant separation in this transparent mutuality of presence. In the "I am" of Jesus, the gulf existing between the realm of the Father and the realm of this world is dissolved: "And the one who sent me is with me; he has not left me alone, for I always do what is pleasing to him" (8:29). The God to whom the Word is turned "in the beginning" (1:1–2), the Father to whom the Son is turned in his mission of revelation (1:18), is himself always turned toward the Son in an unbreakable relationship. There is a zone of peace in the midst of conflicts; a realm of non-judgment, and an interface of love, truth, and life, opening to include the world. Brought thus into the presence of the Father through the words of Jesus, "many believed in him" (8:30). His ever-present Father has drawn believers to him (6:44).

31. Jesus then said to the Jews who had believed in him, "If you abide in my word you are truly my disciples, 32. and you will know the truth, and the truth

190

will make you free." 33. They answered him, "We are descendants of Abraham and have never been in bondage to anyone. How is it that you will say, 'You will be made free'?" 34. Jesus answered them, "Amen, amen, I say to you, every one who commits sin is a slave to sin. 35. The slave does not abide in the house for ever; the son abides forever. 36. So if the Son makes you free, you will be free indeed. 37. I know that you are descendants of Abraham; yet you seek to kill me, because my words find no place in you. 38. I speak of what I have seen with my Father, and you do what you have heard from your father." (8:31–38)

Jesus now addresses the Jews who had begun to believe in him, but who had not yet realized the significance of his relationship with the Father. To continue in this "Fatherward" word until its full utterance is to be truly the disciples of Jesus (8:31). Only in a life of faith can the complete story of the Father be heard. It is spelled out only by following along the way of the only Son in his unbroken, "heart to heart" communication with the one from whom he comes (1:18; cf. also 3:13; 6:46). This journey will terminate in knowing the truth (8:32a).

And it is this truth that will make them free (8:32). True disciples will be free with God, as knowing and loving him who has so loved the world (3:16). They will be set free by becoming "the children of God" (1:12–13) in the knowledge of God's paternal relationship to them. In the past, the Law had brought light and freedom; but now the true light and the fulfillment of freedom are in the incarnate Word of God. True faith means embarking on a new adventure of freedom in openness to what God is bringing about; and in a becoming that can only be described as a new birth from above (3:3–8).

Jesus' opponents protest. They declare their descent from Abraham, and repudiate any suggestion of enslavement (8:33a). Their sarcasm, unaware of any limitation on their liberty, strikes at their supposed liberator: How dare *he* say that *they* will be made free? (8:33b). In this, not only do they refuse the gift of freedom Jesus offers, but they do so in the name of a freedom that they never had—if they are to take seriously their own history of enslavement and exile and the present experience of foreign occupation. The "amen, amen" of Jesus' response underlines the revelatory force of his identity as the Word. He proceeds to uncover the true meaning of enslavement as bondage to sin (8:34b). Unless they accept this diagnosis of their condition, they will never know the true meaning of freedom. However impeccable their physical or spiritual lineage might be, if they commit sin they are enslaved. In rejecting God's Word and in seeking to kill the Son, they are doers of evil, and so in its thrall. In contrast to the true child of God—who enjoys the freedom of the Father's house of many rooms (14:2)—the slave has no secure place in God's household. Only hospitality to the Word ensures the freedom of the Father's house—for only the Son abides forever. As the very embodiment of the truth, he can give release and freedom.

But his hearers are closed to this liberating truth, and unprepared to wait on the unfolding of God's will. Because they even seek to kill the Son, these "descendants of Abraham" are giving evidence of another parentage (8:37–38). Whereas Jesus speaks out of a living communication with his Father, they are acting out of the murderous intent of their father (8:38b), and so denying their Abrahamitic lineage. At the call of God, the great patriarch set out into the unknown (Gen 12:1–9), on a path of such unreserved surrender that he was prepared to sacrifice even his son at the command of God (Gen 22:1–17). But his spurious descendants are trying to kill the Son of God rather than listen to the divine word (8:37b). Abraham welcomed the heavenly messengers (Gen 18:1–18), and accepted the unforeseeable gift of paternity. But his present descendants reject the Word of God, and are closed to the paternity revealing itself to them.

> 39. They answered him, "Abraham is our father." Jesus said to them, "If you were Abraham's children you would do what Abraham did, 40. but you now seek to kill me, a man who has told you the truth that I heard from God; this is not what Abraham did. 41. You do what your father did." They said to him, "We are not born of fornication; we have one Father, even God." 42. Jesus said to them, "If God were your Father you would love me, for I proceeded and came forth from God; I came not of my own accord but God sent me. 43. Why do you not understand what I say? It is because you cannot bear to hear my word. 44. You are of your father the devil, and your will is to do your father's desires. He was a murderer from the beginning, and has nothing to do with the truth because there is no truth in him. When he lies he speaks according to his own nature, for he is a liar and the father of lies. 45. But because I tell the truth you do not believe me. 46. Which of you convicts me of sin? If I tell the truth, why do you not believe me? 47. Whoever is of God hears the words of God; the reason why you do not hear them is that you are not of God." (8:39–47)

For his part, Jesus makes known what he has seen in the Father's presence (8:38): the self-giving of the Father in giving his only Son out of love for the world, in a way that surpasses the scope of Abraham's intended sacrifice. The patriarch's present descendants, allowing no such excess, need to be in truth what they claim to be: "If you were Abraham's children, you would do what Abraham did..." (8:39–40). Since they do not, their real paternity is ominously suggested: "You do what your father did" (8:41). But then they shift the discussion from their patriarchal lineage to claim a divine paternity: "We were not born of fornication; we have one father, even God" (8:42). Their divine paternity is legitimate; that of Jesus is not. He cannot have their God for his father when he is leading the people into apostasy (cf. Hos 1:2; 4:15; Ezek 15:15, 33–44). It is possible, because of his consistent and absolute claim that God alone is his Father, that his adversaries are also anticipating the anti-Christian polemics of later centuries, concerning the illegitimacy of Jesus. Be that as it may, the real point of opposition is this: they are representatives of Israel, "the first born son" of the LORD (Exod 4:22), and are "children of the LORD your God" (Deut 14:1).[11] In contrast, Jesus, with his pretentious claims, is not acknowledging this basic truth in their tradition. But he questions, not the conviction flowing from the pure faith of Israel, but the kind of god its present representatives are claiming as their father: "If God were your father, you would love me, for I proceeded and came forth from God; I came not of my own accord, but he sent me" (8:42). Though, at the dawn of each day of the feast, they turned from the rising sun to adore the God of the Temple, they are now, in fact, turning from the true God who had been acting in their past, and who is now revealed to them in him who came forth from God. Since Jesus was loved by God (3:35), then the children of this God would love him as the only Son of the Father. But, instead of adoring the true God as the source of Jesus' mission, they are making their congealed "theology" into a cause for schism among themselves, and of separation from him. Set against Jesus, the Son and the emissary of the Father, they have become antagonists of God and allergic to his revelation (8:43).

In this they are showing evidence of a diabolic paternity (8:44a). Bent on ridding themselves of the Son whose sole concern is to do the life-giving will of the Father (4:34; 5:36), they have become agents of the murderous force at work in human history, "the father of lies," the ruler of this world (14:30). The diabolical father had brought death into the world through his deceitful influence (Gen 3:1–24; Wis 2:24). By inspiring Cain's envy of his brother, Abel, he was the cause of the world's first murder (Gen 4:15).

The mutually contradictory nature of these two paternal wills is thrown into relief by the stark contrast of origins. The Word, turned toward God in the beginning, is the source of life and light (1:1–5). The devil from the beginning is turned against humankind as the cause of death, murder, and deception. In opposition to this malevolent figure who "has nothing to do with the truth because there is no truth in him" (8:44c), Jesus embodies the fullness of truth in his mission in the service of the one "who is true" (5:32; 7:28b). The Son, by making the Father known (1:14, 17–18; 8:32, 40), and speaking the truth (8:45), is the living contradiction of "the father of lies" (8:44d). How, then, can his adversaries impute sin to him when they have wilfully closed themselves to God and rendered themselves deaf to God's message? Thus, two generations, with their respective paternities, are in conflict. The one is from the true God, the Father of Jesus, the source of life and light. The other is from the false god of death, murder, deceit, and ignorance, who rules in the world of human glory.

> 48. The Jews answered him, "Are we not right in saying that you are a Samaritan and have a demon?" 49. Jesus answered, "I have not a demon; but I honor my Father, and you dishonor me. 50. Yet I do not seek my own glory; there is one who seeks it and he will be the

judge. 51. Amen, amen, I say to you, anyone who keeps my word will never see death." 52. The Jews said to him, "Now we know that you have a demon. Abraham died, as did the prophets; and you say, 'Anyone who keeps my word will never taste death.' 53. Are you greater than our father Abraham, who died? And the prophets died! Who do you claim to be?" 54. Jesus answered, 'If I glorify myself, my glory is nothing; it is my Father who glorifies me, of whom you say, 'He is our God.' 55. But you have not known him; I know him. If I said I do not know him, I should be a liar like you; but I do know him and keep his word. 56. Your father Abraham rejoiced that he was to see my day; he saw it and was glad." 57. The Jews then said to him, "You are not yet fifty years old, and have seen Abraham?" 58. Jesus said to them, "Amen, amen, I say to you, before Abraham was, I am." 59. So they took up stones to throw at him; but Jesus hid himself, and went out of the temple. (8:48–59)

Following this ruthless exposure, Jesus' antagonists, in a further ironic turn, resort to accusing him of being a Samaritan and of having a demon. But it is they who have been shown to be under diabolic influence. Besides, many of the formerly apostate Samaritans have heard the call of the Father in his search for true worshipers in spirit and truth (4:24, 42). Jesus asserts, "I do not have a demon, but I honor my Father, and you dishonor me" (8:49). He is not possessed by a demon, but by the Spirit of God who had descended on him (1:32).

The questions that had previously arisen—Who is sick? Who is mad? Who is guilty?—are posed in another form: Who is demonically possessed? This question, in turn, leads to another, What is true glory? Is it to be found in their defensive clinging to the past? Or is it to be found only in what God is bringing about? The Son honors the Father—even if it means dishonor for him (8:49b). True glory can be found only by looking beyond oneself to the other: just as the Son is intent on the Father's glory, the Father is intent on giving glory to the Son: "...there is one who seeks it and he will be the judge" (8:50b). True glory will be revealed only through God's self-giving love manifest in the self-gift of the Son. Seeking glory in any other form ends in death. Jesus' emphatic statement envisages an experience of life in which death will be revealed as a non-reality in a way that is beyond the ken of those enclosed in the doomed world of human glory: "Amen, amen, I say to you, anyone who keeps my word will never see death" (8:51).

The Word of life provokes a neuralgic reaction in those who had chosen to ally themselves with the force of death, the "murderer from the beginning" (8:44b). They fall back on their all-controlling certitudes, to repeat the allegation that Jesus is demonically possessed (8:52a). Once more the figure of Abraham is introduced by those who had previously claimed him as their father (8:39). But now they are forced to admit that Abraham died, like the prophets after him. Still, how can Jesus claim to offer anything greater than that of their illustrious progenitors? This is a logic previously voiced by the Samaritan woman (4:11–12). Jesus, however, once more turns the discussion back to the Father. While self-glorification is on the way to nothing (8:54a), true glory results from the action of the Father (8:54b). And yet there is a terrible consequence: the God, in whose name they seek to destroy Jesus, is in fact working to glorify him as his Son and revealer. Thus, the God who will glorify Jesus is the God who is unknown to them (8:55a). If Jesus were to disclaim the God he knows, that would make him a liar like those he is calling to account (8:55b).

He appeals to early Jewish traditions which told of Abraham foreseeing all the secrets of the messianic age. So he can claim, "Your father Abraham rejoiced that he was to see my day..." (8:56). In effect, Jesus is here declaring that the whole history of salvation has come to its culmination in him, when the true God would be finally revealed through the Son. Their now frozen pattern of incomprehension makes "the Jews" protest at the impossibility of his seeing Abraham—whereas, for Jesus, it was the patriarch that did the seeing (8:57). At this point, Jesus takes the discussion beyond absurd discussions of time-travel to disclose that other realm of existence in which he dwells: "Truly, truly I say to you, before Abraham was, I am" (8:58). He is not one more actor in the world of "from below." Nor is he one more servant of God conditioned by the flow of time in life and death. The reason has been given: "...what God was the Word also was" (1:1) He is the Word who was with God "in the beginning" (1:1–2). In his coming, the hitherto closed heavens will be opened; and the Word of God has entered the world as the source of eternal life.

His adversaries seek to punish the blasphemy they detect. But who is acting against God? Jesus, moved by another will, conceals himself, and leaves the temple of their failing religion.

7. The Experience of God?

The God whom Jesus reveals is deeply unsettling to a world of previously settled relationships, identities, and theological certitudes. There is an upheaval in the world "from below" in the presence of the one who is "from above." Rifts appear between Jesus and his brothers (7:1–9) and among sections of the crowd (7:10–13). Conflicts intensify between Jesus and "the Jews" (7:14–24). There is no shared point of view among the

Jerusalemites, the authorities, and the crowd (7:25–32), nor among the Pharisees, the Chief Priests, and Jesus (7:32–36). Various other popular parties (7:40–44) come into conflict. There is a crisis of authority between Jewish leaders and the temple police (7:45–47). The united front of the Pharisees is broken by one of their own, Nicodemus (7:50–52), as they are further troubled by the direction Jesus is taking (8:13–31). Some of the Jews experience in him the promise of freedom, while others protest that they needed no liberation (8:31–38). The conflict builds to a dreadful climax—as the children of Abraham find the Son of the Father to be guilty of blasphemy and intend to stone him (8:39–59).

If one thing emerges from this cacophony of conflict and contention it is this: the experience God presented in the Gospel means an agonizing exposure of human evasiveness in all its forms. It continues to be clear that "salvation is from the Jews" (4:22). The Jewish Jesus allies himself with the witness of Moses and Abraham, and, most of all, identifies the Father as the YHWH acting in Israel's history. But this Jesus seeks to give his own people "power to become children of God" (1:12), in the light of the distinctive divine paternity he reveals as unreservedly embracing the whole world. Israel, on its most joyous of feasts, enters into a crucible of decision. What matters now is being born "not of blood, nor of the will of the flesh nor of the will of man, but of God" (1:13). It is a birth that will be experienced as a death, a dreadful renunciation of all that was most prized as Israel's special glory.

In a frenzy of resistance, every possible stratagem was employed. His family suggested that Jesus should settle for a ministry of charismatic healing (7:3–4). Among the different parties celebrating the Feast, some reacted positively to Jesus as "a good man" (7:12), "a performer of signs"(7:31), "the prophet," or the Messiah (7:40–41), and as an astonishing speaker (7:46). Other factions dismissed him as a deceiver (7:12), an ignoramus (7:15), a pretentious proselytizer (7:35), unaccredited (8:13), and of unacceptable or dubious origins (7:41; 8:19); as suicidal (8:22), a Samaritan (8:48), and as one possessed (7:20; 8:48), a deluded visionary (8:57), as deserving arrest (7:30, 32, 43, 45) and the penalty for blasphemy (8:59). In all these instances, he occasioned some momentous disruption in the way things had always been. To relate to the Father in the way he called for meant a change so great that it felt like the ending of a world. If what he said was true, it would mean that those who accepted him had to die to the past, in order that something utterly new could be born within them. How this dying might mean the glory of new life—to be brought into being by the death that Jesus himself will undergo—lacks as yet an essential witness and key source of evidence: "...for as yet the Spirit had not been given, because Jesus was not yet glorified" (7:39). The peace, joy, conviction, and unity that will come with the Spirit are on the far side of the crisis that has occurred. Even as they enjoy the gift of the Spirit, later believers can look back at this time of terrible confrontation when the most radical of all questions arose for God's chosen people: Who, really, is your God? It will mean that they, too, even as they confess the reality of God's paternity in their lives, need to heed the warning: "Little children, keep yourselves from idols" (1 John 5:21).

Here, a passage from Nietzsche's *The Antichrist* provokes radical questions:

> The Christian conception of God—God as god of the sick, God as a spider, God as spirit—is one of the most corrupt conceptions of the divine ever attained on earth. It may even represent the low-water mark in the descending development of divine types. God degenerated into a *contradiction* of life, instead of being its

transfiguration and eternal Yes! God as the declaration of war against life, against nature, against the will to live! God—the formula for every slander against "this world," for every lie about the "beyond"! God the deification of nothingness, the will to nothingness pronounced holy.[12]

This most passionately ambiguous of all philosophers unwittingly provides the key by which to unlock the admittedly unsettling import of this section of John's Gospel—even of the whole Gospel, perhaps. Is the Father revealed by Jesus a contradiction of life or the source of life transfigured and eternally affirmed? Has our cultural denial of death fabricated a god made in our sickly image? Have the tiny preoccupations of what John would term human or worldly "glory" deadened the capacity to experience the true glory of life as it has appeared?

Feeling the force of such questions provokes another self-interrogation; and here, no doubt, we part from Nietzsche: What is the true generative force of our history and culture? Is it human reputation, with its unsleepingly merciless judgments on others? Is our history built on mendacity and murder and violent exclusion of the discomfiting other? On the other hand, has our religious search for life's deepest meaning not amounted to a necrophiliac adjustment to the status quo, but rather led to an all-inclusive hope, to such a fullness of life that death is merely an incidental occurrence in a universe made luminous through the coming of Christ?

It helps, then, to ask, throughout the cacophony of conflict and disputation of these pages of the Gospel: What kind of generativity is Jesus trying to link us to? What kind of "paternity" is he forming within us? Though the answer might be clear, the process is dramatic, demanding levels of renunciation and dimensions of openness for which even the religious are ill-prepared.

There is no question, at least in John's Gospel, of God becoming the Father, or of Jesus becoming the Son. The issue is rather that of our own becoming—whether or not those addressed by the Son allow themselves to be formed in a relationship to life-giving God, the Father of Jesus: "To those who received him he gave power to become the children of God" (1:12) There is no bland assumption in John that "after all, we are all God's children";[13] for its concern is the question: By which "God" have we been begotten, and with what result? Jesus offers a transformation, a divine generativity in terms of life, truth, light, and love on the Father's side, and of total surrender to God's will on our part. God's children are born "not of blood, nor of the will of the flesh nor of the will of man, but of God" (1:13). But other wills are at work, each with its diabolic generativity—death, mendacity, darkness, and hatred, which lead to a self-enclosure that only the force of truth can explode. The flickering light of " human "glory" must yield to the "glory that comes from God" (12:43). For believers of every generation, the fierce therapy of this section of the Fourth Gospel forces into the open questions that so often lie hidden in our capacity to use religion to hide from God, and to reduce the fullness of life to the scope of our own self-serving projects.

This knotty section of the Gospel, while provoking endless exegetical comment, is not usually visited by theology, apart from, say, the reference to the Spirit (7:39), and the "I am" sayings (8:12, 28, 58). Systematic Christology, given the tortuous catalog of conflicts reported in this part of the text, tends to hurry through it, perhaps to dwell on the symbolism of light (8:12), but finding no point of special doctrinal interest. Trinitarian theology is similarly at a loss: after noting a certain reciprocity of relationships between the Father and the Son (8:50), what more is to be said? More than anything, this section is so conflictual that it tends to be quietly set aside, given the more irenic and ecumenical concerns of theology today, one happy feature of which is a dialogue of reconciliation with the Jewish people.

Nonetheless, for the Johannine experience of God, this section of the Gospel[14] does have a special importance, if not on the level of doctrine, then certainly in the texture and movement of faith's experience of God. Here we must insist on our remarks in the introduction on the term "the Jews." This segment of the Johannine writings pierces to a special depth when all readers of this Gospel begin to feel the possibility that they themselves can be numbered among Jesus' antagonists. Whether we be Christians or Jews, priests, theologians, laity, or church authorities, or anyone else in the great drama of human history, a hermeneutics of humility is in order. It is possible for all of us, or any of us at different times, to be contributing to the culture of the Antichrist, as it infects our history and relationships with one another with a murderous lie, to cause the self-centeredness that makes us either indifferent or resistant to the gift of the life-transforming revelation of God in Christ. The task of the church is to communicate this "word of life" (1 John 1:1) to the world. But it is also an imperative for all who consider themselves Christian to ask: Are we merely believing that we believe? What if this "revealed truth" were true? And, if it is, what difference has it made?

In other words, to return to the more technical vocabulary previously employed, the experience of God in the Gospel is informed by a *constitutive* meaning, a remaking and transformation of our identity by the "Father who is still working." It entails a continuing conversion, a renunciation of other "paternities" for the sake of the paternity of the Father whom Jesus reveals: "In your light we see light" (Ps 36:9).

Notes

1. 1:18, 51; 3:13; 4:10; 5:19, 23, 30; 6:28–29, 46, etc.
2. 3:17, 34; 4:34; 5:23, 24, 30, 36–38.
3. Cf. also Isa 10:25; 54:7; Jer 51:33; Hos 1:4; Hag 2:6.
4. See John 8:14, 22; 13:3, 33, 36; 14:4, 5, 28; 6:5, 10, 17.
5. Cf. Ezek 11:19; 36:26–27; 39:29; Isa 44:3; Joel 2:26; 3:1.
6. On the connection of the gift of the Spirit with Jesus' glorification in death, G. D. Badcock, *Light of Truth and Fire of Love,* 31–34.
7. Jacques Derrida, *Of Spirit: Heidegger and the Question,* G. Bennington and R. Bowlby, trans. (Chicago: University of Chicago Press, 1989), in deconstructing the Heideggerian language of *Geist* with its pernicious associations with Nazi ideology, implicitly underscores the theological necessity of connecting the gift of the Spirit to Jesus' self-giving on the cross.
8. On the importance of the symbol of light for Christian theology, Jaroslav Pelikan, *The Light of the World: A Basic Image in Early Christian Thought* (New York: Harper and Brothers, 1962).
9. Cf. LXX Isa 41:4; 43:10, 13; 45:18; 46:4; 48:12.
10. Note here that in Aquinas' presentation of "the divine missions," the Father, though not sent like the Son and the Spirit, is nonetheless "given" in the gift of grace, and thus present with the Son as the source of the missions (*Summa Theol.,* 1, 43, 4, ad 1; ad 2).
11. Cf. also Deut 32:6; Jer 3:4, 19; 31:9; Isa 63:16; 64:7.
12. Friedrich Nietzsche, *The Antichrist,* in *The Portable Nietzsche,* Walter Kaufmann, ed. and trans. (New York: The Viking Press, 1972), 585–586.
13. See James Alison, *Raising Abel,* 63–75; and *The Joy of Being Wrong: Original Sin through Easter Eyes* (New York: Crossroad, 1998), 22–63.
14. We omit 7:53–8:1–11, which however canonically secure and theologically significant is deemed, in general scholarly opinion, to be an insertion in the Fourth Gospel. See F. J. Moloney, *The Gospel of John,* Sacra Pagina 4 (Collegeville: The Liturgical Press, 1998), 258–265.

8

New Sight for the Man
Born Blind (9:1–38)

This celebrated account tells of how a congenitally blind beggar comes to the experience of a new birth and a new vision: "No one can see the kingdom of God without being born again, from above" (3:3). He will be among those who will see "heaven opened" and the "Son of Man" as the way, connecting what is above to what is below (1:51). The "works of God" will bring about in the man-born-blind a new birth, a new vision, a new witness, and a new worship.

1. God Works...

1. As he passed by he saw a man blind from birth. 2. And his disciples asked him, "Rabbi, who sinned, this man or his parents, that he was born blind?" 3. Jesus answered, "It was not that this man sinned, or his parents, but that the works of God might be manifest in him. 4. We must work the works of the one who sent me while it is day; night comes when no one can work. 5. As long as I am in the world, I am the light of the world. 6. As he said this he spat on the ground and made clay of the spittle and anointed the man's eyes with the clay, 7. saying to him, "Go, wash in the pool of Siloam" (which means the Sent One). So he went and washed and came back seeing. (9:1–7)

The setting is still the Feast of Tabernacles, even though Jesus has now moved outside the Temple precincts. The light of the world (8:12; 9:5) sees the man who has never seen. "The true light that enlightens everyone" (1:9) comes into the darkened world of a blind and despised human being. The disciples also see him, but without the vision of their master. Their eyes are clouded by an ancient and enduring religious prejudice. Since God cannot be the author of evil,[1] they ask the logical question about this seemingly "God-forsaken" blind beggar: "Who sinned…?"

Jesus refuses to accept their theological judgment of the situation, with its easy imputation of guilt to the sufferer and of vindictive justice to God. He brings his disciples back to the fundamental truth of what the Father is doing. The true God does not legitimate negative judgment on a suffering human being. The God of salvation is at work within the darkness and blindness shrouding the human condition. In what Jesus will do, God is revealing himself (9:3). God's works are not aimed at judgment, but to bring healing, enlightenment, and new birth into the otherwise hopeless situation of this sufferer. Despite the darkness gathering around him, and the obscurity that will inevitably affect all human beings, Jesus, "the light of the world," associates his disciples with him in his light-giving mission to the world: "*We* must work the works of him who sent me…" (9:4).

After anointing the blind man's eyes with a clay made from the dust and his spittle, Jesus commands him to go and wash in the pool of Siloam—which leads to a happy outcome. The Gospel explains the name *Siloam* in terms of a popular etymology: the Sent One. The symbolism of water and light associated with the Feast of Tabernacles is enriched with new meaning. It is not a ritual libation in the pool of Siloam that effects the cure, but contact with the "living water" (7:37) flowing from Jesus, preeminently "the Sent One" (cf. 3:17, 34; 5:36; 13:8). The "light of the world" (8:12; 9:5) has begun to shine, revealing the works of God.

2. The Cost of the Cure

In the subsequent discussions, the cured man becomes a crux of division (9:8–12). And beyond that, as on previous occasions, the activity of Jesus provokes schism and decision. In the midst of the ensuing conflict, the man reports the truth as he now sees it. He makes clear that *he* is the one who has been cured (9:9b); and that "the man called Jesus" had intervened to give him sight (9:11). As to where Jesus is, he replies, "I do not know" (9:12b). His admission of not knowing is a step toward a fuller seeing—in contrast to the self-sufficiency of his judges, whose all-knowing pretensions will lead to deeper blindness (cf. 9:24–25).

Efforts to verify the identity of the man who had been cured and the whereabouts of the one who cured him lead to a more thorough and threatening investigation. Neighbors bring the previously blind beggar to the Pharisees (9:13). The guardians of the Law learn that Jesus has done this work of healing on the Sabbath (9:14–16). Their interrogation turns to an issue deeper than the marvelous nature of the cure: the origin of Jesus. He cannot be from God if he breaks the Sabbath; and yet, how can he perform such signs if he is a violator of the Law? (9:16). The cured man is questioned: "What do you say about him since he has opened your eyes?" (9:17b). Despite being the object of biting sarcasm, he shows evidence of increasing vision in his affirmation: "He is a prophet" (9:17c). New vision leads to a new courage in giving witness to the Word of God.

Unwilling or unable to imagine anything but deceit and pretense, "the Jews" call on the testimony of his parents. Their response is wisely minimal. They sense that the real trial is not about their son, but about this Jesus, just as they already suspect the likely fate of anyone who credits him with a divine mission (9:18–22). And so they put the responsibility back on their son: "He is of age, ask him" (9:23). His new sight thus brings immediate responsibilities, along with a peculiar isolation in the midst of those who do not see.

3. Witnessing to God

24. So for a second time they called the man who had been blind and said to him, "Give God the praise; we know that this man is a sinner." 25. He answered, "Whether he is a sinner I do not know; one thing I know, that though I was blind, now I see." 26. They said to him, "What did he do to you? How did he open your eyes?" 27. He answered them, "I have told you already and you would not listen. Why do you want to hear it again? Do you too want to become his disciples?" 28. And they reviled him, saying, "You are his disciple, but we are disciples of Moses. 29. We know that God has spoken to Moses, but as for this man, we do not know where he comes from." 30. The man answered, "Why, this is a marvel! You do not know where he comes from, and yet he opened my eyes. 31. We know that God does not listen to sinners, but if anyone is a worshiper of God and does his will, God listens to him. 32. Never since the world began has it been heard that anyone opened the eyes of a man born blind. 33. If this man were not from God, he could do nothing." 34. They answered him, "You were born in utter sin, and would you teach us?" And they cast him out. (9:24–34)

"The Jews" once more interrogate the blind man. The traditional formula, "Give God the praise," rings with special irony, given that the blind man has been cured "that the works of God might be made manifest in him" (9:3). The irony is intensified in the arrogant judgment now made on Jesus, so notably contrasting with the blind man's honest admission of ignorance: "*We know* this man is a sinner (9:24). Questions are implied: Whose "God" is being revealed on this Sabbath? Who knows how God is acting? The man poses such questions in the most unsettling fashion: "Do you too want to become his disciples?" (9:27). Though, in this context, the question drips with dramatic irony, he does not mean to mock. The bounty of God's giving is offered to all. For the once-blind man to receive new sight means that he must witness to the availability of this gift even to those who now judge him. He is no longer the diminished individual presumed to be under a religious cloud, but one acting out a new dignity as a witness to the truth. By performing a sign for him, Jesus has made a witness out of him. His signs inspire faith only as they change believers into living witnesses to the truth in their midst (cf. 2:11, 23–25). It remains possible, however, to see such signs, and yet to remain untouched. But to the degree the truth to which the sign points enters into those who see it, faith emerges in the authenticity of witness.

In any event, the man who honestly witnesses to what Jesus has done is reviled; and the question of the true God dramatically reemerges as this defenseless disciple of Jesus is contrasted to the mighty "disciples of Moses" (9:28). For them, however, another kind of blindness threatens. The Mosaic gift is becoming a blind spot, making the light that now shines intolerable. By clinging to the former gift, they are looking back to what was, rather than opening their eyes to see what is now being revealed. They know where they stand in their religious tradition, whereas Jesus has come from nowhere: "We know that God has spoken through Moses, but as for this man, we do not know where he comes from" (9:29). God's Word has been judged to be limited and contained by their expert knowledge. The truth of the Word become flesh to dwell among them (1:14) is disallowed by what they so confidently know. Both their "we know," in regard to God, and their "we do not know," in reference to the origin of Jesus, are in contrast to the knowing and not-knowing of the man who has been cured (9:25). His honesty was a step toward faith; their admission is a refusal to ask basic questions: Has God's revelation been exhausted in what they already know? Is there no room for this further, this final gift? Have the works of God come to an end?

In the discussion that follows, consideration of the unknown—and, indeed, unexplored—origins of Jesus is the focus. The miraculous gift of sight to the blind man demands a divine explanation. At least he thinks so. The fact that he was cured, that this was effected by Jesus, that it happened on the Sabbath, makes the question of God's involvement in Jesus' action, and of Jesus' relationship to God, inescapable (9:30–33). Jesus cannot be a sinner, since God has listened to him. Anyone able to bring about such an unprecedented cure (biblically speaking), must be uniquely related to the God of creation. If "never since the world began" has such a deed happened, then Jesus must have some connection to what was "in the beginning" (Gen 1:1; John 1:1). The God of the beginning is being made known in "the man called Jesus" (9:11).

Stung into reaction, "the Jews" reiterate the conventional theology previously expressed by the disciples (9:3). It has the advantage, not only of demeaning the man's testimony, but also of precluding other possibilities, above all that of Jesus being from God: "You were born in utter sin, and would you teach us?" (9:34). The man who has borne witness to the light is "cast out" as innately sinful and God-forsaken. The closed, defensive

210

religious world of his interrogators can allow no room either for Jesus, nor for his witness, nor for new vision and new birth from above—nor for the God without whom all would count for "nothing" (9:33).

4. True Worship

35. Jesus heard that they had cast him out, and having found him he said, "Do you believe in the Son of Man?" 36. He answered, "And who is he, sir, that I might believe in him?" 37. Jesus said to him, "You have seen him, and it is he who speaks to you." 38. He said, "Lord, I believe"; and he worshiped him. (9:35–38)

Jesus' initiative continues, for the works of God are to be fully manifested (9:3). He seeks out the man who had been expelled from the circle of those who pretend to see. Though banished from the festive light of the Temple precincts, he will receive a further gift of vision. Jesus asks him whether he believes in the Son of Man (9:35). As in previous instances,[2] this title indicates Jesus' mission to reveal the Father, in the flesh of the human world of questions and conflicts. Once more the man admits to not knowing; but now in the presence of Jesus, expresses his readiness to believe (9:36). His openness to God's revelation and his already courageous witness to a truth that escaped his judges is met with the assurance: "You have seen him..." (9:37). The formerly blind man has now received the full gift of sight: he not only sees, but sees *him*. Though no one has ever seen God (1:34; 3:11, 22; 8:38), Jesus, as the Son, has revealed what he has seen (6:46; 8:38). The vision he communicates is the cure for human blindness. God will be revealed when, in this new vision, the believer will look upon the Son of Man (3:13–15). Darkness has not overcome the light (1:9). In seeing the Son of Man, faith sees heaven made open (1:51).

Seeing the Son of Man also means the new hearing of faith: "...and it is he who speaks to you" (9:37b). As the incarnation of the divine Word (1:1–2, 14), Jesus communicates what he has heard from the Father (3:11, 34; 8:25–26, 38). Therefore he speaks with the word of authority (7:17, 18, 26, 46), of Spirit and life (6:53)—and of judgment, too, for those who give no hearing to his message (cf. 8:40). So involved is God in what Jesus speaks, so generatively present is the Father in what the Son sees and hears, that this Son is God's Word. What was declared to the Samaritan woman, "I am he"(4:26), resonates in this situation as well.

To see and to hear God in Jesus is the gift being offered to the once-blind, doubted, rejected, unknowing, and now excommunicated man. Jesus is no longer someone referred to by him as a man (9:11), nor as a prophet (9:17), nor as someone "from God" (9:33). Speaking as one who now sees in the presence of the light of the world, and hears the voice of the Word in whom all things are created, he confesses, "Lord, I believe," and bows down in worship. The works of God have thus been made manifest in him (9:3). The Father has sought out and found a true worshiper "in spirit and truth" (4:23).[3]

The God revealed by the Son of Man is not indifferent to human suffering, nor constricted by the religious traditions of the past. The Father shines into the human condition with a new and final gift in the person of Jesus: "God is light and in him there is no darkness at all" (1 John 1:5). To face Jesus with the new eyes of faith is to see God made known.

5. The Experience of God?

The vision of faith leads to a radical self-expropriation, the closer the believer comes to the revealed God. The once-blind man in whom "the works of God" are made manifest experiences the advent of God into his life as an extreme dislocation, in regard to his former social identity. He experienced, step by step, a process of being taken out of himself. Jesus finds him at the precise point of his isolation from the community of his neighbors, parents, and religious authorities. When the whole fabric of his former identity seems to have been torn apart, the moment of revelation occurs: "He said, 'Lord, I believe,' and worshiped him" (9:38). Though Jesus' own seeing singled out the blind man for a cure in accord with the unfathomable initiative of God, his recovery of sight means growing estrangement from his own people. When his eyes were opened, it was to see a world grown hostile to him. Like the one who cured him, when he came with new vision to his own, and his people did not accept him (1:11). Their judgment on a congenitally blind beggar as innately guilty and God-forsaken was more theologically acceptable to them than the divinely wrought transformation that occurred. But his eyes were opened—on hearing the voice and feeling the touch (9:6) of "the Son of Man" whose mission it was to reveal God. Seeing the face of Jesus, feeling his touch, and hearing his word, brought him into the presence of another who surpassed the categories and relationships of his former world. He now had to step out into a new identity, and a new world of relationships oriented in accord with the light that had entered his life.

His only security lies in surrender to the Other, in openness to the more and greater in comparison to what was.[4] His cure does not lead to self-regarding enjoyment of sight, for his newly opened eyes turn to God: "If this man were not from God...." (9:33). And in that new attentiveness, he sees, hears, believes, and adores the one in whom God is revealed.[5] From being born into blindness and beggary, he has become one who now sees the

Light of the world, who hears the Word of God, who testifies to what he has seen and heard. Finally, he believes and worships.

What is remarkable in this precious narrative is the extraordinary vitality and assured objectivity of a man who began life in the most abject of circumstances. In terms of the previous chapter, the truth has set him free (8:32). His transformed subjectivity, evidenced in his new capacities to see, to hear, to believe, and to worship, opens onto the objectivity of God's revelation in Jesus standing before him: "Genuine objectivity is the fruit of authentic subjectivity."[6] More than anything else, it is the story of God's formation of a witness to the transforming truth of what is being revealed.[7]

Notes

1. Exod 20:5; Num 14:18; Deut 5:9; Tob 3:3–4.
2. See 1:51; 3:13–14; 5:27; 6:27, 53, 62.
3. Von Balthasar's words are to the point: "A superabundant light beams forth...before which every subjective kind of seeking must lay down its arms," *The Glory of the Lord* I, 191.
4. Ibid., 22.
5. Ibid., 237.
6. B. Lonergan, *Method in Theology,* 292.
7. A valuable reference here is David F. Ford, *Self and Salvation: Being Transformed* (Cambridge: Cambridge University Press, 1999), especially 73–104.

9

<hr>

The Father's En*fold*ing Love, and the Good Shepherd (9:39—10:21)

1. The Shepherd of Israel

The light of the world brings its own judgment on the willful blindness of the Pharisees (9:39–41). Instead of looking toward him, and leading others to the light, they have turned from him and become false guides. By now employing "the figure" (10:6) of the sheepfold and its shepherd, Jesus provocatively underscores the deficiencies of the pretended guardians of Israel (10:1, 5, 6–13).[1]

> 1. "Amen, amen I say to you, anyone who does not enter the sheepfold by the door but climbs in by another way is a thief and a robber. 2. The one who enters by the door is the shepherd of the sheep. 3. To him the doorkeeper opens; the sheep hear his voice, and he calls his own sheep by name and leads them out. 4. When he has brought out all his own, he goes before them, and the sheep follow him, for they know his voice. 5. A stranger they will not follow, but they will flee from him, for they do not know the voice of strangers." 6. This figure Jesus used with them, but they did not understand what he was saying to them. (10:1–6)

The image of the good shepherd appears repeatedly in biblical tradition to describe the manner in which God cares for and leads his people. Despite the grief of exile, the prophets spoke of the all-embracing providence of God in these terms: "He who scattered Israel will gather him, and will keep him as a shepherd a flock" (Jer 31:10).[2] There is a special tenderness associated with this image: "He will feed his flock like a shepherd; he will gather the lambs in his arms, and carry them in his bosom, and gently lead the mother sheep" (Isa 40:11).[3] After the disappearance of the monarch, there were predictions of future Davidic figures who would guide Israel.[4] The prophet Micah saw this role concentrated in a single messianic shepherd (Micah 5:2–5). This one shepherd will bring the scattered people together as one flock (Ezek 34:23–24; 37:24).[5] These prophecies provide the historical and symbolic background in which to understand the culmination of the works of God in the Good Shepherd. He will provide life-giving sustenance to the people (6:10; cf. Ps 23:1–3), and gather into one the scattered flock of God's children (11:52).

2. En*fold*ing Love

7. So Jesus again said to them, "Amen, amen, I say to you, I am the door of the sheep. 8. All who came before me are thieves and robbers; but the sheep did not heed them. 9. I am the door; whoever enters by me will be saved, and will go in and out and find pasture. 10. The thief comes only to steal and kill and destroy; I came that they may have life, and have it abundantly. 11. I am the good shepherd. The good shepherd lays down his life for his sheep. 12. The hireling who is not a shepherd, and does not own the sheep, sees the wolf coming and leaves the sheep and flees; and the wolf

snatches them and scatters them, 13. because he is a hireling and does not care for the sheep. 14. I am the good shepherd; I know my own and my own know me, 15. as the Father knows me and I know the Father; and I lay down my life for the sheep. 16. And I have other sheep that are not of this fold; I must bring them also, and they will heed by voice. So there shall be one flock, one shepherd. 17. For this reason the Father loves me, because I lay down my life that I might take it up again. 18. No one takes it from me, but I lay it down of my own accord. I have power to lay it down and power to take it up again; this charge I have received from my Father." (10:7–18)

After the polemical contrast between the faithless shepherds and the true guardian of the flock, Jesus presents himself as the *good* shepherd. The atmosphere of jarring opposition, betrayal, and death changes to one of mutuality—and of limitless self-giving love. The Good Shepherd loves his sheep, even to the point of laying down his life (10:15). The implication is that only the extreme of self-giving love can counter the stalking evils that threaten the life and unity of the one fold.

The person of the Father enters the picture. He is the one who, in absolute contrast to those who have rejected the Son, loves Jesus in what he is doing, and inspires his self-giving love for his flock. This points a dramatic contrast with the self-promotion of other pretended shepherds. The image of God as the shepherd of Israel, and that of the future Davidic shepherd who was to come, fuse in the one reality—in the mission of the Son. Jesus is loved by the Father in laying down his life for his sheep. The Father loves Jesus in his selfless shepherding; just as he loves the Father as the source of all he does, carrying out the charge the Father had given him (10:18b). All his freedom flows from his obedience to the Father. And the Father, as originating life and love, engenders the Son as the Good Shepherd selflessly guiding all who follow him to the fullness of life.

This *good* shepherd appears not only in contrast to the bad shepherds that have blocked access to true life, but suggests the meaning, unknown to any previous tradition, of what this goodness implies. Most often, it suggests a reciprocity of loving familiarity between Jesus and his own: "I know my own and my own know me" (10:14b). But the bond between the Good Shepherd and his own finds its source and exemplar in the mutuality existing between the Father and the Son: "...as the Father knows me, and I know the Father" (10:15). Thus, the bond between Jesus and his disciples derives from the primordial communion existing between the Father and his only Son. While the image of a good shepherd is something of a commonplace in the expression of past messianic hopes, the unique character of this Good Shepherd reveals a divine milieu of relationships, mutual knowledge, and self-surrendering love. Yet this field of communion is not that of a self-enclosed security. The privileged flock is not removed from the harsh reality of the God-resistant world into which the Son has been sent. Only through Jesus' surrender to the Father in the face of lethal opposition will the promised intimacy and abundance of life result.

The "enfolding" circle of communion—including the Father, the self-sacrificing Son, and the disciples—looks beyond its present realization to a future fullness, to those "other sheep," so that the outcome will be "one flock, one shepherd" (10;16). Where previously God's pastoral love privileged the flock of Israel, it now unfolds beyond former boundaries, and reaches into future times to gather the hitherto "scattered children of God" in an expanding circle of communion (11:52).

In laying down his life for the one emerging flock, Jesus is loved by the Father who himself has so loved the world in an intimate and unreserved act of self-giving (3:16). The Father has given his Son; the Son is laying down his life to accomplish the Father's will. The love of the Father affirms the love of the Son: "For this reason, the Father loves me, because I lay down my life, that I might take it up again" (10:17). Jesus' authoritative assurance, concerning the laying down of his life that he may take it up again, flows from the loving intention of the Father animating every aspect of his mission (10:17).[6] This self-giving love is vulnerable to the world's violence. It cannot but appear as weakness to those outside the one fold. But for those who have been gathered to the God revealed in Jesus, it is the glory of a selfless communion of life which is being shown forth as truly divine.[7]

Jesus is not, therefore, consigning himself to the course of a blind series of malicious events outside his or the Father's control. Although his mission is lived out under the threat of the growing opposition, there is an "hour" in the making which will reveal the true God, identified by Jesus as "my Father." The Baptist had acclaimed Jesus as the Lamb of God who takes away the sin of the world (1:29). He will indeed take away the world's sin, not by simply allowing his life to be taken away, but by giving it up to the Father's purpose: "No one takes it from me, but I lay it down on my own accord. I have the power to lay it down, and the power to take it again. This charge I have received from my Father" (10:18).

The death and the resurrection of the life-giving Good Shepherd are governed by the saving will of the Father. For Jesus to lay down his life does mean genuine death. Still, it is a dying determined by the will of the Father to manifest God's limitless love. Thus the Son's final hour is the revelation of the beginning that otherwise would have remained unknown. His surrender to the Father is not the decision of a human ego simply defying the forces massed against him. Nor is it an act of blind obedience to some extrinsic and arbitrary divine command. It is the voluntary living out of his primordial relationship with the Father. In this he becomes "the way" (14:6) to be followed by all future disciples (1 John 3:16; cf. also John 21:15–19).[8] His "power" to take up again the life he has laid down does not mean that he cancels his previous act of self-abandonment. This "taking up" looks to the essential completion of his mission to fulfill his Father's will. In this his "power" is distinguished from all other human powers and authorities, even that of Israel's patriarchs and prophets, for it flows from the original charge he has received from his Father, and points to their unique relationship (10:18c).[9]

The paradoxical conjunction of Jesus' self-surrender and power, of laying down his life and taking it up again, flows from the freedom of self-giving love transcending all previous categories. As a result, all the religious symbolism of Israel's hope, be it expressed in terms of God's relationship to the Chosen People as their shepherd, or of the coming of the Messiah among them, is given a completely new sense.

3. The Divided Flock

> 19. There was again a division among the Jews because of these words. 20. Many of them said, "He has a demon, and he is mad; why listen to him?" 21. Others said, "These are not the sayings of one who has a demon. Can a demon open the eyes of the blind?" (10:19–21)

Faced with this new and demanding sense of what God is bringing about through the selfless love of the Good Shepherd, "the Jews" are divided. In their prayer they had encountered the menace of another shepherd: "Like sheep they are appointed for Sheol; Death shall be their shepherd" (Ps 49:14). Yet now faced with the alternative, beneficent possibility, some still express utter incredulity regarding the unique "goodness" of the one who is addressing them: only demonic possession or madness could explain such extravagant claims and promises. For others, the words and deeds of this man point to other, more wonderful possibilities: "Can a demon open the eyes of the blind?" (10:21).

And so, the themes of the Feast of Tabernacles comes to a close. In a document contemporary with the Fourth Gospel, there is a poignant expression of Jewish grief over the destruction of Jerusalem and the loss of the Temple. First, we hear the lament of the people:

> ...for the shepherds of Israel have perished, and the lamps that gave light are extinguished, and the fountains from which we used to drink have withheld their streams. Now we have been left in the darkness and in the thick forest and in the aridity of the desert.

Then, the speaker of wisdom courageously replies:

> Shepherds and lanterns and fountains came from the Law, and when we go away, the Law will abide. If you therefore look upon the Law and are intent upon wisdom, then the lamp will not be wanting and the shepherd will not give way, and the fountain will not dry up (*The Apocalypse of 2 Bar* 77:11, 13–16).

This remarkable oracle evidences Judaism's world of postwar struggle to find itself—and the presence of God in the midst of the destruction that had occurred. The path to life must continue in holding fast to the Law. In contrast, the faith of the Johannine community was focused elsewhere. In Jesus Christ, God had brought to perfection the Mosaic dispensation. There is a positive meaning arising out of the rubble of Jerusalem and the dismemberment of its people. Even in such a time of grief and violence, salvation has come to the world. The light shines, the living water flows, and the Good Shepherd leads those who would hear his voice. The Father is still working...

4. What Kind of God?

As with the other "I am..." declarations of Jesus,[10] his self-presentation as the "door" (10:7) and "the good shepherd" (10:14) describes his revelatory and redemptive action. This does not suggest that such symbolic expressions are purely "functional" descriptions of Jesus' relationship to the world, as though the original identity of Jesus and the God from whom he comes are hidden behind such metaphors. The logic of interpretation looks back to the *Logos* in whom all things come into being and have life and light. More often, each of these symbols implies Jesus' primary relationship with the Father, and the Father's ever-generative relationship to Jesus, his only Son, and those given him by the same Father: "I know my own and my own know me, as the Father knows me and I know the Father" (10:14b–15). The abundance of life resides precisely in the life that emanates from the Father, and flows through Jesus to the world (6:57).[11]

In John's Gospel, the distinctions between the immanent reality of God *(in se)* and the economic relatedness of God to the world *(pro nobis),* and between the "ontological" and the "functional" considerations of theology, tend to collapse in the transparent reciprocity of relationships between the Father and the Son. The Son is constituted, as it were, in his identity and mission through his relationship to the Father. For his part, the Father is constituted in his paternal self-giving in relationship to the Son. In every aspect of the being and action of the Word, there is the "verb" of the Father's timeless self-utterance and engendering. The "subsistent relationship" of the Father is revealed in his ceaseless generation of the Son, even while the identity and mission of the Son in intelligible only in his continuing to come forth from the Father, to reveal the loving source of life and light.[12]

In the account of the Good Shepherd, we note the distinctive Johannine emphasis on the initiative of God's love. Only within such a horizon will the commandments to love God and the neighbor make sense. To receive the outgoing love flowing from the Father through Jesus into the world, believers experience the imperative to enter into its movement of self-giving and even of self-dispossession. Since God has first of all 'obeyed' the commandment to love without reserve, all the imperatives inherent in Christian life are only an echo of the charge that Jesus has received from his Father (John 10:18; 12:49, 50). While the Son acts in complete freedom, his freedom is totally at the service of the charge he has received from the Father—to give his life for the world—thus to gather the scattered sheep into one fold. His life, lived as the laying down of life for others, is the form of eternal life flowing forth from the Father (12:50a). The great theological "reduction" of John's Gospel narrative found in the First Letter of John is already in evidence: "We know love by this, that he laid down his life for us—and we ought to lay down our lives for one another" (1 John 3:16). Behind such an exegesis of the *effective* meaning of God lies always the witness of the one who has made God known (1:18).

The love that is thus revealed is not a partial revelation of an otherwise invisible divinity hidden in darkness. The obedience of the Good Shepherd giving himself for his sheep truly manifests what God is: "God is light and in him there is no darkness" (1 John 1:5). The Father so loves the world in giving his only Son

(3:16), and loves the Son in his own self-giving (10:17). This "precedence" of God's love for the world over the Father's love for the Son would be an impenetrable conundrum—unless it is realized that what is being revealed to the world is the very life of the Godhead itself—eternal life now offered to all believers. The measure of faith's experience of God is not limited, even to the most hallowed of religious imperatives (Deut 6:4–6). The Good Shepherd moves in the light of another initiative: "In this is love, not that we loved God, but that he loved us…" (1 John 4:10).[13]

Notes

1. For the strong biblical tradition presenting unfaithful leaders as bad shepherds: Jer 23:1–8; Ezek 34; Zeph 3:3; Zech 10:2–3; 11:4–17, as well as in later Jewish literature (*1 Enoch* 89:12–27, 42–44, 59–70, 74–76; 90:22–25).
2. See also Jer 13:10; 23:2–4.
3. Also Isa 49:9–10; and in the later writings, Zeph 3:19; Mic 2:12; 4:6–7; Qoh 12:11; Sir 18:13.
4. Jer 3:15, cf. 23:4–6; Ezek 34:23–24; 37:24; Zech 13:7–9.
5. Cf. LXX Ps 2:9; *Ps Sol* 17:24, 40; *2 Bar* 77:13–17.
6. As von Balthasar observes, "…this 'authority' is characterized by the commission of the Father. Thereby the trinitarian aspect (including preexistence) of the world of salvation in John is clearly set out, as in the inner nexus between laying down and taking up again, which here appears as the 'power' of the freedom of love to take on the freedom of obedience—a power bestowed by the Father (7:19ff), which can be exercised only as the Father intends." (*The Glory of the Lord VII*, 245, n. 3.)
7. Ibid., 149, 214.
8. Ibid., 247.
9. Ibid., 148, 323.
10. For example, in reference to "the bread of life" (6:35, 51), "the light of the world" (8:12; 9:5), "the resurrection and the life" (11:25), "the way, the truth and the life" (14:6), "the true vine" (15:1).
11. For a theological but deeply biblical reflection on the "I am" sayings, see E. Schillebeeckx, *Christ…*, 384–397.

12. On the necessity of understanding this divine reciprocity of relationships in an active and "verbal" sense, see G. Lafont, *Peut on connaître Dieu...*, 272–277.
13. For an extended reflection along these lines, see von Balthasar, *The Glory of the Lord VII*, 465.

10

========

The Father's Hand
(10:22–42)

Three months after the Feast of Tabernacles, Jesus is walking on a winter morning, during the Feast of the Dedication, in the portico of Solomon (10:22–23). He is just a few hundred yards from where, 200 years before, a terrible sacrilege had been committed. In the reign of Antiochus IV in Syria, the cult of Zeus Olympios had been instituted in Jerusalem; and sacrifice to this pagan deity had been offered in the Temple itself, on an altar built over the altar of holocausts. With the success of the Maccabeean revolt, the pagan abomination was torn down, and the Temple rededicated.

The Feast of the Dedication celebrated the ways of divine providence in enabling Israel to overcome its powerful pagan adversaries, and thus to reclaim the Temple as the site of the true cult of the LORD. Nonetheless, it was impossible to avoid recalling a humiliating failure. A section of Israel had turned away from God to an idol, even in the holiest of places. What happened once remained always a possibility. This sober note sounds in the background in the exchange between Jesus and the Jews about to take place.

1. The Father: Greater Than All

24. So the Jews gathered round him and said to him, "How long will you keep us in suspense? If you are

226

the Christ, tell us plainly." 25. Jesus answered them, "I told you, and you do not believe. The works that I do in my Father's name, they bear witness to me; 26. but you do not believe because you do not belong to my sheep. 27. My sheep hear my voice, and I know them, and they follow me; 28. and I give them eternal life, and they shall never perish, and no one shall snatch them out of my hand. 29. My Father who has given them to me, is greater than all, and no one can snatch them out of the Father's hand. I and the Father are one." (10:24–29)

The celebration of the Feast of Tabernacles, which immediately preceded the present account of Jesus in Jerusalem for the Feast of Dedication, had focused strongly on the question of the Messiah. Now "the Jews" ask him directly, even if ironically: "How long will you keep us in suspense?...tell us plainly" (10:24). What is, in fact, "plain" is that Jesus will not be made to fit into their understanding of the Law (cf. 10:34). Neither can he be allowed to come between them and their God (10:38). Since they will not listen to what he says, he refers them to the works he does in his Father's name. Such works bear witness to him. He has claimed the Sabbath privilege of judging and giving life (5:19–30). He has offered himself as the bread from heaven, bringing to perfection that nourishment once contained in the Law (6:44–50). He gives the water of life, and is the light of the world (7:37–38; 8:12; 9:5). He fulfills and surpasses all the messianic hopes of Israel. But his words and his works, even though performed in the name of his Father, make no difference in this pocket of intense antagonism.[1] His adversaries were unable to move beyond their closed religious system: they know that God spoke to Moses; and they don't know where Jesus comes from (9:29).

He offers a radical explanation of the contradictory responses he meets with. On the one hand, the fundamental antagonism of "the Jews" to him means that they are not numbered among his sheep (10:26). On the other hand, his sheep hear his voice, are known by him, follow him, and receive eternal life from him. They will not come to ruin, nor be snatched from his hand (10:27–28). They will be protected from those intent on deceit and destruction—false shepherds, thieves, robbers, and wolves (cf. 10:1, 5, 8, 12).

Significantly, it is the Father who brings about the flock's acceptance of Jesus. It is as though Jesus' hand (10:28) is made firm in its hold on his own because it is held in the "greater" hand of the Father. Jesus has been given his followers by the one from whom he comes, who is greater than all antagonistic and destructive forces: "...no one is able snatch them out of the Father's hand" (10:29). Once more, the Johannine *greater²* invites the believer into a horizon extending beyond the conflictual and violent exchanges affecting Jesus' mission to the world, to the recognition of the original generative presence of the Father in what is taking place.³ The "holding power" of the Son and that of the Father are two aspects of the one outreach of God: "I and the Father are one" (10:30). The God "who will feed his flock, [who]...will gather the lambs in his arms" (Isa 40:10), and the promised one "who will stand and feed his flock in the strength of the LORD, in the majesty of the name of the LORD his God (Mic 5:4), are one. The Father has reached into history with his saving hand; and that hand opens out to the world in the healing hand of Jesus, even as he does the Sabbath work of God—healing, holding, gathering, protecting, and forming the flock into one fold around one shepherd.⁴

The Father and the Son are one in the divine activity of shepherding Israel, and in reaching out to all who are not of this fold, so that there will be one fold and one shepherd (10:16).

The unbreakable unity of purpose existing between the Father and Son implies a deeper level of communion. Jesus is the recipient of the Father's gift (10:29). Further, the Father loves him as he lays down his life for his sheep (10:17). Indeed, the Father loves the Son and shows him all that he himself is doing (5:20), just as, having life in himself, he has granted the Son to have life in himself (5:26), and given all things into his hands (13:3). The Father's unreserved love for the Son expresses the reality of divine paternity being fulfilled and extended in Jesus' mission to the world. The love of the Father for the world is thereby a joyous consent to the Son's self-giving for the life of the world. God is revealed as "Being-in-love." The relationships existing between the Father and the Son constitute the "love-life" into which believers are to be drawn, to participate in it in their own loving: "God's love was revealed among us in this way: God sent his only Son into the world so that we might live through him" (1 John 4:9). The love that the Father is (1 John 4:8, 16b), is revealed to the world by being enacted in the mission of the Son.

2. "The Father Is in Me..."

31. The Jews took up stones again to stone him. 32. Jesus answered them, "I have shown you many good works from the Father; for which of these do you stone me?" 33. The Jews answered him, "It is not for a good work that we stone you but for blasphemy; because you, being a man, make yourself God." 34. Jesus answered them, "Is it not written in your law, 'I said, you are gods?' 35. If he called them gods to whom the word of God came (and the scripture always remains in force), 36. do you say of him whom the Father consecrated and sent into the world, 'You are blaspheming,'

because I said, 'I am the Son of God?' 37. If I am not doing the works of my Father, then do not believe me; 38. but if I do them, even though you do not believe me, believe the works, that you may know and understand that the Father is in me and I am in the Father." 39. Again they tried to arrest him, but he escaped from their hands. (10:31–39)

The conflict reported here indicates that the implications of Jesus' unique relationship with God have surfaced. He has indeed called God "his own Father" (5:18), although he has never claimed to be, despite allegations to the contrary, either in word or deed, "equal to God" (5:18). His adversaries resent what they take to be Jesus' challenge to their religious authority. They project their resentful imagination onto his relationship with the Father. To their minds, his claim to be one with the Father must mean an assertion of equality born of envy and opposition. The possibility of the Son's being united with the Father in a way that originates with the Father himself is beyond their religious imagination. They are affectively and imaginatively outside the reality being disclosed. For them, the words and actions of this man must be in opposition to the God of the their religious observance. His declaration, that he and the Father are one (10:30), directly contradicts the meaning of the Feast they are celebrating. For this reason they judge that he deserves to be executed for blasphemy. When Jesus asks them which of the Father's good works has merited the death penalty, his would-be executioners reply that that sentence is deserved, not because of good works, but "because you, being a man, make yourself God" (10:33).

Here the irony of the Gospel is double-edged. The guardians of the Law are intent on killing the Good Shepherd who has come to give the gift of abundant life (10:10). They are implicated in the move to add one more to the list of victims of the violent world. For his part, the Father is showing his love by sending his Son to lay down his life for his sheep (10:17). Though Jesus is ever turned to the Father in love and obedience with the sole purpose of making God known (1:18), he is accused of blasphemy. But his adversaries are intent on keeping God contained in the Temple, restricted to the gift of the Law, and limited by the traditions that flow from it. They have confined God to their past history and, as a consequence, to a closed heaven.

In this they are rejecting a new gift and a new possibility. The gift is the all-surpassing revelation of the one true God now taking place in the Son. And the possibility they disallow is that God's heaven has been opened; and that, through works and words of the Son, God is continuing to act within the world by giving an unprecedented gift. Who then is concerned for the glory of the true God? Who is being guilty of blasphemy? If, as Jesus declares, "I and the Father are one" (10:30), a revolution in Israel's religious awareness is called for. "The Jews," celebrating the Feast of the Dedication, have set the criterion of conversion in not desecrating the Temple and in not adoring pagan gods. Now that criterion has shifted: to be converted to the God of Israel in the world, the Father revealed in the Son.

Jesus attempts to reform their imagination by employing a typical rabbinical form of argument. While his adversaries have been using the witness of tradition to reject the revelation of his Father, he exploits that tradition more positively. There is a movement within it that looks to the truth now being revealed. He cites, as an instance of enduring validity of "your law," the words of the psalm: "I said, 'You are gods'" (Ps 82:6). The revelation of God coming through the law is a reality. God has been acting. The divine Word has already reached Israel, calling believers into privileged communion with God, the symbol of which is the rededicated Temple in their midst. But now there is question of a fuller revelation, and of the culmination of God's gifts in Jesus, the Word and Son of God, now in their midst. "The Jews" must now judge according to another logic, that of the *Logos* incarnate. Their past should have made them receptive to this culminating advent of the Word, not close them against it.

How, then, should they judge concerning the one whom the Father has consecrated and sent into the world? In contrast to the consecration of the Temple altar to the honor of God, there has been a divinely wrought consecration of Jesus as the new embodiment of God's presence. There has been a "sending," a new act of God; and it is occurring in their time. But now the beneficiary is not merely the people of Israel, but the *world* itself (10:36). In such a consecration, the holiness of God is involved. In such a sending, the Father's initiative is revealed as a universal love.

Up to a point, Jesus' adversaries show some recognition of Jesus' claim, even though they put into his mouth a statement he has not in fact made, "I am the Son of God" (10:36). For the sake of argument, Jesus grants that it is a true designation of his identity and mission. Far from being blasphemy, it is a true statement of reality of God's all-surpassing gift. The "word of God," which came to Israel and enabled them to be called "gods" according to the expression of its Law, is now revealed to be indeed the Word of God, present among them as the Son of the Father. Nonetheless, Jesus emphasizes that to accept him does not mean paying personal allegiance to him, without reference to the Father who consecrated and sent him: "If I am not doing the works of my Father, then do not believe me" (10:37). But, given his unreserved dedication to the will of the Father, the works of his Father are being performed. He is the living evidence of the Father's working. "The Jews," confined to the world of "appearances" (7:24), cannot but project onto Jesus' existence in the world of the flesh their own self-centeredness and anxious self-promotion. Concerned to defend themselves and control him as a source of continual vexation and bewilderment, they have insisted that he speak "plainly" (10:24). They are now challenged to give weight to the works that have been performed in the name of God: "But if I do them, even though you do not believe me, believe the works..." (10:38).

In this statement, Jesus' unreserved relatedness to the Father is apparent. The way he appears to them is not the crucial issue: they are not to believe him if he is not doing his Father's works. His "plain" speaking seeks to open for them the only horizon in which his mission can make sense. Those called "gods" by the Law, to whom the word of God has come, are being now addressed by God in a new way. They are thus summoned to adore the God whose works are revealed in the words and work of Jesus himself, so that they might "know and understand that the Father is in me, and I am in the Father" (10:38b).[5] God is no longer to be found, let alone confined, in the Temple. The Father is "in Jesus," as one revealed in him, at work through him, and as drawing all to the Son who reveals him (6:44–46). The Son does not witness to the Father as one apart from or behind what he is doing, but as the generative presence involved in his identity and mission. And Jesus is "in the Father," as the beloved Son, as turned toward him in the beginning; as sent by him and as returning to him; and as loved by the Father in his surrender to God's saving will in regard to the whole world. It can be said, then, that the Son is "in the world" by being completely "in the Father," receiving his identity and mission from this paternal source.[6] These "gods"—as the Law named them—are in effect now refusing to allow themselves to be regenerated by the life-giving love of the Father that the Son embodies.

To their minds, the greater the claims of Jesus regarding his intimacy with God, the more he must be in opposition to their conceptions of God. The Fourth Gospel expresses Jesus' relationship to the Father, not in terms of opposition or rivalry, but in those of communion, unreserved surrender, and union of will: he is the Word who is with God from the beginning (John 1:1), and the Son who is lovingly turned to God in the course of his life (1:18). The reality of God is not to be conceived therefore in terms of a mythic rivalry between the God of Jesus and the God of the Jews. The reality of communion and mutual indwelling existing between the Father and the Son must replace an imaginary opposition: "The Father is in me and I in the Father" (10:38; cf. 14:10–11, 20; 17:21–23).

Neither "knowing" nor "understanding" the way Jesus intends (10:38), "the Jews" try to imprison Jesus within their own preconceptions. Just as no one can snatch his followers from his hand, nor from the all-powerful hand of the Father (10:28–29), he slips from other hands that try to hold him: "Again they tried to arrest him, but he escaped from their hands" (10:39).

Having recrossed the Jordan to the place that echoes with the memories of John's testimony to him, Jesus remained there (10:40–41). A sense of closure is apparent as the place—"across the Jordan"—and leading character of the first day of Jesus' ministry—John—are recalled (1:19–28). Having escaped from the city of unbelief, he comes home to the place of faith: "And many believed in him there" (v. 42). Once more it is the case: "…his own people received him not. But to those who received him, who believed in his name, he gave power to become children of God" (1:11–12). Those once declared to be "gods" have refused to be made "children of God"—the Father who is "in" Jesus.

3. The Experience of God

Two major expressions occur that deeply affect any understanding of the Johannine experience of God. The first is a straight declaration on the part of Jesus: "I and the Father are one" (10:30). The second gives expression to his hope that, through his performance of his Father's works (10:37), "you may know and understand that the Father is in me and I am in the Father" (10:38). Neither of these statements collapses the Son's relationship with the Father into undifferentiated metaphysical identity. Nor do they reduce the action of the Father to one of simple collaboration with what Jesus is doing. The Father is "in" the Son, not as contained by him or as confined to his scope of action. Rather, what is at stake is the Father's generative initiative in all that affects the life and mission of Jesus: "My Father...is greater than all" (10:29). Immense and complex theologies have struggled to appreciate each element of these statements. Themes such as the unity of the Son with the Father, the mutual coinherence (perichoresis) of the two, and the sense in which the Father can be understood as "greater" than the Son in a manner that excludes both the Arian and Sabellian extremes, will allow theology no rest.[7] The exploration of such high doctrinal issues begins from and forever returns to the compact experience that is constitutive of Johannine sense of the gift of eternal life emanating from the Father.

Notes

1. In accord with his philosophically modulated theology, Aquinas comes to the same conclusion: properly divine works point to a properly divine "nature," and it is this nature that the Father communicates to the Son (cf. *In Evang. B. Joannis Expositio*, c. 10, 5).
2. See 1:50; 4:11; 5:20, 36; 14:12, 28; 1 John 3:20; 4:4; 5:9.
3. For insightful comment on von Balthasar's theology and reference to a wide range of texts, see Michele M. Schumacher, "The Concept of Representation in the Theology of Hans Urs von Balthasar," *Theological Studies* 60 (1999), 53–71, especially 64–66.

4. See Aquinas's gloss on this text: "…'the hand of the Father and mine are the same…'": first, this text manifests the communication of the divinity made to him by the Father when he says, "The Father who gave them to me is greater than all," namely through the eternal generation, as above: "the Father who has life in himself as given to the Son to have life in himself" (5:26)—"that I be the Word and his only-begotten, and the brightness of his light." Second, he establishes the excellence of the Father's power… "no one can snatch them from the hand (i.e., power) of my Father, nor from me who am the agent *[virtus]* of the Father"—although it is more aptly said of the Father himself. Third, he declares his oneness with the Father…namely in a unity of essence; for the nature of the Father and the Son are the same (*In Evang. B. Joannis Expositio*, c. 10, 4).

5. A crucial aspect of the church's effort "to know and understand" is articulated at the Council of Florence, in its Decree for the Copts (1442), as it enunciates the fundamental trinitarian axiom *In divinis, omnia sunt unum nisi obviat relationis oppositio:* "everything [in them] is one where there is no opposition of relationship." It seems to have originated with St Anselm, in *De Processione Spiritus Sancti* 1 (Neuner-Dupuis, *The Christian Faith,* 325, p. 152, and footnote 1).

6. Though the primacy given to the Father in the Nicene Creed, and in Greek theology generally, is often used to combat the supposed undifferentiated essentialism of the Thomist trinitarian theology, we note that St. Thomas' classic "ordo doctrinae" does not proceed from the One God bereft of trinitarian reference, with the trinity somehow appended. Rather, the *Summa* unfolds from a hermeneutical consideration of "unity of the Godhead"—known through all the divine effects in nature and grace (*Summa Theol.,* 1, 12, 1–13) as making space, as it were, for "the trinity of the persons" to be properly considered, leading through the vitality of divine origination and mutual relationships right to the economic point of the missions, in which the Father is present in the experience of grace as the original source and sender (*Summa Theol.,* 1, 43, 4). Only when such a hermeneutical arrangement is fully appreciated can a striking exegesis of the above points be achieved (cf. *Summa Theol.* 1, 27, prol.). For instances of alternative methodologies, see Wolfhart Pannenberg, *Systematic Theology 1,* Geoffrey W. Bromiley, trans. (Grand Rapids, Mich.: William B. Eerdmans, 1991), 308–327; and John D. Zizioulas, *Being as Communion* (London: Darton, Longman and Todd, 1985), 72–78; 83–89.

7. As Aquinas notes, in reference to 10:30: "A twofold error is here excluded: that of Arius who divided the divine essence, and that of Sabellius who confused the persons. We escape both Charybdis and Scilla, because when he [Jesus] says *"one,"* he frees you from Arius, because if "we" are *"one"* there is no diversity. But in that he says *"we* are," he frees you from Sabellius, for as "we," the Father and the Son are different subjects *[alius et alius]* (*In Evang. B. Joannis Expositio,* c. 10, 4). For an Athanasian treatment of these issues, T. F. Torrance, *The Trinitarian Faith: The Evangelical Theology of the Ancient Catholic Church,* 110–145.

11

The God of Life in the World of Death (11:1–57)

1. A Love Stronger Than Death

1. Now a certain man was ill, Lazarus of Bethany, the village of Mary and her sister Martha. 2. It was Mary who anointed the Lord with ointment and wiped his feet with her hair, whose brother Lazarus was ill. 3. So the sisters sent to him, saying, "Lord, he whom you love is ill." 4. But when Jesus heard it he said, "This illness is not unto death; it is for the glory of God, so that the Son of God may be glorified by means of it." 5. Now Jesus loved Martha and her sister and Lazarus. 6. So when he heard that he was ill he stayed two days longer in the place where he was. (11:1–6)

The two sisters have sent a message to Jesus notifying him of the grave illness of his friend. The reader would expect that his love for this family would take the form of the usual responses of comfort and compassion. Yet Jesus does nothing. The emotional mood of the death-shadowed world—in which both life and love are precarious—is shocked into another level of reality. Another purpose is at work. It owes nothing to death nor social expectations flowing from our mortality: "This illness is not unto death; it is for the glory of God, so that the Son of God may be glorified by means of it" (11:4). Nonetheless, there is indeed an unconditional love at work. Jesus will give life by laying down his life. In the gift that he is, he will break open all human economies based on the limits of human giving and exchange (cf. 15:12–16). His action presumes that neither the Father nor the Son are under the sway of death. The abundance of life (10:10) comes in its own way. As the Son is in the Father and the Father in the Son (10:38), a power greater than death, and a glory greater than any human glory is to be made manifest.

> 7. Then after this he said to the disciples, "Let us go into Judea again." 8. The disciples said to him, "Rabbi, the Jews were but now seeking to stone you, and are you going there again?" 9. Jesus answered, "Are there not twelve hours in the day? Those who walk during the day do not stumble because they see the light of this world. 10. But those who walk at night stumble because the light is not in them." 11. Thus he spoke, and then said to them, "Our friend Lazarus has fallen asleep, but I go to wake him out of sleep." 12. The disciples said to him, "Lord, if he has fallen asleep, he will recover." 13. Now Jesus had spoken of his death, but they thought he meant taking rest in sleep. 14. Then Jesus told them plainly, "Lazarus is dead; 15. and for your sake I am glad that I was not there, so that you may believe. Let us go to him." 16. Thomas, called the Twin, said to his fellow disciples, "Let us also go, that we may die with him." (11:7–16)

Jesus decides to go to Jerusalem, having made it clear that he is motivated only by the will and glory of the Father. The disciples are still moving in that darkening world where death is all-powerful. They are motivated, not by the promised gift of life, but by fear of the death that threatens both him and them (11:8, 16). Though he is going to "awaken" Lazarus from death, the radical motivation of "the light of the world" is a much larger awakening: "...for your sake...so that you may believe" (11:15). Where Jesus, as "the light," is intent on the manifestation of glory and true life, Thomas and the disciples see only the dark threat of death awaiting them. While they understand him to be going to Jerusalem to certain death, he sees himself as going to the Father to become the giver of light and life.

Arriving at Bethany within two miles from Jerusalem, he has reached a point of no return. Lazarus has been dead four days. In every sense, the stench of death (cf. 11:39) is already in the air. In their different ways, the two sisters are affected by it. Martha comes to meet him, supposing that Jesus can remedy the situation only by praying to God (11:22). Though she expresses the conventional Jewish hope that the dead will rise on the last day (11:24), she does not realize that Jesus is in person already the gift and giver of eternal life:

> 25. "I am the resurrection and the life. Those who believe in me, even though they die, will live, 26. and whoever lives and believes in me shall never die. Do you believe this?" 27. She said to him, "Yes, Lord; I have believed that you are the Christ, the Son of God, the one who is coming into the world." (11:25–27)

The deathless life of the Father is so present in the Son that death is a non-reality. Believing in him means never to be under the dominion of death. Death places no limits on the God who has given his only Son to be the source of life for the world (3:16). However exalted Martha's confession of belief might be in terms of traditional messianic expectations, it still falls short of the divine vitality that Jesus incarnates. Though she believes so much *about* Jesus in the best terms of Israel's hope, she does not yet have faith *in* him as the unique focus and source of life. The vision of "greater things" promised to Nathanael (1:50–51) has yet to dawn.

Even Mary, who had promptly responded to the voice of the Good Shepherd (11:28–29; cf. 10:3, 4, 16, 17), eventually capitulates to the power of death and grief. Compared with her sister, she is less knowing and more trusting, as she falls at the feet of Jesus and voices her loving complaint, "Lord, if you had been here..." (11:32). Nonetheless, she lapses into weeping, like her consolers, "the Jews" (11:33a), thus giving a sign of mournful defeat and of her failure to recognize "the resurrection and the life."

2. The Word of Life

33. When Jesus saw her weeping, and the Jews who came with her also weeping, he was deeply moved in spirit and troubled; 34. and he said, "Where have you laid him?" They said to him, "Lord, come and see." 35. Jesus wept. 36. So the Jews said, "See how he loved him!" 37. But some of them said, "Could not he who opened the eyes of the blind man have kept this man from dying?" 38. Then Jesus, deeply moved again, came to the tomb; it was a cave, and a stone lay upon it. 39. Jesus said, "Take away the stone." Martha, the sister of the dead man, said to him, "Lord, by this time there will be an odor, for he has been dead four days." 40. Jesus said to her, "Did I not tell you that if you would believe, you would see the glory of God?" 41. So they took away the stone. And Jesus lifted up his eyes and said, "Father, I thank you

because you have heard me. 42. I knew that you hear me always, but I have said this on account of the people standing by, that they may believe that you did send me." 43. When he said this he cried with a loud voice, "Lazarus, come out." 44. The dead man came out, his hands and feet bound with bandages, and his face wrapped with a cloth. Jesus said to them, "Unbind him and let him go." (11:33–44)

As Jesus pushes on in his divinely-inspired purpose to expose the unreality of death, he sheds tears of frustration—in a kind of passionate impatience with those closest to him. Even his friends have as yet not truly recognized "the gift of God" (cf. 4:10). He is being understood only in accord with the exchanges of worldly love, or merely as a performer of signs and a worker of cures in a world still dominated by death (11:36–37).

At Jesus' command to take away the stone from the tomb, Martha warns of the definitive power of death. After four days, her brother's body will show evidence of irreversible corruption. Jesus meets her sense of defeat in the presence of death by stating in effect that she would "see the glory of God" made manifest in what he is about to do. The limitless vitality and love of the Father is not defeated by the world of death. Beyond the imagination of the world, in which death rules unchallenged and life is reduced to an economy of nonrenewable resources, there is the gift of eternal life.

After his command to remove the stone is carried out, he lifts up his eyes in prayer. In this gesture he is depicted, not as one more good man praying to God who is infinitely beyond all human ken, but as acting in loving intimacy with the infinite source of life. So assured and free is his relationship with God that his prayer is first of all an act of thanksgiving. One with the Father, he lives in no economy of death, defeat, grief, and decay.

His imagination is determined by the superabundant economy of a gift of endless life and light. He does not pray in the hope that God will overcome death on the last day. For his prayer arises from within his relationship to the Father, acting in this present moment to overcome death and to give life. His hearers have hitherto all been deaf to the Word of life and resurrection. But the Father, to whom he is turned from the beginning (1:1), and throughout the whole course of his life (1:18), is lovingly receptive to his only Son to whom all has been given (3:35; 5:19;17:2, 10). He knows that the Father hears him always. For the Father is in the Son, as the Son is in him (10:38). But those standing by, who do not yet dwell in him in perfect union and receptivity, have yet to hear the word of life. Jesus speaks, then, that they may believe that he has been sent by the living Father to be the source of eternal life (11:42; cf. 6:56–57).

After praying, he cried out in a loud voice, summoning Lazarus to come out (11:43). His is the great voice of the Word of God through whom all things came into being. It is the summons of the life that all will have in him (1:3–4). It is the voice that pierces the darkness and decay of the tomb over which the stone had lain. It is the cry of him who gives believers power, beyond all human capability, to become the children of God (1:12–13).

Summoned by the Word, the dead man comes forth. The loud voice now utters the further command to those who hear it, "Unbind him and let him go" (11:44). To continue in his Word is to be truly his disciples, in the knowledge of the truth that liberates and loosens the bonds of death itself (8:31–32). His previous promises begin to take effect: "The hour is coming when all who are in their graves will hear his voice and will come out…" (5:25–29b).

In this account of Jesus restoring Lazarus to life, the action is concentrated on who Jesus is and what he will do. And yet, the issue continues to be the revelation of "the glory of God" (11:4, 40), as the Father is invoked at the climactic point of the episode as the one who hears the Son and sends him on his life-giving mission (11:41–42). The Son has life in himself by the gift of the Father, and so presents himself as the resurrection and the life (11:25). The voice of the Word from the Father resonates in the world of grief and defeat with the question previously addressed to Martha, "Do you believe this?" (11:26). Their brother had meant the world to these sisters; and with his death, that world had collapsed. Now his coming forth from the tomb means a world transformed by the life-giving power of the Word. Many of the fellow Jews believed (11:45). But some did not, and reported this disturbing occurrence to the Jewish authorities, "and told them what Jesus had done" (11:46).

3. Death Transformed through His Death

47. So the chief priests and Pharisees gathered in council and said, "What are we doing? For this man performs many signs. 48. If we let him go on thus, everyone will believe in him, and the Romans will come and destroy both our holy place and our nation." 49. But one of them, Caiaphas, who was the high priest that year, said to them, "You know nothing at all; 50. you do not understand that it is expedient for you that one man should die for the people, and that the whole nation should not perish." 51. He did not say this of his own accord, but being high priest that year he prophesied that Jesus should die for the nation, 52. and not for the nation only, but to gather into one the children of God who are scattered

abroad. 53. So from that day on they took counsel how to put him to death. (11:47–53)

When the Pharisees were apprised of what Jesus had done, they express their powerlessness in the face of what had been going on. They ask themselves what they are doing in response to the "many signs" Jesus has performed (11:47). Jesus has witnessed to the Father's involvement in the signs and works he has performed. The Gospel seems to invite a question here over the role of contrary human agents in the unfolding of divine glory. For their part, the Jewish leaders predict that the unchecked activity of Jesus will occasion the Romans' destruction of what is most dear to them—"our holy place and our nation" (11:48). The "resurrection and the life," who brought Lazarus back to life, is being understood in the irony of John's narrative to be an agent of death. He is undermining his adversaries' security in the world as they know it. They are still so much in the thrall of death that they react to the source of life with dread and alarm.

The irony is sharpened to an even finer point. Caiaphas, the high priest in this decisive time, directs the anxious impotence of his fellow leaders toward a fateful expedient: one man must die for the people so that the whole nation might survive (11:50). In a world bound by death and closed to any other promise of life, the high priest's statement is indeed one of refined worldly calculation, especially given the fate of the Jewish martyrs of the past. But, to the degree that he did not speak "of his own accord...but...prophesied that Jesus should die for the nation" (11:51), he is giving unwitting expression to the will of the Father acting in all these events to bring life to the world.

Jesus will die; but not to add one more death to the sum of the world's dead. He will give himself unto the end "not for the nation only, but to gather into one the children of God who are scattered abroad" (11:52). As he and the Father are one (10:30,

38; 17:20–23), all who will receive the gift of life will not only become the children of God, but will also be enfolded into the unity of the Father and the Son. Jesus' movement toward the Father is openness to the world: his relationship to the Father is a circle of communion open to all believers. The readers of this Gospel already know that the Romans had come and wrought utter destruction on the Holy City and the Temple itself. Yet the man those Jewish authorities sought to sacrifice, in order to avoid this devastating outcome, is alive—"the resurrection and the life" for all generations.

But that gift of gathering, life, and unity must await its time. For the moment, the world of division and violence closes in on itself, as Jesus' adversaries deliberate how to bring about his death (11:53). Yet their decision will be made to serve the radiance of the glory to be revealed. Despite their counsel of despair, the Father is still acting. To await this other time, Jesus withdraws from the world intent on his death, and pauses at Ephraim, a town on the edge of the desert, staying with his disciples (11:54). And yet the Passover drew near, and plans to arrest him were progressing (11:57).

4. Death and the God of Life

The Gospel's narrative of the encounter of the Word of life with the world of death can be taken as a summary of the whole message of the Gospel, "...that believing you may have life in his name" (20:31).[1] The incomprehension it depicts and the multiple ironies it employs lead, in a typically Johannine fashion, into a deeper, more radiant experience of the life that flows from the Father through the Son into the world. As with Jesus' five previous "signs,"[2] this sixth sign points beyond itself to the glory of the Father to be revealed in the self-giving of the Son on the cross. While the other signs dealt with the all-sufficiency of "the gift of God" in situations of human need and infirmity, the problem addressed here resides in the dark fate of all human beings. We die. The early believers in the Gospel of eternal life were confronted with that universal and inescapable fact. Is it to make a mockery of what they proclaimed and worshiped? Or is death itself subsumed into the flow of eternal life—already begun on this side of death—so that the experience of death is transformed in a horizon governed by the gift of the life-giving God?

Death leaves us with nothing of ourselves. At that point of total dispossession, we are dying either into life that only God can give, or simply, but dreadfully, experiencing the ending of the world and the termination of the identity and relationships it gave us. The life of faith works on a level deeper than merely coping with grief.[3] It is important to note the complete passivity of Lazarus in the story. The glory of God is revealed as an initiative that finds him at a point of complete isolation and powerlessness.

In the presence of death—as a horrible interruption to our world, and a complete expropriation of what we have been—the Gospel narrative deals with two possible ways of reacting. The first option amounts to a denial of death. Our existence is reduced to being merely a personal project, characterized by a "vital lie,"[4] excluding death from our consciousness in the anxious self-promotion that John describes in terms of "worldly glory." Paradoxically, by denying death, we fall most under its sway and become most suggestive to the "ruler of this world" (12:31; 14:30). Significantly, "the Jews," the lovers of "worldly glory" (12:43), are notably present as mourners, following the death of Lazarus. They typify the human proclivity to hold back from complete surrender to the generative power of the Father, thus to become addicted to the lure of power and prestige. This leads to a defensiveness all too ready to employ the mechanisms of violence and exclusion—especially in regard to the "Other,"

who alone is the source of life. By refusing an unreserved surrender to the living God, the world fabricates an idol designed
to legitimate the precarious domain of its own making and control: "...for they loved human glory more than the glory that
comes from God" (12:43).

The second option gives death its due as our common fate,
but allows for a transformation in the moment of our unmak-
ing—and so "to be born from above" (3:3–10). At that limit of
human existence, we can cling to nothing of our own. We are
emptied of all mundane identities for the sake of that fullness
that only God can give. At that point of surrender, faith refuses
to create an idol to assuage the existential horror and grief arising from the collapse of one's world. The only way forward is to
adore the Father "in spirit and truth," thereby allowing ourselves to be found as true worshipers of the Father (4:23).

The story of Lazarus invites its readers to identify in turn
with each of the characters it presents. In a broad sense, it acts
as a therapy for faith, recalling believers, whatever their experience of death, to the unconditioned radical reality of the gift
they have received. True life is to be led, not by fixing one's eyes
on the grave, but by giving oneself over to the power of the
gift—greater than any death we know—as we accept our own
mortality, grieve over the loss of those we love, or envisage the
totality of communion of all who have passed out of this world
to the Father. In such an understanding, the person of the
believer is not fundamentally a nodal point of relationships
within the world, but what is called forth by the Word in whom
all have been made, as the life and light of our created being
(1:3–5).

Socrates, as Plato presented this great lover of wisdom to
the ancient world, declared that "genuine philosophers continually practice dying...for they will be of the firm conviction that
only there in the other world will they find the knowledge they

are seeking."[5] In contrast, the Christian experience of God demands a continual practice of *living*, not in search of a knowledge reserved for another world, but in the light of "the fullness of the gift which is truth" (1:14) present in their midst.

The story of Lazarus catches death in the moment of its transformation. On the one hand, the death of the Christian is subject to the power of the Word of life. Faith is summoned to such a point of conviction that death appears incidental to Christian existence, in view of the endless life that has already begun. On the other hand, Jesus gives life by moving closer to what is yet to take place—his own death. His power to vanquish death is not exercised from the outside, as it were, at no cost to himself. He is not a noncombatant in the struggle between the light of life and the tenebrous power of death and its agents. He acts from within. Where both of the sisters had wished that Jesus had been "here" (11:21, 32) to prevent the death of their brother, Jesus shows himself to have been there—from "the beginning" (1:1), which includes every "here," even in its darkest form. As the Word of life and light, his own death will manifest the glory of God's self-giving, life-giving love.

Notes

1. See Brendan Byrne, S.J., *Lazarus: A Contemporary Reading of John 11:1–46* (Collegeville: The Liturgical Press, 1991), 13–33.
2. The changing of the water into wine at Cana (2:1–11), the healing of the pagan official's son (4:46–54), the feeding of the five thousand (6:1–15) the cure of the paralytic on the Sabbath (5:1–9), and the giving of sight to the congenitally blind beggar (9:1–7).
3. For a profound philosophical engagement with the experience of death, see Jerome A. Miller, *In the Throes of Wonder: Intimations of the Sacred in the Post-Modern World* (Albany: State University of New York Press, 1992), 104–161.

4. Ernest Becker, *The Denial of Death* (New York: The Free Press, 1973) is the classic modern reference. For human character as a "vital lie," see especially 47–66.
5. Phaedo, 67e. See Desmond Stewart, *Plato: A New Translation of the Phaedo* (London: Euphorion Books, 1972), 32.

12

The Voice from the
Open Heaven (12:1–50)

1. A Moment of Communion

1. **Six days before Passover Jesus came to Bethany, where Lazarus was, whom Jesus had raised from the dead. 2. There they made him a supper; Martha served, and Lazarus was one of those at table with him. 3. Mary took a pound of costly ointment of pure nard and anointed the feet of Jesus and wiped his feet with her hair; and the house was filled with the fragrance of the ointment. 4. But Judas Iscariot, one of the disciples (he who was to betray him), said, 5. "Why was this ointment not sold for three hundred denarii and given to the poor?" 6. This he said, not that he cared for the poor, but because he was a thief, and as he had the money box he used to take what was put into it. 7. Jesus said, "Leave her alone. The purpose was that she might keep this for the day of preparation for my burial. 8. The poor you always have with you, but you do not always have me." (12:1–8)**

Jesus, moving always in union with the Father, arrives at Bethany, in an atmosphere of a restored communion with those he loved (12:1–2). At a meal, Lazarus is with him at table. Martha is serving, thereby anticipating the role of the

251

true disciple (13:12–17). Mary's loving gesture of anointing Jesus' feet with precious unguents looks beyond the intimacy of the scene to what he himself will soon do for his disciples (cf. 11:2). Jesus will wash the feet of his disciples as he gives them the supreme example of self-giving love (13:14–15). In contrast to the stench of death that Martha had anticipated at the tomb of her dead brother (11:39), the fragrance of Mary's ointment fills the house (12:4). It thus evokes both the spacious hospitality of the Father's house to which Jesus goes to prepare a place for his disciples (14:2–3), and the breath of life they will inhale in the presence of the Risen One (20:22).

Still, anticipation is not fulfillment. Judas complains. Forces inimical to both Jesus and those present with him are at work. The traitor is an agent of the devil (13:2) and "the ruler of this world" (12:31). As a thief encased in his own selfishness, he objects to the selfless extravagance of Mary's gesture. His imagination is paralyzed before the superabundance of the divine gift. Being a creature of another economy based on the dispossession of others, he can neither imagine nor accept the bounty of the gift of God. He has placed himself outside the community of new relationships conformed to the self-giving love of God. His world, governed by death and greed, has no place for the hospitality that is the feature of the Father's house (13:20; 14:2). Jesus rebukes him, "Leave her alone…" (12:7). Another hour is in the making. Mary's gift looks to the ultimate gift that will be realized when Jesus is laid out in the tomb. As for Judas, his inability to give as God gives will leave him forever surrounded by those from whom he takes, the victims of his self-centered greed (12:8).

2. The Coming of the Crowds

The comparative repose of this moment is disturbed by the activity of two "great crowds" (12:9, 12). A large gathering of "the Jews" come to see both Jesus and the miraculously revived Lazarus. This movement toward "the resurrection and the life," however limited it may be, causes the noose to be drawn more tightly around Jesus, to include even Lazarus. For he is the living evidence of the life-giving power at work, beyond the control of "the chief priests" (12:10). The second great crowd is made up of the pilgrims who had come to the Feast. They go out to meet Jesus, who had left Bethany for Jerusalem the day after the first large gathering had arrived. The gathering into one of the dispersed children of God (11:52; 12:11) is taking effect. Traditional messianic expectations, however, are due for disappointment.

The crowd of pilgrims wave the palms of fervent nationalism (12:13a) as they meet Jesus, and hail him as the Messiah they want, the one "who comes in the name of the Lord, even the King of Israel" (12:13b). Yet he comes in the name of his Father, and so makes his entry not in a war chariot, but seated on an ass. In contrast to the exalted Messiah the crowd envisages, his "lifting up" will be of another kind. The palm fronds may be waved, but the grain of wheat must fall into the ground. The king indeed is coming, but his kingship is not of this world (18:36). His triumph will not consist in driving out the Romans, but in revealing the universal, in-gathering extent of the Father's love. The disciples will later recall, in the light of the glorification to which the Father will lead him (12:16), that all this was happening in accord with the scriptural prophecy of Zechariah:

Rejoice greatly, O daughter Sion! Shout aloud, O daughter Jerusalem! Lo, your king comes to you; triumphant and victorious is he, humble and riding on a donkey....He will cut off the chariot from Ephraim and the war horse from Jerusalem....And he shall command peace to the nations; and his dominion shall be from sea to sea....(Zech 9:9–10)

Jesus' lowly entry into the Holy City gives expression to the peaceable expansion of the Father's will working in all aspects of this episode. As they experience a movement beyond any human categories and control, the crowds, however imperfect their apprehension, know that something is afoot: Lazarus has been brought back to life (12:18). On the other hand, the Pharisees are faced with their own powerlessness against the mysterious attraction working in this Jesus who, in the name of God, had brought someone back to life: "You see that you can do nothing; look, the world has gone after him" (12:19). What, in fact, they will do will bring about his death; but that too will be a decisive factor in opening the world to the divine glory.

3. The Hour Has Come

20. **Now among those who went up to worship at the feast were some Greeks. 21. So these came to Philip, who was from Bethsaida in Galilee, and said to him, "Sir, we wish to see Jesus." 22. Philip went and told Andrew; Andrew went with Philip and they told Jesus. 23. And Jesus answered them, "The hour has come for the Son of Man to be glorified. 24. Amen, amen, I say to you, unless a grain of wheat falls into the earth and dies, it remains alone; but if it dies, it bears much fruit. 25. Those who love their life lose it, and those who hate their life in this world will keep it for eternal life. 26. Whoever serves me must follow me; and**

where I am, there shall my servant be also. Whoever serves me, the Father will honor." (12:20–26)

The Gospel had previously reported the Jewish leaders' incomprehension of the goal of Jesus' life and their inability to follow him (7:32–36). When he had spoken of going to the Father, they had wondered whether he was going on a teaching mission to the Greeks in the diaspora (7:33–35). But now, as the great gathering begins to take place, in a strikingly ironic twist, it is representatives of the Greeks who come to him (12:20–22). Attuned to the Father acting in drawing them to him, Jesus declares that the hour of his glorification as the revealer of the Father has arrived (12:23). But this revelation will take place only through his being "lifted up" (3:14; 8:28) in an act of total self-surrender to the will of the Father. The Good Shepherd will lay down his life (10:15). In the decisive hour of glory, the Father will be acting; Jesus will give himself—and his antagonists will see implemented their plans to put him to death (7:30; 8:20). Yet, at every juncture, the timing of this hour chimes with the design and the will of the Father. God will be glorified in the glorification of the Son. Though the voice of the Father is soon to be heard (12:28b), it had already spoken in the oracle of Isaiah that was the subject of meditation for the early generations of Christian believers—those "scattered children of God" who had been gathered into unity through the sacrificial death of the Father's Son:

> See, my servant shall prosper; he shall be exalted and lifted up, and shall be very high. Just as there were many who were astonished at him—so marred was his appearance beyond human semblance, and his form beyond that of mortals, so shall he startle many nations; kings shall shut their mouths because of him;

for that which has not been told them they shall see,
and what they had not heard they shall contemplate.
(Isa 52:13–15)

To be "lifted up" means neither worldly exaltation for
Jesus, brought about by human agency, nor does it represent the
triumph of the worldly powers ranged against him. Although,
"judging by appearances" (7:24), these latter will be most obvious in terms of the execution they effect, the agent of this "lifting up" is the Father himself. He lifts up him whom he has given,
his only Son, and exalts him precisely in the totality of his self-
giving, so as to reveal the glory of God's giving love (3:16;
1 John 4:9–10). Moreover, this up-lifting takes place in a world
in which the idea of glory contradicts the Gospel's notion of
glory. Worldly glory is closed to the demands of unreserved love,
and the conception of God that such love implies. Only God can
counter its laws of gravity. Acting from above, God "lifts up."

In the emphasis characteristic of the Word and Son, the
unique revealer of the Father, Jesus declares, "Amen, amen, I say
to you, unless a grain of wheat falls into the earth and dies, it
remains alone; but if it dies, it bears much fruit" (12:24). To
behold the glory of the cross is to enter another realm. The self-
enclosed barren isolation of a world refusing to be transformed
will be reversed. The grain of wheat, sown in the mysterious
ground of the Father's will, is a long way from the palm
branches of worldly glory. To cling to a life that does not live in
the light of the death that is to take place is to miss out on the
gift of life that is being offered (12:25a). But to stake all on the
glory revealed on the cross will mean finding that the promise of
eternal life with God will be kept (12:25b).

True disciples, therefore, in following Jesus on his way to
the Father, must be united with him both in the heights of his
being "lifted up," and in the depths of his "falling down" into

the earth (12:26). They will be honored by the Father (12:26). From him will come the luminous affirmation of the community of those who will come to the cross and enter into its meaning. The paternal life-giving mystery is thus presented as the ground into which the grain falls. In that ground it sprouts with the energies and fruitfulness of abundant life. By rejecting the superficial glory of this world, believers, as they follow the way of the Son, enter into the dimensions of the glory that only the Father can give (cf. 9:22; 12:43; 16:2).

4. The Voice of the Father

27. "Now is my soul troubled. And what shall I say? 'Father assure my salvation from this hour'? Yes! It is for this reason that I have come to this hour. 28. Father, glorify your name." Then a voice came from heaven, "I have glorified it, and will glorify it again." 29. The crowd standing by heard it and said that it had thundered. Others said, "An angel has spoken to him." 30. Jesus answered, "This voice has come for your sake, not for mine. 31. Now is the judgment of this world; now shall the ruler of this world be cast out; 32. and I, when I am lifted up from the earth, will draw all people to myself." 33. He said this to show by what death he was to die. 34. The crowd answered him, "We have heard from the law that the Christ remains forever. How can you say that the Son of Man must be lifted up? Who is this Son of Man?" 35. Jesus said to them, "The light is with you a little longer. 36. Walk while you have the light, lest the darkness overtake you. If you walk in the darkness, you do not know where you are going. While you

have the light, believe in the light, that you may
become children of light." When Jesus said this, he
departed and hid himself. (12:27–36)

Though the will of God leads disciples of Jesus beyond the
limitations of a self-enclosed world, there is a limit at which
humanity shudders. The ultimate "letting go" of all securities, the
final act of self-transcendence, complete surrender to the will of
the Father acting when and how he will, is a deeply destabilizing
moment in human experience. Love brings its own troubles—and
the dying that is demanded is truly deadly, in a way that recalls but
reshapes the Markan account of Gethsemane (Mark 14:34–36).
Jesus himself faces the "now" of the hour of glory, which causes
the reality of the cross to stand out in stark relief: "Now is my soul
troubled" (12:27a). He is confronted with the full reality of the
passion that he, and those who follow him, must undergo.

The judgment he occasioned had meant divisions on all
sides. Now, at a final lethal extremity, they will tear him apart.
At this juncture, the Gospel depicts what can be described in
human language only in terms of a terrible risk. In the world of
massing violence and increasing malice, all must be staked on
the ultimate victory of love, which at this point cannot but
appear as utterly incapable to withstand the worldly power.
How will his death gather the scattered children of God when
the most obvious movement is toward hatred, division, and
expulsion? How will the Father be revealed as "greater than
all"—greater than the malevolent forces bent on his "lifting up
on the cross," and all too ready to bury him in the ground? And
so this hour brings its own dreadful questioning. At this point of
complete emptiness, only the Father can provide an answer. The
Word experiences himself as a question: "And what shall I say?
'Father, assure my salvation from this hour?'" (12:27b). It is the
hour when all other wills and voices must yield to the glory of

what only the Father can bring about in the face of the naked reality of his being lifted up on the cross and his falling down in death. The "now" of this hour exposes the full dimensions of Jesus' surrender to the one from whom he comes and to whom he is going: "Yes! For this reason I have come to this hour" (12:27c). The loving surrender of the Son is expressed as a prayer signifying the completeness of his devotion to the glory of the one from whom he draws his life: "Father, glorify your name" (12:28a). Where before he had declared that his food is to do the will of him who sent him (4:34), now that will is the only nourishment that can sustain him till the end.

The prayer of the Word made flesh is answered by the voice from heaven (12:28). In the Gospel narrative so far, the Father has been depicted as glorifying his name in the words and works of the Son—from the miracle at Cana (2:11), and the healing of the man born blind (9:3), to the raising of Lazarus from the tomb (11:40). Now that work of glory will come to its completion. God, to whom the Word is turned from the beginning, speaks: "I have glorified [my name], and will glorify it again" (12:28c). Though the disciples have yet to see the opened heaven (1:51), they now hear the voice of the one who fills it. The all-encompassing intent of the Father to open heaven to the scattered children of God has been at work throughout the whole career of Jesus. It is his voice that now resonates in this moment of vulnerability, darkness, and emptiness. God is claiming the Word as his own; the Father is owning his only Son, given in love for the life of the world. Through the words and deeds of Jesus, God has revealed, and will further reveal, who he is for the world. He is originatively and immediately involved with his Son and loves the world through him. In this, the voice of the Father and the Word made flesh speak in unison, for "the Father and I are one" (10:30).

259

The unison of the Word with the voice of the Father is precisely what the crowd of bystanders fails to register. Not yet gathered into the unity that exists between the paternal Speaker and his Word and Son, the crowd can only imagine that God is still hidden in a closed heaven; and that some word of God other than what has been uttered from the beginning is needed. Imagining that an angel has spoken, these potential believers are yet to behold the opened heaven with "the angels of God ascending and descending on the Son of Man" (1:51). Because they envisage divine glory in another guise, they cannot believe that only through the glorification of Jesus in this hour will the glory of the Father shine forth.

Addressing his future disciples, Jesus speaks from the depths of his unbreakable union with the Father: "This voice has come for your sake, not for mine" (12:30). It is not for Jesus' sake, since he is turned toward God "in the beginning" (1:1). The theophany breaks into the world "from above" to open heaven. It manifests the primordial communion that has existed from the beginning. In that divine realm of life, Jesus is the Word in person (1:1–5), while in the realm of the flesh into which this Word has entered, the Son is unceasingly turned toward the heart of the Father (1:18) as the living exposition of God. The God with whom he is so intimately united is the only explanation for the origin and mission of Jesus (1:18; 3:13; 6:62; 8:23): no other explanation will suffice. Because of his divine origin, there will be glory in the lifting up of the Son of Man, and the assurance of divine honor for those who are associated with him in falling down into the earth.

Acceptance of Jesus' divine origin is at the heart of faith. If some reject him as the one sent by the Father, it is because, ignorant of the Father, they "have never heard his voice or seen his form" (5:37). But now the Father has spoken; and just as the voice of Jesus was raised in prayer at the tomb of Lazarus

(11:42), the truth speaks "for your sake" (12:31). The love of God for the world is not reduced to silence. Darkness will not overcome the light, radiating in the glory of the lifting up, and in the honoring that comes in the falling down. In the dimensions of the opened heaven, the lifting up will be an ascent and the falling down will be descent, as the angels of God ascend and descend upon the Son of Man. Both movements have their place in the hour that the Father has determined.

There is another feature in the "now" of the hour that has arrived: "Now is the judgment of the world. Now the ruler of this world is cast out" (12:31). Previously this *now* had referred to the troubling of the soul of Jesus at the onset of his passion, with its implications of violent death, condemnation, betrayal, and desertion. Yet the *now* in this instance is the moment of truth in a different sense. The world will be confronted with a reality that will either inspire the surrender of faith, or cause it to recoil further into violence and mendacity. The light that has come into world brings a time of crisis. In a photophobic rejection of the light, evil will hide further from itself in darkness—while the phototropic search of the good for the good will draw them into the radiance of divine glory (3:19). Although the Father judges no one in his love for the world, the Son as his emissary and agent brings a fundamental division into the world of human liberty (5:22, 24, 27, 30). Will humankind choose to live in openness to the Father, or fall back into an idolatrous self-glorification? Even Jesus, despite the continuous conflicts in which he is embroiled, judges no one (8:15). His mission is to communicate the gift of the truth (3:17–18). But precisely because he is so intimately united with the Father's saving design for the world, a judgment on those who reject him inevitably follows (8:15–16).

With the coming of the hour of judgment of this world, its ruler will be cast out (12:31b). There has been a force at work throughout human history, exercising its control over the world through death, lying, violence, vain glory, and idolatry. It has cut the world off from its true origin, causing history to be closed in on itself. Such a force has made human culture an edifice built on the violent exclusion of the other. Motivated by self-serving glory, its various agents sought to set themselves apart from the Word through which the world was made, so as to turn from the Light that was coming to it (1:9–10). The result is a state of allergic reaction to him who has come to his own (1:11). Up to the present, this evil influence had worked through the Jewish leaders antagonistic to Jesus, to cast out both him and those who followed him. Now this negative force is itself to be cast out of the world—because that world has been so loved by God. What is about to be revealed is that "the world came into being through him" (1:10) to find its true life, radiance, and freedom in the Son of the Father. The light has shone into the darkness that does not overcome it (1:5). The cosmic rule of the evil one is now overcome because the will of the Father is being brought to its fulfillment.

Magnetically drawn to its original and life-giving truth, the world comes to experience the expulsion of its former ruler: "And I, when I am lifted up from the earth, will draw all people to myself" (12:32). The death Jesus is to die results from God's refusal to act in any power other than that of self-giving love. In, and despite, the murderous violence of the world lifting up the Son on the cross, the nonviolent power of the one from above will exercise its attraction in terms of light, truth, love, and life. The Good Shepherd will lay down his life for his sheep, in order that there will be one flock and one shepherd (10:15–16). His death will mean that the scattered children of God will be gathered into one (11:52). The limitless gift of God exceeds all the limited expectations, and even the gifts of the past (12:11, 19, 21). The opened heaven, therefore, will be an all-embracing domain of unity and fulfillment.

And yet, the prospect of divine self-revelation through the lifting up of Jesus on the cross remains a scandal to the end. For those who resist the will of the Father and the cruciform mode of his self-revelation (3:14–15), there can be no messianic significance in such a death. It would be the contradiction of all worldly glory: "We have heard from the law that the Christ remains forever" (12:34). The origin of Jesus' identity and the purpose of his mission have ended with their questions: "How can you say that the Son of Man must be lifted up? Who is this Son of Man?" (12:34). Unable to break the shackles of a closed religious system, they remain outside the fulfillment that the law of Moses prefigured (3:14). As the darkness gathers, the Light of the world makes a final appeal: "...walk while you have the light" (12:35b). Those who turn from the light are deprived of all direction. But in the measure they allow themselves to be illumined by light that shines from beyond the glitter of worldly pretensions, they are born to a new luminous existence. These children of God are begotten out of the light and love that come from the Father, whatever the state of the darkening world: "While you have the light, believe in the light, that you may become children of the light" (12:36).

After these words, the Light will be lost to the crowd. The next time he will be seen will be on the cross (18:1—19:16): "...he departed and hid himself from them" (12:36c). The Gospel thus suggests that Jesus has now hidden himself in the silence and in the utopia, the "no-place," of the Father—the realm above from which the Son comes, and out of which he has spoken. It is inaccessible except through the way that he has opened.

Jesus' withdrawal opens a space to be filled with what the Father is encompassing through the mission of his Son.[1] Jesus had acted in the death of Lazarus whom he loved. But the Father will now act in the death of his Son whom he loved and sent into the world. His death will emerge as "the field of Fatherhood"[2]

263

in which the disciples will be drawn into Jesus' own relationship to the Father (cf. 20:17).[3]

5. Faith or Human Glory

37. Though he had done so many signs before them, yet they did not believe in him; 38. it was so that the word of the prophet Isaiah might be fulfilled: "Lord, who has believed our report, and to whom has the arm of the Lord been revealed?" 39. Therefore they could not believe. For Isaiah again said, 40. "God has blinded their eyes and hardened their hearts, lest they should see with their eyes and perceive with their heart, and turn for me to heal them." 41. Isaiah said this because he saw his glory and spoke of him. 42. Nevertheless many even of the authorities believed in him, but for fear of the Pharisees they did not confess it lest they should be put out of the synagogue: 43. for they loved human glory rather than the glory of God. (12:37–43)

The Gospel, while following Jesus into the silence into which he has retired, looks back at the world he has now left behind. In his dramatic summation of the situation, John does not spare his readers the terrible negativity that has resulted, even if this too is included in the divine design, so as to play its part in the glory of "the hour." The world has had the benefit of "so many signs" performed by Jesus, but faith has not resulted. Still, this widespread failure in faith is subsumed into the plan of God. The earliest Christian tradition understood the ineluctable working of the Father's will, as believers meditated on the prophecy of Isaiah: "Lord, who has believed our report...? (12:38; cf. Isa 53:1 and Rom 10:16). Along with other great figures of the past (8:56), the prophet saw the glory that would be revealed in the words and deeds of Jesus, and interpreted the wavering path of Israel in such terms (12:41). The failure of Israel—"they could not believe" (12:39)—falls under the divine will. Again, Isaiah is quoted: "God has blinded their eyes and hardened their heart..." (12:40).[4] This hour will permit a dreadful dimension of tragedy and self-destruction. The revelation of God has become a judgment. Left to itself, the world turned against Jesus is moving into an ever-deeper darkness. In the flat horizon of "earthly things," limited to what is "from below" (cf. 3:12; 8:23), no light shines. In another horizon, however, open to the will and intention of the Father, there is found the radiance of the ever-greater mystery of saving love. For even in the situation of utter negativity, with its failure to believe, and subject to the dire predictions of the prophet, there are signs of hope: "Nevertheless, many even of the authorities believed in him..." (12:42).

But that "nevertheless" does not mean clear and unreserved acceptance. The whole drama of human freedom must be played out. Hence, contrary forces are evident. Faith hesitates, in fear of the Pharisees and of expulsion from the synagogue. Not only do the "authorities" (12:42) fail to be part of the history of expectation as Isaiah depicts it; they are hiding in a synagogue that has become a prison. The tiny world of human glory has no room for the unimaginable excess of the glory to be revealed: "For they loved human glory rather than the glory of God" (12:43). To accept that divine glory would mean a bad reputation in the defensive and violent world that is still, seemingly, in possession. While there is a stirring of hope in the fact that "many even of the authorities" had come to some tentative belief, the darkness is to become darker yet before the light of glory breaks.

6. Not Judgment, but Eternal Life

44. And Jesus cried out and said, "Whoever believes in me believes not in me but in the one who sent me. 45. And whoever sees me sees the one who sent me. 46. I have come as light into the world, that whoever believes in me may not remain in darkness. 47. I do not judge anyone who hears my words and does not keep them, for I came not to judge the world but to save the world. 48. The one who rejects me and does not receive my word has a judge; the word that I have spoken will serve as judge on the last day. 49. For I have not spoken on my own authority; the Father who sent me has himself given me commandment what to say and what to speak. 50. And I know that his commandment is eternal life. What I say, therefore, I say as the Father has bidden me." (12:44–50)

While failure, hardening of hearts, blindness, fear, and attachment to human reputation bedevil the situation that Jesus has left behind, he calls back to it, with the voice of one exclusively intent on the glory of his Father: "Whoever believes in me, believes not in me but in the one who sent me, and whoever sees me, sees the one who sent me" (12:44–45). Jesus is not making himself an idol in a kind of divine rivalry. He is an icon of the living God, backlit by the mystery of him from whom he is sent.[5] The voice of the Word is totally referred to the one he reveals. At the origin of all his speech and action is the generative, self-giving presence of the Father. Because the Father has sent him, he is, in the words of the Nicene Creed, "light from light," coming as light into the world to make God visible in the darkness. Even for those who reject him, he has come, not to judge the world, but to save it. Whatever the inveterate resistance to him and his message, he is, despite all rejection, the embodiment of universal salvation.

Because of his original relationship to God and his mission from the Father, the language of judgment is foreign to the Word. Judgment will occur only for those who choose to remain outside the sphere of God-willed universal salvation. Those who pass by this hour to await a "last day" will find that their misguided deferral of judgment will be met by the truth already accessible to them: "...the word that I have spoken will serve as judge on the last day" (12:48). They will find that what they have attempted to postpone has already happened.

Thus, Jesus distances both himself and the Father from the role of judge. Such judgment as there is will come about, not as a God-willed, but as a self-imposed reality. The Son has not been sent into the world to confront it as a judge. The defining relationship inscribed into his identity is his being from and for the Father. He is not therefore "judge of the world," but the Son of the Father who "so loved the world" (3:16). In his origins there is no implication of judgment: "I have not spoken on my own authority; the Father who sent me has given me commandment what to say and what to speak" (12:49). At the heart of all that Jesus says there is a hearing and receptivity in regard to what the Father wills. All he communicates, he has received; and what has come from the Father to be received by him and to be communicated to the world is eternal life: "And I know that his commandment is eternal life" (12:50a). Into a world bounded by death and rent with violence and division, the Father is intent on giving deathless life. He is the abiding source, not of judgment, but of life, even as the moment of the Son's death draws near. In all this narrative of rejection, dying, betrayal, and desertion, the Gospel remains a document designed to express the life-giving intention of the Father working through all the events and decisions that it reports. As the primary teller of God's story, Jesus

267

has come neither to die nor to judge, but to save the world, and to quicken it through the Father's gift of endless life: "What I say, therefore, I say as the Father has bidden me" (12:50).

7. Children of Light

In the realm of divine glory, the Son's relationship to the Father implies both receptivity and self-surrender. In him the Father is generatively present. Everything the Son does and says is from and for the Father. His unconditionally "Fatherward" existence is expressed in a self-dispossession contesting the dynamics of human glory. Lifted up beyond the values and judgments that structure mundane identity and reputation, the Son comes as one sent by the Father to give life. In his unreserved openness to the Father he is God's all-inclusive outreach to the world. The Father is in him, as he is in the Father, and one with him (10:30). His essential "non-aloneness" with regard to the Father—with whom he is one and to whose purpose he unreservedly offers himself—models the "non-aloneness" of his followers. Insofar as they are prepared to let go of the defensive limitations characteristic of life in the world of human glory, the realm of the Father's glory awaits them. If they leave the surface-life of isolated and defensive individuality by falling into the generative ground of the Father's will; if they die to the world of their own independence and exclusive privilege; they will not remain a single grain, but bear much fruit. In renouncing life as their own possession, the servants and followers of Jesus will receive the enduring communal life of God's gift (12:25), and be acknowledged by the Father as his own (12:26).

By experiencing God in the glory of self-giving love, human beings are transformed into a new sense of selfhood. Jesus has performed his mission to form them in accord with the Father's generativity: "...that you may become children of light" (12:36). What believing in the light might mean, and what becoming children of light effectively entails, await further clarification as the Gospel unfolds.

Notes

1. See Jean-Luc Marion, "Le don d'une présence," *Prolégomènes à la charité* (Paris: Editions de la Différence, 1986), 163–165. For fuller treatment, Robyn Horner, *Rethinking God as Gift: Jean-Luc Marion and a Theology of Donation*, 290–326.
2. This phrase is taken from G. Lafont, *God, Time and Being*, 244. The section, "The Paternal Invocation" (242–253) is of special importance.
3. Note again, from a feminist perspective, Dorothy A. Lee, "Beyond Suspicion? The Fatherhood of God in the Fourth Gospel," *Pacifica* 8/2, June 1995, 140–153.
4. Cf. Isa 6:9–10. See Mark 4:11–12; 8:17–18; Matt 13:13–15; Luke 8:10; 19:42; Acts 28:26–27; Rom 11:8, 10.
5. We use *icon* in the phenomenological sense previously referred to. John never uses the word for reasons that von Balthasar nicely expresses: "It is not in the created *doxa* that he reflects the uncreated *doxa*: it is the relational being of the (eternal, incarnate) Son/Person that he manifests the glory of the Father. And this is not a Father who is in himself the tranquil *kabod*-glory, but fundamentally the Father who utters himself lovingly in the Son, represents himself in him, and makes known to the world his self-utterance in the Son's gift of himself to the world (3:16)" (*The Glory of the Lord VII*, 377).

13

The Way to the Father (13:1–38)

In the chapters (13–17) making up the "last discourse," we have an extended rhetorical form of the Prologue itself (1:1–18). The words of the Word are addressed to "his own" in a world which, up to this point, has largely rejected the divine invitation he embodied (1:11). Yet to these who are now receiving him, he is giving "power to become children of God" (1:12). God is a generative presence beyond anything the world can fabricate or engender.

In the preceding chapters, it has become clear how the Word, in becoming flesh, has been expressed in many words and signs, and even as a judgment. In this last discourse he will show himself as an "example" (13:15), a "commandment" (13:34), and, in a climactic manner, as a "prayer" (17:1–26). The horizon is filled with the presence of the Father—to whom Jesus is going, and from whom the Paraclete will come. In such a paternal space, the way of Jesus will be explained, and the dark reality of evil will be named and faced. Threaded through Jesus' gifts of the example, the "morsel," the new commandment, and his promises of the advent of the Spirit with the accompanying gifts of knowledge, peace, and joy, there is an all-connecting theme: the unbreakable bond uniting the disciples to Jesus and to the Father. The disciples are in effect being turned toward the opened heaven in which they will have a place. To this realm Jesus goes, with a promise to return. From this realm the Spirit will come to remain forever; and the Father, with Jesus, will come in the fullness of time to those who love him.

1. The Way to the Father

1. Now before the feast of the Passover, when Jesus knew that his hour had come to depart out of this world to the Father, having loved his own who were in the world he loved them to the end. 2. And during the supper, when the devil had already made up his mind that Judas Iscariot, Simon's son, would betray him, 3. Jesus, knowing that the Father had given all things into his hands and that he had come from God and was going to God, 4. rose from supper, laid aside his garments, and girded himself with a towel. 5. Then he poured water into a basin and began to wash the disciples' feet and to wipe them with the towel with which he was girded. (13:1–5)

The programmatic first verse brings together four themes: the significance of the Passover feast, Jesus' awareness of the decisive hour, his departure from this world to the Father, and the affirmation of his consummate love for the disciples. In his mission to reveal God, Jesus has been present at a number of feasts—the Sabbath, Tabernacles, and previous Passovers. In the *now* of this decisive hour, all previous celebrations lead to this crucial Passover in which the generative love of the Father will be disclosed. As Jesus passes out of this world to the Father, he brings to fulfillment the movement that the Exodus of Israel prefigured. But now it is the world as a whole, represented in the loved disciples, which is to see the opening of heaven that had been promised (1:51).

John the Baptist's previous reference to Jesus as the "Lamb of God" now takes on its full meaning. God has given his Lamb into the world of darkness to be a paschal sacrifice of atonement. In his blood the sin of the world will be taken away and its violence disarmed (1:29). Throughout this discourse and in the passion narrative that follows there will be ample evidence of the world's self-destructive predicament. Nonetheless, the cleansing blood of this Lamb is the Father's gift. God has loved the world in giving his Son right into its state of alienation (3:16; 10:17; 1 John 1:7; 2:2; 4:10). The Son, the Lamb of *God*, and the Good Shepherd, lays down his life for those the Father has given him. By "Fathering" the Son in this extreme of self-giving, the generative love of God counters the perversely generative power of evil, and introduces into human existence a new life-form in the gift of eternal life. The "children of light" are born (12:36). Because the Father has gone beyond himself, lovingly to give into the world what is his most intimate possession, namely, his only Son, the way of a final exodus is opened.

The consciousness of Jesus, hitherto stretching forward to the time of the hour, is now concentrated in its actual occurrence: "...when Jesus knew that his hour had come..." (1:1b). It is *his* hour, since it has been at every stage that for which his Father had destined him, and which he himself had unreservedly accepted (2:4; 4:21, 23; 7:30; 12:23, 27). Most radically it is *his* hour, because it is his Father's hour, the time when the character and action of the Father will be made fully manifest. In this hour the whole course of human history will be condensed and fulfilled. Through the sending of his Son—the Word in whom all things came into being (1:3)—the Father creates a new relationship between himself and the world. The gathering of all time and, indeed, of all creation, into this hour flows from the completeness of the union between the Father and the Son, which has been the key to the Gospel narrative from its inception. Since "he was in the beginning with God" (1:2), the union implied in that original beginning overflows to be the field of a new unity among the scattered children of God (11:52).

Jesus' turning to the Father in this hour expresses the fundamental dynamic of his existence, "...to pass out of this world to the Father" (1:1b). In life, and now in the death he is about to die, Jesus has been moving toward the Father. The Word was turned to him in the beginning (1:1). The only Son, in his exposition of the otherwise unseen God, has made the Father known by virtue of the heart-to-heart relationship to the one from whom he came (1:18b). Jesus has passed through a world of conflicts, divisions, rejection, and terminal antagonism in regard to the true God and to himself. Yet he has been ever intent on opening that world to the generative presence of the Father at work in every aspect of his mission. Now the human history of the Word become flesh is coming to its fulfillment. In the passing of Jesus out of the clouded and violent structure of this world, his mission will be accomplished. In this departure, the Father will be revealed to the world as its original lover and as the source of deathless life (3:16).

There is another dimension inherent in Jesus' passing out of the world to the Father. His movement toward the Father brings the maximal manifestation of his love for his own: "...having loved his own who were in the world, he loved them to the end" (1:1c). By going to the God who so loved the world, he embodies the limitless extent of the Father's love. His self-surrender to the Father is the mode of his self-giving for the life of the world. Admittedly, "his own" are set in contrast to the representatives of the world closed to the Word by which it was created, enlivened, and enlightened (1:3–4, 10, 11). Yet, through those who have received him, the world is now opened to the glory of the life-giving love at work. It reaches out to them, as Jesus' love for the Father and for the world goes beyond all limits. The excess of this love will be enacted in the cross itself, "the end" that marks the unreserved measure of God's gift (3:34).

Against this background, the narrative now sets the scene at a final supper. However, between the Gospel's declaration of the limitless quality of Jesus' love and the manifestation of that love in the symbolic gesture of the foot-washing, comes the dramatic interposition of the power of evil at work: "...the devil had already made up his mind that Judas Iscariot...would betray him" (1:2).[1] The Father's will works, not only in the teeth of the murderous designs of the ruler of this world, but even through the disciple's betrayal.

Love goes to the end, even when a murderous force is intent on reaching its end—organizing the world to do away with its Savior. In this hour Jesus must contend with the dark powers of evil at work. Despite the virulence of the forces opposing him, Jesus' consciousness of his identity and mission is expressed in terms of an unreserved indebtedness to the Father in what he has received, and in regard to both his origin and destiny (1:3). Whatever the power of evil, everything is subjected to his Father's design. All things had been given him as the Father's gift. Nothing, and no one, is left in the hands of others—even as they pursue their antagonistic course to the point of Jesus' betrayal and execution.

His departure from this world and his going to God have their explanation in his divine origin. The Father is not simply rescuing a faithful man from the world. There is a deeper truth. The Father is giving his only Son to the world to open it, even at its darkest point, to the realm of God. The filial existence of Jesus is, therefore, not intelligible merely in terms of ascent to a transcendent realm. It is a return to the divine realm from which he has already come as the Father's gift. His passing out of this world to the Father has as its ultimate explanation the Son's exodus from the divine realm. In both phases of the movement, from above and from below, the whole world is implicated. The Father has given *all things* into his hands. In this ascending and descending (1:51), there is nothing left outside the opening of heaven.

The gesture of washing the disciples' feet occurs in a context saturated with the significance of the Father—for Jesus himself, and for the "all things" given into his hands. By laying aside his garments, Jesus is acting in accord with the Father's will and in the mode of his Father's giving. Through this humble action, he radically subverts the glory of this world, thereby giving expression to the only truth that can counter the deceit of the devil's designs. Jesus had come to Jerusalem seated on an ass (12:14). He has identified himself as the Good Shepherd who lays down his life for his sheep. He had spoken of the grain of wheat falling into the ground. The glory of God will be revealed through his being lifted up on the cross. In washing his disciples' feet, he symbolically recapitulates his previous words and deeds, and anticipates the full meaning of the hour that has now arrived. God's glory is a scandal to the world of human glory built on other criteria. The Son's inglorious departure from this world will reveal glory of another kind.

2. The "Example" of Love

6. He came to Simon Peter; and Peter said to him, "Lord, do you wash my feet?" 7. Jesus answered him, "What I am doing you do not know now, but afterward you will understand." 8. Peter said to him, "You shall never wash my feet." Jesus answered him, "If I do not wash you, you have no part in me." 9. Simon Peter said to him, "Lord, not my feet only but also my hands and my head." 10. Jesus said to him, "One who has bathed does not need to wash, but is entirely clean; and

you are clean, but not every one of you." 11. For he knew who was to betray him; that is why he said, "You are not all clean." 12. When he had washed their feet, and taken his garments, and resumed his place, he said to them, "Do you know what I have done to you? 13. You call me Teacher and Lord; and you are right, for so I am. 14. If I then, your Lord and Teacher, have washed your feet, you ought also to wash one another's feet. 15. For I have given you an example, that you also should do what I have done to you. 16. Amen, amen, I say to you, servants are not greater than their master; nor are the ones sent greater than the one who sent them. 17. If you know these things, blessed are you if you do them." (13:6–17)

Still a prey to the expectations and standards of the glory of this world, Peter protests. Jesus replies that what he is now doing for his disciples discloses something essential to their relationship to him. They are called to "have a part in him" (13:8), to be one with him in his relationship to the Father and in his God-given mission. In response, Peter gives extravagant consent to what is being asked, even if he does not yet realize its implications. Still, the point is made: "having a part" in Jesus has echoes of baptism, the necessary condition for experiencing the extreme of Jesus' love for "his own."

Nonetheless, it is a matter of freedom and, necessarily, the capacity to refuse. In recording Jesus' reading of Judas' intentions at this point (13:10–11), the Gospel depicts the determination of love to be true to itself, even in the face of those who hide from it. The divine momentum of this hour must be sought on a plane transcending the machinations of the world's evil. To the degree believers enter into the real meaning of Jesus' gesture, they are conformed to the self-giving, cruciform existence of the one they have accepted as Lord and Teacher. His departure from this world to the Father brings a new form of existence into the world, symbolized in a mutual washing of feet. Christian identity can never be understood in terms of isolated and defensive individuality. Nor is it to be found by obeying the generalized moral imperative to love one's neighbor as oneself. The children of the Father are begotten within the practice of God's actual love binding them to the concrete reality of the other in unity and service. To know the God whom Jesus reveals is to be drawn out of one's self in the conduct of self-forgetful, other-directed loving. To be faced by Jesus on his way to the Father is to be faced by others in the world of God's love.[2] The grain of wheat must continue to fall into the ground if it is not to remain alone. Those who hate their life in this world keep it for eternal life (12:23–25). By going to the Father in this way, Jesus embodies a new existence of loving, humble service in the world. The measure and inspiration of such love is the love "to the end" that the Lord and Teacher has shown. Consequently, following his Fatherward path cannot be limited to a notional acceptance of his words, nor to a verbal declaration of altruism: "Let us love, not in word or speech, but in truth and action" (1 John 3:18). In entering the movement of Jesus' self-transcending love, his disciples are transformed: "We know love by this, that he laid down his life for us—and we ought to lay down our lives for one another" (1 John 3:16).[3] His disconcerting gesture will forever unsettle Christian conscience with the question, "How does God's love abide in anyone who has the world's goods and sees a brother or sister in need and yet refuses to help?" (1 John 3:17).[4] Jesus' enactment of God's self-giving love makes him in person the "concrete universal," forming the community and the generations that follow it in a "gathering" (11:52) which transcends all relationships based on worldly glory and human respect. The life of the opened heaven will be found in self-giving love for others.

The "example" Jesus has given is the example par excellence. It anticipates the Son's self-giving—right up to the limit of death. The imperative inherent in his paradigmatic gesture has its origin in the supreme exemplar of the Son's action, the Father himself: "...the Son can do nothing on his own, but only what he sees the Father doing; for whatever the Father does, the Son does likewise" (5:19–20). On him the Father has set his seal (6:27). To know the Son is to know his Father (8:19; 12:45). Jesus has previously repudiated any suggestion that he has spoken or acted on his own. The Father who sent him is the source of all he says and does in order to actualize the gift of life for the world (12:49–50). Hence, in this climactic instance of Jesus' love for his disciples, there is to be found the original exemplar, the self-giving love of the Father himself.

For the disciples there is a consequence. Just as the Son's action derives from and manifests the life-giving love of the Father, the disciples too must allow themselves to be drawn into such a movement of love and service, "...that you also should do what I have done to you" (13:15). There is no position in which disciples can locate themselves except within the life of self-giving love. In his consciousness of being from and for the Father, and at the extreme limit of his love for his own, Jesus declares that servants are not greater than their master, nor are those who are sent greater than the one who gives them their mission (13:16). The disciples' mission to the world is animated by the exemplary reality of the Father and the Son united in the love that alone manifests the properly divine glory. Objective knowledge of who God is must pass over into the effective living out of such knowledge: "If you know these things, blessed are you if you do them" (13:17): *Ubi caritas et amor, Deus ibi est*. A later community of disciples, in the context of considerable disunity and scandal, are called back to the essential imperative inherent in Christian life: "Beloved, let us love one another, because love is from God; everyone who loves is born of God and knows God" (1 John 4:7).

3. Light in Darkness

18. "I am not speaking of you all; I know whom I have chosen; it is that the scripture may be fulfilled, 'The one who ate my bread has lifted the heel against me.' 19. I tell you this now before it takes place, that when it does take place you may believe that I AM. 20. Amen, amen, I say to you, whoever receives the one whom I send receives me; and whoever receives me receives the one who sent me." (13:18–20)

Though the basic imperative resides in the outgoing, expanding movement of love and service, the reality of opposition must be faced. Love must face rejection and betrayal—not to be defeated by contradiction, but to manifest itself more fully. Though Jesus both chooses and sends his disciples (13:18, 20), there will be resistance: "He who ate my bread has lifted the heel against me" (13:18). The Johannine use of the word *trogein* in the citation from Psalm 41:10 has a eucharistic connotation (cf. 6:53).[5] The bread of life has been offered to all; and those specially chosen by Jesus, in defiance of all human logic, will know fragility and confusion. Jesus reminds his disciples that it is the logic of the Father which determines the unfolding of events. God will be revealed in his proper glory, not only despite, but even because of, the betrayal the Son will suffer, that "...when it does take place you may believe that I AM" (13:19). The generative presence of God, beyond any human computation or decision, is involved.

What is soon to take place will reveal how the God of the Passover and Exodus will become newly invocable in the fulfillment of the hour. The holiest of names—YHWH, "I am he" (Exod 3:14)—resonates with past experiences and future expectations on three accounts. First, the saving intervention of God in the original Passover now fulfills its purpose through the blood of God's own Lamb (Exod 12:3–7; John 1:29). Moses' message to the people is fulfilled in the coming of the Son: "Thus you shall say to the Israelites, 'I AM has sent me to you' " (Exod 3:14b). Second, it suggests the prophetic, and above all the Isaian, conviction of the absolute transcendence of God in relationship to all human powers and categories (Isa 42:8). Third, the form of this name invites the faithful, but fragile, disciples to move forward to the full manifestation that awaits them—the identification of Jesus as one with the Father (10:30). Thomas, one of the disciples now present, will come to express his own passage from unbelief to faith in Jesus when he will confess the Risen One to be, "My Lord and my God" (20:28).

Jesus speaks both from his supraworldly origin and in obedience to his intraworldly mission to reveal God: "Amen, amen, I say to you…" (13:20). But now the language of origin and mission is completed with that of reception and hospitality. As the Father sends the Son, and the Son sends his disciples, whoever receives the disciple receives Jesus and the one who sent him. The chasm between what was above and what is below is overcome. Heaven is opened (1:51) with a descending and ascending communication embodied in the Son of Man. His mission is completed in reception. Through the respective missions of Jesus and his disciples, the movement of God's love reaches into the world. But the mission "from above" must be met with a welcoming "from below"—as the world receives the disciples and, through them, both Jesus and the Father. To receive the disciple is to receive Jesus; to receive him is to receive the Father (13:20).

By means of this welcoming, the scattered children of God are gathered into one (11:52). There is, however, no question of a fusion or merging of identities. In the new communion of life that is in the making, all agents, be it the Father, or the Son he has sent, or the one sent by Jesus, are to be received in their own personal identities. In the realm of the Father's love, distinct identities are not abolished, but affirmed in the hospitality that marks the reality of true communion and the integrity of mutual relationships.

> 21. When Jesus had thus spoken he was troubled in spirit and testified, "Amen, amen, I say to you, one of your will betray me." 22. The disciples looked at one another, uncertain of whom he spoke. 23. One of his disciples, whom Jesus loved, was lying close to the breast of Jesus; 24. so Simon Peter beckoned to him and said, "Tell us who it is of whom he speaks." 25. So lying thus, close to the breast of Jesus, he said to him, "Lord, who is it?" 26. Jesus answered, "It is he to whom I shall give this morsel when I have dipped it." So when he had dipped the morsel he took it and gave it to Judas, the son of Simon Iscariot. 27. Then after the morsel, Satan entered into him. Jesus said to him, "What you are going to do, do quickly." 28. Now no one at the table knew why he said this to him. 29. Some thought that because Judas had the money box Jesus was telling him, "Buy what we need for the feast," or that he should give something to the poor. 30. So after receiving the morsel he immediately went out; and it was night. (13:21–30)

Yet the waves of communion emanating from the Father break on the jagged rock of contingent reality. A diabolic design is also at work. The light will shine, but only in contrast to the deepest darkness. The self-gift of Jesus will be accomplished in the context of intimate betrayal. With his spirit distressed at the onset of the passion and in his consciousness of the fragility of his disciples, he predicts that one of them will betray him. One of his own will set himself outside the communion built on mutual love and welcome. Instead of "receiving," he will opt for betrayal. Indeed, the ensuing discussion indicates the limited horizon in which all the disciples are still enclosed. Nonetheless, Jesus' love for his own remains true to itself. It will not be reduced to anything else; it will go to the end. The will of the Father will be accomplished only in the vulnerability of love: Jesus identifies his betrayer through a gesture of love. He gives Judas the eucharistic morsel (13:26). The traitorous disciple thus rejects the excess of love Jesus has shown him (13:1), "the example" his master has given (13:15), and the conviviality symbolized in the eucharistic "morsel." He chooses to be part of the Satanic design of violence and exclusion. Having opted for an existence of betrayal rather than the hospitality of true communion, the disciple moves from the circle of light—the communion existing among the Father, the Son, and the disciples. He goes into the outer darkness where the ruler of this world waits to accomplish his design. Though this night had fallen, the Son shows an unreserved acceptance of the will of the Father as it works, even in that outer world of violence and death. He frees Judas to act his part: "What you are going to do, do quickly" (13:27). Yet the Father is working. In the glory to be revealed, even this darkness is not dark: "Even the darkness is not dark to you; and the night is as bright as day, for the darkness is as light to you" (Ps 139:11–12).

4. The New Commandment

31. Thus, when he had gone out, Jesus said, "Now is the Son of Man glorified, and in him God is glorified; 32. if God is glorified in him God will also glorify him in himself, and glorify him at once. 33. Little children, yet a little while I am with you. You will seek me; and as I said to the Jews so now I say to you, 'Where I am going you cannot come.' 34. A new commandment I give to you, that you love one another; even as I have loved you, that you also love one another. 35. By this everyone will know that you are my disciples, if you have love, one for another." (13:31–35)

In the logic of the Gospel, Judas's nocturnal exit indicates that the light of glory—of a love that refuses to be anything but itself—begins to shine. As events move toward the lifting up of the Son on the cross,[6] he will be glorified as the revealer of God. The divine glory, subverting the glory of this world and its ruler, will shine forth.[7] The Father and the Son, united in love, act in a reciprocity of glorification (13:32). The mutual love called for in the example of the foot-washing has its radical explanation in the loving relationship existing between the Father and the Son. In this it contrasts with the Satanic glory of this world, which can accomplish its purpose only through deceit, expulsion, and murder.

Still, while the process of glorification is moving forward, it will mean Jesus' departure. He will be violently removed from the scene. Both the Jews (7:34) and the disciples (13:33) will experience his absence. Neither party can understand the Fatherward direction of his path. Only the Son can enter into the realm of the Father. His glory is outside all human capacity and expectation: "Where I am going you cannot come" (13:33). And yet, the realities of his departure and of the subsequent absence experienced by the "little children" he leaves behind, lead him to disclose the way in which his disciples can follow him into the realm of the Father. Because he has chosen the disciples for his own (13:18), they have not allied themselves with "the children of the devil" (cf. 8:39–47). Having received the gift of his "example," they are now given another directive by which to inhabit the realm of the opened heaven: a new commandment.

His going to the Father creates a space in the world for a new community of love. In the midst of the world's darkness, a luminous clearing will be brought about, shaped by the imperatives of Jesus' love for his own. All the commandments and teaching of Jesus originate in the Father (cf. 7:16; 8:26, 29, 38; 12:49–50). By obeying him in the Fatherward direction of his whole existence, they enter into the movement of the Father's all-embracing love, even on the small scale of their own mutual loving. In this they manifest to the world the self-giving love that reigns in the realm of the Father. The logic of Jesus' new commandment is sharply expressed in the First Letter of John, "Those who say, 'I love God,' and hate their brothers and sisters, are liars; for those who do not love a brother or sister whom they have seen, cannot love God whom they have not seen" (1 John 4:20).

One of the disciples will betray him, and the rest will desert him. Peter himself will deny him. Yet despite their ignorance and their various refusals to follow him on his path to the Father (13:36–38), the way will nonetheless be opened: "Where I am going, you cannot follow me now; but you shall follow" (13:36b). Love will follow them "to the end." They will rejoin Jesus in the imperative that ruled his entire existence. They shall indeed follow him (13:37), as they later recognize the glory of the love now being revealed.

5. God and Others

In the arrival of this hour, certain features of the Christian experience of God stand out. God is not presented as an object of "mystical" experience or religious speculation. For the paternal horizon in which Jesus moves is one of radical self-expropriation. The divine other who is the defining pole of Jesus' own consciousness demands his self-surrender for the sake of the many others. These, in an obvious sense, he will leave behind in the world of self-assertiveness and threat. And yet they are summoned into the mode of existence that Jesus' Fatherward movement exemplifies. He opens the space of discipleship: the vertical, Fatherward movement of his path is expressed on the horizontal plane by his washing the disciples' feet. The upward direction of his exodus demands an outward activity of love and service in the community of his disciples. To the degree its members turn with the Son to face the Father, they are imperatively faced with the familiar other—to be loved and served in accord with Jesus' example and new commandment.

The spaciousness of the Father's house (14:2), into which Jesus is going to prepare a place for those who follow him, already breathes an overwhelming hospitality. He has washed the feet of his disciples, and while giving himself to be their food and drink, he offered the morsel to his traitorous disciple. As the Father has sent the Son into the world, Jesus sends his disciples. Yet this mission reaches its term in welcoming and receiving (13:20), in the actuality of living communion.

The experience of God radically destabilizes ordinary identities and relationships. God can no longer be "kept in his place," for the Father has sent his Son into the world. For its part, the world itself has lost its self-made boundaries with this opening of heaven. Nor can Jesus be kept in his place, for he is leaving this world for the Father. Even death ceases to be in place for him as an opaque impenetrable limit to human life. It is now being subsumed into the hour of glory; his dying is integral to the radiance of the love of God revealed in the self-giving of the Son. As for his disciples, though they will suffer the grief of their master's absence, his love "to the end" demands of them an excess of mutual love that will leave them far more disturbed than any grief over his departure can cause. The reality of Jesus' absence leaves a space where no believer can ever live again in self-contained isolation: "Just as I have loved you, you also should love one another" (13:34).

Notes

1. For this translation, see F. J. Moloney, *Glory not Dishonor: Reading John 13—21* (Minneapolis: Fortress Press, 1998), 13, n. 39.
2. David F. Ford, *Self and Salvation: Being Transformed* (Cambridge: Cambridge University Press, 1999) uses the image of "the face" to outline a theology of Christian transformation. See especially 158–200.
3. The word, *hypodeigma* (13:15), found only here in the New Testament, implies the reality of an exemplary self-giving unto death (cf. LXX 2 Macc 6:28; 4 Macc 17:22–23; Sir 44:16).
4. For a more extensive reflection, see Anthony J. Kelly, "'God is Love': A Theological Moral Reading of 1 John," *Studia Moralia* XXXVII/1 (June 1999), 35–72.
5. This is the only other place in which this verb occurs—in the most obviously eucharistic section of the Gospel.
6. Cf. 1:51; 3:14; 6:27, 53; 8:28; 12:23.
7. Cf. 1:14; 2:11; 5:44; 7:18; 11:4, 40; 12:41, 43.

14

To Live in the House of the Father (14:1–31)

1. The Paternal Host

1. "Let not your hearts be troubled; believe in God, believe also in me. 2. In my Father's house there are many abiding places, and if it had not been so I would have told you, for I am going to prepare a place for you. 3. And when I go and prepare a place for you I will come again and take you to myself, that where I am you may be also. 4. And you know the way where I am going." (14:1–4)

Strictly speaking, only now does "the last discourse" begin.[1] On this ominous night, with the onset of "his hour," Jesus speaks to steady the troubled and questioning hearts of his chosen ones. He summons them to believe in God and to believe in him. By believing in him who is uniquely related to God, yet on whom the cross is already casting its shadow, they will be lifted forever beyond the inherently troubled world of human glory, to see God's own glory revealed. Traditional theological beliefs must yield to faith in the Father he has made known, and with whom he is one. Since he is the unique revealer of God, all previous meanings of God and of the way God acts in the world will need to be recast. "God" will be newly defined as the Father of the Son, given in love for the life of the world (3:16).[2]

287

Where before Jesus had simply juxtaposed God and himself as objects of faith, his next words bring the two together within one all-welcoming mystery. By going before his disciples to his Father's house, he is preparing a place for them. He is thereby acting with a unique freedom in God's domain, "his Father's house." Heaven is about to be opened (1:51). In the best Johannine irony, Jesus' departure from the world, where his own have proved so inhospitable (1:11), will bring into being a new era of divine hospitality and welcome. He opens a way of gracious, permanent access to the Father.[3] In that paternal home, there is room for all—the "many abiding places" guaranteed by Jesus' own word (14:2).[4]

Moreover, in the "two-way traffic" of the opened heaven, not only does Jesus go to prepare a place for his followers, but also he will come again to gather them into his company within the spaciousness of his Father's house. He will return to accompany his disciples in their homecoming since he alone is "the way" (14:6). Admittedly, all spatial metaphors of going and returning await their fullest interpretation in the paschal mystery of his cross and resurrection. The glorified Jesus will himself become the new "house of my Father"—the new temple of God's dwelling with his people (cf. 2:13–22). In the gift of his only Son, the Father has sought out—and found—"true worshipers in spirit and in truth" (4:23). The impending departure of Jesus leads to the Father's own coming as well (14:23), as the lovers of Jesus themselves share in the Godly spirit of welcome and hospitality—in regard to the Father, the Son, and their own brothers and sisters (13:20). In the "many abiding places," the life of self-giving love will be the cause of mutual indwelling: "God is love, and those who abide in love, abide in God, and God abides in them" (1 John 4:16b).

To come home to the house of the Father suggests not only an abiding communion with the Father and the Son, but a continuous movement in the company of Jesus as "the way." Entry into the Father's house does not mean the end of history, for a consummation of that history is promised. Still, the metaphors of homecoming and journey interpenetrate. Being able to follow Jesus—along the way that he declares himself to be—is part of the goal. It is an aspect of abiding in the realm of the Father, even if the metaphor of the way is subordinate to that of dwelling and abiding: "And you know the way where I am going" (14:4).

2. Questions from "Troubled Hearts"

5. Thomas said to him, "Lord, we do not know where you are going; how can we know the way?" 6. Jesus said to him, "I am the way, and the truth, and the life; no one comes to the Father but by me. 7. If you have come to know me you shall know my Father also. Henceforth you know him and have seen him." 8. Philip said to him, "Lord, show us the Father and we shall be satisfied." 9. Jesus said to him, "Have I been with you so long and yet you do not know me, Philip? Whoever has seen me has seen the Father; how can you say, 'Show us the Father'? 10. Do you not believe that I am in the Father and the Father in me? The words that I say to you I do not speak on my own authority; but the Father who dwells in me does his works. 11. Believe me that I am in the Father and the Father in me; or else believe for the sake of the works themselves. (14:5–11)

Thomas—conveniently for faithful readers of the Gospel experiencing the troubles of the heart that Jesus addresses (14:1)—expresses his ignorance of both the goal and the path of the way of Jesus. He does not know where Jesus is going, nor how to come to such knowledge (14:5). In reply, Jesus clarifies both the meaning of the way and the demands it will make: "I am the way, and the truth, and the life; no one comes to the Father but by me" (14:6). In the generative, revelatory signifi-cance of his "I am…" declarations, Jesus presents himself as the way precisely because "the fullness of the gift that is truth" is embodied in him (1:14, 17). As this revealing truth, he is the object of the testimony of the Baptist (5:33). Because of his word, the truth is known and liberates (8:32). Those allergic to the truth that he has heard from God have tried to kill him (8:40), in an antagonism that gives birth to violence and lies— all that is opposed to God (8:44–46). Countering the murderous violence by which "the ruler of this world" holds sway is the truth that gives freedom and life. Jesus is, therefore, the way of both truth and life—the way for the world that has come into being through him who is its life (1:4). As the bread of God, he is given from above to give life to the world (6:33, 35). To believe in the truth he reveals means already to be in possession of endless life, and of the promise of final resurrection (6:40, 48, 51). Because he lives from "the living Father," whoever "eats" him, as the stark realism of what's proper to eucharistic rhetoric has it, will live because of him (6:57). His words are spirit and life (6:63); and he alone has the words of eternal life (6:68). To follow his way means walking in the light of life (8:12). As the Good Shepherd giving his life for his sheep, he has come that those who hear his voice may have abundant life (10:10–11). He is "the resurrection and the life" even now, for those who expe-rience the world's grief and the threat of death (11:25).

Jesus' self-identification as "the way" is, therefore, illumined by the truth he witnesses to and the life that derives from him. The gift of the "example" in washing the disciples feet, and his new commandment to love as he loved have already anticipated the way that is here described. Nonetheless, he is not merely a way in which the community of his followers relate to one another. Though indeed he commands such love, he is from beginning to end the way to the Father. Because he is the way in this sense, he is for his followers their way to one another in the community of faith and love.

Still, there is no community of mutual love, nor any access to the Father's house, unless in union with Jesus as the way: no one comes to the Father but by him (14:6b). To refuse to journey on his way of self-giving love is to love one's life in this world; and the grain of wheat will remain alone. Only by participating in his love "to the end," even unto death (cf. 1 John 3:16), do believers have the assurance of living in the realm of "the living Father" (6:57) who loves Jesus, in that he lays down his life in order to take it up again (10:17).

To know Jesus by following him as the way of truth and life means, in practice, knowing and seeing the Father (14:7). The Father is the origin, the end, and the generative source of his Son as "the way." The realm of the Father is the space of limitless love that the way of Jesus travels in coming, going, and returning. Philip's request attempts to place the all-encompassing mystery of the Father within the confines of the world of human control and expectation. He gives voice to the pretensions of human judgment in its eagerness to dominate reality in accord with its own ambiguous criteria: "Lord, show us the Father, and we shall be satisfied" (14:8). In this case, the disciple is not motivated to surrender to the Father's will but to satisfy his own desires. In response, Jesus points to himself as the visible evidence in which the Father can be seen.

Previously the Greeks, in their linguistic and cultural affinity with the Greek-named Philip, had approached the disciple with their request, "Sir, we wish to see Jesus" (12:21). Jesus interpreted their approach as a sign of his approaching hour (12:23). But when Philip makes his request, he is showing himself to be more "Greek" than his fellow Greeks. Whereas they had appreciated the revelatory significance of Jesus, Philip is found looking past him to a God inhabiting a closed heaven, removed, in accord with traditional philosophical and religious criteria, to a realm of inaccessible transcendence. If *that* God is revealed, "…we shall be satisfied" (14:8b).

Jesus' second rhetorical question focuses on the crucial issue: the need to accept the Father as he is self-revealed through the reciprocal indwelling of the Son and the Father: Jesus is *in* the Father and the Father is *in* him (14:10). The Son cannot be understood except in living relationship to the Father; while the only access to the Father is through the way of truth and life that Jesus is in person: "Believe in God, believe also in me" (14:1). There is no need for Philip to be troubled with a metaphysical speculation that bypasses the incarnation of the Word of God. To believe in Jesus who, as the Word, is "what God was" in the beginning (1:1), is to believe in God. It follows that believing in God and believing in Jesus are not two separate activities, but aspects of the one movement of faith, as it embraces the Father and Son in unity. Jesus occupies the Father's house, not as a guest to be welcomed, but as a co-host with his Father. Their reciprocal indwelling suggests a unity between them which both surpasses and underpins the previous metaphor of disciples' many abiding places in the Father's house (14:2–3). So intimate is this unity that, just as no one comes to the Father but by Jesus (14:6), no one can come to him unless drawn by the Father (6:44).

Still, while the Son and the Father indwell one another, there is no implication of a lifeless symmetry or fusion. Though Jesus is about to depart, the ever-active Father is not about to leave the scene; he remains the generative presence in every aspect of this hour, acting in both the words[5] and works[6] of Jesus: "The words that I say to you I do not speak on my own authority; but the Father who dwells in me does the works"

(14:10). The paternal initiative fills his filial awareness: "Believe me that I am in the Father and the Father in me; or else believe me for the sake of the works themselves" (14:11). Jesus commands faith in himself only because he is totally indwelling the Father and indwelt by him. The Father's action is the absolute principle and motive of his mission—so absolute in fact that he effectively repudiates any tendency on the part of believers either to be fixated on himself, or on some abstract consideration of who the Father is. The true character of the Father is disclosed performatively through what he does—in the saving works of gathering the scattered children of God into unity (11:52) and of giving life to the world (1:3–4, 12; 6:51; 10:10).

3. Greater Works

The dynamic involvement of the Father in the works the Son performs, and the transforming effect of such works, is the central consideration. The Father is seen by the disciples as originating and fulfilling the works Jesus performs. The Father's glory does not consist in the world learning exciting new philosophical or theological truths as an extension of its prior theoretical knowledge. For it is the Father who acts, seeking "true worshipers in spirit and truth" (4:23).

> 12. **Amen, amen, I say to you, the one who believes in me will do the works that I do; and will do greater works than these, because I go to the Father. 13. Whatever you ask in my name, I will do it, that the Father may be glorified in the Son; 14. if you ask anything in my name I will do it."** (14:12–14)

The basic dynamism of God's working extends to the activity of the disciples themselves. Jesus' self-effacing dedication to the will of the Father is further instanced in the "greater works" the disciples will perform after his going to the Father (14:12). Faith in Jesus will enable the believer to continue the works the Father has brought forth in him. The actions of the Son in glorifying the Father will be extended and surpassed.[7] His passing out of this world to the Father will, therefore, be the source of boundless creativity. As the community of faith turns in prayer to Jesus—invisible to this world but present to the Father—Jesus will continue to act in his role of glorifying the Father. As the prior "Paraclete" (cf. 14:15), he will be effectively present to his disciples. No longer contained within the limits of this world, he will act from within the realm of the Father, to give life and unity to his followers. Here, his promise anticipates the Father's gift of the "other Paraclete," "the Spirit of truth" (14:16–17), who will be the abiding source of disciples' "greater works."

Jesus' going to the Father means that his unique historical mission will be continued and completed throughout time in the mission of his followers. The other Paraclete will come in answer to his prayer to the Father, and will remain with them forever (14:16). Turned to the Father in intercession on behalf of his disciples, Jesus will be present and active in them. He will glorify the Father through their historical mission as he did in his own earthly existence (2:11; 5:41; 7:18; 8:50, 54; 11:4, 40). Though the disciples will not speak *words* "greater" than those of Jesus—he is the unique Word (1:1)—he subverts the whole self-assertive structure of the glory of this world by allowing for the disciples' "greater works." Having washed his disciples' feet (cf. 13:1–16), he will empower them to surpass his works. He clings to nothing but the glory of the Father, always the source, measure, and goal of his mission (cf. 14:28c). The realm of glory and true life means not only the Son's self-surrender to the Father, but also his self-effacement in the "greater works" to be performed by his followers in the time of another Paraclete.

4. Another Paraclete

15. "If you love me you will keep my commandments. 16. And I will pray to the Father, and he will give you another Paraclete to be with you forever, 17. even the Spirit of truth, whom the world cannot receive because it neither sees him nor knows him; you know him, for he abides with you and will be among you." (14:15–17)

The disciples' love for Jesus entails their obedient acceptance of him as the Word: believing in God, believing in him (14:1), and keeping his commandments (14:15). He commands a hearing as the one who makes the Father known. And not only a hearing, but also a following. He has set a supreme "example" (13:14), and enjoined the practice of mutual love with his "new commandment" of loving one another the way he has loved them (13:34). The Word, in becoming flesh, becomes both an example and a commandment. The "greater works" the disciples will do in his name (14:2) will be the outcome of the love with which he has loved—continued and enlarged to include all his future followers.

Still, his impending departure will inevitably be a cause of fear and desolation for his disciples. For them to be commanded to love him or one another after his example of selfless love, within a world which has had no room for either Jesus or his followers, is no consolation when faced with his absence. His absence will weigh more heavily upon them: his commandment and example are no substitute for his presence, especially as both would expose a humbling human incapacity to live the truth that his life expressed. Their hearts have every reason to be troubled (14:1). Will his going to the Father mean that he will simply disappear? Will what he called "my Father's house" (14:2) prove to be merely a desolating emptiness, especially as his followers must face their own inevitable deaths? How will the love that they are summoned to be possible? Deprived of his presence, will the Father still be present to them; or will they simply be "orphaned" (14:18) in a world formed by other powers?

Jesus addresses these troubling apprehensions. The Father will give another gift to meet the disciples in the depths of their need. The disciples, united in love and committed to the Father's will, will receive "another Paraclete," another counsel for the defense in the great contest with the world over the truth of God (14:16). Previously Jesus had promised to answer the prayers of his followers (14:13–14). But now the emphasis shifts from their prayer to him, to his prayer to the Father for them—that another, and permanent, gift be given them: another Paraclete to remain with them forever.

This other, divinely-given defender will be a permanent counterpoise to the unrelenting opposition the disciples will suffer at the hands of this world and its ruler. "The Spirit of truth" will be an abiding source of evidence for their defense against the lies of a world of frenzied self-justification. And he will remain with them forever. It is not in the nature of this gift that it comes and goes, as was the case in the gift of the prior Paraclete, Jesus himself. In the nature of the case, the Word made flesh is with the disciples for "a little while" (14:19). His physical presence among them has intrinsic limits. Human life must end; and he, in fact, is about to be killed. For it to be otherwise, the physical presence of Jesus would be a distraction from the realm of the Father, obscuring the gift of eternal life with a miraculous extension of mere physical life in this world. As the first Paraclete must depart on the completion of his revealing mission, the other Paraclete not only fills the vacuum caused by the absence of Jesus, but fills it precisely in a giving that makes the Father and Jesus present to the disciples in a new way—the Father as the giver, and Jesus as the intercessor in the Father's presence.

This other Paraclete will be known by his opposition to the antagonistic world that can neither receive, see, or know him (14:17). The Spirit of truth cannot be received by the world bent on rejecting precisely the truth it witnesses to, namely, that Jesus has come from the Father, and that he is the Word *of God*.[8] The Spirit originates outside the self-enclosed realm of worldly glory. It is given by the Father at the prayer of the Son. In terms of his origin and purpose, therefore, this other Paraclete is incomprehensible within the categories of a world hardened in its refusal to adore God "in spirit and in truth" (4:23–24).

In contrast, the disciples, moving with Jesus out of the false consciousness of this world into the realm of the Father, are familiar with the Spirit and the truth in question (14:17). The Spirit that had descended and remained on Jesus himself is the "Holy Spirit" with which he will baptize (1:32–33), the crowning gift that had been promised after the death and glorification of Jesus.[9] It will now abide with the disciples forever. In a gifted life, the community of believers will make its own journey through time and history. The Spirit will be "among them," as the source of unifying truth, mediating to them the double gift— the presence of both the Father and the Son.

5. A Departure and a Coming

18. "I will not leave you desolate; I will come to you. 19. Yet a little while and the world will see me no more, but you will see me; because I live, you will live also. 20. In that day you will know that I am in the Father, and you in me, and I in you. 21. They who have my commandments and keep them are those

who love me; and those who love me will be loved by
my Father, and I will love them and reveal myself to
them." (14:18–21)

Jesus will not leave the disciples abandoned to a world
from which he will now be physically absent. Through the gift
of the Spirit, he will come to them (14:18). The "little while" of
their Master's historical physical presence among them is coming to an end. While the world will see only an absence—the
world will see him no longer (14:19a)—his followers will experience him as a vitalizing presence. They will see him. And
because he lives, they too will live (14:19b). He has not fallen
victim to the reign of death. By dying, he goes from the world to
open it to a new communion of life: "In that day you will know
that I am in my Father, and you in me, and I in you" (14:20).
The "little while" has ushered in the endless day of eternal life.

The former language of example and commandment yields
to that of living communion. His disciples will be united with
him in the life which flows into him from the Father. His previous promise is about to be kept: "As the living Father sent me,
and I live because of the Father, so the one who eats me will live
because of me" (6:57). Abiding in Jesus, believers are united
both in, and to, the source of all life, the Father himself. They
thus share in the communication of life coming from the Father
to the Son. In a world of violence, death, and disunity, the Spirit
witnesses to the true character of life as it exists within the unity
of the Father and the Son: "For as the Father raises the dead and
gives them life, so also the Son gives life to whom he will"
(5:21). The reality of this life is experienced in the worshiping
community, as it prays, follows the example of Jesus, keeps his
commandments, and celebrates his presence in the sacraments of
baptism (3:3–5) and Eucharist (6:51–58).

6. "...We Will Come"

22. Judas (not Iscariot) said to him, "Lord, how is it that you will manifest yourself to us and not to the world?" 23. Jesus answered him, "Those who love me will keep my word, and my Father will love them and we will come to them and make our home with them. 24. Whoever does not love, does not keep my words; and the word you hear is not mine but the Father's who sent me." (14:22–24)

To love Jesus means the praxis of love—"to have and to keep his commandments" (14:21a). The movement of love, toward Jesus and those who love him, brings believers to the ultimate experience of being loved: they will be loved by his Father" (14:21b). As one with the Father, Jesus himself will love them, and reveal himself to them (14:21c). In this luminous context of loving and being loved, the original identity of Jesus will be disclosed in its full relational reality. He is eternally turned toward God, yet, as the light and life of all creation, he includes all in himself—above all the disciples, as will soon be presented in terms of the vine and the branches (15:1–7).

Judas asks how Jesus will show himself to the disciples but not to the world (14:22). This disciple's question presumes that believers will suffer continual antagonism from a world intent on its own self-glorification. Will this clash of perspectives make the self-manifestation of Jesus impossible? The answer is found in the "circulation" of love involving the disciples, Jesus himself, and the Father. Those who love him will keep his word—by believing in God and believing in him (14:1); by following his example (13:1–15); by loving one another as he has loved them (13:34). Loving him in this way, they will be loved by his Father (14:21b). But the great communion of love and life is not yet fully achieved. It looks to a final communication and homecoming: "...and we will come to them and make our home with them" (14:23c). Not only will the disciples find that Jesus has prepared a spacious welcome for them in his Father's house, or even that Jesus himself will return and manifest himself to them, bringing with him the assurance of the still-distant Father's love. The "two-way traffic" of opened heaven means even more than this. *We,* both the Son and the Father, will come to make our home in the community of those who believe and love. The experience of God will unfold in history to its consummation in perfect communion. Jesus' departure, and the way they who love him must follow, leads to a future consummated in a divine advent.[10] Given the abiding presence of the Spirit, and the promised coming of the Father and the Son, the Christian community will itself be under the joyous obligation of receiving the Father, together with his Son and Spirit, into a house of many rooms!

Thus the opened heaven envisages a conjunction of what is from above with what is from below. The "greater things" are in store—in the perfect realization of communion between God and the world redeemed (cf. 1:50–51). The privileged but limited span of the "little time" of Jesus' historical existence with his disciples, the present struggling time supported by the presence of "another Paraclete," and the time soon to come when the crucified Jesus will reveal himself as newly alive, are all leading to a definitive homecoming: "...those who abide in love abide in God, and God abides in them" (1 John 4:16; cf. 3:24; 4:13). The Father, having sought out true worshipers (4:23), will find them, never to be snatched from the hand of him who is greater than all (10:30).

Though history reaches forward to this final homecoming, it still remains a time of choice and conflict: "Whoever does not love me, does not keep my words" (14:24a). Jesus is the way (13:6) of "the truth that will make you free" (8:32). He has prayed that his disciples will receive the Spirit of truth that the world cannot receive (14:16–17). The history of faith will still have to contend with the scandal of refusal. The Father's saving will imposes no automatic program. But his Word is not one more utterance in the vast conflicting conversation of the flesh of this world: to reject Jesus is to close oneself to God's self-communication, so to remain outside the Father's house of many rooms, and to reject the coming of the Father himself.

7. Gifts in the Meantime...

25. "These things I have spoken to you, while I am still with you. 26. But the Paraclete, the Holy Spirit, whom the Father will send in my name, he will teach you all things, and bring to your remembrance all that I have said to you. 27. Peace I leave you; my peace I give you; not as the world gives do I give to you. Let not your hearts be troubled, neither let them be afraid. 28. You heard me say to you, 'I go away and I am coming to you.' If you loved me you would have rejoiced, because I go to the Father; for the Father is greater than I. 29. And now I have told you before it takes place so that when it does take place you may believe. 30. I will no longer talk much with you, for the ruler of this world is coming. He has no power over me; 31. but I do as the Father has commanded me so that the world may know that I love the Father. Rise, let us go hence." (14:25–31)

Jesus is still with the disciples, yet his death draws near. "His own" are still in the world. Faced with their own fragility and the threat of death and violence, their future seems uncertain. The full meaning of what he has communicated awaits an interpretation exceeding what is possible in this present time of confusion, questioning, and heart-troubling lack of evidence. What is happening in this moment will need to be remembered in the context of the "all things" of the Word's communication in the flesh (14:26). Nonetheless, a full grasp of the Gospel's message exceeds human comprehension. Only the Father can be the source of a complete understanding of his Word. Hence, the Paraclete is sent by the Father to bring out the God-given significance of "all things" that Jesus has said, done, and suffered.

The disciples will perform deeds greater than the deeds of Jesus (14:12); but their knowledge of the words the Word has spoken will always be in progress, for the gift of truth is unsurpassable (1:14). The "Holy Spirit," the gift of the "holy Father" (17:11), the one with whom Jesus baptizes (1:33), will guide the disciples to an ever-fuller appropriation of his message. The Paraclete will be sent by the Father, who is the transcendent origin of all gifts, and who is himself "spirit" (4:24). His search for worshipers in "spirit and truth" (4:23) will be accomplished through the gift of the truth incarnate in his Word, and in the associated giving of the Spirit of truth. The Father will show himself to be the "God [who] is true...[who] gives the Spirit without measure" (3:33b–34).

To the Spirit-assisted pilgrim community, Jesus now promises the gift of his own peace. It results from the interrelated gifts of his own presence and that of the Spirit (14:27a). He has already given the gifts of his "example" and new commandment; and in the gift of the morsel, the eucharistic gift of his own flesh for the life of the world is implied. He has just promised the Father's gift of the other Paraclete, to be the permanent guide and defender of the disciples in his absence. All these gifts come together to amount to a new, unbreakable bond of communion with himself and the Father, impregnable to the violence that threatens both him and his followers. It is *his* peace, the peace that has enabled him to do the will of the Father and to love his own unto the end. Such a peace originates from his unbreakable union with the Father: "And the one who has sent me is with me; he has not left me alone, for I always do what is pleasing to him" (8:29).[11] Further, he gives his peace, in a way different from that in which the world gives, and promises peace—"not as the world gives..." (14:27a). The peace of the world is built on an endless history of violence and victimization. It has come to demand even the death of the Son (11:48–52). In contrast, the peace of Jesus and the way he gives it consist not in making other victims, but in his self-offering on behalf of all (11:53). In this he is the true Son of the Father. For God has given what is most intimate to himself—his only Son—for the world's salvation (3:16). Hence, the peace of Jesus, and the way he gives it, consists not in violent self-assertion at the expense of others—after the pattern of worldly glory—but in washing the feet of others and loving others "unto the end." His gift of peace is deeply subversive of the world's peace, even as it steadies disciples' hearts, troubled by the challenge ahead of them (14:27b).

If the peace of this world demands his violent removal (11:50), it will need other scapegoats in the future. The disciples are left with what seems a fragile consolation: "You heard me say, 'If I go away, I will come to you.'" (14:28a). Their disconsolate acceptance of his departure can hardly envisage the reality of his life-giving return, a situation mirrored in the lives of Christians in every age. But where faith cannot yet go, love is invited to bridge the gap and live, not in sorrow, but in joy: "If you loved me, you would have rejoiced, because I go the Father; for the Father is greater than I" (14:28b). Inasmuch as his disciples re-center their lives in the Father—the center of Jesus' own life—their "pain will be turned into joy" (16:20). If their love follows him on his way to the Father, they will not fall victim to the defeated sadness of the world of violence and human glory.

Jesus' departure, though it means his dying, will lead to glory for him, and to the glorification of the Father in a supreme moment of revelation. Surrender to the Father's will, for him and for his followers, means joy and the fullness of life. It is dying into the ever-greater mystery of life and love. The grief marking this world of departures and death yields, in the presence of the Father, to joy.

For Jesus is going to him who "is greater than all" (10:30). He says, therefore, in the logic of the one who knows that the Father has given all things into his hands, and that he has come from God and is going to God (13:3), that "the Father is greater than I" (14:28). Though he has been reproached for making himself God's equal (5:18; 10:33), and though he has declared, "The Father and I are one" (10:30), the language of the Son emerges from his filial consciousness. In all that he is and does he is from and for the Father. He has never asserted himself, as his adversaries charged, against the Father. For they know only the language of this world's glory. But in this other realm, in the sphere in which the glory of God will be revealed, relationships are otherwise. It is a world of communion, loving relationships, and service of the other. To live is not to be set against the other in envy and competition, but to exist for the other in loving mutuality. With such a sense of life, Jesus can say not only that the Father is greater than he, but that the disciples will do greater works than he has done (14:12). To him who has washed his disciples' feet as an "example" of the way of truth and life, the language of self-assertion is foreign and violent. Admittedly, the realism of trinitarian faith will have to struggle hard, in the three centuries following the time of the Gospel, to develop a notion of God as the limitless self-communication of life and love. Theological language will have to free itself from all the limits of even the greatest philosophies, if it is to appreciate the glory of the self-giving love that has been revealed.[12]

Jesus' promise of the gifts of the Spirit, peace and joy, directs the fragile disciples into the progress of the mystery now reaching its dénouement: "...so that when it does take place, you may believe" (14:29). The decisive hour is about to occur, when "the ruler of this world" will no longer be countered by the words of Jesus alone, but by the power of the Father, who, despite all evil, will offer that world its true life. The full dimensions of the conflict between the agents of death and the paternal giver of life are still to be realized. The Word will be revealed, not so much by further words, but by a largely silent surrender to the will of the Father. His all-encompassing will is about to be accomplished—even through the violent death in store for the Son—as the design of the ruler of this world takes effect. For Jesus acknowledges no ruler except the Father. In his love for his Father, he is not about to be reduced within the world to anything less than the Father's Son, and God's Word of revelation. He does, therefore, as the Father commands, so that the world may know that his whole being is love for the world-loving, life-giving, non-judging Father.

"Rise, let us go hence" (14:31b). As "the Way," Jesus summons his followers to make their way with him into the realm of the Father, and to the knock-down-drag-out confrontation with evil that impends. A journey from the darkness and ambiguities of this world into the realm of life and truth has begun. The fulfillment of all Passovers is about to happen.

Notes

1. Tradition has rightly considered John 13—17 in toto under the heading of "the last discourse." While there are the different genres of narrative, discourse, and prayer, the unity of the whole is guaranteed by the author's careful literary and theological usage of the material (cf. F. J. Moloney, *Glory not Dishonor: Reading John 13—21* (Minneapolis: Fortress Press, 1998), 1–7.

2. For an incisive and accessible commentary on the whole of "the last discourse," see Stanley B. Marrow, *The Gospel of John: A Reading* (Mahwah, N.J.: Paulist Press, 1995), 248–318.

3. Compare with M. Coloe, *God Dwells with Us*, 157–178.

4. This point is nicely articulated in Christopher Morse, *Not Every Spirit: A Dogmatics of Christian Disbelief* (Valley Forge, Pa.: Trinity Press International, 1994), 342–343.

5. Cf. 3:34; 5:23–24; 8:18, 28, 38, 47; 12:49.

6. Cf. 5:20, 36; 9:3–4; 10:25, 32, 37–38.

7. This bold Johannine position deeply affects the course of Christian theology in its formulation of the immanence of God in the activity of the created cause. Aquinas notes that "to detract from the perfection of the creature is to detract from the perfection of the divine power at work" (*Summa contra Gentiles*, Lib. 3, c. 66).

8. Cf. 1:35–51; 3:1–21, 31–36; 4:10–15; 5:19–30, 36–38, 43–44; 6:41–51; 7:25–31, 40–44; 8:12–20, 21–29; 9:24–34; 10:31–39.

9. Cf. 7:39; 11:4, 51–53; 12:23, 32–33; 13:1, 31–32.

10. The informed exegesis that would stress the eschatological nature of this coming of the Father and the Son seems at first glance to be contrary to a long history of trinitarian mysticism founded in an experiential sense of the divine indwelling as, say, it is represented in Elizabeth of Dijon. However, it is as well to keep in mind at this point the Thomist doctrine of the divine missions. On this side of the "beatific vision," there are as many divine "comings" as there are continuing outpourings of grace (cf. *Summa Theol.*, 1, 43, 6 ad 2). Further, in terms of the spatial metaphor implied, Aquinas writes, commenting on this verse, "God is said to come to us not because he is brought near to us but because we are brought near to him. Someone comes to a place where before he was not present; but this does not fit the divine case, because God is everywhere...God, therefore, is said to come to someone insofar as he is there in a new way...namely through the effect of grace. Through the working of grace it is he who makes us come to him" (*In Evang. B. Joannis Expositio*, c. 14, lect. 6, n. 8).

11. For a richly suggestive reflection, see Brian V. Johnstone, "The Resurrection as Source for a Theology of Peace," *Studia Moralia* XXXVI/2, December, 1998, 441–460.

12. For a concise account of the development of the Christian notion of God, see Joseph Ratzinger, *Introduction to Christianity*, J. R. Forster, trans. (London: Search Press, 1969), 94–127.

15

<hr>

The Father: Source of Life and Fruitfulness (15:1—16:3)

1. The Heavenly Vine-Dresser

1. "I am the true vine and my Father is the vine-dresser. 2. Every branch of mine that bears no fruit he takes away, and every branch that does bear fruit he prunes that it may bear more fruit. 3. You are already made clean by the word I have spoken to you. 4. Abide in me, and I in you. As the branch cannot bear fruit by itself unless it abides in the vine, neither can you unless you abide in me. 5. I am the vine, you are the branches. Those who abide in me and I in them bear much fruit, because apart from me you can do nothing. 6. Whoever does not abide in me is cast forth as a branch and withers; and the branches are gathered, thrown on the fire, and burned. 7. If you abide in me and my words abide in you, ask whatever you will and it shall be done for you. 8. By this my Father is glorified, because you bear much fruit and so prove to be my disciples." (15:1–8)

As with Jesus' other *I am* statements,[1] the self-designation, "I am the vine," indicates the generative action of God working in and through him (cf. 14:11). Doing the works of the Father, he has been sent to make God known and to glorify him as the

One from whom he comes. As the true vine, he presents himself as the God-given source of life and fruitfulness. As the *true* vine, he is in contrast to the barrenness of the once-fruitful vine of Israel.[2] Though it had formerly brought forth salvation (4:22b), it is now separated from its life-giving source. The Father, unceasingly at work, is depicted as tending the health and fruitfulness of the vine. As the ultimate and decisive agent, he prunes it—and gets rid of dead branches, so that the vital union of the disciples with Jesus will be maintained and enhanced. Apart from the vine, the branch neither lives nor bears fruit, and the prospect of "greater works" (14:12) is diminished.

Yet the disciples are already "cleansed" by the word of Jesus (15:3); and are now listening to him at table because the Father has already been in action. Now they are to abide in Jesus just as he abides in them. Enlivened through union with the vine, the branches are not doomed to barren inactivity in the Father's vineyard. In a communion of life and growth, those united to Jesus are necessarily involved in the life-giving praxis of keeping his commandments. In this they will be the object of the Father's nurturing care and generosity: "…ask whatever you will, and it shall be done for you" (15:7). The bounty of the grape harvest will be to the glory of the vine-dresser: the Father will be glorified because disciples of Jesus bear fruit in abundance (15:8).

> 9. "Inasmuch as the Father has loved me, so I have loved you; abide in my love. 10. If you keep my commandments you will abide in my love, just as I have kept my Father's commandments and abide in his love. 11. These things I have spoken to you that my joy may be in you, and that your joy may be complete."(15:9–11)

The quickening sap moving through the vine to its branches is the life of love flowing from the Father himself. The

Father has loved Jesus who abides in his love; Jesus has loved his disciples who are to abide in his love. The language of life is redoubled in the language of love. Previously, in the context of another symbolic expression, it has been declared that just as the living Father sent Jesus, and he lives because of the Father, so those who receive him as the living bread will live because of him (6:57). That life is now identified with love. Just as the loving Father has loved his only Son, so the Son loves his disciples. The Father, the Son, and believers are united in the dynamic of love. Though everything they have and are has been received from Jesus as the Father's original gift—"...apart from me you can do nothing" (15:5)—this gift must be productive, bringing forth appropriate fruit—through obedience to Jesus' commandments, believing in God, and believing in him (14:1b), and in loving others as he has loved them (13:34). In a reciprocity of love and life, not only will the disciples be enlivened as branches of the vine, but that "true vine" itself will achieve its intended fruitfulness in "the greater works" (14:12) of its branches.

From Jesus' loving obedience to the loving Father derives the disciples' obligation to prove their love in practice. If the Father's love is at the root of the love of both Jesus and his disciples, obedience to the Father's will is the essential imperative—both for Jesus himself and those who follow him. Yet his words are for the communication of joy; that his joy will be in the disciples who abide in his love and words, and that their joy will be complete (15:11). Inasmuch as the disciples are one with Jesus, they will experience the joy of true life. "These things" of which he has spoken—his dwelling in the love of the Father and surrender to his will—are the abiding source of his joy. Despite the dreadful conflicts and rejection they will experience, those united to the true vine and to the "love-life" that courses through it will live in a zone of joy, made complete in the awareness that in all that occurs the Father's all-encompassing will is being realized.

2. Loved by the Father

Just as Jesus' joy—"my joy...in you"—is delight in the glory of the Father, so their joy too will have its unshakable foundation in the Other who has so loved the world (3:16). The "completion" of such joy is to be found in self-giving love. The grain of wheat must fall into the ground and die if it is not to remain alone (12:24). Hence, Jesus repeats what he had previously issued as his "new commandment" (13:34).

> 12. "This is my commandment, that you love one another as I have loved you. 13. No one has greater love than this: to lay down one's life for one's friends. 14. You are my friends if you do what I command you. 15. No longer do I call you servants, for the servant does not know what the master is doing; but I have called you friends, for all that I have heard from my Father I have made known to you. 16. You did not choose me, but I chose you and appointed you so that you should go and bear fruit and that your fruit should abide, so that whatever you ask the Father in my name, he may give it to you. 17. This I command you, to love one another." (15:12–17)

His joy is realized in the disciples' mutual loving (15:12), through participating in his love for his own "unto the end" (13:1). For that reason, it is characterized by an excess, laying down one's life for one's friends (15:13; cf. 1 John 3:16). The disciples are addressed as "friends" (15:14–15). By living in intimate communion with their Master, they share his loves—for the Father, and for "his own" (13:1c). They are drawn into his intimate relationship with the Father. They are not left in ignorance, as though on the outside of what is going on between him and the Father. They are part of a heavenly exchange, for they are taken into the original communication of the Father to the Son in his mission to give life to the world: he has made known to them all he has heard from his Father (15:15b).

In the light of this primary communication, Jesus has chosen them (15:16a). They have not broken into the primordial "friendship" existing between the Father and the Son, but have been invited into it, and thus, united to the true vine, they are appointed to bear lasting fruit (15:16b). The Father's vital communication to the Son branches out into the world to continue in history. Yet this will unfold only if the community of faith and worship is open to the inexhaustible generosity of the Father whom Jesus has revealed: "...whatever you ask the Father in my name, he may give it to you" (15:16c). United in the true vine, the disciples must turn to the Father, the generative origin of all that Jesus has said and done. Though in prayer they face the Father who is revealed in the Son, they must continually find one another in the light of the love that has been made known: "This I command you, to love one another" (15:17).

From the realm of the Father has come, and will come, many gifts: the truth itself, the Spirit of truth, peace, and "the new commandment." But each is confronted by the counterforce working in the realm of worldly glory. It has denied the truth of Jesus' origin in the Father. The world cannot receive or recognize the Holy Spirit. Nor can it give the peace Jesus gives. In its self-centered rejection of God's glory, it contradicts Jesus' command to love as he has loved. If the disciples are united with Jesus and to the Father in a great communion of life and love, their lives, going on in a world of contradiction, must be ready for the consequences. The disciples must bear fruit in stony ground. Jesus, therefore, addresses the dismal prospect of their being hated as he was before them.

3. The World and Its Plight

18. "If the world hates you, know that it has hated me before it has hated you. 19. If you were of the world, the world would love its own; but because you are not of the world, but I chose you out of the world, therefore the world hates you. 20. Remember the word that I said to you, 'Servants are not greater than their master.' If they persecuted me, they will persecute you; if they kept my word they will keep yours also. 21. But all this they will do on my account, because they do not know the one who sent me." (15:18–21)

Because the followers of Jesus can no longer be complicit in the false peace built on idolatrous absolutes; because they are not one with the world in rejecting the Word that has come to it; because they have been called out of the self-serving concerns of worldly glory, they can expect no love from that quarter (15:19–20). The world's allergic reaction to the Word is the result of an idolatry bearing the distinctive fruits of murder and lies. There remains a cosmic antagonism to the God that has been self-revealed in Jesus (15:21). In failing to recognize the Father, the world is locked in hatred; and the disciples, like their master before them, must expect to be made scapegoats for the self-justifications of the world that has rejected him.

22. "If I had not come and spoken to them, they would not have sin; but now they have no excuse for their sin. 23. Anyone who hates me hates my Father also. 24. If I had not done among them the works that no one else had done, they would not have sin; but now they have seen and hated both me and my Father.

25. It is to fulfill the word written in their law, 'They hated me without cause.'" (15:22–25)

The word of Jesus has exacerbated the plight of the world. It has chosen to turn from the light to the darkness it preferred. Mere ignorance has become deliberate rejection (15:22). The rejection of Jesus has meant rejection of the Father himself. The representatives of the God-denying world are "the Jews" who have expressed their terminal antagonism to Jesus in his words and works. Their closed religious system had prevented them from recognizing the culminating revelation of the true God of Israel.[3] Jesus has urged his antagonists to look beyond his words to the works he performed in healing and giving life and light.[4] But to no effect. They have rejected both Jesus and the one who has worked in him, "...me and my Father" (15:24). The revelation of God to Israel in the Mosaic Law (5:46)—as in the vision of Abraham (8:56) and the prophets (12:38–41)—had looked to this hour of fulfillment. But in refusing that fulfillment, the pretended representatives of the patriarchs, the Law, and the prophets have turned against their God and the one he has now sent. In the process, they nullify their case, and even deny their own identity: "They have hated me without cause" (cf. Ps 35:19; 69:4–5).

4. Witnesses to the Truth

26. "But when the Paraclete comes, whom I shall send to you from the Father, even the Spirit of truth who proceeds from the Father, he will bear witness to me; 27. and you also are witnesses because you have been with me from the beginning. (15:26–27.)

The Paraclete, as counsel for the defense,[5] comes into this situation of hatred and misrepresentation. The full gift of the truth (1:14) involves the coming of "the Spirit of truth" as sent by Jesus, "the truth" (14:6) from the Father who is true (5:33; 8:26). Like the Word itself, the Paraclete proceeds from the Father. Since the Spirit of truth and the Word of truth have the same origin, the Paraclete will bear witness to the Word as the incarnate revelation of God.[6] From within this gifted experience of truth, which includes the respective initiatives of the Father, Son, and Spirit, the disciples will have their distinctive role in mediating the revelation that has been given from a realm beyond this world: they have been with Jesus from the beginning (15:27).

16:1. I have said this to you to keep you from falling away. 2. They will put you out of the synagogues; indeed, the hour is coming when those who kill you will think that by doing so they are offering worship to God. 3. And they will do this because they have not known the Father, nor me." (16:1–3)

The first three verses of chapter 16 conclude all that has been said up to this point, while at the same time, they lead more deeply into the drama of Jesus' impending departure. The violence inherent in the theological logic of the adversaries ranged against Jesus and his witnesses is unmasked. He has promised the gift of the Paraclete to keep them from falling away under the pressure of the rejection that awaits them. Given the murderous energy of the world's hatred of Jesus (15:18), and even of the Father himself (15:23–25), the disciples will feel the dead weight of a world that has removed Jesus from its midst, and closed itself against the God he has come to reveal. In the darkness of this double rejection of what the disciples must witness to, only the permanent gift of the Paraclete can enable them to resist the self-enclosure of the world, and find their home in the house of the Father. Though they have been promised life and love and fruitfulness through union with Jesus and the Father, that life of transcendent communion and unity will be lived out in a world of exclusion and lethal threat (16:2–3).

5. Contrasting Forms of Existence

While the history of the Johannine community's experience of such suffering can probably never be fully known, the Gospel here points to the root cause of the world's animosity. It follows another "god"—the idols of false absolutes (cf. 1 John 5:21)[7]— legitimating the violent removal of all who disturb its sacred order. To preserve its ever-precarious peace, the world needs scapegoats, if its conspiracy against the only true God is to be maintained, and if its "unity" is to be untroubled by the demands of love and true justice (cf. 11:49–50). Acting in this way, the world neither knows nor loves the Father (cf. 1 John 2:15–17). For the true God welcomes the whole world into a house of many dwelling places. In his love for the world, the Father has refused to be part of the world's endless process of victimization by unmasking it once and for all in the cross.[8] Through the gift of his only Son (3:16), God has inspired a new experience of true life and love. The Spirit of truth has been given. But in neither knowing nor receiving that Spirit, the representatives of the world's violence cannot receive true peace. They have chosen not to know the Father and the one he has sent to be the world's savior. Thus they have cut themselves off from the source of the love that alone can undo the world's culture of death and violence. The security of the world's idolatrous projections can be maintained only by excluding all who challenge it—the Father, the Son, the Spirit of truth—and the disciples themselves.

To sum up: two contrasting forms of existence are in terminal contention. A closed religious system seeking to worship its "god" (16:2), while having no room for Jesus, nor the Father (15:23–24; 16:3), nor the Spirit (14:17), it turns with hatred on the disciples and expels them from its midst (15:18–20; 16:2). In contrast, there is the open system of the life, love, and friendship emanating from the Father and enfolding the disciples into its life-giving communion. As these two forms of existence collide, the disciples will be tempted to falter (16:2). But they will be strengthened to witness to the true source and form of life by the perduring gift of the Spirit (15:26–27). While the world that has rejected Jesus is bent on hatred and exclusion, the disciples' mission is to be implemented through mutual love—to share in the mission of gathering the scattered children of God into one (11:51–52; 17:20–23).

Notes

1. See 4:26 (the word of God); 6:35, 51 (bread of life); 8:12; 9:5 (the light of the world); 10:7, 9 (the gate for the sheep); 10:11, 14 (the good shepherd).
2. Cf. Jer 2:21; Ezek 19:10–14; Ps 80:18–19; Isa 27:2–6.
3. See 5:19–47; 8:12–20, 21–30, 39–47, 54–59; 9:24–34, 39–41.
4. See 5:36; 7:21–24, 50–52; 9:24–34; 10:31–39.
5. For a stimulating account of the Spirit's role, see James Alison, *Raising Abel*, 65–68.
6. For current theological approaches to the relation of the Spirit to Christ in the economy of salvation, see Gary D. Badcock, *Light of Truth and Fire of Love*, especially 145–169.
7. On this point, Kelly, "'God is Love': A Theological Moral Reading of 1 John," 37–42.
8. James Alison, *Raising Abel*, 34–49, and Gil Bailie, *Violence Unveiled*, 217–233, are key references.

16

=====

The Peace of God (16:4–33)

Having forewarned believers of the violence and hatred in store, the Gospel now doubles back on a number of previous themes (cf. 14:1–31) as it presents Jesus' "plain speaking" (16:25) on the subject of the Father's presence to the grief-stricken disciples.

1. The Spirit in a Dispirited World

The disciples are still missing the point. They are unable to go beyond Peter's previous question with its focus on death (13:36a). They give no evidence of any inside knowledge of what is taking place. To them the death of Jesus appears as ultimate defeat and his departure from them a path to nowhere. They fear that he will be expelled from their world, his voice silenced, and his deeds performed in vain. To them the realm of the Father is just another name for death, defeat, and a void made more vast by the violent death which now looms. In this dispirited atmosphere, Jesus declares, "Now I am going to him who sent me, yet none of you asks me, 'Where are you going?' But because I have said these things to you, sorrow has filled your hearts" (16:5–6).

As if conceding that a feeling of all-pervasive sorrow will be inevitable, Jesus confronts the problem by stating that this grim state of affairs will be to their advantage. The very emptiness, darkness, and powerlessness of the situation make room for another Paraclete:

> 7. "Nevertheless I tell you the truth: it is to your advantage that I go away; for if I do not go away the Paraclete will not come to you; but if I go I will send him to you. 8. And when he comes he will expose the world concerning sin and righteousness and judgment: 9. concerning sin, because they do not believe in me; 10. concerning righteousness, because I go to the Father and you will see me no more; 11. concerning judgment, because the ruler of this world is already judged." (16:7–11)

The "advantage" the disciples are to enjoy cannot be appreciated in the undisturbed world of human glory (14:17). Only when that world is shaken out of its self-enclosure by the glory of self-giving love can the Spirit of truth be known for what it is. Jesus' departure is not one more addition to the sum of the world's sorrows, but the condition of the coming of a gift that will make *the* difference to their spiritless and bereft existence. The Gospel has already linked the sending of the Spirit to Jesus' departure: "As yet the Spirit had not been given, because Jesus was not yet glorified" (7:39). His death is the occasion of glory, for both the Father and the Son (11:4). Unless a grain of wheat falls into the earth and dies, it will remain just a single grain (12:23–24). When Jesus is lifted up, he will draw all to himself (12:32–33). The Paraclete will come as the crowning glory of Jesus' mission, to realize in his disciples' lives the meaning of his words and deeds. This other presence will fill the void that Jesus' absence will create. But this further gift is not just a remedy for his absence, nor merely a consolation for the grieving disciples. For Jesus will send the Paraclete as the essential fulfillment of his revelatory mission to them—and to the world to which they will be sent. Such will be the advantage that awaits them, not as a consolation, nor as a substitute, but as the fulfillment to which everything is moving.

2. Exposing the World

First of all, the coming of the Spirit will mean a radical disturbance of the world's self-assurance. It will be exposed for what it is. It has turned from the opening of heaven, refusing to be drawn out of itself into the realm of the Father, and to enter on "the way" of Jesus. The Paraclete brings into the open the false consciousness of the world; and, in so doing, serves the mission of "the light of the world": "...all who do evil hate the light, and do not come to the light, so that their deeds might not be exposed" (3:20–21).[1]

While the disciples will be guided by the Spirit into all truth (16:13), the self-imposed limitations of the world's version of truth will be exposed through his coming: the untruth it has chosen and the truth it has refused will be brought into the open (cf. 12:45–47). Like Jesus himself, the other Paraclete will confront pretended judges and teachers with the truth about themselves (3:19; 5:22, 27, 30, 44–45; 8:16; 9:39). The radical cause of the world's sin will be made clear. The doers of evil will be shown to be doing their "...father's desires," the "murderer from the beginning" who is alien to the truth, a liar and the source of lies (8:44). The unholy generativity at work in the world, in its encounter with the Holy Spirit, will be identified as a web of violence and idolatrous untruth, in allergic reaction to the nonviolent, life-giving truth of the love offered it (3:16).

There is a second crucial consideration: "concerning righteousness." The Paraclete reveals the peculiar religious

319

self-righteousness of the world. It has condemned Jesus for blasphemy in breaking the Sabbath and calling God his Father (5:18). It has declared him to be demonically possessed (8:48), and a sinner (9:24b). In their refusal to receive the gift of God, the "righteous" ones of this world have clung to a pretended justification in claiming to be the children of Abraham, rather than receive the Son of the Father (8:39–59). They have claimed to be the disciples of Moses (6:30–31; 9:28–29) but have not accepted the full gift of the truth as it has come in Jesus (1:17). They reckoned themselves to be obedient to the Law[2] rather than allowing the word of the One whose voice they have never heard, whose form they have never seen, abide in them (5:37–38). In the tiny world of their self-glorification, they would shut their own people out of the synagogues of Israel, rather than welcome the glory that comes from God (12:43). They show no awareness of the Father's house of many dwellings.

In the third place, "concerning judgment": even though the world will bring about the death of Jesus through a quasi-judicial execution, the coming of the Paraclete will not allow the verdict of the world's judgment to remain in possession. The cross will not be seen as a vindication of worldly justice, since through it, the Son of Man will be lifted up for the world's salvation (3:14; 8:28; 12:32–33), and the true God will be revealed in the hour of glory (11:4; 12:23; 13:31–33). Though the execution of Jesus appear as the triumph of his enemies' plans to remove him and to scatter his disciples, it will result in gathering into one the scattered children of God (11:50, 52; 12:11, 19), as the Crucified draws all to himself (12:32). Far from being the infliction of divine punishment, his death will accomplish his return to the Father (13:1), opening heaven to dimensions of peace and joy that the closed world cannot imagine.

As a result, the cross will be the radical reversal of the history of the self-serving, murderous judgments of human glory. The age of sacred violence is over; for its "god," the ruler of this world. is already judged (16:11; cf. 14:30). Grim though this exposure might be, the action of the Paraclete will ensure that history will continue to be the theater in which the glory of God will be experienced. Exposed to the counteraction of the Paraclete, the world will nonetheless continue to find itself as the object of God's love (3:16).

3. Toward "All Truth"

> 12. I have yet many things to say to you, but you cannot bear them now. 13. When the Spirit of truth comes he will guide you into all the truth, for he will not speak on his own authority, but whatever he hears he will speak, and he will declare to you the things that are to come. 14. He will glorify me, for he will take what is mine and declare it to you. 15. All that the Father has is mine; therefore I said he takes what is mine and will declare it to you." (16:12–15)

The coming of the Spirit does not end in a purely subversive role in regard to the self-assurance of the world in its resistance to God. This further gift has an overwhelming positive significance in relation to the disciples, to Jesus himself, and to the Father. First of all, the Spirit of truth will guide the disciples into "all truth" (16:13c). Second, as the Spirit of *truth,* he will glorify Jesus, taking what is his to declare it to the disciples (16:13b). Third, in declaring the truth of Jesus, he will be declaring "all that the Father has" (16:15). In the light of these relationships, the Spirit is, so to speak, a luminous field of presence in the history of faith, through which the disciples will penetrate more deeply into what has been going on between the Father and the Son. Post-biblical doctrinal developments will speak of the Spirit as a "subsisting relationship" between the Father and the Son.[3] But already at this stage of faith's expression, the Spirit is identified as "in-between-ness," making possible the believers' entry into communion with God and into the full bounty of the divine gifts. He is the God-given presence of the "revealed-ness" of what the Father has communicated to the Son and, through him, to the disciples.

And yet the full significance of this hour of glory will take its own time: "I have yet many things to say to you but you cannot bear them now" (16:12). Though the whole truth of Jesus' words will be the truth that heals, frees, and gives life, the disciples at this time find themselves on the dark side of the cross. In sorrow and fear they have a foreboding anticipation of their Master's violent exit from the scene. The full truth of the revelation to be accomplished in his death and resurrection is beyond what they can either imagine or expect. God's self-revelation takes time; and all the events of the hour must run their course. Even if the disciples were to receive verbal instructions from the lips of the Master, the "many things" yet to come cannot be fully communicated (16:13c). The Word made flesh will be fully incarnate among them only when in the flesh of his existence he will be glorified in the event of the cross. Mere words can go only so far on the eve of the passion. Their meaning must look to the time when such words will be able to catch up with what is about to be enacted. History is in the making, and the work of the Father is to be accomplished. The words of Jesus anticipate the paschal event of the cross, and the realization of this event looks to the coming of the Spirit for it to be grasped in its abiding significance.

Given into the limited horizon of the disciples, the Spirit will abide in them and be among them (14:18). As the field in which the full meaning of what is taking place will be progressively unfolded, the Spirit will guide the disciples into "all truth" (16:13a). The Paraclete not only acts against the darkness, but for the light, bringing home to the community of faith "the fullness of the gift of truth" that Jesus embodies (1:14–18; 14:6). He will guide the followers of Jesus into the way of living truth opened up through his passing over to the Father (14:6). Hence, the Spirit will not speak independently, but will communicate only what he himself hears (16:13b). The Spirit has come, not to replace the message and mission of Jesus, but to make it a living reality in the history that is to unfold. In this sense, the Spirit is the light in which the opened heaven will be seen in all its truth (1:51).

Nonetheless, neither Jesus,[4] nor the Paraclete, is the originator of revelation. Both are sent by the Father (14:16, 26; 15:26), each serving the one revelatory communication of the Father: the Son, in the course of his coming from God and going to God (13:3); the Spirit, by coming after the departure of Jesus to bring out the saving fact that "the Father had given all things into his hands" (13:3). The Spirit will remain with the disciples as the Father's permanent gift, in the "forever" (14:16) which is in contrast to the "little time" (16:16–19) of Jesus' physical presence to them. Because of the coming of the Spirit, time is no longer a pointless succession of instants, nor a continuing cycle endlessly repeating itself, nor a memory of a privileged past. Time is experienced as moving to a divine fulfillment, for the Spirit comes to declare what is to come (16:13c). There is a dynamism inscribed in time that looks to the fullness of divine revelation. Jesus and the Father will come to make their home with those who, despite the conflicts that history will produce, have made the persistent, yet peaceful, journey of faith (14:23). With the gift of the Spirit released through the death and glorification of Jesus (7:39), the worshiping community will move to meet the Father "in spirit and truth" (4:23–24).

Guiding the disciples in all truth, the Spirit of truth "unpacks" the full meaning of the Word incarnate in the historical conversation of faith. The Spirit will glorify Jesus, to communicate all that he has and is to the present and future believers (16:14b). Coming from the Father, the Spirit does what the Father does. He glorifies Jesus in all the dimensions of the truth he embodies. This truth has been variously expressed. As the Son, he makes the Father known (1:18; 14:9–10). As the Way, he leads his followers to find an abiding place in the house of the Father (14:2, 5). As center of a new community, he unites his disciples through the example of love that he has given (13:15, 34). As sent by the Father, he is the impetus to a continuing mission of witness to the world (15:8).

Working in all these dimensions of the truth of Jesus, the Spirit brings out the most original truth—that of Jesus' oneness with the Father. For not only does the Son do what he sees the Father doing, in perfect conformity to the divine will (5:19, 30), not only does he receive all things from the Father (13:3), but his oneness with the Father is so complete that he can claim, "All that the Father has is mine" (16:15a). He thereby utters the innermost essence of the Gospel (1:1–2, 18; 10:30, 38).

The Spirit is given into the world from the heart of this unity.[5] He proceeds from the Father and is sent by Jesus (16:7; cf. 15:26). As their joint gift, he is the first witness to the unity that reigns between the Father and the Son, the natural communicator of that all-enfolding unity to the world. The Father is not hidden, as one unknown, behind the mask of the Son. Rather, under the guidance of the Spirit, the community of faith finds in Jesus the true face of the Father turned lovingly toward it.

4. The Joy of New Life

16. "A little while and you will see me no more; again a little while and you will see me." 17. Some of his disciples said to one another, "What is this that he says to us, 'A little while and you will see me no more, and again a little while and you will see me,' and 'because I go to the Father?'" 18. They said, "What does he mean by 'a little while?' We do not know what he means." 19. Jesus knew that they wanted to ask him, so he said to them, "Is this what you are asking yourselves, what I mean by saying 'A little while and you will not see me, and again a little while and you will see me?' 20. Amen, amen, I say to you, you will weep and lament, but the world will rejoice; you will be sorrowful, but your sorrow will turn into joy." (16:16–20)

Although the Spirit will come as gift, witness, and guide to serve the Father's communication to the world, the disciples still have to contend with their own confusions and sorrow. With the work of God still in progress, they still have little sense of the unity and direction of the divine purpose and the phases of its timing (16:15–19). The manner of Jesus' going to the Father compatible with the two "little times"—when he will be first invisible to them, and then made visible—is beyond them. How can impending departure, let alone his death, permit such a promise? Or, on the other hand, if he is truly going to God, how and why does God permit such a violent interruption?

Without the presence of the Spirit, they cannot imagine any future visibility explicable on his terms—"...because I go the Father" (16:17c). What dominates their experience of the world is the opaque finality of death—the silence, darkness, defeat, and terminal separation from him. Still on the outside of the Father's house, still without the benefit of the Spirit's guidance, still incapable of entering into the imagination of Jesus, they interpret any promised "little time" as the long time of death—when the dead stay dead, and human fate is wrapped in dread and obscurity. They have no eyes to look forward to the visibility of the glorified Jesus that is to result from his going to the Father, and to his subsequent return as a source of life outside the limits of death. In the history of faith, they are not the last to express the limitations of both their vision and their patience: "We do not know what he means" (16:18b).

The dispirited sadness of the disciples is met with the vitality and confidence of another imagination, drawing its energy from the deathless realm of the Father. At the depths of apparent defeat, and in the face of the world's celebration of victory, a great transformation will occur. The glorification of Jesus will mean a transformation of the consciousness and very imagination of the his disciples: "Amen, amen I say to you, you will weep and lament, but the world will rejoice; you will be sorrowful, but your sorrow will turn into joy" (16:20). A world-transforming birth is about to occur:

> 21. "When a woman is in travail she has sorrow because her hour has come; but when she is delivered of the child she no longer remembers the anguish for joy that a child is born into the world. 22. So you have sorrow now, but I will see you again and your hearts will rejoice and no one will take your joy from you. 23. In that day you will ask nothing of me. Amen, amen, I say to you, if you ask anything of the Father, he will give it to you in my name. 24. Hitherto you have asked nothing in my name; ask and you will receive, that your joy may be full." (16:21–24)

Isaiah had foretold that "the earth will give birth to those long dead" (Isa 26:19).[6] Jesus had addressed his own mother as she made known the shortage of wine at the marriage feast, "O woman, what have you to do with me? My hour has not yet come" (2:4). Yet in her unconditional faith she instructed the servants, "Do whatever he tells you" (2:5). The result was "the first of his signs" through which he "manifested his glory" (2:11). In this hour determined by the Father, new life is being brought forth. Genuine believers, modeling their faith on the mother of Jesus, will participate in a joyous birth. Their present sorrows are not symptoms of terminal distress but of the travail connected with being born from above to abundant life (10:10).

Despite the inevitable darkness of history, the light will bring its joyous evidence. The cross will reveal the glory of God; and the life that streams from the Crucified will lead to its consummation in perfect joy. The followers of Jesus will experience their lives unfolding in the sight of Jesus—"I will see you again" (16:22)—in a kind of eye-to-eye contact unclouded by any darkness, in a vision that pierces the veil of death and defeat. They will not be found looking into an empty tomb or up to a closed heaven. In that day, the times of questioning will be over—even the time of hope-filled prayers. A fulfillment beyond the need for further prayers will have been given: on that day believers will ask for nothing more (16:23a).

But now is the time-in-between, with its struggles and ambiguities. Still, the joy is not moved indefinitely into the future. The journey of faith in time, whatever its conflicts, will unfold in the presence of the gracious Father. He will be turned to the disciples—as Jesus has revealed him, and as the Spirit witnesses. Believers will no longer experience themselves as outsiders to the communion existing between the Father and the Son, needing to address Jesus in order to contact the Father. Through Jesus they will be drawn into an immediate relationship with the Father, "for it is not by measure that he gives the Spirit" (3:34). Whatever the prayer addressed to the Father, it will be answered in the name of Jesus (16:23b).

Though the day for the fullness of joy is reserved for the future, the time between the glorification of Jesus and his return will have its own joy, in anticipation of what is to come. The community of believers will move through history, worshiping the Father, following Jesus' example of selfless love, keeping his commandment to love as he has loved, and guided by the Spirit of truth. Above all, the faithful will live in a horizon filled with welcoming and bountiful presence of the Father himself, unconditionally gracious to those who follow the way of the Son. From the Father flows all the gifts that will be the cause of an ever-renewable and growing joy.

5. Speaking Plainly of the Father

25. "I have said this to you in figures; the hour is coming when I shall no longer speak to you in figures but tell you plainly of the Father. 26. In that day you will ask in my name; and I do not say to you that I shall pray to the Father for you, 27. for the Father himself loves you because you have loved me and believed that I came from God. 28. I came from the Father and have come into the world; again I am leaving the world and going to the Father." 29. His disciples said, "Ah, now you are speaking plainly, not in figures! 30. Now we know that you know all things and need none to question you; by this we believe that you came from God." 31. Jesus answered them, "Do you now believe? 32. The hour is coming, indeed it has come, when you will be scattered, each to his own home, and

will leave me alone; yet I am not alone, for the Father is with me. 33. I have said this to you that in me you may have peace. In the world you have tribulation; but be of good cheer, I have overcome the world." (16:25–33)

Jesus' departure from this world will give his disciples a new and immediate familiarity with the Father as the loving source of past and future gifts. The time of speaking in figures will yield in the coming hour to a time of transparency when Jesus will speak "plainly" of the Father (16:25). Hitherto, he has made the Father known in the language of figures, as in the "example" of the foot-washing, and likewise through the symbols of the paternal house, the heavenly vine-dresser, the woman in travail. Now the hour of the public display of the Father's glory is coming. The symbols will be verified in the reality. The glory of God will shine forth through what is no longer a figure—the Word fully incarnate in the flesh of the Crucified.[7] In the hour of revelation, the disciples' relationship to the Father will be transformed. Belief in Jesus' word *about* the Father will be interiorized in an immediate knowledge of the Father, through immediate experiential familiarity with the God who has been revealed. Sought out by the Father, true worshipers will adore "in spirit and truth" (4:23–24). Though they will pray in the name of Jesus, it is not as though he prays for them as had been the case up till then. He had made the Father known in the world before the time of "that day" (16:26a). But now, in the light of this new day, all exteriority, all lesser forms of mediation, will yield to a new freedom and intimacy with the God from whom Jesus has come. In their vital union with Jesus, the true vine—abiding in him and he in them, and receiving the Spirit proceeding from the Father and sent by him—they will find themselves to be the direct objects of the Father's love: "...for the Father himself loves you, because you loved me, and believed that I came from God" (16:27). In their love for Jesus, they are in contact with his divine origin, thus brought into a loving relationship with the Father as the source and goal of the Son's entire existence in the world (16:28). The incarnation of the Word in the flesh of the world has dissolved all frontiers, as far as access to the Father is concerned (14:23).

The disciples are quick to respond to this hitherto unimaginable intimacy with God. Their sense of being far removed from God's heaven is replaced with an awareness of the decisive revelation Jesus has brought about. Now he is speaking plainly (16:29). Yet a certain unreality remains. The gap has been narrowed, but heaven is not yet fully open to them. They have not fully entered into the meaning of "that day." Their presumption and impatience still locks them in a time scale and frame of reference unaligned to what is in fact coming to be. In this regard, they are still in a situation of notional belief, and have not yet arrived at the full surrender of faith (16:30). They voice a belief *about* Jesus as an authority who, as a heaven-sent messenger from God, knows "all things." Consequently, they pretend to an evidence that now needs none of the questions that arose in the previous time of unbelief.[8] They feel, too, that they have moved beyond their own previous questions.[9] For all their self-assurance, they are not yet ready to surrender fully to the way of Jesus as he returns to the Father, giving himself "to the end" for the life of the world. Nor have they grasped the true status of their own relationship to the Father and its essential connection to Jesus' original relationship to God. What they are to become will depend less on their "we know," and more on what they ask and receive as the Father's gift. Though they express their readiness to accept that Jesus is the supreme authority on God (16:30), they are as yet unconverted to revolutionary reality of the God who will be revealed by following Jesus into the realm of the Father.

Though they have no further questions for Jesus, he has one for them: "Do you believe?" (16:31). As long as they do not accept his going to the Father as the necessary outcome of identity and mission, his followers will be enclosed in a world too small to appreciate the event of God's glory taking place as the fulfillment of this Passover. For them it will follow that if the shepherd is struck down, the sheep will be scattered (cf. Zech 13:7).[10] As they seek refuge in their own homes—forgetting their place in the Father's house (14:2)—and leave him alone, the truth of the Prologue is borne out: Jesus came to his own and his own did not receive him (1:11). But though they are scattered, the Father and the Son are gathering them into one through the power of the cross. Neither the disciples, nor all of God's children (11:52), will be left in disarray. At the heart of all that is happening is Jesus' return to the Father from whom he has come. In this, he is not alone (cf. 8:16, 29), for the Father is with him. In the scattering and death that will occur, something else is going on.

Jesus has questioned his fragile disciples for one purpose: "...that in me you may have peace" (16:33a). Provided they locate themselves "in him," they will live in a space, not enclosed in death and defeat, but opening out to the life and love that have their source in the Father himself. All this will be in contrast to the closed, violent sphere of the world. There will be an outcome to the travail they will suffer. It remains that the main actor in all that will take place is the Father. Between him and Jesus there is an unbreakable bond: "I and the Father are one" (10:30). Since the Father himself, who is greater than all, has given the disciples to Jesus, no one can snatch them from the Father's hand (10:29). The world is still subject to his all-directing will, acting in the events that will occur. The forces of violence that have ruled in that world are now to be met with the Father's pacific intention to be realized in the self-giving of the Son: "...that in me you may have peace" (16:33). The sadness of defeat and false peace is contrasted with the "good cheer" appropriate to a new world in the making.

There will be tension and suffering in the meantime. But all negativity will, in the end, be overcome, for Jesus has overcome the world (16:33). By passing over into the realm of the Father, he will be a life-giving presence for the community of love and worship.[11] All who follow him will share in his victory (cf. 1 John 5:4–5).

Notes

1. Cf. 5:22; 7:7; 8:24; 9:39; 12:31.
2. Cf. 5:16–18, 39–40, 45–47; 7:12, 18, 20–24, 48–49; 8:58–59; 9:16, 24; 10:24–38; 11:48–50; 16:2.
3. For a thorough survey and comment, see Gary D. Badcock, *Light of Truth and Fire of Love*, 35–82; 145–170. Rowan Williams, in his *On Christian Theology* (Oxford: Blackwell, 2000), insightfully compares Johannine pneumatology with the Pauline and the Lukan types. See especially pp. 115–121.
4. Cf. 3:32–35; 7:16–18; 8:26–29, 42–43; 12:47–50; 14:10.
5. For an illuminating account of Holy Spirit in the immanent Trinity, drawing on Eastern and Western positions, see Gary D. Badcock, *Light of Truth and Fire of Love*, 234–256.
6. Cf. the whole passage, Isa 26:16–19.
7. For example, 11:4; 12:23, 32–33; 13:1, 31–32.
8. Cf. 5:12, 18; 6:5, 7, 9, 30–31, 34, 41–42, 52; 7:3–4, 20, 25–27, 31, 35–36, 40–42, 45–51; 8:13, 19, 22, 25, 33, 39, 41, 48, 52–53; 9:40; 10:6, 19–21, 33.
9. Cf. 13:22–25, 36, 37; 14:5, 8, 22; 16:16.
10. See the parallels in Mark 4:27; Matt 26:31.
11. See 14:18–21; 16:16–19, 23b–24.

17

The Realm of the Father:
Expanding Life (17:1–26)

In this final prayer, the earliest themes of his last discourse with the disciples are replayed and developed with fresh clarity (13:1–4): the meaning of the Passover, the arrival of the hour, Jesus' limitless love for his disciples, his confrontation with the evil one, the unreserved nature of the Father's gift to him, his own divine origin and destiny. It is as though the summons that had oddly interrupted his previous communication is reissued at a higher register—as he raises his eyes to the heaven where the Father dwells: "Rise, let us go hence!" (14:31).

As Jesus raises his eyes to heaven in a traditional attitude of prayer, heaven, in the person of the "holy" and "righteous" Father (17:11, 25) is, as it were, looking down. From within the world, those following the upward gaze of the Son are "seeing heaven opened" (1:51), to glimpse the glory that is promised—and future generations will look back. The Father has not left Jesus alone (16:23b). On the point of leaving behind the world he has overcome (16:33), he is also about to enter the luminous realm of the Father's glory.

1. This Is Eternal Life

1. **When Jesus had spoken these words he lifted up his eyes to heaven and said, "Father, the hour has come; glorify your Son that the Son may glorify you, 2. since**

you have given him power over all flesh, to give eternal life to all whom you have given him. 3. And this is eternal life, that they know you the only true God, and Jesus Christ whom you have sent. 4. I glorified you on earth, having accomplished the work that you gave me to do; 5. and now, Father, glorify me in your own presence with the glory I had with you before the world was made. (17:1–5)

In the first section of the prayer, now that "the hour" has arrived, the Father is immediately invoked. He alone can consummate the great action that has been taking place in the world through the coming and, now, in the departure, of the Son: "Father, the hour has come" (17:1). "The hour" implies the climactic completion of what both the Father and the Son have been bringing about. It marks the transcendent time frame in which the prayer is uttered (13:1; cf. 12:23). As the prayer celebrates the full meaning of the hour, the impending tragedy of the cross is subsumed into the glory to be revealed. Glory is the keynote. Jesus prays for his own glorification at the hands of the Father in order to accomplish his essential mission: to glorify the Father by making him known to the world: "…glorify the Son that the Son may glorify you…" (17:1b).

As Word and Son, Jesus has received the God-given powers of exercising authority over all creation, and of giving eternal life to all those who have been given to him (17:2). With his whole being bent on the glorification of the Father, he expresses his awareness of the twofold gift the Father has made to him. First, there is the gift of a universal power to give life (cf. 5:19–30; 6:57); and second, there is the gift of those who are to be its beneficiaries. The Father has given him power over all flesh, "to give eternal life to all whom you have given him." (17:2). In the realm of the Father, gifts are joined with gifts. All have their source in the Father as the original giver, and lead to endless life. The generosity of the economy of heaven thus contrasts with the mean and murderous powers of this world also at work in this hour.

In a hermeneutical aside, the Johannine understanding of eternal life is declared in terms of the Son's essential relationship to the Father: "And this is eternal life, that they know you, the only true God, and Jesus Christ whom you have sent" (17:3). In these two poles of the experience of eternal life, the way that God is God, and the way that God is one and true, will be newly defined.[1] Both the unity and the truth of God are communicative. In the truth of what has been revealed, Jesus is one with the Father in a unity beyond the imagination of a world frozen in envy and confrontation. In contrast, the unity of heaven, realized in the oneness existing between the Father and the Son, while being transcendent, is not exclusive: it enfolds others into it (17:21).[2] Out of this primordial oneness the Father is revealed by sending his only Son. What is most intimate to God becomes a communication to what is completely other—the world.

For his part, Jesus Christ is only truly known as the one uniquely sent by the Father. To know him means to acknowledge his origin. Hence, for faith, the only true God and Jesus Christ are not juxtaposed as two unrelated truths. In the realm of eternal life, they exist in the one reality of perfect communion: "...as you, Father, are in me, and I in you" (17:21). The source and form of eternal life is this original communion. Not only are the Father and the Son dwelling in one another; they are united in a reciprocity of glorification: "I glorified you on earth, having accomplished the work that you gave me to do" (17:4) The Father glorifies the Son, and the Son glorifies the Father (17:1, 5).

The unity based on such a relationship radically subverts the world of human glory, in which self-assertion must always regard the other as a threat to one's own status. But eternal life flows from the communion of the Father and the Son, to extend to the whole world of believers (17:23). It precedes "the foundation of the world" (17:5, 24c), which the world has imagined in terms of its own pride borne out in the violent divisions caused by its idolatrous self-assertion (cf. 1 John 2:15–17). Jesus Christ, sent as the Word made flesh, existing before the foundation of such a world, opens the world of the flesh to the unity and communion of eternal life.[3] Now that Jesus has completed his mission to glorify the Father on earth (17:4), he prays that the original union he enjoys with the Father be manifest as the unifying principle of all time, history, and creation: "...glorify me in your presence with the glory I had with you before the world was made" (17:5). Since he was "in the beginning...with God" (1:1–2), since "all things were made in him through him" (1:3), since "what happened in him was life, and the life was the light of humankind" (1:3b–4), the Son can pray that his timeless glory in the presence of the Father will be revealed as the fundamental reality in which the darkened world can find itself anew: "the light shines in the darkness, and the darkness has not overcome it" (1:5).[4]

His prayer does not envisage leaving the world without revelation as though, in departing for an exclusive realm of transcendence, he is leaving the world behind. His reunion with the Father in original glory continues to be a revelation to the world. He is the expression of the God-willed universe in which the world can awaken to its original meaning and purpose. The glory proper to the realm of God beyond time floods into the world created in time, to be its unifying principle (1:1–2; 6:62; 8:58). The eternity of God is revealed as that which holds time together and gives it direction.[5] Heaven opens itself to enfold the world into the relationship that precedes all creation, that of the Father to his Son and Word.

The reality of this relationship has been lived out in time in the Word made flesh. The unseen God has been made known by him who is closest to the Father's heart (1:18). The depth of this relationship has been historically extended in the words and deeds of Jesus throughout the whole course of his mission to the world. It is soon to be concentrated in "the hour" when he will be "lifted up." He will reveal the glory of God, and will himself be glorified in accomplishing his mission (11:4; 12:23, 32–33; 13:31–33). In the dramatic transactions of that hour, the limitless extent of Jesus' love for the Father, as well as for "his own," will become apparent (13:1, 18–20; 14:30–31; 17:1–2).

2. The Disciples' Mission

So far the prayer has turned on two absolutes. Jesus' mission is accomplished; and he is returning to his original glory in the presence of the Father (17:4–5). Both these factors throw into sharp contrast the fragile relativity of the disciples gathered now in his presence, but soon to experience the void his departure will cause:

> 6. "I have manifested your name to those whom you gave me out of the world; they were yours and you gave them to me, and they have kept your word. 7. Now they know that everything that you have given me is from you, 8. for the words that you gave me I have given to them, and they have received them and know in truth that I came from you, and they have believed that you sent me." (17:6–8)

There will indeed be an ending. Jesus' revealing mission within the world is complete (12:36b). But history is not at an end. There is a further phase in the working out of God's saving design. It is represented in the group gathered around the praying Jesus. He presents them to the Father as "those whom you gave me out of the world" (17:6). They have been chosen

337

(15:16). They are both the Father's gift to Jesus, and the recipients of Jesus' own giving. To them has been revealed the name of the Father (17:6); and to them has been given the words Jesus himself has been given by the Father (17:8a). Their presence with Jesus is the outcome of the Father's initiative actualized in an unstinting series of gifts. In that realm of grace, the disciples are invited to understand themselves as a gifted circle enfolded into the communication of the Father and the Son. They have received the name of God, the words of the Father, and Jesus' mission from the Father for their sake (17:8b).

For the disciples to be the beneficiaries of such a chain of graces would seem to leave little room for the fragility that has marked them in the past—and will mark them in the future. Nonetheless, Jesus depicts them here as the exemplary community of faith, aware of its gifts, and conscious of the great communication of God to the world. To these who have been called out of the darkness and violence of the world (17:6a), Jesus has made the Father an invocable and intimate reality: "I have manifested your name to those whom you gave me..." (17:6), thus completing the work the Father has given him to do (17:4). Through their association with him, they have come to know the very identity of God. Still, as Jesus is now leaving them to go to the Father, and as they are left to continue his mission in the world inimical to what he has been and what they are called to be, Jesus prays for them:

> 9. "I am praying for them; I am not praying for the world but for those you have given me, for they are yours; 10. all mine are yours, and yours are mine, and I am glorified in them. 11a. And now I am no more in the world, but they are in the world and I am coming to you." (17:9–11a)

Jesus' task is finished; but, in the design of the Father, the task of the disciples is about to begin. Hence, they are the special object of the Son's prayer. He prays for them, acknowledging both that they are the Father's special gift to him, and that they are included in his surrender of all to the Father. In them the Son's revealing work will be prolonged and bear fruit: "...and I am glorified in them" (17:10).⁶ As the Father is glorified in Jesus, Jesus himself will be glorified in his followers. With his public ministry at an end, he is no longer in the world. The forces that will cause his death are irrevocably at work in the world. Yet his leaving the world and going to the Father will mean for his disciples a new way of dwelling in the world as bearers of God's revelation to it.

The Son prays to the Father, not from some timeless moment, but within the timing of God at work in the succession of events making up the climactic "hour" of revelation (13:1; 17:1). Precisely when the world is most confident of removing Jesus from its midst, it will discover that a divinely wrought action has been taking place. While Jesus is to be lifted up on the cross (3:14; 8:28; 12:32), a great gathering into unity will take place.⁷ The glory of the Father will be revealed in the self-giving of the Son; and the Son himself will be glorified as the perfect instrument and expression of the Father's saving will (11:4; 12:23; 13:31–32; 17:1, 5). Consequently, the self-containment of the world is undermined, both by the dawning revelation of the Father, and in the manner of Jesus' departure. Unbroken communication between the Father and the Son will be shown to be at the heart of the meaning of God, of life, and even of the world itself.

3. In the Father's Keeping

11b. "Holy Father, keep them in your name, which you have given me, that they may be one, even as we are one. 12. While I was with them, I kept them in

your name, which you gave me; I have guarded them, and none of them is lost but the son of perdition, that the scripture might be fulfilled." (17:11b–12)

Jesus has come to the limit of his being in the world. Yet, he is at the frontier of passing out of this world to the Father. His prayer expresses his love for his own unto the end (13:1). His mission is accomplished that their mission might begin. They are to become bearers of the new possibilities of divine life and grace that he has opened up for all. What he has been for the world, they must now continue to be.[8] In the timing of the hour, the ending of Jesus' existence within the world means, for the disciples, the beginning of a new phase of inhabiting the world as the sphere of God's saving action. Though Jesus does not pray for the world directly, this does not mean that the world has ceased to be the object of God's life-giving love. But that love is brought home to it only through the mission of the disciples of Jesus. The world without the incarnation of the Word, and without the mission of the disciples to continue the mission of the Son, would be a world closed in on itself, deaf and blind to the promise of endless life (14:30; 15:18–19, 21; 16:3). Of itself, that world offers no true peace (14:30). Of itself, it is enclosed in a vicious circle of violence and locked in an arrogant ignorance of the true meaning of God (15:18–19, 21). In the service of its idols, it expels the messengers of God (16:3). But into that world the disciples must go. They are sent by him who has been sent by the Father.

Since they will be entering into a world of violent contradiction, ignorance, and disunity, the followers of Jesus are in a precarious situation. Only the Father, who is greater than all (10:29), can keep them safe.

Jesus turns to God as "Holy Father" (17:11b). In Israel's tradition, God has been proclaimed as "the Holy One," the guarantor and transcendent object of temple worship: "O Holy

340

One, Lord of all holiness, keep undefiled forever this house that has been recently purified" (2 Macc 14:36; cf. also 3 Macc 2:2). Now that the hour has arrived in which the Father will seek true worshipers in spirit and truth (4:23), the transcendent holiness of God is disclosed in new dimensions of generosity, immanence, and universality. The only true God provides no legitimation for the violence and exclusion perpetrated in the name of religion. For the *Holy* Father is revealed in giving—not a temple for the exclusive worship of Israel—but his only Son—for the salvation of the world (3:16). He will send the *Holy* Spirit in the name of Jesus (14:26).

The holiness of God will thus be the effective source of unity. For the disciples of Jesus are to be enfolded into the oneness existing between the Father and the Son: "...that they may be one, even as we are one" (17:11b). The transcendent realm of divine life reaches into the world to bring into being a new vital unity amongst all believers. The holiness of the Father, far from being the quality of a supreme being infinitely distant from the world, is to hold the fragile disciples in loving care: "...keep them in your name..." (17:11b). Jesus thus asks his Father to "father" those he leaves in the world.

The Father's name has been revealed: Jesus has made known all that is to be known of the person of the Father. As a result, God is now intimately invocable because he has sent both his only Son and his Holy Spirit into the world. Accessible in this manner, the Father is known as the giver of all gifts, even "the gift of God" (4:10). He has given his only Son to the world. He has given the disciples, along with all things, to the Son. Moreover, he will give the Holy Spirit to the disciples. Because God has been revealed in such giving, the Father can be so named. In his consciousness of the identity and character of his Father, Jesus has kept and guarded his followers (17:11b–12), so that none of them is lost.

There is one exception: "...none of them is lost but the son of perdition, that the scripture might be fulfilled" (17:12c). While an overly judgmental piety has rushed to identify this lost one with Judas Iscariot, it must be remembered that Jesus has never made such a judgment of his disciple. In the context of many betrayals and desertions, however traitorous the intentions and actions of Judas may have been, his feet had been washed by Jesus; and he too had been given the gift of the morsel in the final meal (13:26–27). He too had been loved to the end (13:1). It would seem, then, that the only adequate referent for the phrase "son of perdition" must be the figure who is totally opposed to "the Holy Father," namely, the "ruler of this world who has been driven out" (12:31), "the murderer from the beginning" and "the father of lies" (8:44–46). Satan had inspired and accomplished Jesus' betrayal through the agency of Judas (13:2, 27; cf. 2 Thess 2:3, 8–9). He is, or works through, the antichrist of the Johannine letters (1 John 2:18, 22; 4:3)— "The one who denies the Father and the Son..." (1 John 2:22b). In the present context, Jesus identifies him as "the evil one" (17:15b).[9] Whatever the love of God for the world, whatever the unity that is prayed for, there is no pretense on Jesus' part that evil is good or that the lie is the truth.

Yet, however murderous and deceptive the power of the evil one, it is subservient to the Father's design: "...that the scripture might be fulfilled" (17:12d; cf. 13:18). The glory of God will be revealed, but not in terms of worldly violence or human glory. The Father's action is not contained within the vicious circle of the world's darkness. God's love, acting from above, is neither thwarted by some intraworldly power play, nor conformed to it (11:49–50, 57; 12:9–11). Operating on its own terms, the work of the Father subverts the self-assertive dynamics of human pride. For what the Father is bringing into being is manifested in a love that gives of its own and goes to the end. A divine circle of life is opened to all who will enter it: "...that they may be one, even as we are one" (17:11b). Precisely in exposing the violence, the lies, and evil of the world for what it is, the "Holy Father" is glorified in terms of that peace, love, and unity that are not of this world, but that are his unique gifts.

4. Life in the World

13. "But now I am coming to you; and these things I speak in the world that they may have my joy fulfilled in themselves. 14. I have given them your word, and the world has hated them because they are not of the world, even as I am not of the world. 15. I do not pray that you should take them out of the world, but that you keep them from the evil one. 16. They are not of the world, even as I am not of the world. 17. Make them holy in your truth; your word is truth. 18. As you sent me into the world, so I have sent them into the world. 19. And for their sake I make myself holy that they also may be made holy in truth." (17:13–19)

Jesus does not promise his hearers an escape from the world of extreme contradiction. He sends his disciples into it, with the assurance that he has commended them to the Father's care (17:15). They are in the world; they witness to it; but they are not "of it." The disciples live out their mission in the world in the loving presence of the one to whom Jesus is returning (17:13–16). Although their encounter with the world will mean an experience of hatred and rejection, Jesus' prayer envisages nonetheless a joy of a special kind: "...that they may have my joy fulfilled in themselves" (17:13). Despite the inevitable conflict inherent in being in the world, Jesus' own joy will sustain them (15:7–11; 16:24). Their mission is beginning; but his is complete: "But now I am coming to you..." (17:13a). To enter the realm of the Father is to move in the experience of joy fulfilled and shared.

Experiencing the buoyancy of Jesus' joy, the disciples continue to live in the world. Yet they are to live beyond any horizon determined by worldly criteria, in the luminous realm now opened to them through the Son's going to the Father. Their consciousness is flooded with the Father's all-fulfilling presence. At every moment of Jesus' own life, this paternal presence has been the horizon determining all his words and actions. The Father is now asked not only to keep the disciples safe from the influence of the evil one (17:15b), but to make them holy in the truth (17:17). The sanctifying power of truth contrasts with the deceptions and vainglory of the ruler of this world. More positively, this truth is the Father's "word" (17:17b) through which God has communicated both his name and his will through the mission of his Son. Consequently, Jesus' mission reaches its completion through his sending the disciples to continue what the Father has begun in him. As the Father sent him into the world, so he sends his disciples (17:18).

The *terminus a quo,* the source of such an expanding communication, is the Father; its *terminus ad quem* is the world itself. Given the cosmic scale of the task awaiting the disciples, Jesus makes himself holy that they may be made holy in truth (17:19). That they could continue his Father-given mission, Jesus has completely dedicated himself to the Father's will (4:34; 5:36; 17:4). He has done nothing on his own, but only what he sees the Father doing in terms of judging and giving life (5:19–30). As the Word turned toward God in the beginning (1:1), as the only Son given in love for the life of the world (3:16), the whole existence of Jesus is communicative. In his unreserved openness to the Father, his destiny is to embrace all the Father has given him (17:2). His self-sanctification has consisted in his being unconditionally surrendered to God for the sake of the world. In moving toward the Father he is unrestrictedly related to all—"for us and our salvation," as the Nicene Creed will later express it.[10] If the disciples are to be true to their mission, they too must become holy as both God and Jesus are holy, in the sanctity of a self-giving love for others. The truth of God's revelation is manifested in the holiness of costly love (cf. 1 John 4:7–12).

5. The Glory of Love

20. "I do not pray for these only, but also for those who believe in me through their word, 21. that they may be one, even as you, Father, are in me and I in you, that they also may be in us, so that the world may believe that you sent me. 22. The glory that you have given me I have given to them, that they may be one, even as we are one, 23. I in them, and you in me, that they may become perfectly one, so that the world may know that you have sent me and have loved them even as you have loved me." (17:20–23)

The prayer now opens to the wider circle of present believers who are not present. In this sense, "the hour" to which this prayer gives expression reaches out into all the times of faith, and into all its different journeys. While no actual missionary activity of disciples has been recorded in this Gospel (in contrast to the Synoptics), it is presupposed. The disciples are declared to enter into the fruitful labors of Jesus and John the Baptist (4:35–38). In what his disciples have already become, and through what they will later do, a new community, based in the unity of the Father and the Son, comes into being.

Significantly, the outreach of this actively witnessing community extends to the world that has hitherto been presented in

345

ambiguous terms. The word of their witness, flowing from their union with the Father and the Son, has a goal: "...that the world may believe that you sent me" (17:21). The united community and its unifying mission are meant to bear witness to the unique communication the Father has made to the world in sending his only Son. In continuing the mission of the Son, the community of disciples attests to the intimate and unreserved character of God's love for the world. Though Jesus did not pray for the world as an abstract entity (17:9), the world as potentially open to the Father's gift has been present—at times negatively, at times positively—as the sphere in which the design of the Father is to be realized. It is not being abandoned to its darkness, but summoned to the light "...that the world may believe...."

In a further reference to God's life-giving design for the world (17:23), Jesus re-introduces the related themes of glory and unity. In contrast to the vainglory of this world, the glory Jesus has received from God derives from his complete surrender to the will of the Other who has sent him, to whose cause he is unreservedly dedicated.[11] The world is thus confronted with an alternative sense of life and relationships that are incomprehensible to it, given its defensive holding on to what is its own (12:43). This other glory cannot be won from God as a personal adornment or possession. It is purely the gift of the Father. Such is the glory that Jesus, the original receiver, now gives to his disciples: "The glory that you have given to me I have given to them..." (17:22a).

The realm of the Father is depicted in terms of a continuing exchange of gifts. There is no holding on to what is one's own—neither in the case of the Father, nor of the Son, nor of the disciples. The glory of God is revealed, but not in one self asserting itself against another in a dynamic of murderous violence and exclusion. The communication of true glory makes for unity and inspires self-surrender for the sake of the other: "...that they may be one even as we are one, I in them and you in me, that they may become perfectly one..." (17:22b–23a). As this glory originates in the living and affective unity of the Father and the Son, it becomes the unifying principle of new life.

The indwelling of Jesus in the disciples, and the indwelling of the Father in Jesus, replace the externality and limitation of traditional sacred habitations—"...neither on this mountain nor in Jerusalem" (4:21). Though there is a new intimacy and freedom of access to God, the glory appropriate to this new existence is that of the grain of wheat falling into the earth so as not to remain alone, but to bear abundant fruit. It is a glory that will enable the followers of Jesus "to hate their life" in the world of false glory, in order to keep it for eternal life (12:24–25). United with Jesus in the glory of self-giving love, the disciples will be honored by the Father (12:26), and share in the paradigmatic oneness of life and communication existing between the Father and the Son: "...perfectly one..." (17:23a).

Nonetheless, the glory of this perfect communion is not turned inward. It is not an undifferentiated symbiotic fusion, self-sufficient and exclusive. Jesus himself communicates to his disciples the glory he has received and his union with the Father. His gifts and his self-giving look beyond all present realization to an expanding circle of communication. It looks to the world coming to know that the Father has sent his Son, and loved his disciples as he has loved Jesus himself (17:23b). The "only true God" has sent his Son, Jesus Christ, into the world to be the source and form of eternal life (17:3). For their part, the disciples of Jesus have a mission to awaken the world to the gifts which they have received, but as destined for all. Both the sending of the Son and the Son's sending of the disciples into the world are the outcome of the Father's unreserved love—for Jesus, for the disciples, and for the world itself.

24. "Father, I desire also that they, whom you have given me, may be with me where I am, to behold my glory, which you have given me because you loved me before the foundation of the world. 25. O righteous Father, the world has not known you, but I have known you; and these know that you have sent me. 26. I made known to them your name, and I will make it known, that the love with which you have loved me may be in them, and I in them." (17:24–26)

Jesus prays that the disciples, received by him as the Father's gift, will be transported into a new sphere of existence—to be where he is—and to receive the gift of a new vision—to behold his glory (17:24a). Jesus desires that his followers will live in a new luminous horizon, their outlook determined not by the conditions and categories of the world in time, but by the Father's limitless original love for him. In the consummation of this hour, they will behold what has been the fundamental reality of his whole life: his union with God "in the beginning" (1:1), "before the foundation of the world" (17:24b). If the Word is turned toward the Father in the beginning (1:1), the Father is also turned toward the Son. He will glorify his Son by giving him disciples who will understand his "hour" as the outcome of God's original love.

The process of history, and the progress of events in the life of Jesus himself, are held together in the Father's timeless love. Though the disciples will continue to experience the fractured and conflict-ridden existence of the life in the world, there will be a dimension of wholeness, peace, and joy, based on the assurance that the eternal project of the Father will be realized. Believers will be in the world, but not "of it," in their awareness of love in which the world was made, and of the life for which it is destined (17:11, 14–15, 16). By leaving them, Jesus has in effect relocated them.[12] They live now in the heavenly realm of life and communion, the

Father's house of many dwelling places (14:2–3). Believers can anticipate a luminous consummation of their faith, with a hope founded on the desire and prayer of Jesus himself. In this prayer, his followers will accompany him into the presence of the Father, "...my Father and your Father, my God and your God" (20:17).

The "righteous Father" (17:25a) to whom Jesus turns is the source of the Paraclete sent to expose the unrighteousness of the world in its various stratagems of self-justification (16:7–11). In turning from Jesus, the world has not known the true God (17:25a). It has locked itself in a willful and idolatrous ignorance of the truth. In contrast, Jesus has known and revealed the name of God (17:25b), and set his disciples on the right path of knowledge of the Father (17:25c). In their respective ways, the "righteous" Father, Jesus, the Paraclete, and the disciples contest the false glory of the world, to reveal the truth of God's own glory. Jesus sums up his mission, as it has been up to the present, and as it will be continued in his disciples: "I have made known to them your name, and I will make it known" (17:26a). In him are embodied a justice and truth that are entirely counter to the false justice characteristic of worldly glory.

What he is and will be can be understood only in terms of the original love of the Father. The purpose of his revelation of the Father's name is "that the love with which you have loved me may be in them, and I in them" (17:26b). Through their union with Jesus, the disciples are drawn into the universe of love. The Father's love for the Son overflows into those who believe in him; and his love for them will be enacted in their love for one another (13:34–35; 15:12, 17).

Key words in the Gospel feature in the prayer of Jesus: glory (17:1, 5, 24), eternal life (17:3), knowing God (17:3, 23), the divine name (17:6, 11b), mutual indwelling and unity (17:11b, 22–23), truth (17:17, 19), holiness (17:11b, 17, 19), and righteousness (17:25). They are each redefined in terms of the Father's original love and the disciples' active participation in it. While the notion of love has redefined all else, the event of the cross has yet to define love in its fullest meaning as the innermost expression of the divine name (cf. 1 John 4:8, 16).

Still, the stage is set for revelation of the divine glory that is the origin, end, and heart of all creation (17:5, 24). With the Father glorified in the Son (17:1, 5), and the Son glorified in the disciples (17:11), the distinctive form of divine glory will be made known to the world in the unity characteristic of eternal life (17:22–23). Such "perfect" oneness (17:23) is brought into being only by the self-giving love of the Father for the Son (17:23–24, 26), and of the Son for the Father; in their respective love (17:23) for the disciples; and in their love for Jesus himself and for one another (13:34; 14:21).

6. The Open Invitation

The first words of the Word to the disciples was the question, "What are you looking for?" (1:38b). In response to their question, "Rabbi, where are you staying?" Jesus issued the invitation, "Come and see" (1:38–39). Now, his final words in the presence the disciples are a prayer. His prayer expresses for those who have followed him to this point—not without questions, confusion, and foreboding—the holy space that Jesus inhabits. The Father's house to which Jesus is going in one of perfect unity and communion. It is the fullness of truth to which the Spirit is leading, as the disciples are enfolded into the mutuality of love and life that characterizes the relationship of the Father and the Son. The thick forest of darkness and threat opens into a bright clearing illuminated by the glory of another realm. It also discloses a path yet to be travelled. Neither the journey of Jesus, nor that of his followers, is yet complete.

In this regard, the prayer implies a kind of intradivine dialogue in which the followers of Jesus are drawn. They are the subject matter of the conversation of the opened heaven. As Jesus is departing this world for the Father, to be united with him in the glory that was his before the world was made, he takes with him, in effect, those whom the Father has given him. The open heaven is disclosed as an open circle. The unity existing between the Father and the Son appears as an expanding field of life, love, and truth. Into it the disciples are drawn, and through them, successive generations of believers, that the world might come to know the mysteries unfolding in its midst.

Notes

1. R. W. Jenson, *The Triune God,* 93, 109.
2. How much the true knowing of God is a process of unlearning, and of breaking out of our habitual categorizations of reality, is often the theme of the mystics. For a refreshing doctrinal approach, see Christopher Morse, *Not Every Spirit: A Dogmatics of Christian Disbelief,* 73–84; 113–194.
3. Cf. 1:14, 16–18; 3:14–15, 16–17, 31–36a; 4:13–14; 5:24–25; 6:35, 51; 7:37–38; 8:12; 9:5; 10:27–29; 11:42; 13:18–20; 14:6–7.
4. For further reflections on the mutual glorification of the Father and the Son, see von Balthasar, *The Glory of the Lord VII,* 246–250.
5. For an alternative, but complementary, approach, see David F. Ford, *Self and Salvation,* 157–162.
6. Cf. 13:34–35; 15:1–11, 18–19, 21; 16:3.
7. Cf. 10:16; 11:52; 12:11, 19, 32.
8. Cf. 13:15, 34–35; 15:12, 17; 17:10.
9. Cf. 12:31; 14:30; 16:11; 1 John 2:13–14; 3:12; 5:18–19.
10. Cf. 3:16–17; 10:14–18; 13:1; 15:13.
11. See 2:11; 5:44; 7:18; 8:50–54; 11:4, 40.
12. James Alison, *Raising Abel,* is particularly good on this point. See especially "The Creation of Meaning and the Forging of Love," 69–76.

18

<hr/>

The Father's Cup
(18:1—19:42)

The prayer of Jesus to the Father, with its various themes of glory, unity and confrontation with evil, throws light on this night journey. It will lead to the evening of the next day in another garden (19:41). The immemorial symbolism of a garden as the place of God's presence (Genesis 3:8) evokes a sense of another dimension—the genesis of the opened heaven brought about by the generative action of the Father. Though the Father is no longer addressed, and mentioned only once by name (18:11), the events of this hour unfold under his gaze and direction. The divine will, intimated in the various scriptural prophecies, is being realised (18:9, 27, 32; 19:24, 36). The assurance evident in Jesus' confrontation with his adversaries, judges, and executioners brings home this point. A kingdom not of this world is coming into effect. In what Jesus suffers, an Other is acting with him and in him. A progressive silence underscores the completeness of the Son's surrender to the Father's action and his unbroken communion with the only true God who is to be revealed in the glory of this hour (see 1:14, 18).

1. Confrontation

1. When Jesus had spoken these words he went forth with his disciples across the Kidron valley to where there was a garden, which he and his disciples entered.

2. Now Judas, who betrayed him, also knew the place, for Jesus often met there with his disciples. 3. So Judas, procuring a band of soldiers and some officers from the chief priests and the Pharisees, went there with lanterns and torches and weapons. 4. Then Jesus, knowing all that was to befall him, came forward and said to them, "Whom do you seek?" 5. They answered him, "Jesus of Nazareth." Jesus said to them, "I am he." Judas, who betrayed him, was standing with them. 6. When he said to them, "I am he," they drew back and fell to the ground. 7. Again he asked them, "Whom do you seek?" And they said, "Jesus of Nazareth." 8. Jesus answered, "I told you that I am he; so if you seek me let these others go." 9. This was to fulfill the word he had spoken, "Of those whom you gave me I lost not one." 10. Then Simon Peter, having a sword, drew it and struck the high priest's slave and cut off his right ear. The slave's name was Malchus. 11. Jesus said to Peter, "Put your sword into its sheath; shall I not drink the cup the Father has given me?" (18:1–11)

In a first act, those representing a world in opposition to the Father's will—Judas, the band of soldiers, and the officers from the Jewish authorities—go out with their lanterns and torches and weapons to confront "the light of the world" (8:12; 9:5). But it is Jesus, attuned to his Father's initiative, who confronts them: "Whom do you seek?" (18:4). In willful ignorance of Jesus' divine origin, these designate him only in terms of their familiar world, namely, "Jesus of Nazareth" (18:5; cf. 1:46). But his self-identification, "I am he" (18:5–6), locates him on the holy ground of divine revelation (cf. Exod 3:5). The history of the revelation of the divine name (Exod 3:14) will culminate in him. What Jesus had foretold, is being accomplished: "...when it does occur you may believe that I am he" (13:19). Unable either to stand or understand the in-breaking presence of God, Jesus' would-be captors fall back (Ps 56:9). With the assurance that the Father has heard his prayer for his disciples (17:12; cf. 6:69; 10:28), he commands those who had come for him to let them go. In the plan of God, they have a mission to complete, inspired by the events that are taking place.[1] He will not allow their mission to be thwarted.

The mission of the disciples to witness to the self-giving love of God pertains to the essence of the divine design (17:23, 26). However, they are not yet on the inside of what is taking place. Responding to demands of what he still imagines as a worldly kingdom, Peter slashes with his sword at the slave of the high priest. But the love of the Father can only be revealed on its own terms. Violence on the part of the disciple adds only to the darkness of the world. Such is not the way of the Father. This point is brought home in Jesus' command and question, "Put your sword into its sheath; shall I not drink the cup the Father has given me?" (18:11b; cf. 12:27).

Having secured the freedom of his disciples, Jesus himself is now seized and bound (18:12). The cup the Father has given him contains those ingredients of evil that will make the glory of love appear. The Father's action is moving forward even as the plans of evil, expressed in the counsel of Caiaphas, are being realized: "...it is expedient for you that one man should die for the people, and that the whole nation should not perish" (11:50). The deeper mystery is at work: that "...Jesus should die for the nation, and not for the nation only, but to gather into one the children of God who are scattered abroad (11:51–52).

Even as Peter follows violence with denial (18:15–18; 25–27), the words of Jesus are borne out: "And at once the cock crowed (18:27; 13:38). An action is afoot that even the frailty of the disciples cannot compromise. Indeed, despite their frailty, they are still declared by Jesus, in his answer to the high priest, to be the continuing mediators of the revelation that has been made: "Ask those who have heard me what I said to them; they know what I said" (18:21). Jesus thereby implies that this disreputable group knows something that has passed the high priest by. The point is not lost on "one of the officers" standing by, as he strikes the prisoner (18:22).

In the occurrence of this hour, Jesus' judges are judged. What they insist on interpreting as blasphemy on his part ("speaking wrongly," 18:23),[2] has in fact been an open revelation to the world, of the name of God: "I have spoken openly to the world" (18:20).

2. Judgment

28. Then they led Jesus from the house of Caiaphas to the praetorium. It was early. They themselves did not enter the praetorium so that they might not be defiled, but might eat the Passover. 29. So Pilate went out to them and said, "What accusation do you bring against this man?" 30. They answered him, "If this man were not an evildoer we would not have handed him over." 31. Pilate said to them, "Take him yourselves and judge him by your own law." 32. The Jews said to him, "It is not lawful for us to put any man to death." This was to fulfill the word that Jesus had spoken to show by what death he was to die. (18:28–32)

The scene shifts to a larger theater of judgment. Jesus is led to the praetorium. Though they are intent on bringing about the death of the Lamb of God (1:29, 34), his antagonists show the religious nicety of not entering a pagan building lest they suffer defilement on the eve of the Passover. The strange creativity of religious ideology, prepared, on the one hand, to make the Roman official complicit in its murderous intentions, yet, on the other, delicately observing ritual externals, is presented with piercing irony. It leaves the reader of the Gospel wondering what each actor in the drama is imagining God to be. How is it possible to miss both the experience and the meaning of the divine action in progress? How has the Passover itself, in the practice of these ritually observant Israelites, come to such a dead end?

The Gospel has in fact offered its own explanations as it records the increasingly virulent hostility of "the Jews" to Jesus. But in the progress of this hour, it is not explanation but revelation that predominates, as the divine logic unfolds in what is taking place. In a first exchange between Pilate and the parties intent on lynching their prisoner (18:29–32), crucifixion looms as the desired outcome. Given the previous attempts to plot his death, or even to bring it about through stoning, the modest disclaimer, "it is not lawful for us to put anyone to death" (18:31), is hardly credible. But what is emerging to the vision of faith is the revelatory and transforming character of the death Jesus is to die: "This was to fulfill the word that Jesus had spoken to show by what death he was to die" (18:33). When Jesus is lifted up from the earth he will gather everyone to himself (12:32). The subversive presence of God's non-violent and supremely self-giving love is to be manifest in Jesus, victimized by both Jews and Romans. The sacred violence that holds in place both the temple and the imperial authority will be used to expose the unrighteousness of the world. In the crucifixion that results, the glory of God will be revealed as something completely at odds with a worldly kingdom. Within the divinely wrought action by which the Lamb *of God* takes away the sin of the world (1:29), the true dimensions of the sin of the world are to be brought into the open.

3. The Realm of Truth

33. Pilate entered the praetorium again and called Jesus, and said to him, "Are you the King of the Jews?" 34. Jesus answered him, "Do you say this of your own accord, or did others say it about me?" 35. Pilate answered, "Am I a Jew? Your own nation and the chief priests have handed you over to me; what have you done?" 36. Jesus answered, "My kingship is not of this world; if my kingship were of this world my servants would fight that I might not be handed over to the Jews; but my kingship is not from the world." 37. Pilate said to him, "So you are a king?" Jesus answered, "You say that I am a king. For this I was born, and for this I have come into the world, to bear witness to the truth. Everyone who is of the truth hears my voice. 38a. Pilate said to him, "What is truth?" (18:33–38a)

Reentering the praetorium, Pilate asks his strange prisoner whether he is the King of the Jews. The character of Jesus' kingship explicitly emerges, in marked contrast to the murderous intentions of his supposed subjects. Yet it connects with Jesus' previous exemplary action in washing the disciples' feet (13:12–15), and refers back to the Baptist's designation of him as "the Lamb of God" (1:29, 34). His rule is different. He had evaded the people's effort to take him by force and proclaim him king (6:15). And then, when the great crowd, assembled for the Passover, had gone out to meet him and acclaimed him "the King of Israel," he chose to seat himself on a young ass (12:13–14). The Gospel looked back to the puzzlement of the disciples themselves, concerning the nature of his kingship: "His disciples did not understand this at first; but when Jesus was glorified, then they remembered that this had been written of him and had been done to him" (12:16).

Now, in the process of what was being "done to him," Jesus distances himself from any regal pretension in a univocally political or religious sense (18:34, 37b). His regal status is not explicable in terms of a personal claim to worldly power operating through violence. It is, therefore, a kingship not of this world, upheld not by the military power of its subjects, but by the truth that Jesus witnesses to (18:36). His authority looks beyond this world to the realm of the Father. When Peter had acted in the violence of a behavior typical of a worldly kingship, Jesus restrained him for the sake of the cup the Father had given him to drink (18:10–11). Neither his disciples nor he are "of this world" (17:14). The power of the kingdom embodied in him is invisible and inaccessible, except to those who are born again, from above (3:3), of water and the Spirit (3:5). In this kingdom, his authority consists in being unreservedly surrendered to the Father. It is exercised in loving his own "unto the end" (13:1).

In declaring that "Everyone who is of the truth hears my voice" (18:37b), Jesus further suggests the kind of kingly authority he exercises. For this king is the Good Shepherd who gives abundant life by laying down his life for his sheep (10:10–11). In the violent world of thieves, robbers, and wolves (10:8, 12), there is another realm of truth. The sheep hear his voice and he calls them by name (10:3). He knows his own and they know him (10:14). In laying down his life, the Father loves him; and gives him the power to give his life and to take it up again to accomplish the divine purpose (10:17–18). The authority of such a kingship and role of the Good Shepherd are joined in the service of the sheep the Father has given him. His kingship, though not of this world, consists in the community of believers who, within this world, have received him and heard his voice, and so have come to know the Father who is acting through him.

Pilate's retort, "What is truth?" (18:38a), despite all the dramatic and literary interpretations of this question, is probably best construed in its most banal significance. The Roman senses that he is caught in the middle of some immense conflict. On the one side, there is the harsh political truth of an influential political and religious group obviously intent on enlisting him for its murderous purposes. On the other side, there is the truth of another authority, not of that world, refusing to respond in kind to the threat of violence. This other kind of truth is beyond the imagination of the pragmatic world of the Roman administrator. For him, especially in this maddeningly complicated part of the empire, bargains have to be struck and compromises achieved—if anyone is to live in peace. What is truth, indeed? And where is the God of truth to be found in what is taking place?

4. Terminal Conflict

38b. After he had said this he went out to the Jews again and told them, "I find no crime in him. 39. But you have a custom that I should release one man for you on the Passover; will you have me release for you the King of the Jews?" 40. They cried out again, "Not this man, but Barabbas!" Now Barabbas was a robber. 19:1 Then Pilate took Jesus and had him scourged. 2. And the soldiers plaited a crown of thorns and put it on his head, and arrayed him in a purple robe; 3. they came up to him, saying, "Hail, King of the Jews!" and struck him with their hands. 4. Pilate went out again and said to them, "See, I am bringing him out to you that you may know that I find no crime in him." 5. So Jesus came out, bearing

the crown of thorns and wearing the purple robe. Pilate said to them, "Behold the man!" 6. When the chief priests and the officers saw him they cried out, "Crucify him, crucify him!" Pilate said to them, "Take him yourselves and crucify him, for I find no crime in him." 7. The Jews answered him, "We have a law, and by that law he ought to die, because he has made himself the Son of God." (18:38b—19:7)

There is enough of the truth in Pilate to declare Jesus innocent (18:38b). Yet Pilate is still beholden to the political reality of his situation, so he offers to release the innocent prisoner in accord with the Passover custom. Perhaps a deal could be struck and the unsettling question of truth would go away. But a terminal conflict is taking place. So intent are Jesus' accusers on his execution, that they declare their option for Barabbas, a man of violence (18:40). He was probably associated with the Zealots whose false messianic pretensions, in the opinion of the historian Josephus, would cause God to abandon his people. In this case, the world of violence chooses one of its own. The thief and the bandit wreaking havoc on the fold (10:1, 8) is preferred to the Good Shepherd who lays down his life for his sheep (10:11). There is no room for the other truth.

Perhaps in an effort to occupy the middle ground between the two versions of the truth represented before him, Pilate has Jesus scourged (19:1). This action gives the soldiers the opportunity to perform a mock coronation. The crown of thorns is pressed on his head; he is arrayed in a purple robe; and his tormentors, in a parody of the military salute, *Ave Caesar!* strike out at him: "Hail, the King of the Jews!" (19:3). Pilate goes out once more to confront the Jews, declaring that no crime has been detected in the prisoner he intends to bring out to them (19:4). As a defenseless victim of the kingdom of this world, the King within

360

that other realm appears, wearing the crown of thorns and the purple robe (19:5a). He is not brought out, but comes out, of his own accord. And with a word usually reserved for the honorable or regal bearing of clothes or armor, Jesus is said to "bear" the insignia of his kingship, which he will wear till the end. The truth is appearing in its own power and on its own terms: God's glory owes nothing to the kingdom of this world.

Pilate announces, "Behold the man!" (19:5b). At one level, Pilate, in addressing Jesus' accusers, may well be calling for a consideration based on common humanity, and represented in the tortured, humiliated figure before them. More likely, because of his repeated declarations of Jesus' innocence (18:38b; 19:4, 6), "the man" is an honorific title, an acknowledgement of the rectitude of the accused. However, in terms, of the revelation taking place in this hour, it indicates that Jesus' prophetic words are being fulfilled: "When you have lifted up the Son of Man, then you will know that I am he" (8:28). When the Greeks came to see him, he had declared, "The hour has come for the Son of Man to be glorified" (12:23). The process of glorification is taking place: "When I am lifted up from the earth I will draw everyone to myself" (12:32). It is precisely this "lifting up" that his antagonists now demand, in calling on Pilate to crucify him (19:6).

In the subsequent exchange between Pilate and the Jewish leaders, while the Roman judges are in favor of the accused, the crucial point of terminal antagonism between Jesus and those rejecting him emerges: "We have a law, and by that law he ought to die, because he has made himself the Son of God" (19:7). Jesus has to go—because, in the judgment of his accusers, he cannot be from God. God cannot be revealed like *this*. Divine revelation cannot allow this kind of subversion of their traditional religious identity and security. The clashes between Jesus and "the Jews," dramatically documented in 5:1—10:42, have come to a dénouement. Jesus is no longer denounced simply as an "evildoer" (18:30), but as one pretending to be "the Son of God," the bearer of another revelation, the embodiment of another holiness. *That* cannot possibly be true.

> 8. **When Pilate heard these words he was the more afraid; 9. he entered the praetorium again and said to Jesus, "Where are you from?" But Jesus gave no answer. 10. Pilate therefore said to him, "You will not speak to me? Do you not know that I have power to release you and power to crucify you?" 11. Jesus answered him, "You would have no power over me unless it had been given you from above; therefore the one who delivered me to you has the greater sin."**
> (19:8–11)

Pilate seemingly recognizes the dimensions of the problem in which he is involved. The truth has beckoned, but is now passing him by. He becomes "the more afraid" (19:8). His subsequent question expresses the one radical consideration from which everything taking place has to be judged: "Where are you from?" (19:9a). If there is an answer to that question, and if the answer should lead to Jesus' divine origins, everything would be changed. But this question can no longer be answered in human words. The time for words had passed; and Jesus remains silent. Pilate attempts to pull Jesus back from the kingdom of truth into his own domain of worldly words and power: for him not to speak to the judge is to refuse to communicate with one who has power of life and death over him (19:10). When Jesus does speak he refers to the one who is at work in the unfolding of this hour, and to the various actors who have a place in it. Pilate would have no power over him unless it had been given him from above (19:11). The authority of Pilate is under the sway of another will which works its purposes despite all human evil.

The giver of power from above will reveal his glory, not just despite, but even *through* "the greater sin" of those who have planned to do away with Jesus, as has occurred in the action of Caiaphas (11:49–53; 18:27–28). Despite the ultimate opposition of the evil one, the son of perdition (17:12), the Lamb *of God* will take away the sin of the world (1:29) in the fulfillment of the Passover now taking place.

Again the Gospel suggests that Pilate steps to the frontier of another realm, another authority, another truth, and another glory: "Upon this, Pilate sought to release him..." (19:12a). But the familiar world of human power and glory pulls him back: "If you release this man, you are not Caesar's friend..." (19:12b). The world of human glory can understand itself only in terms of violent confrontation: "Everyone who makes himself a king sets himself against Caesar" (19:12c). All other possibilities are ruled out: to be in the world yet not of it goes beyond the imagination of both judge and accusers. For them, "God" is the legitimating idol of worldly power. That the only true God should give his only Son to reveal himself and disclose their world for what it is—and thereby offer the world-transcending gifts of peace and communion—all that has ceased to be worthy of consideration.

> **14. Now it was the day of preparation of the Passover; it was about the sixth hour. He said to the Jews, "Behold your king!" 15. They cried out, "Away with him, away with him, crucify him!" Pilate said to them, "Shall I crucify your king?" The chief priests answered, "We have no king but Caesar." 16a. Then he handed him over to them to be crucified. (19:14–16a)**

And so the judgment takes place on the eve of the Passover. Pilate presents "the Jews" with "your king." Their reply contradicts everything sacred to the Mosaic tradition: they proclaim that they have only Caesar as their king (19:15c). As the paschal lambs are being slaughtered in the temple precincts about the sixth hour, they cry out for the blood of the Lamb of God. The logic of the Gospel's previous explanation of antagonism to Jesus is complete: "For they loved human glory rather than the glory of God" (12:43).

Thus, as Pilate hands Jesus over to them to be crucified in the Roman form of execution (19:16a), he is turning against the truth of his own judgment. And the Jewish leaders are making an option for what most undermines their own tradition. The irony is complete. In condemning Jesus they are making a judgment on themselves. They have refused the truth, and closed themselves to what is at work "from above" (19:11).

5. The New Community

The journey to Golgotha takes place: "So they took Jesus, and he went out bearing his own cross, to a place called the place of a skull..." (19:16b–17). But another movement is in progress, attracting all to the crucified one: "There they crucified him, and with him two others, one on either side, and Jesus between them" (19:18). Significantly, his two cosufferers are not named in John's Gospel as criminals or sinners, for they are associated with Jesus in a supreme moment of glory. The sheep "not of this fold" are being enfolded into the keeping of the Good Shepherd who lays down his life for his sheep (10:14–16). Jesus is dying "...not for the nation only, but to gather into one the children of God who are scattered abroad" (11:52). On being lifted up from the earth, he "will draw all people" to himself (12:32). Even Pilate, who had hitherto remained notoriously outside the domain of the truth, brings to the public gaze his judgment of the universal significance of Jesus. In the three official languages of his world, he designates Jesus of Nazareth as "the King of the Jews" (19:19–20). Despite the protest that such a title only legitimated the claims of an imposter (19:21), he insists on his original version of the truth, initially formulated as a charge, now presented as a fact and a promise: "What I have written, I have written" (19:22). Like Caiaphas before him (11:49), the Roman governor acts under the sway of the power at work from above (19:11).

Subsequent events indicate the irresistible momentum of the hour. As the soldiers divide the outer garment of Jesus, and cast lots for the tunic (19:23–24), scripture is fulfilled in accord with the Psalm, "They parted my garments among them, and for clothing they cast lots" (Ps 22:19). Yet there is a hint of another fulfillment, the coming into being of the unbreakable unity that the Father and the Son have shared with the disciples, symbolized in the indivisible seamless tunic (19:23b–24). The Father's answer to the prayer of Jesus "…that they may be all one, even as you, Father, are in me, and I in you, that they also may also be in us, that the world may believe that you have sent me" (17:21), is to become evident in what is about to take place.

> 25. But standing by the cross of Jesus were his mother, and his mother's sister, Mary the wife of Clopas, and Mary Magdalene. 26. When Jesus saw his mother, and the disciple whom he loved, standing near, he said to his mother, "Woman, behold, your son!" 27. Then he said to the disciple, "Behold, your mother!" And from that hour the disciple took her to his own home. (19:25–27)

A new community is represented by those standing by the cross of Jesus: his mother, her sister, Mary Magdalene, and the Beloved Disciple. Seeing his mother and the Beloved Disciple standing there, Jesus speaks to them. His going to the Father is an act of love for his own "unto the end" (13:1). Those who had shown unconditional faith in him will never be left alone. As he goes to prepare for them the many dwelling places in his Father's house (14:2), after having promised the sending of another Paraclete (14:16–17), those left bereft of his earthly presence will be united in a new community as the Spirit of truth abides in them (14:17b). They are to be one, as the Father and he are one (17:21). In their different journeys to faith, they are given as gifts to one another: "Woman, behold, your son" (19:26b). The woman of unconditional obedience to the word of Jesus—"Do whatever he tells you" (2:5)—receives this final instruction, to be mother to him whom Jesus loved (13:23). In the universe of the Father's love, her motherhood is immeasurably extended. She is not given by her Son to be a sister to the disciple, but to be his mother.

Then the disciple is addressed: "Behold, your mother!" (19:27a). His faith is to be enriched and supported by the woman of faith. A new community of faith and care takes flesh in the world. The response of the disciple is unreserved. From that hour he takes the mother of Jesus to his own home (19:27b). From that hour, indeed *because* of that hour (12:23; 13:1; 17:1), the welcoming house of the Father takes human shape in the hospitality of the new community of faith. Jesus "had come to his own home, and his own people received him not" (1:11). Now, through his passing from this world to the Father, the home of each believer becomes a place of love and welcome for others. The seamless garment will not be divided. The scattered children of God are gathered into a new God-given unity.[3]

> 28. After this, Jesus, knowing that all was now finished, said (to fulfill the scripture), "I thirst." 29. A bowl full of vinegar stood there; so they put a sponge

full of vinegar on hyssop and held it to his mouth. 30. When Jesus had received the vinegar he said, "It is finished"; and he bowed his head and handed over the spirit. (19:28–30)

The Father has moved everything to a great fulfillment: Jesus knows that his mission is achieved.[4] All has been brought to its completion by the Father working in the events determining this hour. Jesus has drunk the cup the Father had given him (18:11), and completed the work of him who sent him (4:34; 5:36; 17:4). He had loved unto the end (13:1). In fulfillment of the scripture, he says, "I thirst" (19:28b). As the Gospel has promised, his thirst would lead to the gift of living water (4:6, 10). The sponge filled with vinegar given to him on the hyssop suggests the lamb of the Passover (Exod 12:22–23; cf. 2:17), and the prophecy hidden in Israel's ancient prayer, "For my thirst they gave me vinegar to drink" (LXX Ps 68:22).[5]

With his mission now brought to completion, Jesus initiates the new age that will have its beginning in this hour: "...and he bowed his head and handed over the spirit" (19:30). As he inclines his head toward the little community, representing the great circle of a new unity of all in the Father and the Son, Jesus hands over the Spirit of new life that he had promised. The stream of living water now begins to flow from him into the community of faith (7:37–39). What the Gospel had previously foreshadowed is now taking place: "Now this he said about the Spirit that those who believed in him were to receive; for as yet the Spirit had not been given, because Jesus was not yet glorified" (7:39). In the glory of this hour, the Father's gift to the world of his only Son is prolonged into the world. It will be kept alive through the Spirit of truth "...who will take what is mine and declare it to you" (16:15). While the death of Jesus will leave a gaping hole in the experience of the disciples, that void will be filled by the luminous presence of the Spirit. And the gift of the Spirit will guide believers into the open horizon of "the things that are to come" (16:13); above all, to that consummation when the Father and the Son will come to make their home in them (14:23).

6. The Flow of Gifts

In terms, however, of the flesh that the Word was made of, all that remains of him, in the world that he has become, is his crucified corpse. On this level of the flesh, "the Jews" act once more, to remove Jesus in death, as they had encompassed his removal in life. His corpse must not defile the Sabbath, nor compromise the celebration of the Passover (19:31). In their keen sense of ritual purity, they petition Pilate to have the legs of the crucified men broken "that they might be taken away" (19:32). The Lamb of God who had been sent to take away the sin of the world (1:29) is to be taken away by the sin of the world, represented by those of his own people who had rejected him.

> 34. **But one of the soldiers pierced his side with a spear, and at once there came out blood and water. 35. He who saw it has borne witness—his testimony is true, and he knows that he is telling the truth—that you also may believe. 36. For these things took place that the scripture might be fulfilled, "Not a bone of him shall be broken." 37. And another scripture says, "They shall look on him whom they have pierced."** (19:34–37)

When he is found to be already dead, the soldier recognizes the fact by spearing his body in the side: "...and at once there came out blood and water" (19:34). In the hour of revelation, this physical detail is perceived as of huge symbolic import. The narrator cannot resist projecting himself into the account of the incident, to bring home to future believers the truth here embodied. From the side of Jesus flows blood and water. What Jesus had promised, as the Gospel has previously explained, is now realized:

> "Let anyone who is thirsty come to me, and let the one who believes in me drink. As the scripture has said, 'Out of his heart shall flow rivers of living water.'" Now this he said about the Spirit....(7:37–39)

Previously the Spirit had not yet been given because Jesus had not yet been glorified. But now the promised gift of the Spirit takes place. The community of believers receives the gifts of water and the Spirit (3:5) in which to be reborn, and the blood to nourish them to life eternal in continuous union with the Crucified One (6:53–56). In the coming of the Spirit, believers can recognize that the physically absent Jesus is present through the sacraments of Eucharist and baptism. Indeed, as the First Letter of John expresses it, these three factors are brought together in the "testimony of God": "There are three that testify: the Spirit and the water and the blood; and these three agree. If we receive human testimony, the testimony of God is greater..." (1 John 5:7–9). Each gift, in its own way, testifies that Jesus has completed his work in making the Father known.

And in every moment of this decisive hour, the Father is at work, seeking and finding true worshipers in Spirit and in truth (4:23). The divine design climaxing in this moment had been expressed in scriptural prophecy: "Not a bone of him shall be broken" (19:36). God's Lamb, given to take away the sin of the world, is the fulfillment of the Paschal sacrifice (Exod 12:10, 46; Num 9:12). The righteous sufferer has been glorified (Ps 34:20–21). As the community of believers gazes on the Crucified

One, it finds in him the source of the Spirit, and of the water and the blood. The prophecy of Zechariah is fulfilled in the new era of faith: "They shall look on him whom they have pierced" (19:37; cf. Zech 12:10).[6]

Hints of this "looking on," on the Crucified Jesus, are given in the closing scene. Not only is the truth of Jesus made public in the hour of glory, but former disciples—Joseph of Arimathea (19:38) and Nicodemus (19:39; cf. 3:1)—who had previously been enclosed in their own fears, now enter the public scene as witnesses to his origin and mission. In final recognition of his identity they give him a royal burial—implied in the enormous amount of precious spices Nicodemus brought, and the new tomb in the garden (19:39–40).

7. Silence and Anticipation

His being buried in accord with "the burial custom of the Jews" (19:40b) is an enigmatic closure. He has been killed at the instigation of "the Jews," and buried according to the traditions that have held sway. Yet there is an anticipation of something more. Jesus' mission is accomplished. But is this the end of the story? Is the glory of the king to end in the tomb? Will the burial clothes hold him bound? (cf. 11:44; 20:5–7). What further glory is in store? What further word awaits his friends in this garden of burial? How will they will hear "the sound of the LORD walking in the garden at the time of the evening breeze"? (Gen 3:8). If "the wind blows where it wills, and you hear the sound of it, but you do not know whence it comes or whither it goes..." (3:8), is there still room for the surprises of God? If this is "the Jewish day of preparation" (19:42), what other great preparation is taking place?

As his friends leave the garden in which they have just buried the body of Jesus, binding it in the vesture of death and laying it the new tomb, they will return to find things otherwise. The grain of wheat falling into the earth will not remain alone (12:24).

Notes

1. Cf. 13:20, 34–35; 15:5–8, 16, 26–27; 17:18–19, 20–23.
2. Cf. Exod 22:7; Lev 19:14; 20:9; Isa 8:21; 1 Macc.
3. See 10:16; 11:49–52; 12:11, 19, 20–24, 32–33.
4. See Gil Bailie's profound meditation on this theme in *Violence Unveiled,* 217–233. He is of the view that "John's Gospel provides the New Testament's most breathtaking vista on the universal meaning of the crucifixion and its eventual impact on the world" (219).
5. Note the whole of Ps 69 in this context.
6. David F. Ford in *Self and Salvation,* reflecting on the symbolism of the face from philosophical, biblical, and theological perspectives, writes: "This face as dead matter is like a 'black hole' for all familiar and comforting images of this event. It sucks into it other reality....If this dead face of Jesus is intrinsic to salvation, then there is needed a radical critique of concepts of salvation....They may indeed all be sucked into the black hole in order to be reconstituted with reserve as appropriate metaphors, but the dead face is a vital criterion of appropriateness and signifies a radical rupture at the heart of relating..." (205–206).

19

My Father and Your Father
(20:1–31)

1. Three Journeys to the Tomb

1. Now on the first day of the week Mary Magdalene came to the tomb early, while it was still dark, and saw that the stone had been taken away from the tomb. 2. So she ran, and went to Simon Peter and the other disciple, the one whom Jesus loved, and said to them, "They have taken the Lord out of the tomb, and we do not know where they have laid him." 3. Peter then came out with the other disciple and they went together toward the tomb. 4. They both ran, but the other disciple outran Peter and reached the tomb first; 5. stooping to look in he saw the linen cloths lying there, but he did not go in. 6. Then Simon Peter came, following him, and went into the tomb; he saw the linen cloths lying there, 7. and the napkin which had been on his head, not lying with the other linen cloths but rolled up in a place by itself. 8. Then the other disciple, who reached the tomb first, also went in, and saw and believed; 9. for as yet they did not know the scripture, that he must rise from the dead. 10. Then the disciples went back to their homes. (20:1–10)

The first day of the week, celebrated in the Christian liturgy as the Day of the Lord, is, in this instance, the day following the Passover—which that year had fallen on the Sabbath (19:31). The early hour of this new day promises a new beginning; but, in the language of the Gospel narrative, "it is still dark" (20:1b). Full-bodied faith has yet to be born. Throughout the Gospel, darkness had been associated with what was inhospitable to "the light of the world" (8:12). The darkness of unbelief has contended in vain against the light (1:5). The uncomprehending Nicodemus had come to Jesus by night (3:2). In the darkness of the storm, the disciples had experienced their separation from Jesus (6:17). He had promised to all who follow him an escape from darkness (8:12b), just as he had predicted the nighttime of powerlessness and stumbling for those who do not recognize the luminous day of his presence (9:4; 11:10; 12:35, 46). Judas, his betrayer, had disappeared into the night (13:30). Though Nicodemus had begun to turn to the light (19:35), it is still dark. Jesus is dead and buried; his enemies had triumphed; and his friends were left only with memories of their previous relationships with him, whose dead face and pierced body they had seen.

And yet there is a hint of the opening of heaven in what Mary Magdalene saw: the stone had been taken away (20:1b). Despite the darkness, there is this intimation of first light, the dawn of the first day of a new creation.[1] But Magdalene runs away from the tomb, and goes to the two most important disciples in the story: Peter, the Rock, who had last appeared in the darkness of his denial,[2] and the Beloved Disciple,[3] who had stood beneath the cross, who had been bidden to take the Mother of Jesus into his own home, and who, with her and the other Marys, had been part of the small representative community to receive the gift of the Spirit as Jesus died (19:25b–30). How this Spirit will guide the disciples into the full truth of the things that previously could not be borne

(16:12–13), and declare "the things that are to come" (16:13), the story will now unfold.

For the moment, Mary can think of the ending of Jesus' story only in terms of a final act of robbery perpetrated by those who had done away him: "They have taken the Lord out of the tomb, and we do not know where they have laid him" (20:2b). "They" are the agents of death and violence; and the "we" are the vulnerable subjects of a kingship not of this world (19:36). These followers of Jesus are still at the point of powerlessness, ignorance, and confusion. They have no inkling of how God has acted, especially when the powers of this world are preventing them, it seems to them, from giving due reverence to the body of the Lord.

But a positive movement begins. Peter and the other Beloved Disciple begin their journey. Magdalene's running away from the tomb, from the place of God's action, is reversed. The Crucified One is attracting all to himself (12:32); and the Father is drawing the disciples to come to him (6:44). In the movement of the two disciples, different journeys to faith, and different responsibilities within the community of faith, are represented. The Beloved Disciple, who moves with the greater urgency, born of the special love he has received from Jesus, stoops down and looks into the tomb to see the empty vesture of death, and waits. Peter arrives in his wake, enters the tomb, and sees the linen cloths, with the head covering rolled up in a separate place. The grave had not been robbed; but *someone* had been at work. In this empty tomb, in contrast to the case of Lazarus (11: 44), the grave cloths are already unraveled. Then the other disciple enters the tomb to share Peter's vision of things, with the result that he saw and believed (20:8). Enjoying a special intimacy with the Lord, and having received the gift of the mother of Jesus, the first of the believers (2:5), and taken her into his own home (19:26–27), and with her having received the outpouring of the Spirit (19:30), he believes. The glory has been revealed.

The Gospel reaches beyond this privileged manner of coming to faith, to the situation of future generations of believers. It suggests the all-sufficiency of the scriptures, instanced both in the Old Testament prophecies and in the Gospel of John itself, for genuine faith: "For as yet they did not know the scripture, that he must rise from the dead" (20:9). Later disciples will have no need to look into the empty tomb and see the grave cloths unraveled. For the witness of these original disciples will reach them. As they read the Gospel and interpret the action of God revealed in all the scriptures, they will enjoy the guidance of the Paraclete who will be with them forever (14:16–17, 18–21). Despite his physical absence (14:2–3, 28; 16:5, 28), Jesus will be present through the Spirit (14:16–17).

In a full-bodied life of faith, the emptiness of the tomb will not be an ambiguous puzzle, nor will the resurrection be a happy ending to an otherwise tragic story of defeat and rejection. Under the guidance of the Spirit, and sustained by the blood and water flowing from the side of the Crucified (19:34–35), believers will celebrate the love of the Father at work, in the whole of previous history, to bring about the salvation of the world. Adoring the Father in Spirit and in truth (4:23), they will know the divine will at work, "...that he must rise from the dead" (20:9).

2. The Witness of Magdalene

As the disciples return to their homes, the stage is now set for the proclamation of another dimension of faith. The stone has been rolled back, the grave cloths are unraveled, the tomb is empty. But where is the Crucified Jesus now? The answer to this question is found in the witness of Magdalene, who now reenters the story.

11. But Mary stood weeping outside the tomb, and as she wept, she stooped to look into the tomb; 12. and she saw two angels in white, sitting where the body of Jesus had lain, one at the head and one at the feet. 13. They said to her, "Woman, why are you weeping?" She said to them, "Because they have taken away my Lord and I do not know where they have laid him." 14. Saying this, she turned round and saw Jesus standing, but she did not know it was Jesus. 15. Jesus said to her, "Woman, why are you weeping? Whom do you seek?" Supposing him to be the gardener, she said to him, "Sir, if you have carried him away, tell me where you have laid him and I will take him away." 16. Jesus said to her, "Mariam." She turned and said to him in Hebrew, *"Rabbouni!"* (which means Teacher). 17. Jesus said to her, "Do not cling to me, for I have not yet ascended to the Father; but go to my brethren and say to them, 'I am ascending to my Father and your Father, to my God and your God.'" 18. Mary Magdalene went and said to the disciples, "I have seen the Lord"; and she told them that he had said these things to her. (20:11–18)

The narrative of events here seems to dwell on Magdalene's inability to enter into what is taking place. In contrast to the two other disciples, she is presented as fixated in her grief and sense of abandonment. For her "it was still dark" (20:1); her lamentation is similar to hopeless wailing that accompanied the death of Lazarus (cf. 11:31, 33) which occasioned the dramatic frustration of Jesus (11:35) in the face of the unbelief, which was incapable of either recognizing him as the resurrection and the life (11:25), or of discerning the glory of God to be revealed (11:4, 40). And yet the attractive power of the Crucified One

(12:32), and of the Father (6:44), is having its effect. Her initiative in bending down to look into the tomb is met with the sight of the two angels looking out at her, light-clad mediators of the divine presence now occupying the space where the corpse of the Crucified Jesus has lain. She is being invited to behold "the greater things" as promised to Nathanael (1:50), the vision of "heaven opened, and the angels of God ascending and descending on the Son of Man" (1:51).

And yet her horizon is still restricted to the loss of what she once had. The angels express both a question and a summons to move beyond her present position: "Woman, why are you weeping?" (20:13a). To explain her grief, she reiterates her previous explanation (20:2): "they" have taken away the body of Jesus (20:13b). Unaware of how the Father has acted, she speaks of an all-victorious, violent *they* as the object of her fearful concern. But compared to her previous response, there are two notable differences. "They" have taken away, not "the Lord," but "*my* Lord"; and it is no longer "we" who do not know where "they" have laid him, but *I* (20:13b). In the pent-up intensity of her grief, she does not recognize Jesus when he speaks to her, as he echoes the question of the angels, and reiterates a question central to the Gospel: "Woman, why are you weeping? Whom do you seek?" (20:15a; cf. 1:41; 18:4). With characteristic irony, the Gospel has her imagining that Jesus is the gardener, a party to the mischievous removal of the body of "her Lord" (20:15b). Her desperate hope is still for herself—that she may take him away for a decent disposal of his corpse.

While she is engrossed in the concerns of death, her interlocutor speaks with the voice of life. The Good Shepherd knows his own and his own know him, just as the Father knows him and he knows the Father (10:14–15). With the voice of him who is recognized by his own, who calls his own sheep by name and leads them out (10:3), he utters her name: "Mariam" (20:16a).

A moment of recognition follows; yet her way of addressing Jesus is still according to her previous experience of him: "Rabbouni" (20:16b)[4]—pointedly translated once again as "Teacher" (cf. 1:38; 20:16). She is yet to acknowledge him as "the Lord" (20:18), in whom the glory of the Father is revealed. Jesus summons her into the luminous darkness of a new relationship to him: "Do not cling to me, for I have not yet ascended to the Father" (20:17a). She is to relate to him, not in terms of past experience, but as the one who has come from the Father and is now returning to him. He is to be clung to as the way, not as the end (14:6). Though his task is completed in making God known,[5] the hour is not yet complete. The fruits of his glorification are yet to appear, for he has not yet fulfilled the promise of returning to the Father (14:12, 28; 16:10, 28). Believers relate to him now, not as one *with* them in the flesh, but as one *for* them in the realm of the Father, to give them "power to become the children of God" (1:12).

And so Mary is to leave him as she had previously known him, to become a messenger of a new "Fatherward" relationship: "...go to my brethren and say to them, "I am ascending to my Father and your Father, to my God and your God" (20:17b). Through the fulfillment of this hour, believers are empowered to invoke his Father as "our Father," and his God as "our God." They are no longer disciples, nor even friends (15:15), but his brothers and sisters in the one communion of divine life. Jesus, the only Son of the Father, given in love for the world (3:16), is gathering into one the scattered children of God (11:51). And the Father is answering his prayer, "...that they may be one, even as we are one" (17:22).

So Mary leaves the familiar presence of "her Lord" to announce to the disciples that she had seen "the Lord" (20:18a). She thereby witnesses to the new, all-embracing mystery of life and love in which they were related, as she tells the disciples what she had heard from the Lord (20:18b).

3. The Disciples' House Transformed

19. On the evening of that day, the first day of the week, the doors being shut where the disciples were for fear of the Jews, Jesus came and stood among them and said to them, "Peace to you." 20. When he had said this he showed them his hands and side. Then the disciples were glad when they saw the Lord. 21. Jesus said to them again, "Peace to you. As the Father has sent me, even so I send you." 22. And when he had said this he breathed on them and said to them, "Receive the Holy Spirit. 23. If you forgive the sins of any, they are forgiven; if you retain the sins of any, they are retained." (20:19–23)

On the evening of this Day of the Lord, the disciples are where Mary had found them when she brought her good news. Still, the fear arising from the violence that had been inflicted on Jesus keeps them hidden behind closed doors. The Lord may have risen, but they had not; and certainly their world had not been changed. The ominous "they" whom Magdalene had feared (20:2, 13) are still the major threat, while the "we" (20:2) are adrift in an atmosphere of rejection and persecution (15:18—16:3). They are not yet released to enter the world as agents of peace and reconciliation (cf. 20:22–23). Still living under a closed heaven, they have not yet occupied the Father's house.

Now "Jesus came and stood among them..." (20:19b). He appears at the beginning of Mary's mission to the disciples, and at its conclusion. Behind his seemingly conventional *shalom,* "Peace to you" (20:19c), is the fulfillment of his promise to give

379

his peace to those he has left (14:27). Despite the sorry performance of his disciples, they are still his: the Father has not left him alone (16:32). Even in that fear-filled, locked room, his followers are to find peace in him, for he, the source of new courage, has conquered the world (16:33). Neither the tomb, nor the grave cloths, nor the locked doors restrain him. He embodies the truth that will set them free (8:32). The walls of their former world no longer stand.

Jesus then identifies himself by showing his wounds. He is the same as the one who had been raised on the cross, and whose side had been pierced with a spear. He presents himself as the one in whom the glory of God has been revealed, in a love surpassing all the capacities of human evil to negate it. And the disciples begin to "look on him whom they have pierced" (19:37). A great transformation is taking place: "The disciples were glad when they saw the Lord" (20:20b). In this encounter with the Crucified One among them, they receive his joy, and their joy is complete (15:11). Mary's message has been confirmed with the appearance of the one who had sent her to them.

Jesus' second greeting of peace is followed by his words of mission: "As the Father has sent me, even so I send you" (20:21). He is present among them, as sent by the Father, bearing the wounds of the cross. The Father has acted, and given him to them in this new mode of peace and joy. If the Father is to be "my Father and your Father" (20:17), then they too must be sent on the path of self-giving love so as to be to the world what he has been. The house of the Father (14:10) is open to the world, as he attracts all to the Crucified Jesus in a new life of unity. Remaining in the locked room is no longer an option. Just as Magdalene's meeting with the Risen One led to her being sent to the disciples, so the disciples' meeting with Jesus entails a mission beyond the locked doors of their fears, into the world that is loved by God

(3:16). They are to be to the world what Jesus has been (13:20; 17:18)—witnesses and agents of the opened heaven.

Yet there is a vital further factor. The words of the Baptist, in his report of the divine communication he had received, resonate with new significance: "He on whom you see the Spirit of God descend and remain is the one who baptizes with the Holy Spirit" (1:33). The Crucified Jesus had handed over the Spirit to his new family gathered around the cross (19:30b). From his pierced side, the fountain of living water had gushed (19:34). Glorified by the Father, he has become the source of the Spirit for all who believe (7:39). The "measureless gift of the Spirit" (3:34) continues to be given: "...he breathed on them and said to them, 'Receive the Holy Spirit'" (20:22).

As the Risen One breathes forth the Spirit over the disciples, creation is brought to its fulfillment. The Spirit of new life enters them.[6] Jesus' prayer to the one now declared to be "my Father and your Father" (20:17), had asked that his disciples be protected from the evil one (17:15), and so to be in the world but not of it (17:15a). Now the *Holy* Father (17:11c) empowers the glorified Jesus to give the *Holy* Spirit to counter the powers of evil which will still make the world as dangerous for the disciples as it was for him (17:18). More positively, they will be made holy in the truth (17:17–19) through the coming of the other Paraclete, the Spirit of truth which the world cannot receive (14:16–17). This Holy Spirit, sent by the Father in the name of Jesus, will teach the disciples everything and inspire in them an ever richer recollection of the Word (14:25–26). The Spirit of truth is the principal witness to Jesus, remaining with the disciples in their own mission (15:26–27). The presence of the Spirit will be experienced as an advantage, even though Jesus himself will be absent in the manner in which he had previously been present (16:7). The truthful Spirit will glorify Jesus, the recipient of all that the Father has given him (16:12–15)—so that the world might believe (17:21, 23).

The Lord of peace and joy has now come to his disciples, bearing the gift of the Holy Spirit of truth, in the midst of the world's violence and evil. Despite the murderous rejection of the Son, God's love for the world has not been changed into something other. Its radiance is intensified through its encounter with the powers of darkness. The light shines with its own glory. It brings peace to the disciples in their anxieties and joy in their sorrows. For the Holy Spirit is breathed into them to enable them to live beyond the failure, betrayal, and disbelief of their former lives, and so to carry out their new mission to the world.

The transformation wrought in the disciples now becomes the source of transformation for others: "If you forgive the sins of any, they are forgiven; if you retain the sins of any, they are retained" (20:23). In the mission they receive from the Son, as in the mission he received from the Father, God is at work—"...my God and your God" (20:17). Through the forgiven, God works to forgive; through their experience of the evil they have caused or suffered or confronted, they are now equipped by the Holy Spirit of the Holy Father to unmask the evils of the world.[7] The Spirit of the risen Christ manifests both the true character of God's forgiving love, and the true character of the world, in its self-enclosure against God's will. When both the Spirit and the disciples testify on behalf of Jesus (15:26), the dimensions of sin, its spurious righteousness and its false judgment, are to be brought to light (16:7–11). The truth, accordingly, both frees and judges. Because it is manifest only in a world of freedom, it calls forth a decision. In the Gospel narrative, failure and hesitation have been a fact of life. But in the light of the resurrection, as with the gift of the Spirit, the last word is left with a love intent on forgiveness and life.

4. True Faith

24. Now Thomas, one of the twelve, called the Twin, was not with them when Jesus came. 25. So the other disciples told him, "We have seen the Lord." But he said to them, "Unless I see in his hands the print of the nails, and place my finger in the mark of the nails, and place my hand in his side, I will not believe." 26. Eight days later, his disciples were again in the house, and Thomas was with them. The doors were shut, but Jesus came and stood among them, and said, "Peace to you." 27. Then he said to Thomas, "Put your finger here and see my hands; and put out your hand and place it in my side; do not be faithless, but believing." 28. Thomas answered him, "My Lord and my God!" 29. Jesus said to him, "You have believed because you saw me. Blessed are those who have not seen and yet believe." (20:24–29)

A further dimension of the divine self-manifestation in the glorified Jesus is brought home in this episode involving Thomas. Ostensibly it deals with how he comes to faith. Yet more radically, it is about the manner in which he is changed by God's self-revelation. Not only had he not encountered the risen Lord; he had been deprived of the witness of Mary Magdalene. The Holy Spirit had not been breathed on him. He had not been among those commissioned to bear witness to Jesus in the world. The Gospel presents him simply as "not there when Jesus came" (20:24). When the other disciples attempt to tell him that they have seen the Lord, their report has no effect.

He will not believe—unless his own criteria are met (20:25). The enthusiastic announcement of what others have seen have left him unmoved. Unless he has his own encounter with Jesus, not as

383

one mysteriously risen and transformed, but as someone palpably identifiable as the one who had been crucified, he will not believe. For him to believe is not a matter of hearing the witness of others, nor of meeting a being so transformed that there is no continuity with the Jesus he had known. His kind of faith demands the recognition of the full-bodied reality of the man who had been crucified. Thomas lives behind his own locked doors, shutting out whatever is outside the range of his imagination.

A week passes, with Thomas still enclosed in his view of the possibilities of the situation. Moreover, he is in the company of fellow disciples who, whatever the insistence of their testimony to having seen the Lord, are still defending themselves against any unwelcome interest in who or where they are (20:26). Initiative on both sides is exhausted. He will not believe, and the companions' efforts to explain otherwise have failed.

But another actor enters the story, the bearer of another, more crucial initiative. Jesus comes into their midst and greets them (20:26b). He declares the peace that is already with them, keeping them, whatever their fears and incomprehension, open to what might be. Then, he addresses Thomas, surprisingly offering to meet the criteria that the disciple had set: "Put your finger here and see my hands; and put out your hand and place it in my side" (20:27a). In his Father's house there are evidently many dwelling places (14:1). Still, in offering to meet Thomas's criteria, he calls him to an ultimate point of self-surrender: "Be not faithless but believing" (20:27b). The decisive reality is not the conditions set by the disciple in order to believe, but the conditions in which God manifests his glory on his own terms. The act of faith is only explicable by the act of the free self-disclosure of God.[8]

Leaving behind the conditions he had laid down, Thomas ecstatically proclaims his unconditional acceptance: "My Lord and my God!" (20:28). In fulfillment of the prophecy, both of Israel's scripture and of the Gospel, the disciple is looking "on him whom they have pierced" (19:37). Jesus' prediction is ful-filled: "When you have lifted up the Son of Man, then you will realize that *I am he*" (8:28; cf. 4:26, 28, 58; 13:19). The unity of life and love existing between the Father and the Son shines forth: "I and the Father are one" (10:30, 38). Thomas's encounter with Jesus in this moment captures the significance of all his previous words and deeds and signs, of everything he had done and suffered, to verify what the first words of the Gospel had announced: "In the beginning was the Word, and the Word was turned toward God, and what God was, the Word was also" (1:1–2). To the previously unbelieving but now adoring disciple, it is evident that "the Word [that] became flesh and dwelt amongst us...[is] the fullness of the gift that is truth" (1:14). Thomas has entered the company of those who "have gazed upon his glory, the glory as of the only Son of the Father" (1:14b). He too is seeing the opening of heaven.

Still, something more is now called for. The disciple's act of self-surrendering adoration leads Jesus to summon him and all believers to authentic faith. True faith must reach beyond all earthly conditions. Thomas has believed because he has seen Jesus. But the crucified and risen one blesses those "who have not seen and yet believe" (20:29). The hour has come when true worshipers will worship the Father "neither on this mountain nor in Jerusalem" (4:21), nor in the conditions laid down by Thomas in this locked room. The hour has now arrived when true worshipers will worship the Father in Spirit and in truth, "for the Father seeks such as these to worship him" (4:23).

Just as Magdalene progressed from her clinging to *her* Lord and teacher (20:13b, 16b) to her proclamation "I have seen *the* Lord" (20:18a), so Thomas is being summoned beyond the lim-ited subjectivity of "*my* Lord and *my* God" (20:28), to the cor-porate faith of the community he had previously refused (20:29). The Father has given the Son power over all flesh, to give eternal life to all those given to him in the Father's gift (17:2). Not the tiny world of what is "mine," with its limited expectations and restrictive conditions—"Unless *I* see...*I* will not believe" (20:25b)—but the unbounded community of the *all*, is the proper dimension of eternal life, in which *they* will know "you, the only true God, and Jesus Christ whom you have sent" (17:3).

The wider word of pure faith relies, not on any individual vision, but on the scriptures, on the Spirit, and on those witnesses associated with the Spirit in testifying to the truth (cf. 15:26–27). Those who believe in this way are blessed, for they receive everything as given, beyond all worldly conditions, from "my Father and your Father, my God and your God" to whom Jesus ascends (20:17).

5. The Gospel's Purpose

30. Now Jesus did many other signs in the presence of the disciples which are not written in this book, 31. but these are written that you may go on believing that Jesus is the Christ, the Son of God, and that believing you may have life in his name. (20:30–31)

The Gospel concludes by reiterating its intention to sustain faith in Jesus, and to promote acceptance of the gift of eternal life given through him (cf. 1:4, 9, 12, 16, 18; 19:35). The conclusion expresses a quite practical intention, "that you may go on believing" (20:31a). The life of faith, the reality of knowing the only true God, does not consist in a nostalgic fixation on the way things were. Under the guidance of the Spirit, believers must move on to greet "things that are to come" (16:13). Such faith is centered neither in Jesus' death nor one's own, for anyone who has begun to live and believe the Resurrection and the Life, "will never die" (11:26). By believing, Christians are possessing life in his name, united to him in whom the plenitude of the gift of the truth has been offered. If Socrates had counseled that "the unexamined life is not worth living,"[9] life, in the terms of the Gospel, is both examined and summoned to its highest reach, namely, communion with the Father and the Son: "...that they may be one even as we are one, I in them and you in me, that they may be perfectly one..." (17:22–23).

In confessing that Jesus is both the Christ and the Son of God (20:31), faith affirms that the Word has become flesh, both to fulfill the revelation of the past and its messianic hopes, and to lead to existence in the world open to the ultimate horizon of God's self-giving love (3:16). He is the Son of *God*.

Notes

1. René Girard, in *Des choses cachées depuis la fondation du monde* (Paris: Bernard Grasset, 1978), gives a valuable pointer toward a theology of the Empty Tomb with the words, "Culture always starts from the grave. The grave is always the first human memorial, which has been erected over the victim who has been driven out, the first, most elementary, most fundamental layer of cultural signs. No culture without a grave, no grave without culture" (91).
2. Cf. 1:40–42; 6:8, 66–69; 13:5–11, 24, 36–38; 18:10–11, 15–18, 25–27.
3. Cf. 1:35; 13:23–25; 18:15–16; 19:25–27.
4. Cf. 1:38, 49; 3:2: 4:31; 6:25; 9:2; 11:8.
5. See 4:34; 5:36; 17:4; 19:30.
6. Wis 15:11; cf. LXX Gen 2:7; LXX Ezek 37:9–10.
7. Note the use of the divine passive (cf. 20:1, 6–7, 23).
8. This scene suggests how a striking phenomenology of revelation could be developed, for "passion that leaves the mark of a scar is that place where the impossible takes place" (Jacques Derrida, *"Sauf le Nom,"* in Thomas Dutoit, ed. (Stanford: Stanford University Press, 1995), 59–60.
9. *Apology,* 38A.

20

Conclusion: God Is Love

Though there are many ways of relating the First Letter of John to the Gospel, it is at least a kind of theological reprise of the great themes of the Gospel narrative. From one point of view, the Gospel story is complete. From another, in the life of this early community, struggling to assimilate the original message that "we have heard and proclaim to you" (1 John 1:5; cf. 2:8a; 3:11; 5:11), it continues. The existence of John 21, added to the Gospel before it made its first appearance, indicates that the Johannine proclamation within a developing and changing context called for further refinement.[1] The Letters of John continue this process. They envisage a different situation compared to that of the Gospel. The adversary is no longer "the Jews," but "the Antichrist," uncomfortably present within the community itself. The rhetoric of "glory" that had so marked the Gospel's presentation of divine revelation has been replaced by one in which the words "life," "light," "love," and "truth" occur in special combinations and emphases, above all when God himself is declared to be "light" (1 John 1:5) and, in a most remarkable fashion, "love" (1 John 4:8, 16).

The group of believers addressed in 1 John is beginning on a theological quest—in two senses. First of all, the comparatively isolated and beleaguered community has to make sense of itself and its faith in a new experience of limits: internal divisions, isolation, failure, and the dying out of the first generation of believers. And second, in ways related to all this, the very meaning of the God who was revealed in Jesus is being examined in a manner so fresh and radical that some of the boldest theological affirmations of the New Testament come to be made. While the Gospel story of Jesus is not replaced by theological statements, but always presupposed, the character of the God of the Gospel has now become a new focus, and the community's authentic experience of that God, troubled by the lure of idols (5:21), has become a question needing an answer.[2]

Every generation of faith will have its own questions, either because it feels the attraction of its own idols, or more positively because, when confronted with the challenge, they will want to give the most meaningful account of the Light that has shone upon it. In a concluding reflection, we return to the question that animated this study: What experience of God do the Johannine writings suggest?

1. Seven Features of the Johannine God Experience

The community of faith exists because "God is love." Its communal existence shares in the divine "being-in-love," and its life flows from the "love-life" that circulates between the Father and the Son. To specify further the facets of this experience, we suggest the following seven features, without implying thereby any strict temporal sequence in their ordering.[3]

I. The Father

First, "God is love" in terms of the divine originality and initiative of the Father. All is given, and is to be received, as "the gift of God" (John 4:10): "In this is love, not that we loved God but that he loved us and sent his Son..." (1 John 4:10). God exists and loves in an absolute "beginning." This love precedes, not only all creation and human action but also, as the Gospel repeatedly stresses, the Father acts as the generative initiative involved in the life, action, speech, and mission of Jesus himself.[4] Where Jesus in the Gospel spoke of himself as light (John 8:12; 12:46), life (11:25; 14:6), and the truth (14:6), 1 John concentrates the gifts that Jesus embodies in the source from which they flow: God is love as the light (1 John 1:5), and as "…true God and eternal life" (5:20). Because of the absolute originality and initiative of God, Christian experience must look beyond everything that restricts or diminishes its confidence in the one who "…is greater than our hearts" (1 John 3:20; cf. 4:4, 18; 5:4, 9). The horizon of Christian faith is filled with a gift from beyond this world.

II. The Son

Second, God is love in the self-giving and self-expressiveness manifest in the giving of his only Son.[5] So intimately connected is the Son to the Father's self-revelation, that 1 John can state: "No one who denies the Son has the Father; everyone who confesses the Son has the Father also" (1 John 2:23). To experience the self-communication of God is to enter into the intersubjective communion that exists between the Father and the Son, and to be enfolded into its unity (John 17:20–24). Believers are in communion "with the Father and with his Son Jesus Christ" (1 John 1:3). In such an experience of divine love, the Son is the unique self-expression and self-gift of the Father: "God's love was revealed among us in this way: God sent his only Son into the world so that we might live through him" (4:9). The whole of Christian experience turns on an utterly unreserved, personal self-communication of God to the world, a self-giving in a most radical and self-expressive form. The Word, who is what God is, is made flesh in the conversation of human history.

III. The Cross

Third, God is love to an unconditional extreme: the cross marks the divine power of this love working in the maximal experience of evil. It is a love that keeps on being love "to the end" (John 13:1b), outstripping all human limits and contrary forces. In the cross, this love shows itself most as the light that not only is not overcome by hatred and rejection (1:5), but itself overcomes the power of evil and violence by being what it is. While it remains the gift of endless life, it subsumes death into itself, not as a limit blocking our relationship with God, nor as a defeat for God's communication with us, but as the extreme to which God's love has gone. Death is thus transformed into an occasion of love, a condition of limitless loving into which believers themselves are drawn: "We know love by this, that he laid down his life for us—and we ought to lay down our lives for one another" (1 John 3:16). By being exposed to the power of evil, and not being overcome by it at such an extreme of vulnerability, the "Lamb of God takes away the sin of the world" (John 1:29) to become the "atoning sacrifice for our sins...but also for the sins of the whole world" (1 John 2:2). Though his self-giving death, a great reversal in the vicious circle of self-destruction, begins in human history: "If anyone does sin, we have an advocate with the Father, Jesus Christ the righteous one" (2:1b). Though there is a sober and truthful realism woven into the texture of Christian experience, through its intimate familiarity with the conflict between an ever-vulnerable love and the violence of human selfishness, the love manifested in the "lifting up" of the cross remains ever greater. Such unconditional love swallows up all human conditions: "...we will reassure our hearts before him whenever our hearts condemn us; for God is greater than our hearts..." (3:19–20).

IV. The Resurrection

Fourth, God is love in the transformation it has brought about—in Jesus and in the disciples themselves. Love has not been defeated. The tomb is empty. Jesus has returned to his own as "the resurrection and the life" (John 11:25), giving his peace, joy, and victory over the world, to become the way to "my Father and your Father" (20:17). The crucified and risen Jesus is the revelation of the divine glory, for he overcame death, and introduced his disciples into the communion of life and love that unites the Father and the Son. Transformed himself and transforming others, Jesus is "the Word of life," of the "life [that] was revealed," "of the eternal life that was with the Father and was revealed to us" (1 John 1:1–2). God is love—as the life-force that rolled back the stone of all human defeat, so as to make even the wounds of the Crucified emblems of its life-giving power.

V. The Holy Spirit

Fifth, God is love by giving into human history the permanent presence of its "Spirit of Truth." The Paraclete guides those who follow the way of love into an increasingly fuller realization of the form of true life, strengthening them in the midst of a world to which such love-life is at once a nonsense and a threat to its self-enclosure. The historical community of witnesses will not lack *this* witness, the ever-greater testimony of God (1 John 5:9) concerning what God has revealed through the incarnation of his Word: "By the Spirit that he has given us" (3:24; 4:13), those who have "this testimony in their hearts" (5:10) are conscious of living from a new center focused on the love that God is. For they abide in God and God abides in them (4:13). The God-given gift of the Spirit permeates Christian experience. Yet it is intimately connected with the presence of the Son as the incarnate "way" to the Father. John the Baptist had declared his witness to this Spirit, descending from heaven and remaining on Jesus, to be the medium with which he would baptize (John 1:32–33). Accordingly, in the experience of God's love, the Holy Spirit is a living stream emanating from the glorified Christ (7:37–39). The coming of the Spirit is the "advantage" that would follow the departure of Jesus from the earthly scene (16:7), so that his coming is associated with the last breath of the Crucified (19:30) and the first breath of the Risen One (20:22). Emanating from Jesus, the Spirit always connects Christian God-consciousness back to the form of love incarnate in the life and death of the Son (16:14; 1 John 4:2–3; 2 John 1:7).

VI. The Community

Sixth, God is love through a historical embodiment in a community of mutual love and mission. The gathering of believers, identified by their celebration of baptism and the Eucharist, is sent into the world with its own distinctive mission, thus continuing the mission that Jesus himself has received from the Father (20:21). The transcendent love that is the object of Christian witness is inherently bound up with the practical realization of such love in the mutual relationships of the members of the community.[6] Their unity, as it participates in the primordial unity of the Father and the Son, witnesses to the world the love that has been made known (17:23, 26).

VII. Eternal Life

Seventh, God is love as leading to an eschatological consummation, even though the stream of eternal life has already begun to flow. Along with the peace and joy of Christian existence, and the gift of the Paraclete, vistas of eschatological hope permeate the horizon of those who live in the world but are not of it (1 John 3:3). Jesus' desire is still to be fulfilled: "Father, I desire that those also whom you have given me, may be with me where I am, to see my glory…" (17:24). The world as loved by God (3:16), the world to which Jesus has come as its savior (4:42; 1 John 2:2), has yet to respond to the love that has been shown it: "…so that the world may believe that you have sent me" (John 17:21). Even though believers are already "God's children," it remains that "…what we will be has not yet been revealed" (1 John 3:2a). In the assurance of their present relationship to God, a fulfillment of revelation is promised: "What we do know is this: when he is revealed, we will be like him, for we will see him as he is" (1 John 3:2b). The courage of faith in Jesus' victory over the world (John 16:33) manifests itself in a hope that this cosmic triumph will be fully displayed (1 John 5:4–5). Though faith can locate itself under the opened heaven, the world as a whole has yet to lift its gaze to glory that has been revealed. Only when the word of Jesus will be fully kept, will the love of the Father be manifest—"And we will come to them and make our home with them" (John 14:23).

In summary, then, the experience, objectified in the affirmation "God is love," can be expressed under the above-mentioned seven headings. Any account of the Johannine experience of God would be distorted if any one of these seven aspects was omitted or downplayed. While granting the possibility of any number of different orderings and nuances when exploring the depths of the Johannine writings, these seven headings are signposts, guiding an exploration of those depths, and within the limits of any one reading, they conveniently summarize our findings.

2. Dimensions of Meaning

To take the above description a step farther, there is a further question if theology is to proceed with its ever-unfinished task: What dimensions of theological meaning, however implicit, inform such an experience and how can they be expressed? A full-blown trinitarian theology will emerge in the centuries to come, as will various patterns of trinitarian mysticism.[7] How such accounts will be interpreted and developed is far beyond the scope of this particular investigation. Still, whatever the new directions that might open up, we offer a brief remark on the four functions of meaning, especially as they are discernible in the theology of 1 John.[8] While this will mean bearing in mind the data that have emerged from our reflection on the Gospel, it will emphasize the inherently multidimensional nature of theology that both arises out of, and ever returns to, the distinctively Christian experience of God. Previously we referred to these four "functions of meaning"[9] as cognitive, constitutive, communicative, and effective. Though it would be artificial to maintain any strict sequence in the manner in which the complex meaning of God arises in the horizon of the Johannine experience, there is some justification for beginning with the "effective" aspect of what God means, if the full realism of John's witness is to be respected.[10]

3. Effective Meaning: Knowing God in Action

The First Letter of John describes the experience of God as light, love, and truth in ways that intrinsically demand that it be lived out through a many-sided Christian praxis. Believers must walk in the light (1 John 1:7), and confess their sins (1:9). They must obey the commandments (2:3; 5:2–3), and do the Father's will (2:17).

Hearkening to the original message (2:24; 4:6), they are to abide in Christ so as not to be put to shame at his coming (2:28). They are to recognize the Father's already effective love in making them his children (3:1–2), yet look forward in hope and self-purification to a final visionary evidence (3:3). In the meantime, they are to do what is right (3:7), above all through mutual love (3:11–18). The love in question is at once characterized as unreserved self-sacrifice after the example of Jesus (3:16), and by practical realism (3:17–18). This effective meaning is crystallized in the command to believe in the name of God's Son, Jesus Christ, and to obey his commandment to love (3:23; 5:13). In the light of this criterion, spirits are to be tested (4:1–3), and the presence of the Spirit of truth recognized. Abiding in love (4:16), the faithful are invited into a growing assurance of the true character of God through a love that expels all fear (4:18). They are to appreciate their faith as a victory over the world (5:4–5), as they receive both the truth of Jesus' coming "by water and blood" (5:6), and the God-given testimony of the Spirit (5:12). In the assurance that God hears and answers their requests, believers are summoned to be confident in prayer and intercession (5:14–15). In loving the Father and his children (5:1–2), the "little children" are warned not to "love the world and the things of the world" (2:15), and to keep themselves from idols (5:21).

In each of these commands and exhortations, the effective meaning of the revealed God is a continuing movement of self-transcendence. Living in God means renouncing the world and its idols. It means a confession of the incarnate Son and discernment of the Spirit. It means acknowledging sinfulness and growing in hope. Above all, it means loving one's fellow Christians in self-sacrificing generosity.

But to leave the matter there as though knowing God meant only a series of moral imperatives to transcend the lies, the pretensions, the lovelessness, and the defeats that threaten

Christian conscience, would be to understand the data of the Johannine writings merely as moral exhortation along the lines of an ethical tract. For the summons to self-transcendence is linked to an experience of a self that is transformed.

4. Constitutive Meaning: Godly Identity

A word then on the constitutive function of the meaning of God. Ethical conformity to the will of God follows from a subjective conformity to the divine intersubjectivity itself. The meaning of God not only inspires action, but affects the roots of Christian identity, informing the believing consciousness with a sense of dwelling in God, and of God's dwelling in it. Christians come to have a new experiential and intersubjective identity. In this, their self-understanding is newly constituted.

The features of this godly identity can be suggested in the following summary fashion. Christian consciousness is illumined by the light that God is (1:5), so that believers walk in the light (1:7), and, by loving their fellows, live in it (2:10). In the light of him who is "faithful and just" (1:9), "righteous" (2:29), and "pure" (3:3), they are offered the assurance of being forgiven, cleansed, purified, justified, confirmed in sinlessness (cf. 1:9; 2:2; 3:3, 7, 9; 5:16, 18).

Fundamental to Christian identity is a sense of being "beloved" (2:7; 3:2; 4:1, 7, 11), and a conviction of knowing the revealed truth. The root of this conviction is their reception of the "christening" and interior witness of the Spirit of God, who is the truth (2:20, 26; 3:24b; 5:6, 10). Hence, believers understand themselves to abide in the Father and the Son (2:24; 3:24). And so they already participate in the eternal life (2:25; 3:14; 5:11–13)—which God is (5:20), and which is found in the Son (5:11–12). Even though they must live in hope, they are already

God's children (3:2–3), aware of God's love manifest to them and abiding within them (3:17; 4:9–10, 16a). Consequently, they face the world as being "from God," in the assurance of a final victory over all evil (4:4; 5:4).

As the faithful are conformed to God who is love (4:8, 16b), they are born of God, live in God, and know God (4:7, 16b). In this light, they enjoy an unreserved freedom with God. They grow in an assurance that casts out all fear (2:20; 4:18) and inspires unconditional confidence in prayer (5:14). Thus, the meaning of God constitutes Christian identity by informing the believer's consciousness with a new self-understanding: "...as he is, so are we in this world" (4:17).

5. Communicative Meaning: Living Communion

As the meaning of God in 1 John is effective in inspiring a godly way of life, just as it constitutive in affecting the consciousness of believers with a new godly identity, so too it is communicative. It is formative of a new godly communion, the *koinonia*, which unites present believers with the witnesses of the past—"...from the beginning..." (1:1; 3:11)—with communities in other places (2 and 3 John), and, most of all, with the Father and the Son (2:23–24). The field of communication in question has historical, geographical, interpersonal, intergenerational, transcendent, and cosmic dimensions. A word on each of these.

First, *historical*: communication takes place in history. The impact of past witnesses, voiced in the author of 1 John (cf. 2:1, 7, 8, 12, 21, 26; 5:13), affects the present community: "We declare to you what was in the beginning...that you may have fellowship with us" (cf. 1:1–3). From their privileged immediate contact with "the word of life" (1:1), these witnesses of the past are declared to be "from God" (4:6a), so that "whoever knows God listens to us" (4:6b). The fellowship of faith unfolds in history.

Second, the communication has its own *geography,* as the Presbyter writes to "the elect lady and her children" (2 John 1) and to "the beloved Gaius" (3 John 1), in order that the fellowship of faith will be actualized in a hospitality overcoming geographical separation and localized conflicts (cf. 2 John 10—11; 3 John 5—8).

Third, the meaning of God is communicative in that it promises and demands an *interpersonal* communion: "If we walk in the light as he himself is in the light, we have fellowship with one another..." (1:7). The insistent emphasis on mutual love produces the explosive declaration, "...those who do not love a brother or sister whom they have seen, cannot love God whom they have not seen" (4:20).

Fourth, allied to the above, the *intergenerational character* of communion. The communicative meaning of God affects children, young people, and fathers (2:12–14). Whether such a distinction is to be taken in a biological sense, or as a metaphor for different degrees of Christian maturity, is not the issue. The fact that the meaning of God unites believers in their different experiences of life or faith points to its communicative function.

Fifth, understood as the source, form, and goal of communion in eternal life, the meaning of God is communicative in a *transcendent manner:* "this life was revealed...and [we] declare to you the eternal life that was with the Father and was revealed to us" (1:2). Comprehending all time and space, the communion which makes all such fellowship possible is that which exists between the Father and the Son: "...and truly our fellowship is with the Father and his Son Jesus Christ" (1:3). Eternal life means abiding in the Son and in the Father (2:23–24). Indeed, the communion which exists between the faithful and the Father and the Son results from the original life-giving communication of the Father himself: "God gave us eternal life, and this life is in his Son. Whoever has the Son has life" (5:11–12; cf. 4:9–10).

Finally, there is a *cosmic* or global dimension inherent in the communicative meaning of God. The beleaguered state of this particular community is obviously not conducive to a full appreciation of the universality of the divine communication. Yet the fact is that the cosmic dimension figures at all points to the persistent power of the original message: "God so loved *the world…*" (John 3:16). In 1 John the cosmic scope of the divine communication is largely tacit, except for some notable asides: Jesus Christ "…is the atoning sacrifice for our sins, and not for ours only, but for the sins of the whole world" (1 John 2:2). Despite the extremely negative evaluation of the world, given the parlous situation addressed by the author (cf. 2:15–17; 3:13; 4:4–5; 5:19), the world, for all its threat and ambiguity, is still the realm into which God has sent his only Son (4:9). As if to counter the tendency to restrict the cosmic character of God's love, the writer voices the testimony of the original witnesses: "And we have seen and do testify that the Father has sent his Son as the Savior of the world" (4:14). By recalling the community to the cosmic extent of its faith, it can at least live in the world with confidence (4:4; 5:4–5). There is, therefore, a cosmic significance in the meaning of the revealed God.

The meaning of God, then, in these writings of John, is communicative. It holds in its range of discourse past witnesses, present relationships with those both near and far, communion with the Father and the Son, and, more implicitly, a relationship with the world itself.

6. Cognitive Meaning: The Truth of God Revealed

Underpinning the effective, constitutive, and communicative manners in which Johannine theology functions is the cognitive function. It expresses not only what God commands, not only a new godly identity and community, but also the transcendent truth that God is. This has been implicit in the other three functions of meaning: the God-given commandment to walk in the light, to love, to do the deeds of righteousness, and so on, derives from the primal truth that God is in himself light, love, and righteousness. For Christians to enter into a new self-understanding as the children of God, implies an understanding of God as their Father. For the faithful to coexist in a historical, geographical, social, theological, and cosmic field of communication, implies a primordial, paradigmatic communion existing between the Father and the Son, in which the community in time abides through the witness of the Spirit.

Moving from the implicit to the explicit in terms of cognitive meaning, we observe the following: the distinctive Johannine accent falls on the truth, and the criteria for judging it—above all the truth of confession, "God is love," and the kind of love that God is and shows. The subjectivity of Johannine faith is marked with a salvific objectivity concerning the reality of God, and what is divinely revealed and willed. It is a striking instance of Lonergan's axiom, "objectivity is the fruit of authentic subjectivity."[11]

In this regard, we note the vigorously objective rhetoric with which the letter begins. It recaptures the revelatory language of the Gospel, thus setting the tone in which the various themes of the Johannine discourse will be treated. What God has revealed from the beginning has been seen, gazed upon, touched, and heard (1:1–3a). This privileged immediacy is characteristic of the foundational witnesses: "...truly our fellowship is with the Father and with his Son Jesus Christ" (1:3b). The joyous conviction of the past is communicated to the present generation of faithful through the force of an original and transforming truth (1:4).

The experience of this truth is expressed in the primal metaphor of light: "God is light" (1:5). The consciousness of faith is irradiated by the divine reality as it exposes sinfulness and brings forgiveness (1:7–8), and gives both sight and direction (2:11). The commandment of mutual love is both old and new, and "is true in him and in you" (2:8). Believers are commanded to be what God is. Both the "fathers" and the "children" of the community know the Father (2:13–14), and the young have "the word of God" abiding in them (2:14b). By doing the will of God, believers move beyond the ephemeral and illusory projections of mundane experience into the realm of lasting life (2:17).

In their openness to the divine light, love, and life, the faithful are anointed by the Holy One, and "have all knowledge" and "know the truth" (2:20–21, 27). Yet such a knowledge does not place believers in some kind of gnostic heaven; for it is always beholden to the incarnate reality of God's only Son, Jesus Christ. Indeed, to confess the incarnate reality of the Son is the essential condition for knowing and "having" the Father as well (2:23), and for dwelling in both, (2:24)—thus to enjoy the promised eternal life (2:25).

Anchored in the incarnate character of the truth, the consciousness of faith, though abiding in its divine object, expands into a hope for what is yet to be revealed in an eschatological advent (*parousia*) (2:28). When Christian praxis is consistent with the truth of the one who is righteous, believers have an assurance of being born of God into a radical sinless-ness (2:29; 3:7–9). Faith lives from the conviction that the love of the Father has already brought about a transformation: "Beloved, we are God's children now" (3:2a), even as it awaits the full evidence concerning both God and his children, when "...we will be like

402

him, for we will see him as he is" (3:2b). The time of waiting is one of self-purification, the better to be conformed to him who is "pure" (3:3). From the present actuality of divine birth, the dynamics of Christian conduct derive, as manifest in authentic activities of righteousness, hope, self-purification, and resistance to error and deceit (3:7). Christian praxis is therefore the existential acknowledgement of the reality of God as light, true, pure, righteous, and loving.

The meaning of what God is brings about a sharp division in human history. The true children of God are revealed in their mutual loving judged in the light of Jesus' self-giving love; the children of the devil reveal themselves in the works of hatred, violence, and murder (3:10–18). The problem with such a criterion is that it might unwittingly enclose believers in their own inevitably troubled and ambiguous consciences. But conscience is not left to itself. It is judged, encouraged, and sustained by the truth and the knowledge that reside in God himself: "By this we will know that we are from the truth and will reassure our hearts before him...For God is greater than our hearts, and he knows everything" (3:19–20). A gift continues to be given to the increasingly emboldened faith of God's children: "...and we receive from him whatever we ask..." (3:22).

While the effective meaning of God is essentially connected to keeping his commandment to believe in the name of his only Son Jesus Christ and to live in mutual love (3:23), and while such obedience leads to a relationship of reciprocal indwelling between God and his children (3:24a), the God-given Spirit is the medium and assurance of the believers' knowledge of God's indwelling presence (3:24b; 4:13; 5:6–8). The Spirit is received as coming "from God," and being "of God," as it leads to the confession that "Jesus Christ has come in the flesh" (4:2). It follows that the genuineness of faith's knowledge of God is founded at one and the same time on the gift of the Spirit and the incarnational presence of the Son in the world. In its relation to the truth incarnate in Jesus Christ, "the Spirit of truth" can be objectively and cognitively distinguished from "the spirit of error" (4:6b).

After the Johannine author's careful and somewhat complex presentation of the modes of self-transcendence that lead to the true knowledge of God, he moves to the core condition from which all else depends. Since "God is love" (4:8), and since love is from God, the divine life can be lived, and the true God can only be known, by loving (4:7–8). The possibility of reducing the agapeic and properly divine extent of love to the measure of human subjectivity is carefully precluded. God has revealed the kind of love he is by the sending of his only Son into the world to be the source of life (4:9). The self-revelation of the Father is made through his sending of what is most intimate to himself—"his only Son"—into what is most distant from him, namely "the world" (cf. 2:15–17).

The divine initiative acknowledges no human conditions, neither that of a prior human, loving search for God ("...not that we loved God"), nor even that of a prior innocence in those who have been so loved ("...to be the atoning sacrifice for our sins" (4:10)). As they participate in the reality of divine *agape* through mutual love, believers are drawn by the invisible God into the divine life; and the self-communicating love of God achieves its purpose (4:12). Once more the gift of the Spirit and the sending of the Son (4:13–15) figure in the Letter's presentation of the originating and life-giving nature of God's love: "So we have known and believe the love that God has for us" (4:16a). *Our* knowing depends on God's action; and the reality of *our* loving derives from love's initiative, as the Father gives of his Spirit and sends his Son to be the Savior of the world.

The originating reality, "God is love" (4:16b), is the transforming truth. In a transcendent objectivity it counters the subjective projections of human fear and the distorted calculations of human justice (4:17–18), so that believers can transcend their doubts to both affirm, "We love because he first loved us" (4:19), and to carry their love for the invisible God into fraternal love within the visible community (4:20–21). For them, love becomes a way of life because, in God, love and life are two dimensions of the same truth: "God is love" (4:8, 16b), and "...the true God and eternal life" (5:20b).

The Letter's various affirmations of God as light, as pure, as righteous, as love, as true, and as life, accumulate in the conviction that believers genuinely know God: "We know that we are God's children..." (5:2). "We know that the Son of God has come and has given us understanding so that we may know him who is true; and we are in him who is true, in his Son, Jesus Christ" (5:19–20). Evidently, then, for the author of 1 John the meaning of God is emphatically cognitive. While the effective meaning of God demands and inspires action, while its constitutive meaning informs the consciousness of believers with a new identity, while its communicative meaning unites them in a shared life and love, the cognitive meaning of God is eminently objective.

God is more than the inspiration to moral action, more than a feature of human identity, more than the bond of human community. Though no explicit doxological formulae of praise and thanksgiving are found in this letter,[12] the intent of its author is governed by the all-transcending objectivity in what has been revealed. The confession, "God is love," is a judgment of reality. While its meaning is closed to those who do not believe or do not love, for those who believe and whose faith expresses itself in the praxis of love, it is the original and abiding truth. God has been truly revealed: "...the darkness is passing away and the true light is already shining" (2:8).

Where 1 John ends, theology must always begin anew: "Little children, keep yourselves from idols!" (5:21).

7. Conclusion

The vigilance needed for believers to keep themselves from idols and to know the God disclosed in the Word and through the Spirit, suggests an ongoing experience along the lines of a journey, or a path of pilgrimage. The way opens both to an all-deciding culmination or fulfillment—"we have gazed upon his glory, glory as the only Son from the Father" (John 1:14)—and to the provisionality and perseverance of faith: "Blessed are those who have not seen and yet believe" (John 20:29).

We have reread the Johannine writings with this question in mind: What experience of God do they suggest? Though the perspectives opening from such an exploration find ready support in many varieties of theological and mystical tradition, they are of special relevance to the Christian faith today, characterized increasingly by interreligious dialogue. In a sense, this whole work is a protracted way of agreeing with Karl Rahner's judgment that the "experience of God really constitutes the very heart and center of Christianity itself and also every living source of that conscious manifestation that we call 'revelation'".[13]

Similarly, Lonergan's methodological description of how the experience of God occurs within the experience of self-transcendence finds remarkable support in the Gospel's narrative of the unsettling challenges faced by Jesus' disciples. Their experience of the divine glory "dismantles and abolishes the horizon in which their knowing and choosing went on and sets up a new horizon in which the love of God will transvalue our values and the eyes of that love will transform our knowing."[14] To experience God and to see the divine glory revealed meant, for the disciples, a radically new level of self-transcendence, of knowing God by being drawn out of themselves. Von Balthasar referred to this as "the movement away from myself, the preference of what is other and greater...."[15] He concedes that the

406

criteria of experience in the writings of John "continually circle around each other, always pointing one to the other."[16] This is above all true in reference to the Father, Son, and Spirit. To say that either of the three is central to the experience of God in its Johannine presentation would be to find that the metaphor of the "center" would suggest different but interrelated meanings in each case. Speaking more generally, it is impossible to adequately systematize that Johannine data into an adequate theoretical synthesis—an impossibility instanced in the interweaving themes and mutually conditioning perspectives of this present work. But what is also clear is that the "sythesis" of our experience of God is, for John, a preeminently practical matter: doing the will of the Father, and loving as God loves: "God is love, and those who abide in love abide in God, and God abides in them" (1 John 4:16).

This extended reflection is intended to enhance a two-way access between meaning and experience. By focusing on the experience of God in the writings of John, we hoped to refresh our spiritual and theological capacities to articulate the meaning of God for Christian faith. On the other hand, limited as we are to words and to the theological contexts associated with them, we saw the value of reimmersing the meaning of our words in the ineffable excess of meaning characteristic of the theology of John. It has been throughout a matter of learning at a new level, both how to speak of what must be spoken by Christian believers in the world, and how to be silent, intent on what the Word has revealed beyond the capacity of all human words to express.

Notes

1. For a discussion of the place of John 21 as an "Epilogue" to John 1:1–20:31, its role in the development of the Johannine community, its interpretation, and a survey of contemporary scholarship, see F. J. Moloney, *Glory not Dishonor: Reading John 13—21*

(Minneapolis: Fortress Press, 1998), 182–91, and *The Gospel of John* (Sacra Pagina 4; Collegeville: The Liturgical Press, 1998), 545–568.

2. For a study of the Johannine Letters from one of the authors of the present book, see F. J. Moloney, *From James to Jude* (The Peoples' Bible Commentary; Oxford: The Bible Reading Fellowship, 1999), 108–167.

3. For a comparatively brief account of his distinctive love-orientated theology, see Hans Urs von Balthasar, *Love Alone,* Alexander Dru, ed. and trans. (New York: Herder and Herder, 1969).

4. For example, John 1:18; 3:16, 35; 4:23, 34; 5:18–21, 26–28, 30, 36–37; 6:32–33, 37–40, 44–45, 57, 65; 7:16.

5. See John 1:18; 3:16; 8:19, 38; 10:17, 30; 12:45, 50; 14:7, 10–11; 16:28.

6. See 13:14, 34–35; 15:12–13; 1 John 2:7–11; 3:10–18; 4:7–8, 11, 20; 5:1–2, 16; 2 John 1:5; 3 John 5–8.

7. For the original link between trinitarian theology and mysticism, see Bernard McGinn, *The Foundations of Mysticism* (New York: Crossroad, 1997), 150–158; 243–248. A striking instance of the fusion of the mystical and the theological is found in a metaphor employed by St. Catherine of Siena. She presents the Father speaking: "I am their bed and table. This gentle loving Word is their food...the food I have given you...The Holy Spirit, my loving charity, is the waiter who serves them my gifts and graces" (*Catherine of Siena: Selected Spiritual Writings,* Mary O'Driscoll, ed. [New York: New City Press, 1993]), 110–111.

8. For a more extended theological reflection, see Anthony Kelly, "'God is Love': A Theological Moral Reading of 1 John," *Studia Moralia* XXXVII/1, June 1999, 35–71.

9. Bernard Lonergan, *Method in Theology* (London: Darton, Longman and Todd, 1971), especially 76–81.

10. By way of contrast, the meanings of God in John's Gospel tend to unfold in the reverse order, beginning with a strong accent on the cognitive (e.g., 1:1–18), moving to the constitutive (e.g., 3:1–10; 4:7–27), and then to the communicative (e.g., 10:1–19; 15:1–11; 17:20–24)—though with the effective increasingly stressed (e.g., 8:12, 31–33; 9:35–36; 12:44–50; 13:31–35; 20:19–31).

11. *Method in Theology,* 265, 292.

12. There is an interesting exegetical question here: Does 1 John refrain from doxological language because of the danger of removing God to a false transcendence? Or is the doxological dimension so typical of the Gospel simply taken for granted?
13. Rahner, "The Experience of God Today," 164.
14. Lonergan, *Method...*, 106.
15. Von Balthasar, *The Glory of the Lord I*, 237.
16. Ibid., 238–239.

References

Alison, James, *Raising Abel. The Recovery of the Eschatological Imagination.* New York: Crossroad, 1996.

———. *The Joy of Being Wrong: Original Sin through Easter Eyes.* New York: Crossroad, 1998.

Aquinas, St. Thomas, *Summa Theologiae.* Alba: Editiones Paulinae: Rome, 1962.

———. *Summa Contra Gentes.* Marietti Edition: Turin, 1946.

———. *In Evangelium B. Joannis Expositio.* Marietti Edition: Turin, 1925.

Ashton, J., "The Identity and Function of the *Ioudaioi* in the Fourth Gospel." *NT* 27, 1985, 40–75.

———. *Understanding the Fourth Gospel.* Oxford: Clarendon, 1991.

Badcock, Gary D., *Light of Truth and Fire of Love: A Theology of the Holy Spirit.* Grand Rapids, Mich.: William Eerdmans, 1997.

Bailie, Gil., *Violence Unveiled: Humanity at the Crossroads.* New York: Crossroad, 1997.

Balthasar, H. U. von, *A Theology of History.* London: Sheed and Ward, 1964.

———. *Love Alone,* Alexander Dru, trans. New York: Herder and Herder, 1969.

———. *The Glory of the Lord: A Theological Aesthetics: I: Seeing the Form,* Erasmo Leiva-Merikakis, trans. New York: Crossroad Publications, 1982.

References

————. *Theo-Drama: Theological Dramatic Theory, I–III.* Graham Harrison, trans. San Francisco: Ignatius Press, 1988, 1992.

Becker, Ernest, *The Denial of Death.* New York: The Free Press, 1973.

Bouësse, H., *Le Sauveur du monde: La place du Christ dans le plan de Dieu.* Chambéry-Leysse: College Théologique Dominicain, 1951.

Brady, L. Augustine, "Martin Buber and the Gospel of John," *Thought* 201, September 1978, 283–292.

Brown, Raymond E., *The Community of the Beloved Disciple: The Lives, Loves and Hates of an Early Christian Community.* New York: Paulist Press, 1979.

Buckley, Michael J., *At the Origins of Modern Atheism.* New Haven: Yale University Press, 1987.

Byrne, Brendan, *Lazarus: A Contemporary Reading of John 11:1–46.* Collegeville: The Liturgical Press, 1991.

Cadman, W., *The Open Heaven: The Revelation of God in the Johannine Sayings of Jesus,* G. B. Caird, ed. Oxford: Blackwell, 1969.

Celan, Paul, *Poems,* M. Hamburger, trans. Manchester: Carcanet, 1980.

Coloe, Mary L., *God Dwells with Us: Temple Symbolism in the Fourth Gospel.* Collegeville, Minn.: Liturgical Press, 2001.

Dedek, J., "*Quasi-Experimentalis Cognitio:* An Historical Approach to the Meaning of St. Thomas." *Theological Studies* 22, 1961, 363–370.

Derrida, Jacques, *Of Spirit: Heidegger and the Question,* G. Bennington and R. Bowlby, trans. Chicago: University of Chicago Press, 1989.

————. *"Sauf le Nom,"* in Thomas Dutoit, ed. Stanford: Stanford University Press, 1995.

Durrwell, F.-X., *The Spirit of the Father and the Son: Theological and Ecumenical Perspectives,* Robert Nowell, trans. Middlegreen, Slough: St. Paul Publications, 1990.

————. *Holy Spirit of God: An Essay in Biblical Theology,* Benedict Davies, trans. London: Geoffrey Chapman, 1986.

Fitzmyer, Joseph A., "Paul's Anthropology," *The New Jerome Biblical Commentary,* Raymond E. Brown, Joseph A. Fitzmyer, and Roland E. Murphy, eds. London: Geoffrey Chapman, 1989.

Ford, David F., *Self and Salvation: Being Transformed.* Cambridge: Cambridge University Press, 1999.

Galot, Jean, *Abba, Father: We Long to See Your Face: Theological Insights into the First Person of the Trinity,* M. Angeline Bouchard, trans. New York: Alba House, 1992.

Gaventa, B. R., "The Archive of Excess: John 21 and the Problem of Narrative Closure," in R. A. Culpepper and C. C. Black, *Exploring the Gospel of John: In Honor of D. Moody Smith.* Louisville: Westminster John Knox Press, 1996.

Girard, René, *Des choses cachées depuis la fondation du monde.* Paris: Bernard Grasset, 1978.

Griggs, E. L., ed., *Collected Letters of Samuel Taylor Coleridge,* vol. 2. Oxford: Oxford University Press, 1971.

Horner, Robyn, *Rethinking God as Gift: Marion, Derrida and the Limits of Phenomenology.* Fordham: Fordham University Press, 2001.

Jenson, Robert. W., *Systematic Theology I: The Triune God.* New York: Oxford University Press, 1997.

Johnstone, Brian V., "The Resurrection as Source for a Theology of Peace." *Studia Moralia* XXXVI/2, December, 1998, 441–460.

Kaufmann, W., ed. and trans., *The Portable Nietzsche.* New York: The Viking Press, 1972.

References

Kelly, Anthony J., *Trinity of Love: A Theology of the Christian God*. Wilmington, Del.: Michael Glazier, 1989.

———. *An Expanding Theology: Faith in a World of Connections*. Newtown, NSW: E. J. Dwyer, 1993/ Ridgefield, Conn.: Morehouse Publishing, 1993.

———. "'God is Love': A Theological Moral Reading of 1 John." *Studia Moralia* XXVII/1, June 1999, 35–72.

Lafont, Ghislain, *Peut-on connâitre Dieu en Jésus-Christ*. Paris: Les Editions du Cerf, 1969.

———. *God, Time and Being*, Leonard Maluf, trans. Petersham: Mass.: Saint Bede's Publications, 1992.

Lash, Nicholas, *The Beginning and the End of Religion*. Cambridge: Cambridge University Press, 1996.

Lee, Dorothy A., "Beyond Suspicion? The Fatherhood of God in the Fourth Gospel." *Pacifica* 8/2, June 1995, 140–153.

Lonergan, Bernard, *Collection: Papers by Bernard Lonergan, S. J.* London: Darton, Longman and Todd, 1967.

———. *Method in Theology*. London: Darton, Longman and Todd, 1972.

———. *A Third Collection: Papers by Bernard J.F. Lonergan, S.J.*, F. E. Crowe, ed. New York: Paulist Press, 1985.

Louth, Andrew, *Maximus the Confessor*. London: Routledge, 1996.

Marion, Jean-Luc, "Le don d'une présence," *Prolégomènes à la charité*. Paris: Editions de la Différence, 1986.

———. *God Without Being: Hors-Texte*, Thomas A. Carlson, trans., Chicago: University of Chicago Press, 1991.

———. *Phénomènologie et théologie*. Paris: Criterion, 1992.

Marrow, Stanley B., *The Gospel of John: A Reading*. Mahwah, N.J.: Paulist Press, 1995.

McGinn, Bernard, *The Foundations of Mysticism*. New York: Crossroad, 1997.

Milbank, John, *Theology and Social Theory: Beyond Secular Reason*. Oxford: Blackwell, 1993.

———. *The Word Made Strange: Theology, Language, Culture*. Oxford: Blackwell, 1997.

Miller, Jerome A., *In the Throes of Wonder: Intimations of the Sacred in the Post-Modern World*. Albany: State University of New York Press, 1992.

Moloney, Francis J., *The Johannine Son of Man*, Second Edition. Biblioteca di Scienze Religiose 14; Rome LAS, 1978.

———. "Johannine Theology," in R. E. Brown, J. A. Fitzmyer, and R. E. Murphy, eds. *The New Jerome Biblical Commentary*. Englewood Cliffs: Prentice Hall, 1989, 1417–26.

———. *Belief in the Word: Reading John 1—4*. Minneapolis: Fortress Press, 1993.

———. *Signs and Shadows: Reading John 5—12*. Minneapolis: Fortress Press, 1996.

———. *Glory not Dishonor: Reading John 13—21*. Minneapolis: Fortress Press, 1998.

———. *The Gospel of John*. Sacra Pagina 4. Collegeville: The Liturgical Press, 1998.

———. *From James to Jude*. The Peoples' Bible Commentary. Oxford: The Bible Reading Fellowship, 1999.

Morse, Christopher, *Not Every Spirit: A Dogmatics of Christian Disbelief*. Valley Forge, Pa.: Trinity Press International, 1994, 342–343.

Murray, John C., *The Problem of God*. New Haven: Yale University Press, 1964.

Neuner, J. and J. Dupuis, eds., *The Christian Faith in the Doctrinal Documents of the Catholic Church*. London: Collins Liturgical, 1982.

Oakes, E. T., *Pattern of Redemption: The Theology of Hans Urs von Balthasar*. New York: Continuum, 1994.

References

O'Driscoll, M., ed., *Catherine of Siena: Selected Spiritual Writings*. New York: New City Press, 1993.

O'Leary, Joseph S., *Questioning Back: The Overcoming of Metaphysics in the Christian Tradition*. New York: Seabury, 1985.

———. *La vérité chrétienne à l'âge du pluralisme religieux*. Paris: Cerf, 1994.

Pannenberg, Wolfhart, *Systematic Theology* 1–II, Geoffrey W. Bromiley, trans. Grand Rapids, Mich.: William B. Eerdmans, 1991–1994.

Pelikan, Jaroslav, *The Light of the World: A Basic Image in Early Christian Thought*. New York: Harper and Brothers, 1962.

———. *The Emergence of the Catholic Tradition 100–600*. Chicago: University of Chicago Press, 1971.

Placher, W. C., *The Domestication of Transcendence: How Modern Thinking About God Went Wrong*. Louisville: Westminster, 1996.

Rahner, Karl, "The Concept of Mystery in Catholic Theology," *Theological Investigations IV*, Kevin Smyth, trans. Baltimore: Helicon Press, 1966, 36–73.

———. *Hearers of the Word*, J. B. Metz, ed., Ronald Walls, trans. London: Sheed and Ward, 1969.

———. "Christology within an Evolutionary View of the Word," *Theological Investigations V*, Karl-H. Kruger, trans. Baltimore: Helicon, 1966, 157–192.

———. "The Experience of God Today," *Theological Investigations XI*, David Bourke, trans. London: Darton, Longman and Todd, 1974, 149–165.

Ratzinger, Joseph, *Introduction to Christianity*, J. R. Forster, trans. London: Search Press, 1969.

Rensberger, D., *1 John, 2 John, 3 John.* Abingdon New Testament Commentaries. Nashville: Abingdon Press, 1997.

Rolnick, P. A., *Analogical Possibilities: How Words Refer to God.* Atlanta: Scholars Press, 1993.

Schillebeeckx, Edward, *Christ: The Christian Experience in the Modern World.* John Bowden, trans. London: SCM Press, 1980.

Schumacher, Michele M., "The Concept of Representation in the Theology of Hans Urs von Balthasar." *Theological Studies* 60, 1999, 53–71.

Stewart, D., *Plato: A New Translation of the Phaedo.* London: Euphorion Books, 1972.

Studer, Basil, *Trinity and Incarnation: The Faith of the Early Church,* Matthias Westerhoff, trans., Andrew Louth, ed. Collegeville, Minn.: Liturgical Press, 1993.

Thunberg, Lars, *Man and the Cosmos: The Vision of Maximus the Confessor.* Crestwood, N.Y.: St. Vladimirs Seminary Press, 1985.

Torrance, T. F., *The Trinitarian Faith: The Evangelical Theology of the Ancient Catholic Church.* Edinburgh: T. & T. Clark, 1988.

Tracy, David, *The Analogical Imagination: Christian Theology and the Culture of Pluralism.* New York: Crossroad, 1981.

———. *Pluralism and Ambiguity: Hermeneutics, Religion, Hope.* San Francisco: Harper and Row, 1987.

Turner, Denys, *The Darkness of God: Negativity in Christian Mysticism.* Cambridge: Cambridge University Press, 1995.

Ward, G., ed., *The Post-Modern God: A Theological Reader.* Oxford: Blackwell, 1997.

Williams, Rowan, *On Christian Theology.* Oxford: Blackwell, 2000.

Zizioulas, John D., *Being as Communion.* London: Darton, Longman and Todd, 1985.

Index of Authors

Biblical Citations

Individual verses within the chapter by chapter reflections on the Fourth Gospel will not be cited. Readers seeking comment on these verses can trace the relevant verses within the pages of the respective chapters indicated below.

Old Testament				
		22:2	81	
Genesis		22:7	81	
1:1	30, 210	22:8	81	
1:1—2:3	30	22:12	81	
1:2	30	22:13	81	
2:2–3	119, 120	22:14	81	
2:16–17	45	22:14–19	81	
2:17	141	28:12–17	69, 100	
3:1–7	45	33:19	98	
3:1–24	195	48:22	98	
3:8	352, 370			
3:22–24	45	*Exodus*		
4:15	195	3:2–6	183	
11:4	40	3:5	353	
11:6–8	40	3:14	105, 280, 353	
11:9	40	4:22	194	
12:1–9	192	12:3–7	280	
18:1–18	193	12:10	369	
22:1–17	192	12:22–23	367	
22:1–19	81	12:46	369	
		13:21	183	

15:24	152
16:2	152
16:4	148
16:7	152
16:8	153
16:15	148, 154
17:3	152
19:11	151
19:20	151
20:8–11	117
25:8	48
40:35	48

Leviticus
24:16	121

Numbers
9:12	369
11:13	143
15:30–31	121
35:30	184

Deuteronomy
4:12	133
4:15	133
5:15	117
6:4–6	224
14:1	194
17:6	184
18:15–18	143
32:39	125
34:5–8	154

Joshua
24:32	98

2 Samuel
21:1–14	82
21:2	82
21:3	82
21:6–9	82
21:14	82

2 Maccabees
14:36	341

Nehemiah
9:15	148

Psalms
22:19	365
23:1–3	43, 216
29:3	144
34:20–21	369
35:19	313
36:7–9	184
36:9	184, 203
41:10	279
49:14	220
56:9	354
68:22 (LXX)	367
69:4–5	313
77:17–19	144
78:24	148
82:6	231
107:29–30	145

3:11–15	154		3:33–34	302
3:11–21	161		3:34	10, 32, 113, 123, 179, 206, 212, 259, 274, 381
3:12	163, 265			
3:13	129, 146, 163, 191, 260			
3:13–15	211		3:35	123, 129, 150, 193, 243
3:14	108, 129, 146, 156, 255, 263, 320, 339			
			3:35–36	107
			4:1–4	87
3:14–15	363		4:1–54	80, 97–114
3:15	129		4:6	367
3:16	16, 19, 50, 53, 54, 107, 110, 113, 123, 150, 151, 156, 177, 186, 191, 224, 240, 256, 267, 272, 273, 287, 303, 310, 315, 319, 321, 341, 344, 378, 381, 387, 394, 400		4:9	87
			4:10	1, 16, 87, 94, 143, 150, 166, 341, 367, 389
			4:11–12	197
			4:13	300
			4:13–26	180
			4:14	23
			4:15	149
			4:18	116
			4:21	186, 272, 347, 385
3:16–17	107, 110, 132			
3:16–21	129		4:22	16, 54, 153, 199, 308
3:17	110, 112, 206			
3:17–18	261		4:23	67, 130, 133, 137, 153, 164, 212, 248, 272, 293, 300, 302, 341, 369, 375, 385
3:19	261			
3:19–21	185			
3:20–21	319			
3:22	2:11			
3:24	111, 300			
3:29	165		4:23–24	13, 19, 186, 297, 323, 329
3:30	110			

6:50	39		8:12	23, 206, 207, 227, 290, 353, 373
6:51	47, 290, 293			
6:51–58	298			
6:53	212, 279		8:15	13, 158, 261
6:53–56	369		8:15–16	261
6:53–58	47		8:16	319, 331
6:54	39		8:19	278
6:56–57	243		8:20	255
6:57	222, 290, 291, 298, 309, 334		8:23	260, 265
			8:24	105
6:57–58	39		8:25–26	212
6:62	260, 336		8:26	284, 314
6:63	290		8:27–29	14
6:66	170		8:28	40, 105, 179, 255, 320, 339, 361, 385
6:68	290			
6:69	354			
7:1—8:59	169–204		8:29	284, 303, 331
7:2	136		8:31	17, 103
7:16	40, 284		8:31–32	243
7:17	212		8:32	40, 214, 290, 380
7:18	212, 294			
7:24	158, 232, 256		8:38	211, 212, 284
7:26	212		8:38–59	320
7:30	255, 272		8:39–47	284
7:32–36	255		8:40	212, 290
7:33–35	255		8:42	2
7:34	283		8:44	319
7:37	206		8:44–46	290, 342
7:37–38	227		8:48	320
7:37–39	367, 369, 393		8:50	294
7:39	318, 323, 367, 381		8:54	294
			8:56	264, 313
7:46	212		8:58	105, 336

Experiencing God in the Gospel of John